BALTIC SEA

EAST PRUSSIA

Berlin

POLAND

Dresden

CZECHOSLOVAKIA

BOHEMIA

AUSTRIA

HUNGARY

Boundaries showing post-war zones of
occupation: N.W. Germany — BRITISH;
S.W. Germany — FRENCH; S. Germany
— AMERICAN; E. Germany — RUSSIAN

Rail

Reichsbank gold route
Berlin to Mittenwald

Road

1944-5 Frontiers of the GREAT GERMAN
REICH (NAZI GERMANY)

GERMANY 1944-5

NAZI GOLD

The Story of
the World's Greatest Robbery—
and Its Aftermath

Nazi Gold

Ian Sayer and Douglas Botting
with the London *Sunday Times*

CONGDON & WEED, INC.
New York

Copyright © 1984 by Ian Sayer and Douglas Botting

Library of Congress Cataloging in Publication Data

Sayer, Ian.
Nazi gold.

Bibliography: p.
Includes index.
1. Bank robberies—Germany—History—20th
century. 2. Reichsbank (Germany)—History.
I. Botting, Douglas. II. Sunday times (London,
England) III. Title.
HV6665.G32S29 1945b   364.1'62   84-21497
ISBN 0-86553-138-2
ISBN 0-312-92567-0 (St. Martin's Press)

Published by Congdon & Weed, Inc.
298 Fifth Avenue, New York, N.Y. 10001

Distributed by St. Martin's Press
175 Fifth Avenue, New York, N.Y. 10010

First published in Great Britain 1984
by Granada Publishing Limited, London

Contents

Introduction

The robbery of the German Reichsbank, the State Bank of the Third Reich, in 1945 was not only the biggest robbery in history but for many years the least known to the world at large.

The Nazi era inspired almost as many myths of gold and treasure as the buccaneer days of the Spanish Main—myths of SS loot at the bottom of Alpine lakes, of sunken U-boats stuffed with jewels, of Rommel's gold buried beneath the Libyan sands. A few of these legends have a basis in fact—those surrounding Lake Toplitz in Austria, for example. Millions in counterfeit English pound notes were recovered from this deep lake in the Tyrol some years ago, and at the time of writing, more mysterious treasure chests have been sighted on the lake bed, lying beside the wreckage of a German plane, whose pilot's skeleton has remained perfectly preserved in the undisturbed depths. Probably it is to Lake Toplitz that most people's minds turn at the mention of Nazi treasure. But *Nazi Gold* is about a very different kind of treasure, and its subject is a story which has lingered for years in the half-light of rumor and speculaton—the disappearance of millions of dollars' worth of gold and currency from the Reichsbank reserves buried somewhere in the mountains of Bavaria.

In the chaos of the German collapse at the end of the Second World War, and in the administrative confusion of the American occupation that followed, any facts that were known about the loss of part of the Reichsbank reserves were largely ignored, and belated efforts by the American military and German civil authorities to put two and two together in the postwar years were dogged by ignorance of what had gone awry, because of the lack of coordination between investigative agencies, and by the total disappearance of key witnesses from the scene.

The first public utterance on the subject of Reichsbank treasure seems to have been an article by Henriette von Schirach (the wife of Hitler's former Youth Leader) entitled "What Happened To The Reichsbank Gold?"

which appeared in the now defunct picture magazine, *Wochenend*, in 1950. This article at least posed the right questions, even if it did not actually answer them, and it seems to have provoked the Munich Criminal Investigation Division (CID) of the Bavarian Police to carry out their own investigation into certain aspects of the case. But even they had only limited facts at their disposal, and they were unable to bring any prosecutions and never made their report public.

While the CID investigation was in progress, the story was taken up again by a German journalist, Ottmar Katz, in an article — "Where is the Gold from the Walchensee?" which appeared in *Quick* magazine in 1952. Before long this came to the attention of an English writer, William (Billy) Stanley Moss, who began his own private investigation into the Reichsbank robbery and its aftermath. The resulting book, *Gold Is Where You Hide It*, was published in London in 1956. It was incomplete and in parts misleading. But it was the first attempt at a coherent account of the Reichsbank affair and the first to appear outside of Germany. Indirectly it lead to this present more definitive history.

Billy Moss, author of a best-selling war adventure, *Ill Met By Moonlight* (an account of his part in the daring kidnapping of the commander of the German Forces in Crete), first stumbled on the Reichsbank robbery through an intermediary — a Polish-born, naturalized Briton by the name of Andrew Kennedy. During the war Andrew Kennedy had served as the head of an escape organization in Hungary and later as a member of the British resistance organization, Special Operation Executive (SOE). After the war he lived and worked as a business in Germany, forming a wide circle of friends, including Billy Moss and two inhabitants of the Bavarian mountain resort of Garmisch-Partenkirchen — Gusti Stinnes and her English husband Eric Knight. It was from Eric and Gusti Knight that Kennedy and Moss first got wind of the story of the Reichsbank treasure.

Billy Moss labored under several disadvantages. He was not in the best of health, nor did his financial resources stretch as far as a project of this scope required. Above all, he was denied any kind of cooperation from the United States authorities, whose various archives it was thought might contain vital information about the Reichsbank robbery. Indeed, the U.S. government denied, and have continued to deny, that such a robbery ever took place or that any U.S. Army personnel had any part in it or the events that followed. The archives, the government maintained, possessed no records that bore on such a case. Denied the crucial documentation the investigation needed, Moss's book was inevitably somewhat skimpy and speculative. Nevertheless, for nearly thirty years it was to remain the best attempt at a solution to the mystery of what happened to the Reichsbank treasure.

Soon afterwards, the *Guinness Book of Records* picked up a Reuter message on the story in the Press Association-Reuter files in London and recorded it in earlier editions under the heading "Robbery: Biggest Unsolved." The entry accused officers of both the American Army and the former German Army of taking part in the theft and rightly pointed out that no one had ever been charged with it, though its inventory of what had been taken was wide of the mark. The entry was reprinted in the Guinness book in various forms in every subsequent year (except one), and it was there that the present authors, independently of one another, first came across the germination of the remarkable events which form the subject of *Nazi Gold*.

Douglas Botting, a writer and traveler, first noticed the Guinness entry in 1969 following a visit to Brazil in which he believed that he had discovered the whereabouts of Hitler's missing Party Secretary, Martin Bormann. Like Moss, Botting got nowhere with the U.S. archives, came to the conclusion (wrongly, it turned out) that the Reichsbank robbery was the product of anti-American propaganda by the Soviet-controlled East German press—an entry to that effect was carried in the 1970 edition of the Guinness book—and turned his attention to other themes in immediate postwar Germany.

Five years later, just before Christmas 1974, Ian Sayer, a transport executive who was born in the year of the Reichsbank robbery, bought his first copy of the Guinness book. His interest was immediately stirred and, with the help of a colleague, Harry Seaman, he immediately embarked on a private investigation of the Reichsbank case—a project which soon became a compulsive quest to find out the truth once and for all. This was easier said than done. Sayer started from zero. He did not even have Billy Moss's advantage of personal contact with some of the *dramatis personae* in the Reichsbank affair. He knew none of the real names of the people involved and nothing of the techniques of historical and criminal research, the means of tracing foreign nationals in faraway countries or of extracting sensitive records from military and police departments in such places as Washington, Berlin, and Buenos Aires. But he was hooked, and he persevered.

At first it was a thankless task, days of foot-slogging through the Public Records Office and Colindale Newspaper Library, endless hours poring through the international telephone directories. Many people had died in the intervening years, including Billy Moss. But, although he was not aware of this for some while, history proved to be on Sayer's side. The debacle of Richard Nixon's second presidency and the wreckage of the Watergate cover-up led indirectly to the enactment of the Freedom of Information Act, which provided for a virtual open-sesame to the archives of the U.S. government and to the various departments and agencies of state.

This was the first breakthrough. With infinite gradualness over a period of months and years, the archives began to yield their secrets. Though the Department of the Army in Washington continued to deny that the Reichsbank robbery had ever taken place or that American soldiers played any part in the events described in the book, one document led to another, one name led to five more names, until Sayer began to build a growing dossier of crime, corruption, and cover-up in American-occupied Germany after World War Two. In 1976, in order to make a personal search of the national and military archives in Washington and neighboring Maryland and Virginia, Sayer set sail for America on the QE2 (he prefers not to fly). He found himself in curious situations that he had not envisaged before — inside the Pentagon, ringing up the CIA, knocking on the doors of the Secret Service, Military Intelligence, and a host of other U.S. government and military agencies. The documentation led off on many murky tangents. Often it was heavily sanitized. In certain areas where the records had been deliberately destroyed it dried up altogether. This was balanced by Sayer's discovery of the data stored in the Defense Department's computer — the basic means of tracing individuals across a gulf in time.

Back in England the transatlantic telephone became the medium of contact. The scores of former American Army personnel from the old Bavarian days were located in this way, in places as far apart as Locust Valley in Long Island, Anchorage, Alaska, Concrete in Washington State, Drake Falls, Virginia, Liberty Lake, Hollywood, New York, El Paso, Fort Worth, St. Petersburg, and Palm Springs. Almost without exception, individual Americans (like U.S. government agencies) were unflaggingly courteous and cooperative. After more than thirty years, some could recall little; others were gifted with almost total recall. Most were astonished that the case had been resurrected after so long. All were astonished that the case had been resurrected by an Englishman. This was tolerantly viewed as a typical example of British eccentricity.

Ian Sayer's breakthrough in America was paralleled by a similar breakthrough in Europe. This was made possible by establishing contact (through the goodwill of Billy Moss's running-mate, Andrew Kennedy) with a former Polish national, Ivar Buxell, who was close to the action in postwar Bavaria and had subsequently emigrated to Venezuela. Buxell had remained in touch with old friends from his German past, the hub of a wheel from which radiated many spokes. He was to prove a tireless and unfailingly helpful source of information for many of the events described in this book. From men with a sense of history like Buxell, or William C. Wilson (a former agent in the U.S. Army Criminal Investigation Division with a remarkable and astonishingly accurate memory of events and personnel) or Tom Agoston (an English newspaperman who first broke the story of the Garmisch affair and led Sayer to the memoranda and correspondence of Guenther Reinhardt, a crucial figure in the later stages of this story), it proved possible to fill in some of the gaps in the official archives and to enliven the historical documentation with more human and anecdotal material than might otherwise have been salvaged from the past.

The net extended to four continents and to places as widely dispersed as Caracas and Buenos Aires, Harare in Zimbabwe, Rome and Livigno in Italy, Graz and Innsbruck in Austria, and Garmisch and Mittenwald in Bavaria. But it was not all easy sailing. There were times when the project seemed to have run into a brick wall, when months passed without progress and no way forward could be found. As a private individual it was difficult for Sayer to probe official institutions and reconstruct events which had been the subject of a cover-up several decades before. Certain people, not unnaturally, objected to inquiries into their past, and one or two caused difficulties which were potentially embarrassing in the extreme. In March 1981, for example, following a meeting in Innsbruck with a German journalist to discuss aspects of *Nazi Gold*, Ian Sayer's name was given to the London *Daily Mail* by a person or persons unknown as someone who could help the police inquiries into the disappearance and suspected kidnapping of an Englishwoman, Jeanette May, in Italy during the preceding winter.

Mrs. May, whose first marriage had been to a member of the Rothschild family, had disappeared with a woman friend while driving through the remote mountain region of Italy in a blizzard in the winter of 1980. Needless to say, Sayer had absolutely nothing to do with Mrs. May's disappearance, nor did he know who had given his name to the *Daily Mail*, though he had his suspicions. In July 1981, he was interviewed for the first time by two members of the Carabinieri from Italy and two members of the Serious Crimes Squad from London. There the matter rested until the remains of the two women were discovered in the mountains in January 1982. A year later, the Italian police reopened the case as one of suspected

murder. In March 1983, Sayer was summoned to Scotland Yard for interrogation by representatives of the Italian police, and he was implicated by
the Italian press not only in the death of Jeanette May but even in the
death of the Italian banker, Roberto Calvi, and in the activities of Propaganda 2, (P2), a right-wing Masonic lodge, in articles which would have
been hilarious had they not been so blatantly untrue and appallingly de-
famatory.

Though Sayer had no difficulty in establishing his innocence with the
Italian police, he was left in little doubt that all this had occurred as a result
of his involement with the *Nazi Gold* project — as a warning, perhaps, not
to probe deeper into the affairs of the past.

In the beginning, Ian Sayer had had no thought of producing a book
out of his investigations. He had been motivated purely by a spirit of adventure, the thrill of the chase, and a desire to discover the real truth about
an episode which, with its dope-peddling, corruption, murder, and "Third
Man" atmosphere, seemed to contain all the elements of fiction and modern myth. But as the files of archive documents, interview transcripts,
court-martial and investigative records, and eyewitness correspondence
grew until they occupied forty feet of shelving space and over one hundred
hours of tape time, it became obvious that they contained historical material of interest to a wider audience and that it should ideally be organized
into book form.

Slowly this material was arranged into a rough narrative line. Early efforts to produce a book proved abortive. Then one summer, at Agatha's
waterfront tavern in Nissaki, a small village on the remoter northeast coast
of the Greek island of Corfu, Ian Sayer struck up an acquaintance with
Douglas Botting, whose earlier efforts to crack the Reichsbank mystery
were already known to him, and the present collaboration was born. The
research had taken eight years. The writing of the book — a task of considerable complexity and magnitude — was to take two more years. While the
resulting work can reasonably claim to be the most definitive study of this
remarkable case to date, it is not an exhaustive one. The story of the
Reichsbank mystery remains in part a mystery. No one was charged with
complicity in the robbery and few have volunteered to confess. There are
gaps in the evidence. Some archival material has been destroyed; some has
proved extremely difficult to locate; some could not be printed because of
the laws of libel.

The research behind this book had begun as an attempt to discover the
truth about the world's greatest robbery. It was never envisaged that it
would eventually reveal a story of corruption in the American occupation

of Germany and of deliberate cover-up by the U.S. European Command in Berlin and the Department of the Army in Washington. The authors had never set out to indict American military government in Germany after the war. Both authors were fully aware of the huge contribution made by the government and people of the United States to the defeat of Nazism in World War Two and the salvation of Western Europe in the years that followed. They were also aware of the sincere and dedicated efforts made by a great many Americans working in military government towards the restoration of order, decency, and hope in the American Zone of Germany during the period of havoc and privation immediately after the war. Nevertheless, the evidence revealed much that was wrong with the U.S. Occupation and a degree of corruption on the part of a portion of American military government personnel that was highly relevant to the story of *Nazi Gold* and could hardly be overlooked. Some American readers of this book may perhaps feel as a consequence that the book is anti-American in tone. The authors contend that this is not so. It simply attempts to tell the truth as clearly as the complex and often opaque raw material will allow and in the process sheds new light on a little-known byway of modern history.

From conception to publication *Nazi Gold* has taken ten years in the making. That it ever reached completion at all is due largely to the help of a great many people, whose names are listed in the Acknowledgments, and whose contributions are gratefully acknowledged here. Particular thanks are due to Mary Sayer, for her steadfast encouragement and active support of the project throughout all its stages; to Melanie Bryan, who kept the complex mass of research material from ever lapsing into chaos and anarchy and typed thousands of pages of research notes and draft versions of the book; to Gail Lynch and Pamela Shaw, who fished so patiently and to such excellent effect in the Washington archives; to Alastair Brett of the *Sunday Times*, who through thick and thin continued to have faith in the book and was an unfailing source of strength; to Antony Terry, who lent the great weight of his experience and expertise as the former *Sunday Times* correspondent in Germany and who conducted interviews and undertook research for the project in Europe; to Andrew Thompson, the *Sunday Times* man in Buenos Aires, who courageously persevered with delicate and difficult lines of inquiry in spite of the adverse working climate brought about by the Falklands conflict; and to Katy and Anna Botting for finding the location of the Walchensee treasure and for their enthusiasm when the going was rough.

Ian Sayer
Douglas Botting

18 July 1983

Authors' Note

The Reichsbank robbery was not a single robbery headed by a single mastermind but a series of separate incidents involving different portions of the Reichsbank gold and currency reserves between May 1945 and March 1947. It might help the reader to envisage the Reichsbank treasure as a dead whale attacked by sharks. There are big sharks and little sharks and they take big bites and little bites. They are all devouring the same carcass at about the same time but they are acting independently, not in collusion.

To help the reader further in comprehending the magnitude of the sums of gold and currency mentioned in this book, we have given both the 1945 values and/or their corresponding 1983 values in U.S. dollars. With the assistance of the Bank of England and the United States Embassy in London we have calculated that the value of the 1945 £1 sterling is £11 in 1983; the 1945 $1 is worth $5.50. *Additionally, the value of the 1945 £1 sterling was equal to $4.0350 1945 dollars.* *

The price of gold in 1945 was $35 per ounce. The prevailing rate in January 1983 was $487 ½ per ounce — or about 14 times the 1945 *statistical face value.*

To simplify the figures in this story, the value of all other foreign currencies has been converted to its 1945 U.S. dollar equivalent.

* Editor's italics.

Acknowledgments

The authors are profoundly grateful to many people and institutions in a number of countries throughout the world who unstintingly gave up a great deal of their time and energy to answering—by letter, telephone, and personal interview—a remorseless stream of questions about complicated events of many years ago. To all of these people—and especially to those who on occasion ungrudgingly allowed their privacy to be invaded—the authors extend their very genuinely felt gratitude and appreciation. In addition to those mentioned in the Introduction, thanks are due to the following:

Private Individuals

United Kingdom
Mike Bennett, Michael Cuddy, David Forwell, Roy Furness, Brig. Sir James Gault (deceased), Gene Gutowski, Sir Frank McFadzean, Norris McWhirter, Andrew Mollo, Fred Nolan, Peter Pringle, Winston Ramsey, Mrs. T. Reedy, Eric Runacres, Keith Salter (deceased), Harry Seaman, Colin Simpson, Anthony Smith, Dr. D. A. Spencer, Lorana Sullivan, Franklin Wood

United States
Robert M. Allgeier, Ward S. Atherton, Theodore H. Ball, Jack Bennett, James S. Billups, Edward E. Bird, Vernon J. Blondell, Charles I. Bradley (deceased), William G. Brey, Earl S. Browning, Paul O. Bruehl, Ralph Carlin, Lawrence Carls, Lucius D. Clay (deceased), Pat Conger, Harry Cottingham, Henry D. Cragon (deceased), John M. Curran, H. A. Deck, Walter R. Dee, Alan Dinehart, Jr., Werner C. Duke, William E. Eckles, Hal Faust, H. H. Frey, Frank C. Gabell, David A. Gallant, Frank

Gammache, Dale M. Garvey, Hobert R. Gay, Mrs. H. R. Gay, Alfred Geiffert, III, Hon. William Geiler, Gordon Gray, Louis Graziano, John E. Grindell, Alphonse Hartl (deceased), Edwin Hartrich, Thomas Hasler, Charles R. Hayes, James H. Hea, Joseph W. Hensel, Robert R. Hensley, Arthur Horn, Walter N. Israel, Edward A. Jesser, William A. Karp, E. P. Keller, Jack Ketcham, Leo de Gar Kulka, Thomas M. Lancer, Morton K. Lange, Anthony W. Lobb, Russell R. Lord (deceased), Gail Lynch, Milton S. Marcus, Max L. Marshall, Paul H. Marvin, F. J. McDonnell, Bernice McIntyre, Werner Michel, Charles B. Milliken, William J. Moran, Thomas V. Mullen, Robin E. Mullins, Woodrow L. Nelson, Lester M. Nichols, Melvin W. Nitz, Eli Nobleman, Albert "Nick" Nokutis, Charles M. O'Donnell, Harry J. Painter, Oliver S. Patton, Rev. G. Hurst Paul, Mrs. Alice Peccarelli, Frank Purcell, Roger Rawley, Tom Reedy, Jonathan B. Rintels, Mrs. Kenneth C. Royall, Fred Schnackenderg (deceased), Val Seeger, III, George M. Seignous, Pamela Shaw, Robert B. Shawe, John W. Sheffield, Raymond T. Shelby, George C. Sheldon, Bruce B. Simmons, Albert Singleton, Leonard H. Smith, Herbert L. Snapp, Charles W. Snedeker, Sidney N. Steinbach, Arthur C. Timbo, Frank L. Tracy, Ed Valens, Murray Van Waggoner, Hans von Euen, Clarence J. Wardle, Arnold H. Weiss, William C. Wilson, Clifton H. Young, Thomas H. Young, Leon Zackrewski, Lester C. Zucker

Germany

Tom Agoston, Christl Belwe, Eugene K. Bird, Don Brooks, Karl Dönitz, Dr. Sieglinde Ehard (*née* Odorfer), Barbara Freem, Willie Gerl, Leo M. Goodman, Klothilde Hallmann, Dr. Robert M. W. Kempner, Andrew Kennedy, Eric Knight, Ernest Langendorf, Hans Neuhauser, Dr. Maximilian Ott, Gunter Peis, Franz Pfeiffer, Josef Pinzl, Michael Pössinger, Elmer G. Pralle, Ardo Rousselle, Robert R. Seeger, Albert Speer, Jakob "Jaky" Stubel, Kenneth G. Van Buskirk, Hubert von Blücher, Henriette von Schirach, Armin Walter

Austria

Hans Fischer, Fritz Rauch, Dr. Phillip Schenk, James W. Shea, Josef Veit, Simon Wiesenthal

Italy

Walter (Mucki) Clausing,

Spain

Mrs. Chiquita Sitwell

Mexico

Juan A. A. Sedillo

South Africa
Lüder von Blücher
Zimbabwe
Don and Susan Miller, Andrew Searle, Lizbeth Searle, Brigadier M. H.
F. Waring (deceased)
Venezuela
Ivar Buxell
Switzerland
Terence Taylor

Organizations — United States

U.S. Army Criminal Investigation Command — Falls Church, Virginia
Major Brigham S. Shuler, *Chief of Public Affairs*; Captain Terry McCann;
Major Harlan J. Lenius, *Chief of Public Affairs*; Major John E. Taylor, *Chief of Public Affairs*; Russell A. Powell, *Chief, Release of Information Division*;
Leonard F. Gunn, *Acting Chief, Release of Information Division*; G. M. Anderson, *Chief, Release of Information Division*

U.S. Army Judiciary, Falls Church, Virginia
James D. Kemper, Jr., *Clerk of Court*; Mary B. Dennis, *Deputy Clerk of Court*

Office of the General Counsel
Bland West, *Deputy General Counsel (Military and Civil Affairs)*

Office of the Adjutant General and the Adjutant General Center
Rome D. Smyth, *Director, Administration Management*

U.S. Army Military History Institute, Carlisle Barracks, Pennsylvania
Joyce L. Eakin, *Assitant, Director for Library Services*; John J. Slonaker, *Chief, Historical Reference Section*

Office of the Chief of Information, Public Information Division
Lt.-Col. Hugh G. Waite, *Chief, News Branch*

U.S. Army Intelligence Agency, U.S. Army Intelligence and Security Command, Fort George G. Meade, Maryland
Thomas F. Conley, *Chief, Freedom of Information Center*; James L. Selechta, *Chief, Freedom of Information Division*

Naval Investigative Service, Alexandria, Virginia
Captain L. E. Connell, *Director, NIS*

Department of the Air Force, Headquarters Air Force Office of Special Investigations, Washington, D.C.

Rudolph M. Schellhammer, *Director of Plans, Programs, and Resources*; Lt.-Col. Thomas M. Slawson, *Deputy Director of Plans, Programs, and Resources*; Robert T. Walker, *Information Release Division Director of Plans, Programs, and Resources*

National Archives and Records Service, Washington, D.C.

James J. Hastings, *General Archives Division*; William H. Cunliffe, *Assistant Chief Modern Military Branch, Military Archives Division*; George G. Chalou, *Assistant Chief, Reference Branch, General Archives Division*; Frederick W. Pernell, *Reference Branch, General Archives Division*; William G. Lewis, *Reference Branch, General Archives Division;* Janet L. Hargett, *Chief, Reference Branch, General Archives Division;* Steve Bern

Office of the Secretary of the Treasury, Washington, D.C.

Dennis M. O'Connell, *Acting Chief Counsel, Office of Foreign Assets Control*; J. Robert McBrien, *Special Assistant, Special Legislation and Projects, Office of Enforcement*; Stanley L. Sommerfield, *Acting Director, Office of Foreign Assets Control*; Robert W. Vayda, *Assistant to the Director (Legislative Programs)*; Henry C. De Seguirant, *Assistant Director of Personnel (Executive Manpower and Employment)*

U.S. Secret Service

Thomas A. Troubly, *Freedom of Information and Private Acts Officer*

Department of State, Washington, D.C.

Ely Maurer, *Assistant Legal Adviser*; Homer R. Nue, *Records Specialist, Office of Management, Bureau of Personnel*

Federal Bureau of Investigation, Washington, D.C.

Clarence M. Kelley, *Director*; E. L. Grimsley; Allen M. McCreight, *Chief, Freedom of Information-Privacy Acts Branch, Records Management Division*

Central Intelligence Agency, Washington, D.C.

Gene F. Wilson, *Information and Privacy Coordinator*; George W. Owens, *Information and Privacy Coordinator*

Alien Property Unit

John R. Franklin, *Chief*

Miscellaneous

Immigration and Naturalization Service, Milwaukee, Wisconsin; National Personnel Records Center (Civilian Personnel Records), St. Louis, Missouri; State of California, Department of Health Services, Office of the State Registrar of Vital Statistics; National Personnel Records Center (Military Personnel Records), St. Louis, Missouri; Mission of the United States, Berlin Document Center, Berlin, Germany; Daniel P. Simon, *Director, Veterans Administration, Milwaukee, Wisconsin*; B. E. Pile, *Veterans Ser-*

vices Officer; Federal Reserve Bank of New York, New York; Carl Back-lund, *Chief, Correspondence Files Division*; Library of Congress, Washington, D.C.; Military Bookman, New York

Organizations — Europe

W. D. Frank, *U.S. Embassy, Bonn, Germany, Personnel Officer*; E. M. Kelly, *Curator, Bank of England, Administration Department, Museum and Historical Research Section*; Paul D. Mortimer-Lee, *Bank of England, Economics Intelligence Department*; Metropolitan Police Office, New Scotland Yard; Public Records Office, Kew, Surrey; Landeszentralbank in Bayern, Munich; Deutsche Bundesbank, Frankfurt; Deutsche Dienststelle (WAST), Berlin; Bundesarchiv, Aachen; Auswärtiges Amt, Bonn; Wiener Library, London; Imperial War Museum Library, London; British Museum Library, London; British Museum Newspaper Library, London; City Business Library, London; Westminster Central Reference Library, London; Ministry of Defence Library, London; U.S. Army Library, Heidelberg, Germany; Stars and Stripes Library, Darmstadt, Germany; Feltham Public Lending Library, Feltham, Middlesex; History Bookshop, London

Illustrations

The photographs are from Ian Sayer's collection. Thanks are due to the following for providing photographic prints:

U.S. Army Signal Corps (for photos of the Merkers Mine)

U.S. Army Intelligence Agency (for photo of Dr. Walther Funk)

Berlin Document Center (for photos of Brig.-Gen. Josef Spacil, Lt.-Col. Friedrich (Fritz) Rauch, Helmut Groeger, Hubert von Blücher)

Albert Singleton (for photos of Displaced persons in Mittenwald, Three ex-officers recovering weapons, Three ex-officers bringing down the weapons)

Ottmar Katz (for photo of Tree stump which marked one of the secret treasure caches)

Rolf Höhne (for photo of The main gold hole on the Steinriegel)

Alfred Geiffert III (for photo of Major William Geiler, Capt. George Garwood and Capt. Walter Dee and of American soldiers on the forestry track beside the gold hole)

Francis White (for photo of Helmut Schreiber)

Col. Charles M. O'Donnell (for photo of Col. Russell Lord with Brig.-Gen. Muller)

Col. Robert M. Allgeier (for photo of himself)

Garmisch Police (for photo of Zenta Hausner)

After the Battle magazine (for photos of Haus Hohe Halde and The apartment where Zenta Hausner was found dead)

Frank Purcell (for photo of The boys from the CID at a wedding)

William C. Wilson (for photos of Philip Benzell and Walter Snyder)

Lt.-Col. Frank Tracy (for photo of Brig.-Gen. Muller presiding over a meeting.

NAZI GOLD

I. THE ROBBERY

1

The Destruction of the Reichsbank

On the morning of 3 February 1945, an anonymous young American air force bombardier in the Plexiglas nose of a B-17 Flying Fortress crossing Berlin on a course parallel to and a little south of the city's most fashionable boulevard, the Unter den Linden, depressed his salvo-release bomb switch and, with the traditional bombardier's cry — "Bombs away! Doors closing! Let's get the hell out of here!" — unwittingly set in motion the greatest robbery in history, and a mystery and a cover-up which threatened to involve the United States Army in Germany, and the Pentagon and the Department of the Army in Washington, in a scandal that predated Watergate by nearly 30 years.

Until that fateful morning there had been no major air raid on the German capital for nearly two months. For much of the winter a continuous cloud had covered the city for days on end and the British and American heavy bomber groups had turned their attention to easier targets nearer to home, leaving the Berliners free to concentrate their anxieties on the Russian armies, then pushing rapidly and with overwhelming force towards the banks of the River Oder, only 55 miles to the east. Unfortunately for the Berliners the arrival of the Red Army on the Oder coincided more or less exactly with a break in the weather over Berlin, and for the morning of 3 February the weather forecast was clear skies followed by intermittent cloud and rain later in the afternoon — conditions good enough to permit a massive daylight air strike against the city in support of the Russian push. By destroying military installations, government buildings and transportation centers — especially the Tempelhof marshaling yards — the Allies aimed to bring about a complete disruption of German preparations for a counterattack against the Russian positions. To achieve this, the 8th

U.S. Army Air Force launched the first 1,000-bomber raid ever to be directed on Berlin in daylight.

Though 3 February was a Saturday it was still a working day in the German capital. Shops, banks, offices, and ministries were open for business and the streets were crowded with office workers and bewildered German refugees who had fled to the capital from the advancing Russians in the east. The Berliners' first intimation of danger was an announcement on the radio. It took the usual form: "Attention! Heavy formations of enemy aircraft approaching from the area Hanover-Brunswick." Later, as the bombers drew nearer, the ominous wail of the air-raid sirens announced the first public warning, followed in a short while by the general warning. The railways and tram cars stopped. The office workers tumbled down into their cellars. The refugees ran aimlessly from street to street in a vain search for shelter. The crews of the flak batteries elevated their guns, warmed up their radar sets, and fused their shells. At the Zoo the sound-detecting devices on the huge flak towers began to swing around like giant ears. Hospitals, fire services, civil defense, and police were put on alert. Hot soup and shrouds were sorted in readiness and emergency mortuaries prepared. As the leading bombers appeared over a seemingly lifeless city, towards ten o'clock the guns began firing almost as one.

Nine hundred and fifty Flying Fortress bombers with an escort of 575 Mustang fighters roared over Berlin that morning. One thousand and three had taken off for Berlin from their bases in England, but 25 had had to divert to targets of opportunity and 28 turned back. (On the same morning 362 B-24s of the 8th U.S. Army Air Force had come in the same bomber stream but stopped short at Magdeburg, where they bombed the synthetic oil installations.) They came in at 26,600 feet, so high above the ground that they looked at first like tiny glistening points of light, in formations like perfect triangles, tiny clear-cut patterns remote and unattainable, vapor trails streaming behind them from all four engines. Steadily they droned on high above the city in an endless stream that stretched back in a line across almost the whole of Western Europe to the Zuider Zee, and small sooty smudges erupted in their midst and blossomed into tiny round black clouds of flak as the 1,200 antiaircraft guns, pounding away all over the city, tried to get their range and height. In intensity and accuracy this was the most fearul flak concentration yet encountered by the 8th Air Force and as the raid developed, one or two planes in each formation were hit and seen to fall. Now and again the planes dropped white markers and what looked from the ground like tiny marbles—high-explosive bombs, fragmentation bombs, incendiary bombs, incendiary clusters, and mines.

Berlin was a bomb-aimer's delight. A very broad artery 15 miles long known as the East-West Axis, rebuilt by Hitler in 1938 for his victory marches in the early months of the war, led straight as a die to the very heart of the city, the Brandenburg Gate, clearly visible because of its conspicuous position even from 20,000 or 30,000 feet up. In this central area the key buildings stood out prominently because of size—the Reichstag, the Reich Chancellery, Goering's huge Air Ministry, the Propaganda Ministry and other principal government ministries on the Wilhelmstrasse. Eastwards from the Brandenburg Gate ran the Unter den Linden, which was virtually an extension of the East-West Axis. Four blocks to the south of this avenue another prominent edifice stood out clearly—the Reichsbank, the heart of Nazi Germany's banking system, the citadel of its national treasure, and a tempting target to any plane which had completed half its run across Berlin and not yet dropped its bomb load. Bombing visually in good conditions with the city center laid out sharp and clear as a map beneath them, the Americans dropped 2,265 tons of bombs in the heaviest bombardment Berlin had experienced in the war to date.

The city was ravaged. Houses were sliced through like a knife through a layer cake, whole blocks reduced to a pile of bricks no higher than a man, whole streets turned to rubble, from which came the cries of the trapped and the dying in cellars blocked by mounds of immovable concrete. The bombing had been so intense that railway cars weighing 200 tons had been lifted bodily off the rails and the air was full of charred paper from eviscerated offices to a height of 1,000 feet. Roads were blocked by collapsed buildings and yawning bomb craters, severed water mains gushing like geysers and rescue teams everywhere digging frantically through hot masonry. The fires burned so fiercely that bodies were glued to the surface of the streets by the heat, white-hot sparks shot hundreds of feet into the sky, rivets exploded like bullets, and brandy detonated in the cellars with the force of a *Panzerfaust*. There was the smell of air raid everywhere—an overpowering unmistakable stench of compacted earth, thick smoke, acrid brick dust, charred wood, spent cordite, burst sewers, musty cellars, and escaping gas. When the steel doors of the bunkers were unlocked, the survivors emerged blinking into a vision of Armageddon, a medieval picture of hell fire. A thick pall of smoke hung over the city to a height of 20,000 feet. Blue-black columns of smoke, lit by flickering tongues of orange-yellow flame, obscured visibility to a few yards ahead. Olive-green dust and whitish plaster-rubble covered the streets several feet deep and when it started to rain this turned to a sticky paste.

It was so dark in the center of the city that no one noticed when evening fell. Photographs taken during the day look as though they had been taken in the middle of the night—the steel-helmeted fire-fighters of the Luftschutzpolizei silhouetted against the flames consuming the smoking ruins in the Alexanderplatz; the dome of the French Church streaming with fires and smoke like a gigantic Olympic torch; above the unscathed Kaiser Friedrich Museum a dust cloud towering as monstrous as a Saharan sand storm. A Swedish journalist filed the first press report of the raid:

Indescribable scenes occurred in Berlin on Saturday when American bombers launched the heaviest attack of the entire war. When the attack came—at a time when the Russians were advancing into areas where many Berliners had their weekend cottages before the war—it quickly became apparent that the ARP was seriously disorganized and short of staff. Only a very few fighters went up. The undermanned fire brigade had great difficulty in fighting the gigantic fires. Many Berliners were so shocked by this last visitation that they refused to emerge from their shelters.

Two thousand Berliners died in the great raid of 3 February—almost one for every ton of bombs—and 120,000 were made homeless. At least one returning bomber crew expressed anxiety about the civilian casualties they had inflicted, writing in their log book: "Berlin, Saturday, barrage flak, weakening as each group went over. No damage to ship. Visual! 5 × 1,000 pounders. Shacked women and children." Whole districts were flattened, and the bombs had scored several notable hits. One was the Gestapo headquarters in the Prinz Albrechtstrasse, which was set on fire. Another was the People's Court, where the Court's President, the infamous Nazi jurist Dr. Roland Freisler, was killed. Freisler was the man who had tried and sentenced to death hundreds of suspects accused of complicity in the 20 July plot on Hitler's life the previous year. That cataclysmic morning of 3 February he was crushed to death by collapsing beams in the air raid shelter beneath the courtroom, still clutching the file of one of the plotters, Fabian von Schlabrendorff, whom he had been about to cross-examine before the air raid suddenly interrupted the court proceedings.

Hitler's Chancellery did not escape unscathed. The morning after the raid Martin Bormann, the Party Secretary and "Hitler's Mephistopheles," wrote to his wife in Berchtesgaden describing the damage:

I have just this minute taken refuge in my secretary's office, which is the only room in the place that has some temporary windows. Yesterday's raid was very heavy. The Reich Chancellery garden is an amazing sight—deep craters, fallen trees, and the paths obliterated by a mass of rubble and rubbish. The Führer's residence was badly hit several times. The new Reich Chancellery was also hit several times and is not useable for the time being. The Party Chancellery buildings, too, are a sorry sight. Telephone communications are still very inadequate, and the Führer's residence and the Party Chancellery still have no connection with the outside world. To crown everything, in this so-called government quarter, the light, power, and water supply is still lacking! We have a water cart standing before the Reich Chancellery, and that is our only supply for cooking and washing up! And the worst thing of all is the water closets. These Commando pigs use them constantly, and not one of them even thinks of taking a bucket of water with him to flush the place.

From this evening I am apparently to have a room in the bunker in which to work and sleep...

The greatest damage in Berlin was caused in the area around the Templehof railway station, but other important targets were hit, among them — a fact of great significance in the story of the Great Reichsbank Robbery — the Berlin headquarters of the Reichsbank itself.

The Reichsbank was a solid, grandiose, turn-of-the-century edifice, as big as the Old Chancellery and almost as big as the Reichstag, and it took twenty-one direct hits to demolish it on the morning of 3 February. It is not clear whether the entire bomb load of one B-17 fell on the headquarters of the Third Reich's banking and financial interest — Flying Fortress bombardiers claimed they could "drop bombs into a pickle barrel from four miles up" using their advanced Norden bombsights — or whether the building succumbed to a series of hits from a number of different bombers during the course of the raid. What is certain is that to the 5,000 employees of the bank huddled in the basement bunker where they had taken shelter, it seemed that the end of the world had indeed arrived. The walls of the cement cavern in which they were entombed wobbled like cardboard, a choking cloud of white dust fell from the ceiling, the lights went out, and women screamed with terror or wept continuously as the bombs exploded directly on top of them and walls and floors collapsed on the basement roof. Amazingly, no one was killed when the bank was hit, though the Reichsbank's President, Dr. Walther Funk, was to admit afterwards: "It was only by a miracle that I was able to reach the surface from this deep cellar together with 5,000 other people."

After the raid, the bank building itself presented the same dismally shattered aspect as much of the rest of the smoking city: pyramids of rubble, exposed offices, broken furniture, wash basins, hanging by their pipes, windows without glass in leaning walls, smoldering door frames, charred papers smoking in the drizzle. As bank workers picked over the remnants of files and archives, the bank directors considered their unprecedented predicament. The presses used for printing German bank notes had been destroyed. Worse, with the walls of the temple, as it were, rent asunder, the treasure of Hitler's Reich, the wealth of the nation, the assets, deposits, reserves, gold and precious metals, cash, currency, and bonds which Germany required to continue the war and to survive the peace, lay vulnerable and exposed. The raid of 3 February had left the Reichsbank's vaults and strong rooms and their priceless contents intact. But it would only require one more raid and a few more bombs for a large part of the concentrated wealth of Nazi Germany to go up, literally, in a puff of smoke and be lost for good.

As the State's own bank, the Reichsbank was the leading bank of Germany and one of the great banks of the world, resembling in certain respects its larger and more august peer, the Bank of England. Like the Bank of England, it involved itself in a curious mixture of governmental and private financial affairs. It handled Reich financial transactions on a worldwide basis, carried out large-scale maneuvers such as foreign exchange control, manipulated exchange rates and tariffs, and provided the finance for the government ministries. Like the Bank of England, the Reichsbank was obliged to buy gold at a fixed minimum price and declare its rates in gold; and it acted as the keeper of the country's gold reserves and lender of last resort. Unlike the Bank of England, however, the Reichsbank also operated as a retail or commercial banking operation for ordinary German citizens, providing banking services for private depositors at 100 main banks and more than 4,000 smaller banks throughout the country.

In 1939, a State decree placed the Reichsbank directly under the control of Adolf Hitler. Soon afterwards the President of the Reichsbank, Dr. Hjalmar Schacht, and most of his fellow directors lost their jobs in an argument with Hitler over the financing of the German war program. Hitler replaced Schacht with a more compliant economist, Dr. Walther Funk, who became both Reich Minister of Economics and President of the Reichsbank. Funk's first job was to fire most of the remaining top executives of the bank, except for the Senior Vice-President, Emil Puhl. Puhl was a banker of the old school; he stood for good order and had long been convinced that the war was lost and the regime doomed—but refused to do anything about it out of loyalty to the "Herr Minister." Puhl became Funk's acting deputy and the man who actually ran the Reichsbank, for Funk himself knew next to nothing about banking and achieved the distinction of having never attended a single meeting of the Bank's Board of Directors.

It was Puhl who, as the war progressed, extended the functions of the Reichsbank to embrace activities organized along peculiarly Nazi lines, including the acquisition of monetary loot from conquered nations and from exterminated persons. Soon after the outbreak of the war the German national gold reserves, already substantially increased by the acquisition of Austrian gold holdings following the *Anschluss*, were significantly augmented by forcible acquisitions from abroad. The Nazis took $2,596,608 of gold from the gold reserve of the Czech National Bank, and $32,000,000 from the National Bank of Hungary. They looted part of the gold reserves of Albania, Holland, the USSR, and other countries overrun by the victorious *Wehrmacht*, and after the conquest of France they stole $200,000,000 worth of gold, comprising part of the Belgian national gold reserves, which had been deposited in the Banque de France for safekeeping by the Belgian government. The Belgian gold was taken to the Reichsbank in Berlin and resmelted. Each bar was then stamped with the letter RB (for Reichsbank), the German eagle, the retrospective date 1938, and its weight to three points of decimals. Later, when the Germans were forced to withdraw from southern Italy in the face of the advancing Anglo-American forces, they took with them $100,000,000 in Italian gold, which also ended up in the Reichsbank's reserves. At the height of the Nazi conquest of Europe the gold reserves held by the Reichsbank were estimated to total as much as $500,000,000 — by today's values the equivalent of $7,500,000,000 — much of it looted from the subject nations of Europe, though the exact figure was never known for sure. (For these and other relative values see the Authors' Note on p. xiv.) Not all of this gold was kept in the headquarters bank in Berlin, for part of the gold reserves had been distributed to various Reichsbank branches (known as special storage points) throughout central and southern Germany in 1943. But Berlin, in spite of these precautions, remained the main holding branch for Reichsbank bullion.

The Berlin headquarters were also the principal repository for deposits of currency, gold, and other valuable belonging to the German Army (*Wehrmacht*), the Military Intelligence Service (*Abwehr*), the Foreign Office, and other affiliated bodies, as well as providing a uniquely macabre banking service for the SS. Early in the war, Reichsbank Deputy President Puhl had worked out an arrangement with his near namesake, General (Obergruppenführer) Dr. Oswald Pohl, Head of the Economic and Administrative Department of the SS, the department responsible for administering the concentration camps. By this arrangement the Reichsbank would receive and dispose of bank notes, securities, gold teeth, jewelry, and other SS loot shipped from Auschwitz and other extermination camps and the SS would be credited with the proceeds. In 1943 the SS carried out an operation known as *Aktion Reinhardt*. They systematically stripped concentration camp inmates of currency, gold coins, jewelry, and clothing, and as a result were able to add a total of $10,004,700 worth of foreign exchange to the SS deposits held in Berlin. Emil Puhl was aided in this patriotic task by being, in addition to the active head of the Reichsbank, a German director of a private international bank in Switzerland — the Bank for International Settlements based at Basle. This gave him the ideal opportunity to act as a fence in disposing of concentration camp gold after it had been melted down into gold bars by the Reichsbank.

Following the bombing of the Reichsbank headquarters in Berlin, Funk decided to authorize the removal of the Reichsbank reserves (and personnel) from Berlin to a place of safety; his deputy, Puhl, was given the task of implementing it. The decision was made quickly, even while the smoke hung over the rooftops and the firemen were still dousing the fires. Officials from the most important departments in Berlin would be evacuated to Weimar and Erfurt and run the Reichsbank from there, while the Third Reich's gold and monetary reserves would be shipped to a new site for safe-keeping — a very deep and a very extensive potassium mine at Merkers, in Thuringia, some 200 miles to the southwest of Berlin, and 30 miles south of Mühlhausen, the nearest sizeable town.

Less than a week after the raid, arrangements for the registering, packaging, and transportation of the German State reserves held in the strong-rooms of the ruined Reichsbank in Berlin were sufficiently advanced for the first consignment — the currency reserves, totalling a billion paper Reichsmarks bundled in a thousand sacks, and a considerable quantity of foreign currency, including over $4,000,000 in U.S. dollar notes — to be dispatched to Merkers on 9 February. Three days later the bulk of the gold reserves followed. They were worth over $200,000,000, weighed around 100 tons, needed 13 railway flat cars to transport them, and 72 hours to unload them and transfer them, in twenty 10-ton trucks, to a special vault designated at Room No. 8, deep inside the Kaiseroda Mine. By 18 February the transfer was completed. For the next seven weeks, while the Anglo-American bomber fleets inflicted even more devastating and ever more frequent air attacks on Berlin and the Russian hordes smashed their way towards the eastern suburbs of the capital, the bulk of Germany's wealth remained securely entombed in a cold cavern hewn out of salt rock half a mile below the Thuringian plain.

Any sense of security the leaders of the Reich might have felt for the safe keeping of the State reserves soon proved hollow when the German front in the west began to collapse. On 22 March units of the U.S. Third Army under its charismatic but controversial commander, Lieutenant-General

George S. Patton, crossed the Rhine, Germany's last natural defensive barrier in the west, in a surprise attack at Ludwigshafen. Slicing through weakening German resistance, Patton's army raced eastwards and on 4 April broke into the Thuringian plain and advanced on Gotha. The Nazi leadership reacted very belatedly to the threat the American advance posed to the State reserves at Merkers. At the last minute Reichsbank officials began a frantic race to remove the entire reserves back to Berlin, but they were handicapped by the speed of the American advance and the partial shutdown of the German railway system due to the Easter holidays. Even by the standards of Nazi administration at the time, this was bizarre. When Goebbels heard the news he exploded: "One could tear one's hair when one thinks that the Reichsbahn is having an Easter holiday while the enemy is looting our entire stocks of gold." The bank officials soon gave up all hope of moving the gold and concentrated on the paper currency, especially the Reichsmarks, which were in short supply in Germany because of the destruction of the printing presses in the 3 February raid. Four hundred and fifty of the 1,000 sacks of paper marks in the mine were got away safely, but there was no time to remove the other 550 before the Americans arrived and they were abandoned at the bottom of the main shaft while the Reichsbank officials attempted to make good their escape.

Merkers fell to the 90th U.S. Division at 11 o'clock on the morning of 4 April. It was not a place that meant anything at all to anyone in the Third Army, and in the normal course of events it could have been a long while before the Americans undertook any systematic search of the mines there. But a day or two later a chance encounter by two American military policemen in Merkers village led to the accidental discovery of the mine and its fabulous contents.

One of the first things the Americans did in Merkers was to establish a curfew and restrict the movement of civilians in the area. On the morning of 6 April two military policement, Privates First Class Clyde Harmon and Anthony Kline, were driving around Merkers on a routine jeep patrol intended to enforce army orders against civilian circulation when they overtook two women on a road outside the town. Since both women were French displaced persons, and one of them was pregnant, the MPs decided to give them a lift. The women were first taken to the command post for questioning, then driven back into Merkers by a Private Mootz. On the way the passed one of the entrances to the Kaiseroda Mine and one of the women exclaimed: "That's the mine where the gold bullion is kept." So the story came out. By noon the news had passed all the way up to the Chief of Staff and within a few hours had been confirmed by other displaced persons and a British sergeant—one of 200 prisoners of war from the 51st Highland Division employed in the mine—who had helped unload the gold when it first arrived. When it was learned that "reportedly the entire reserves of the Reichsbank in Berlin" were hidden in the Kaiseroda Mine, immediate steps were taken to secure the 30 miles of underground passageways and the five entrances to the mines. The 712th Tank Battalion was assigned to guard the entrance at Merkers and the whole of the 357th Infantry Regiment, comprising some 600 to 700 men, covered the other four.

The Americans went into the mine on 7 April. In the space of a minute a double-tier elevator took a party of 90th Division's headquarter officers, accompanied by German mining officials, to the bottom of the main shaft 2,100 feet—the best part of half a mile—beneath the surface. Rarely in history could an invading army have stumbled on an Aladdin's cave of treasure comparable to this one. Stacked against the walls of the main passageway lay huge piles of sacks—550 in all—containing German paper currency totalling the best part of a billion Reichsmarks. Moving down the tunnel the inspection party came to the main vault. The vault was blocked by a brick wall three feet thick with a heavy steel door set in the middle of it. Army engineers were summoned and with a modest half-stick of dynamite blasted a hole through the hole, entered so-called Room No. 8, and peered about them.

They found they were in a great cavern hewn out of dry salt rock 150 feet long, 75 feet wide, and 12 feet high. The floor of the cavern was covered knee-high with over 7,000 numbered bags, laid out in rows. The Americans counted 20 rows in all, some of them two or three sacks high, stretching right to the back of the cavern. Inside each bag were gold coins or gold bars, weighing between 55 and 81 pounds to the bag. There were over 8,527 gold bars altogether, weighing 110,387 tons and valued at more than $112,000,000. The minted gold coins—later officially valued at more than $126,000,000—included a million Swiss francs, a billion French francs, and 711 bags of U.S. $20 gold pieces, $25,000 to a bag. Altogether the gold bars and coin weighed 250 tons. Baled paper money was stacked against one wall, and at the back, crammed into suitcases, trunks, and boxes, was a large quantity of gold and silver plate looted from private homes and institutions all over Europe. All the articles had been flattened with hammers to save storage space, then tossed into the containers until an opportunity came to melt them down into gold and silver bars. There were sacks of gold teeth fillings and gold dental bridges and suitcases crammed with diamonds and pearls and other gems ripped from the victims of the SS death camps, as well as looted eyeglasses, watches, wedding rings, and cigarette cases.

A senior Reichsbank official captured by the Americans, a Dr. Werner Veick, estimated that the total currency reserves captured in the Merkers mine amounted to:

2,700,000 marks in paper money worth over $187,500,000
2,000,000 U.S. dollars
98,000,000 French francs
£110,000 in British money
4,000,000 Norwegian crowns
and smaller amounts of Turkish pounds, Spanish pesetas, and Portuguese escudos

A tentative American estimate at the time put the value of the entire hoard at about $315,000,000—which made it one of the greatest deposits in the world. A more systematic count later put the value of the gold alone at $238,490,000.

The reserves were not the only treasures the Americans seized that day in the Kaiseroda Mine. An enormous number of paintings and other pieces of art, 400 tons in all, were stored in one of the other tunnels, some of them wrapped in paper and burlap, others simply stacked together like sheets of plywood. The paintings had been collected from 15 German museums and included works by Rembrandt, Titian, Van Dyck, Raphael, Dürer, and Renoir. The entire collection was beyond price, but the most priceless of all the items was not a painting but a diminutive 3,000-year-old ancient Egyptian statuette representing Queen Nefertiti, the single most precious art object in Germany. Other finds were made in neighboring mines in the Merkers area, including 400 tons of records from the Reich Patent Office, sufficient to fill 30 railroad cars and potentially as valuable as the gold, along with German Army High Command records, two million books from Berlin, the Goethe collection from Weimar, and much else.

The discovery of the gold and monetary reserves of the Third Reich—or a substantial part of them—was sufficiently important for the Supreme Commander of the Allied Expeditionary Forces, General Eisenhower, and his two senior generals, General Omar N. Bradley (commanding the U.S. 12th Army Group) and General Patton, to take time off from the war to have a look for themselves. They were met at the mine head by two more generals, Generals Eddy and Weyland, and also a Colonel Bernstein from the Finance Section of SHAEF (Supreme Headquarters Allied Expeditionary Force). Patton's aide-de-camp, Colonel Charles R. Codman, recalled the nightmare descent:

The party was ushered into a primitive freight hoist [he wrote to his wife], operated by an unprepossessing German civilian. General Patton began counting the
stars on the shoulders of those about him as the jittery elevator rattled with ever-
accelerating speed down the two thousand feet of pitch-black shaft. He glanced up
at the single cable now barely visible against the diminishing patch of sky.

"If that clothesline should part," he observed thoughtfully, "promotions in the
United States Army would be considerably stimulated."

A voice from the darkness, that of General Eisenhower, "OK George, that's
enough. No more cracks until we are above ground again."

When the five generals stepped out into the dimly lit tunnel at the foot of
the shaft, the GI on guard took one look at the inordinately heavy concentration of top brass in front of him, saluted, and in the subterranean silence
was heard by all to mutter: "Jesus Christ!"

The party moved on down the tunnel into a high-vaulted cavern full of
art treasures. Patton cast a bored glance at a few paintings. "The ones I
saw were worth, in my opinion, $2.50," he was to recall in his memoirs,
"and were the type normally seen in bars in America."

Pointing to a dozen large bales of Reichsmarks in a corner by themselves, Eisenhower demanded: "What are those?"

A German mine official explained that they were earmarked to meet future German Army payrolls.

"I doubt," interjected General Bradley, "the German Army will be meeting payrolls much longer."

The generals entered Room No. 8 and looked around in awe at the captured gold from the Reichsbank reserves that filled the vault. "If these were
the old free-booting days, when a soldier kept his loot," Bradley quipped
to Patton, "you'd be the richest man in the world." And later, back on the
surface, Bradley leaned across to Patton and asked him, half seriously:
"George, what would you do with all that money?" Patton chuckled. Half
his men wanted the gold made into medallions, he said — "One for every
sonuvabitch in Third Army." Eisenhower laughed at that, never dreaming
how oddly prophetic Patton's remark would turn out to be, or just how
much of the Reichsbank reserves would finally adhere to the exceptionally
sticky fingers of a few of his Third Army comrades-in-arms.

It was clear that the treasure could not stay in the caves at Merkers in-
definitely. Patton insisted that Eisenhower send someone up to take responsibility for the vault. Guarding it was tying up a whole regiment, he
said, and knocking hell out of one of his divisions. It was decided that the
entire hoard should be transferred immediately to a place of safety, and the
Reichsbank building in Frankfurt, which had fallen to the Americans on

26 March, was chosen for that purpose. At 9 o'clock on the morning of 14 April the move began, under conditions of rigid security. Down in the mine, jeeps with trailers hauled the treasure from the vault to the shaft, where the loaded trailers were put on board the lifts and brought to the surface. Working nonstop for 20 hours, American troops brought the entire contents of the mine to the surface—gold, currency, works of art in a total of 11,750 containers—inventoried them and loaded them onto thirty-two 10-ton trucks. The next morning the convoy set off for Frankfurt escorted by five platoons of infantry, two machine-gun platoons, ten mobile antiaircraft guns, and an air cover of spotter planes and Mustang fighter bombers. In Frankfurt two infantry companies cordoned off the Reichsbank while each item was unloaded, checked off and moved down into the vaults of the bank. The operation was completed during the night of 15 April. In spite of the extraordinarily heavy guard, the rumor persisted for years afterwards that one truckload of gold or works of art vanished in transit to Frankfurt. But it was the gold and currency reserves still in German hands that were to suffer this kind of indignity. These surviving reserves now became the subject of considerable concern to both Americans and Nazis alike.

The Americans expressed grave doubts that the Merkers hoard represented the entire German gold and currency reserves in existence, and these doubts were confirmed after the interrogation of the Reichsbank officials captured at Merkers. A special team of U.S. Treasury and Bank of England experts under Colonel Bernard Bernstein raced up to Frankfort and from there fanned out into occupied Germany in an urgent quest for other hoards. The Gold Rush, as they termed it, was on.

2

The Flight to the Redoubt

The capture of the Reichsbank reserves at Merkers had proved a devastating blow to the Nazi leadership. Propaganda Minister Goebbels was beside himself with fury and wrote in his diary on 8 April, the day after the capture: "Sad news from Mühlhausen in Thuringia. Our entire gold reserves amounting to hundreds of tons and vast art treasures, including the Nefertiti, have fallen into American hands there. I have always opposed the removal of gold and art treasures from Berlin but, despite my objections, Funk refused to take advice. Probably he was talked into it by his staff and advisors. Now by criminal dereliction of duty they have allowed the German people's most treasured possessions to fall into enemy hands. If I were the Führer I should know what now has to be done."

But Goebbels misjudged Hitler. Far from demanding Funk's head, the Führer allowed himself to be talked into yet another major evacuation of what remained of the Reichsbank reserves — the gold and foreign currency still in German hands in the special storage points in central and southern Germany.

Though it was Funk who put the proposal to Hitler, it was not his original idea. This seems to have come from a 39-year-old colonel in the Schutzpolizei, or Security Police (a branch of the regular police force), Friedrich Josef Rauch, popularly known as Fritz, who since 1942 had acted as adjutant to the Chancellery Secretary, Reich Minister Hans-Heinrich Lammers, one of the twenty most powerfully placed men in the Third Reich, and had recently become Hitler's personal security officer. Rauch is destined to loom large in the story of the Great Reichsbank Robbery, though his role appears at first sight at odds with his impeccable credentials — impeccable, that is, by the standards of the National Socialists.

Friedrich Rauch was born in Munich on 1 September 1906, the son of a senior police inspector. At the early age of 15, while still at school, he joined a right-wing paramilitary organization, the Freikorps, and in this he received his first military training. A year later in November 1922 he joined the Nazi Party (then only two years old) with membership number 11053, and later became a member of the SA, the Nazi Party's private army. In 1923 he was awarded the highly-prized *Blutorden* (Blood Order) for his participation in the march to the Feldherrnhalle in Munich during Hitler's first unsuccessful "Putsch" of 9 November.

From an early age Rauch was a convinced and fervent supporter of the Nazi cause. "Even as a boy," he was to write in a short biography for his employers in 1940, "the unhappy outcome of the World War and the quickening decline of the German nation affected me very deeply. As a result, there was awakened in me very early an interest in political matters. I have remained firmly attached to the National Socialist outlook." Until Hitler seized power in 1933 Rauch's Nazi convictions were a handicap rather than a springboard to his career as a young policeman in the Munich police force. "In my official career," he wrote, "I labored under the odium attaching to me as a known National Socialist."

Things looked up in 1933 when Germany turned to the Nazis. Six foot tall, upright in bearing, an outdoor type without suspect intellectual pretensions, a keen and accomplished horse rider, skier, and mountaineer with all the right political and nationalistic views, Friedrich Rauch was just the kind of man the New Order welcomed to its ranks. He was promoted to inspector, then to captain in the Security Police, and in 1940 he was sent to Berlin to assist with security duties on the staff of the Head of the Reich Chancellery, Dr. Lammers. At the same time he was admitted to the Allgemeine SS with the rank of SS Captain (Hauptsturmführer). In December 1940 Rauch left headquarters duties in the capital at his own request and joined the Flak Regiment of one of the most prestigious formations of the Waffen-SS, the SS Division Leibstandarte "Adolf Hitler," which had its origins in Hitler's elite personal guard battalion in Berlin. For the next six months he was on active service at various fronts in Rumania, Greece, Bulgaria, Yugoslavia, and (very briefly) Russia. A letter Rauch sent back to his superior general in March 1941, from the Dobrudja area on the Black Sea coast of Rumania, gives a good idea of his line of thought at this time. He was then a commandant of a sizeable town — a post, he claimed, "that will be of value to me in my future work with the Security Police." Rauch wrote:

The morale in the unit is fabulous. The resolution to die for the sake of victory imbues officers and men to the innermost recesses of their hearts. The fighting spirit of the [Nazi] movement, arm in arm with other soldierly virtues, will win victory in the war we are fighting for Germany's greatness and her right to live. That is what points the way for all of us — the quiet and determined conviction resulting from these beliefs. I am very glad that I was granted the opportunity of taking part in this great event as a frontline soldier.... We all await the decisive events for which we long.

On 4 July 1941, barely a week after that most decisive of all events — the German invasion of Russia — Captain Rauch was back in Berlin, this time for good, bringing with him a medal, the Yugoslav National Order 5th Class. Once again he took up his Security Police work with the Reich Minister and Head of the Reich Chancellery, Dr. Lammers, who soon formed a glowing opinion of his protege. "Rauch has proved himself first rate," Lammers wrote in a personal assessment to Rauch's superiors at Security Police headquarters towards the end of the month. "His grasp of his duties, his disposition, and his natural characteristics cannot be faulted. His upright military bearing, on and off duty, his excellent and tactful manner of relating to superiors (members of the Reich Government, the Diplomatic Corps, etc.), his way of dealing with subordinates, and his social behavior show him as particularly suited to his present post. He has the ability necessary for making oral reports to me and for dealing in writing with the matters which he has to handle, the power to grasp information rapidly, and the necessary knowledge in the sphere of administrative life and the laws affecting public bodies."

By early 1942 Rauch was a Major of Police and by the spring of 1944 he had reached the rank of Lieutenant-Colonel, his promotion ratified in a certificate signed by Hitler himself and countersigned by Himmler. "IN THE NAME OF THE GERMAN PEOPLE," the certificate ran, "I nominate you, Friedrich Rauch, as Lieutenant-Colonel of Police. I ratify this document in the expectation that the above-named will fulfill the duties of his office with loyalty to his oath of service.... At the same time I assure him of my special protection. The Führer [signed] Adolf Hitler."

It was this same Colonel Rauch, dyed-in-the-wool Nazi, conscientious Third Reich bureaucrat and fanatical patriot, who dreamed up the idea of shipping the remaining Reichsbank reserves lock, stock, and barrel down to the so-called Alpine Fortress, the national redoubt in the Alps where a few die-hards believed that National Socialism would make its last Wagnerian stand. In this impregnable natural fortress, Rauch contended, the treasure of the Third Reich could be used to finance the continuation of the war or the formation of a Fourth Reich — ideally on the side of the Anglo-Americans against the Russians—when the war was over. Rauch put his idea to his immediate superior, Dr. Lammers, who liked it so much that he put it in turn to Economics Minister and Reichsbank President Funk. Funk, too, was impressed and decided that he would put the matter to the Führer himself.

Strictly speaking, the idea of an Alpine Fortress was more a creation of American Intelligence than of Germany's leaders. The first word of such a concept—of a national redoubt of 20,000 square miles of impregnable Alps in southern Germany, western Austria and northern Italy, with Hitler's mountain home, the Berghof at Berchtesgaden, in the center—was circulated by a detachment of the American Office of Strategic Services (OSS) in Switzerland. Their erroneous intelligence report was intercepted by the Germans and subsequently exploited by Goebbels for its propaganda nuisance value. Though the word *Alpenfestung* (Alpine fortress) was almost unknown in Germany and few German generals had the slightest idea what was meant by it or believed in it if they did, Supreme Headquarters Allied Expeditionary Forces (SHAEF) intelligence became convinced of its existence and in the American press it was to become an *idée fixe*. In the Allied Armies there was a growing fear that the Third Reich would hold out for years embattled in the mountains, the Hitlerian regime defended by regular die-hard SS formations and a formidable guerrilla army of fanatical partisans called "werewolves." By April 1945 even the Supreme Commander, General Eisenhower, was in thrall to the idea and altered the strategy of the final campaign in Germany by shifting the main thrust of the American advance southwards to deal with it. But in fact, though some of the ministries in Berlin had evacuated some of their staffs and files to the south, and a few defense works had been thrown up at the western end of the so-called Alpine Fortress, the whole thing was more illusion than reality.

To give Rauch his due, though the national redoubt itself was a myth, the idea of sitting out the final *Götterdämmerung* in some Alpine retreat remote from the battle was not outrageously out of step with the times. As long ago as August 1944, at a meeting at the Hotel Maison Rouge in Strasbourg, leading Nazi financiers and industrialists had met to make long-range plans to safeguard Nazi assets from Allied confiscation. Predicting the defeat of Germany, these men arranged for considerable funds and looted assets to be transferred to neutral and nonbelligerent countries, including Switzerland, Spain, Portugal, Turkey, Argentina, and other Latin American states, where the money could be reinvested and held in reserve for a future Nazi Party revival. By the spring of 1945 the SS, increasingly a law to itself, had been salting away its ill-gotten assets in the Bavarian Alps and the Austrian Tyrol, sneaking concentration camp loot and departmental and personal fortunes in gold, currency, and narcotics to hideaways in the area of the proposed national redoubt — most especially to the region around the Austrian village of Alt Aussee, where the Reich Security Head Office (RSHA) chief, Ernst Kaltenbrunner (the second most powerful SS leader after Himmler), had his private residence. The RSHA was the main security department of the Reich, the branch of the SS which controlled the Gestapo, the security services and the military intelligence service (*Abwehr*). The gold and other precious metals in its possession, as well as gems, art treasures, millions of American dollars, and lesser numbers of genuine and forged sterling notes were already being hidden all over the mountainous areas of southern Bavaria and northern Austria — at the bottom of mines and lakes, in holes in the ground, in the roofs and under the floors of barns and houses. The mountainous south became a treasure house of the collapsing Reich as valuables of all kinds from all kinds of sources poured down from the hard-pressed north. Recently the RSHA had begun to compile records of assets transported south. Only one document purporting to list RSHA treasure survived the end of the war, but it gives an idea of the sheer size of the consignments being spirited away:

50 cases of gold coins and gold articles, each case weighing 100 pounds
2 million U.S. dollars
2 million Swiss francs
5 cases full of diamonds and precious stones
A stamp collection worth at least 5 million gold marks
110 pounds of gold bars

All that Colonel Rauch was proposing and Dr. Funk seconding, therefore, was that the Reichsbank should jump on the same bandwagon that the SS had already started rolling, and get their assets out of the capital — as a purely precautionary measure, of course — while the going was good. In practice this meant that the flight of Nazi gold and other valuables would follow two parallel — and on occasion confusingly intertwined — migratory paths southward to the Bavarian mountains and Austrian Tyrol, one stream consisting of SS (including RSHA, *Scherheit dienst* (SD), and *Abwehr*), Foreign Office, and other reserves, the other of Reichsbank reserves. Rauch always insisted he was no more than a middleman in this operation and that his motivation was patriotic duty rather than personal self-interest. It is not clear whether it was now or later that he first perceived that the more portable and negotiable portions of the Reichsbank reserves could be put to other uses than the ones he had first proposed.

On 8/9 April, it seems that Funk and—almost certainly—Bormann attended a meeting with Hitler in the *Führerbunker* in Berlin to present their case. It was a sticky session. Funk was not Hitler's favorite minister, the fate of the nation's gold bars and banknotes was not uppermost in Hitler's mind, nor was that mind in the best of sorts anymore. Virtually buried alive in the surrealistic netherworld of the bunker, imprisoned amid the rising sour odors of damp, stale boots and disinfectant in tiny cement catacombs lit by lightbulbs which glared night and day without distinction, the head of an empire that had once stretched from the Channel to the Volga now lived the troglodytic life of a U-boat captain stranded on the ocean bottom, all sense of time, season, and weather gone, all contact with the reality of actual events and the actual war fading fast.

The Führer-figure that presented itself before the three visitors was that of a prematurely aged, sick, hysterical, shambling, broken creature, with bowed head and sunken eyes, trembling hands, and a trailing foot—a creature which in its dying moments still clung with feverish intensity to outworn concepts and unrealistic hopes. The idea of moving the Reichsbank reserves out of Berlin was downright defeatism, Hitler snapped. Berlin would not fall, victory was assured, the move was unnecessary. In any case, such a move played into the hands of the nation's enemies, of the traitors that were everywhere in its midst even now. Once in Bavaria, the Führer argued—not without a glimmer of reason—Rauch might hand over all the reserves to Bavarian separatists who could use the treasure to promote a breakaway Bavarian nationalist movement in opposition to the Nazi regime. (Only three weeks later the Bavarian underground was to rebel against the Nazis and the Bavarian populace was to welcome the American Army in the streets of Munich with garlands and wine.)

But Funk's common-sense reasoning eventually prevailed. The exhausted Hitler wearily conceded a grudging consent to the move. The emissaries of the Reichsbank's interests were casually dismissed and the Führer returned to the study of his hateful maps and hopeless war games.

The closing balances of the Berlin Reichsbank's Precious Metal Department before the building was destroyed by bombing had shown that the *official* gold reserves held by the Third Reich totalled $255.96 million. Of this, some 93.17 percent, totalling $238.49 million, was subsequently captured by the Americans after its removal to Merkers, leaving 6.83 percent, amounting to $17.48 million (consisting entirely of looted Belgian gold) still in German hands in the vaults of various Reichsbanks in central and southern Germany on 8 April. Additionally, the Reichsbank still had in its possession many millions of dollars worth of paper Reichsmarks and foreign exchange and continued to act as repository for the precious metal and currency deposits of the *Wehrmacht*, the SS, the *Abwehr*, and the Foreign Office, which represented a huge but—in the absence of precise documentation—unquantifiable amount of valuables. The minute Hitler gave his assent to the transfer of the surviving Reichsbank reserves to Bavaria, orders were relayed to the Reichsbank branches to make immediate shipment of their remaining gold and currency stocks back to Berlin, from which the entire reserves would then be sent south in one shipment.

The branch officials made frantic efforts between 4 and 13 April to comply. For some of the more westerly banks that lay in the line of the American advance it was already too late. Eschwege and Coburg fell before the banks could respond to their directive and their gold bullion and other assets passed into American hands. But from branches in towns and cities farther removed from the American thrust—Goslar, Magdeburg, Erfurt, Adoda, Weimar, and elsewhere—780 gold bars were shipped back to the temporary new Reichsbank headquarters in Berlin and preparations were made to send 730 of these bars south at once. Fifty bars (worth $711,000 in 1945) were held back for possible contingencies, along with another 40 bars (worth $567,000) which had never left Berlin in the first place, and many millions of gold coins (valued at $2,156,625). The total value of the 730 bars and gold coins earmarked for shipment to Bavaria was nearly $10 million; the value of the bars and coins destined to stay was $3,434,625.

So the stage was set for the next act. Dr. Funk, the nominal President of the Reichsbank, and all the senior officials of the bank's Berlin headquarters were ready with bags packed to leave the doomed city for the move south. Huge quantities of paper marks, dollars, and other currencies were packed and stacked in readiness for shipment. Probably it had always been intended that the whole of the reserves—gold and currency alike—should be transported south by train on 13 April. But as some of the gold was still in transit to Berlin on the 13th it was finally arranged that the paper currency and the bank personnel would leave for Munich by train and that the gold would follow by road on 14 April. The idea was for Munich to serve as a base from which to distribute much-needed German currency to Reichsbank branches in Bavaria and as a springboard from which the gold, foreign currency, and other valuables would be propelled to their final hiding place, as yet to be decided.

At two different stations in the southern suburbs of the capital—Berlin-Michendorf and Berlin-Lichterfelde-West—two special trains code-named *Adler* and *Dohle* stood with steam up, awaiting the signal to go. An air raid was in progress when the operation finally swung into action. Through a gauntlet of bombs and fire, conveys of trucks laden with a greater part of the banknote wealth of the Fatherland made a headlong dash to the waiting trains. It is not difficult to picture the scene — the trucks, sealed and sentried, a steel-helmeted trooper up front, more by the tailgate, racing through the emptying streets, klaxons honking, the slow to a crawl down endless diversions, around smoking craters, bombed-out blocks, thoroughfares choked with rubble and signs reading *"Achtung! Minen!"*, the bombs falling, the shrapnel pattering on the cab roof like iron hail, the final dash down Potsdamerstrasse, mouths dry and hearts thumping, the barked orders in the station precincts, *Raus! Schnell! Raus!*

The trains waiting impatiently in the southern suburbs between them carried a prodigious quantity of paper money, including 520,000,000 Reichsmarks (valued at $52,000,000) for normal internal currency exchange and — of far greater negotiable value to the Reich and far greater importance to the future development of this story — 146 bags of foreign exchange. At Berlin-Lichterfelde-West, *Adler* (meaning eagle) was complete with a baggage car which was to hold one part of the Reichsbank's currency reserves (including 105 bags of foreign currency — 52 of them belonging to the RSHA) and a passenger car which was to accommodate most of the Reichsbank senior staff, including its President, Dr. Walther Funk, his assistant Dr. August Schwedler, and the official in overall charge of the evacuation, Reichsbank Director Hans Alfred von Rosenberg-Lipinski, one of Funk's right-hand men in the Reichsbank. *Dohle* (meaning jackdaw), already loading up at Berlin-Michendorf, carried the other part of the Reichsbank's currency reserves, including 41 bags of foreign exchange. *Adler's* role was to distribute much-needed paper money to the nearly dried-up Reichsbank branches in the south of Germany, *Dohle's* to replenish *Adler* as required and transport what was left direct to the Munich Reichsbank, where it would link up with the gold convoy coming from Berlin by road.

If this was the plan it seems to have misfired. Because of the worsening military situation the trains could not take the direct route from Berlin to Munich via Nuremberg and had to be diverted along a route which swung to the southeast through Saxony and Czechoslovakia. The total distance was some 500 miles and under normal circumstances the journey by train would have taken no more than a day. But in the second half of April, as the Third Reich collapsed on all fronts and Germany's railway network everywhere was subject to interdiction and delay as a result of bombing from the air, fighting on the land, and priority through-routing for troop and ammunition trains racing to the front, it took the Reichsbank specials,

Adler and *Dohle*, not a day but a fortnight to reach their destination. And by then a substantial part of these remaining Reichsbank reserves, the gold and monetary treasure of the nation, had been, or was about to be, stolen.

So the two special trains drew away from the ashen wreckage of the shattered capital. Their departure did not go unnoticed — even by western intelligence. After the trains had gone, a field detachment of the OSS, the U.S. secret intelligence and special operations service, logged the following signal from a secret agent located somewhere in the Reich: "Two special trains carrying the *Führungstab Oberste Reichsbehörden* left Berlin 14 April. These officials are now in Imsterberg, which has been closed to all but Party members. [From copy of the Secret Order]." (The agent would probably have been a member of the OSS team code-named GREENUP which was parachuted into the Tyrolean Alps near Innsbruck, Austria, in February 1945. GREENUP was one of the most successful of the Allied spy teams to penetrate the Third Reich. It formed contacts with the local Austrian Resistance and the remarkable Resistance organizer, OSS agent, and courier, Fritz Molden, transmitting consistently useful intelligence back to base until the team was deactivated by the Germans just before the end of the war — surviving, however, to hand over the surrender of the Tyrolean capital, Innsbruck, to the advancing Americans early in May 1945.)

If the Allies had but known it, this signal possibly contained their first glimpse of the Reichsbank affair which was later to engage their investigators in a vain quest for the truth over a period of years.

The journey to Munich was no joy ride. To move by day was difficult. From sunrise to sunset low-flying American and Russian fighter bombers scoured the countryside for prey, strafing anything that moved on road or rail. At night the trains could carry no proper lights, not even in the compartments, whose occupants often had to make do with candles to see by. The scenes at the halts along the track doused the hopes of even the staunchest optimists. Everywhere were images of cataclysmic destruction and absolute defeat. Station platforms were packed from end to end with rows of wounded, their paper bandages, saturated with blood, dissolving around still gaping wounds. Country roads were choked with refugees fleeing from the Russians, tangled melees of horse-drawn carts, bombed cars, old trucks laden with household chattels, baby-carriages, pushcarts, wheelbarrows, old men on bikes, intermingled with ragtag troops on the move, Hitler Youth, Volkssturm Homeguards, rear echelon troops looking for their front-line units. Passing through Dresden the Reischsbank officials, long hardened to the piecemeal destruction of Berlin, peered aghast

at the desolation of this once beautiful and historic city, now razed to the
ground in the course of a nonstop air raid lasting 48 hours which had killed
over 135,000 people. The empty shells and windowless, fire-blackened facades of this dead city loomed like a specter of the imminent future. If anyone on the two trains had entertained any hopes for Germany's national
salvation when they pulled out of Berlin, few could have sustained them
after they had passed through Dresden. Germany, it was clear, was
doomed. In a few days, a few weeks at most, the nation would perish. And
in the havoc that would be bound to follow, to what masters would the
present guardians of the Reichsbank owe allegiance? The Soviet hordes?
The Anglo-Saxon armies? Some Nazi government in exile or Third Reich
caucus in the national redoubt? But what caucus and what redoubt?

It may have crossed the minds of a few of the men on board *Adler*, as it
hissed and rattled through the narrow corridor of territory that was now all
that was left of unoccupied Germany, that in the world following the final
collapse there would be no orders to be received or to be obeyed, that for
each and every one of them it would be a case of every man for himself,
and that in that connection the Reichsbank treasure might be, in a manner
of speaking, a free-for-all.

That at any rate seems to have been the line of thought which wormed
its way through the head of the Reichsbank official most directly involved
in the handling of the currency reserves on board *Adler* and *Dohle*, Reichsbank Director von Rosenberg-Lipinski. On 16 April, when *Adler* was held
up ten miles outside Pilsen, in Czechoslovakia, and the train commander
indicated that it would be some time before the journey could be continued, it was Rosenberg-Lipinski who took the initiative and off-loaded 11
sacks of foreign currency belonging to the Reich Security Head Office
(RSHA) and sent them off to Germany by road in a requisitioned truck
bound for the Reichsbank branch at Regensburg. As the progress of the
trains grew even more tardy and erratic, Rosenberg-Lipinski and his boss,
Dr. Funk, grew increasingly restless and impatient. Between 18 and 19
April, while the trains were held up again just inside the Bavarian border,
Rosenberg-Lipinski ordered 53 bags of Reichsbank foreign exchange from
Adler and 41 bags from *Dohle* to be unloaded and driven by truck to Munich (in company with Funk and Schwedler) in order to rendezvous with the
gold convoy coming down by road from Berlin. (Forty-one bags of foreign
exchange belonging to the RSHA were left on board *Adler*, and 11 more
bags of RSHA currency, which had been taken from *Adler* a few days previously, were still in Regensburg.)

Compared with the trains, the gold convoy had made good time on its journey south. The convoy of five or six Opel-Blitz trucks belonging to the Berlin Police had left Berlin on 14 April in the charge of Police Lieutenant George Krüger and was accompanied by three Reichsbank officials — George Netzeband (Senior Cashier), Friedrich Will (Senior Clerk), and Emil Januszewski (Senior Inspector). It was followed by Lieutenant-Colonel Rauch making his own way south. The trucks followed much the same route as the trains, via Dresden, Karlsbad, and the Bohemian Forest, and by 19 April were safely drawn up outside the front entrance of the Reichsbank building in bomb-ravaged Munich, where they were met by Funk and Schwedler.

The convoy stayed only long enough to take on board the 94 bags of foreign currency taken off the trains and to receive instructions about the next destination. No definite destination for the Reichsbank treasure had been worked out before it was shipped from Berlin, although it had been hoped that when the gold and currency reached Munich it could be stored in the so-called Bormann Bunker; but Bormann refused permission and new plans had to be hastily worked out. By the evening of 19 April the treasure was on its way again, bound for Peissenberg, near Weiheim, some 50 miles south of Munich, where it was thought a secure hiding place could be found in the tunnels of the local lead mine.

At this stage the treasure was believed to consist of:

365 bags, each containing 2 bars of gold, the whole weighing nearly 9 tons and worth over $10,000,000
9 envelopes containing records of the gold
4 boxes of bullion
2 bags of gold coins
6 cases of Danish coins
94 bags of foreign exchange
34 printing plates (for Reichsmarks) and a quantity of banknote printing paper enough for 100,000 bills)

When the convoy finally reached Peissenberg the mine manager advised against stowing the treasure in the mine. The shaft was already waterlogged, he explained, because recent air raids had cut the electricity supply and put the pumping machinery out of action. While the treasure was unloaded for temporary storage in a building on the mining estate, Schwedler telephoned Funk for new instructions. It was agreed that the banknote printing plates and the paper ought to be returned to Munich. The rest of the consignment, Funk suggested, should be driven down to a small town called Mittenwald in the Bavarian Alps near the Austrian border, where the barracks of the Gebirgsjägerschule — the Mountain Infantry Training

School—was located. Funk considered the commander of the school, a certain Colonel Franz Pfeiffer, to be a completely trustworthy *Wehrmacht* officer who was ideally placed to assume responsibility for the treasure and make arrangements for its concealment in the mountainous regions surrounding Mittenwald.

So on the afternoon of 21 April—while Reichsbank officials Netzeband and Will returned to Munich with the banknote printing plates and paper —the nine tons of gold bullion, the boxes of gold coins and the voluminous hoard of foreign currency were once again loaded on to the Opel-Blitz trucks for the final stage of their journey to the south, this time under the baleful eye of the remaining Reichsbank official, Januszewski.

The convoy rolled past unending streams of refugees and over bridges with demolition charges already in place. On the winding road to Kochel the drivers refreshed themselves from bottles of brandy, champagne, and wine and admired the spectacular mountain scenery, so different from the flat countryside around Berlin. At the foot of the Kessel Mountains they refueled with the last of the gasoline from their gas cans, and at Urfeld they passed a group of evacuated Berlin children who waved cheerily when they recognized the Berlin truck's registration plates. Burping champagne bubbles and breathing deeply of the clean Alpine air in the relative peace and security of the south, the Reichsbank treasure party were glad to be clear of the doomed capital. They did not know then that none of them would ever return there.

In the meantime, the trains *Adler* and *Dohle* continued to battle their way to Munich along a railway line incessantly bombed and strafed by marauding enemy planes. (They eventually arrived on 27 April after two weeks on the line.) Whenever the trains stopped, which was often, Rosenberg-Lipinski and his companions seemed to have run a complicated shuttle service between *Adler* and the various Reichsbank branches in Bavaria, handing out German banknotes on the one hand and juggling in a complicated way with the potentially more valuable foreign exchange on the other. On 21 April, 13 sacks of foreign exchange and five boxes of valuables were taken from *Adler* and driven by car to the Munich Reichsbank. On the same day the 11 bags of foreign currency left in Regensburg were transferred to the Munich branch. On 22 April, when *Adler* was held up on the north bank of the Danube, the tireless Rosenberg-Lipinski picked up the 14 sacks of foreign currency which had been deposited in the Munich bank the day before and drove out to Lindau at the eastern end of Lake Konstanz. When Rosenberg-Lipinski returned, he brought with him 25 boxes containing 100 bars of gold bullion which had been stored in the

Konstanz Reichsbank, as well as the 24 sacks of foreign currency with which he had set out. Eleven of these sacks were duly checked into the Munich branch. But one sack (containing SS foreign funds) was retained by Rosenberg-Lipinski "for certain reasons" which he did not enlarge upon, and the remaining 12 sacks were not logged in by the bank. Not long afterwards both they and the sack "retained" by Rosenberg-Lipinski had vanished. So had the five small boxes (which may have contained some of Himmler's private papers) originally taken from *Adler* with the 13 sacks of currency. Though part of the missing 12 sacks were destined to turn up again, neither Rosenberg-Lipinski's sack nor the five boxes were ever heard of again.

As for the 25 boxes of bullion which Rosenberg-Lipinski had brought from Konstanz, it had always been intended that they should be added to the main body of Reichsbank assets despatched south from Munich. But when Rosenberg-Lipinski eventually arrived at the Peissenberg mine to hand over the 25 boxes on 22 April he found that the treasure and trucks had moved on. They had disappeared somewhere into the Alps, but where he did not know.

April 22nd was a significant date in the development of the Reichsbank story, for on or about that day a collective shudder seems to have gone through the uppermost echelons of the SS in Berlin. The original impetus may have come from Reichsführer SS Heinrich Himmler himself, who was even then deeply involved in the secret surrender negotiations through emissaries of the western powers. It certainly became apparent in the office of Ernst Kaltenbrunner by that day that Berlin was indeed lost, that whoever did not get out at once, and whatever was not taken out at once, was destined to stay, trapped inside the tightening Russian ring.

The immediate cause of the reverberations of 22 April could be found in the erratic behavior of the Führer during the preceding two days. It had always been understood in the Reich Chancellery that when Berlin became militarily untenable all the bunker people (Hitler, his closest ministers and aides, and their staff and families) would evacuate *en masse* to the relative security of the second "capital" in the south — the mountain retreat on the Obersalzberg above Berchtesgaden, the hypothetical command center of the so-called national redoubt. Responsibility for the move rested with Martin Bormann and as the days went by and the situation in Berlin worsened he became increasingly anxious that the transfer should be made as soon as possible. To the bunker secretaries he indicated that the Führer's fifty-sixth birthday on 20 April would mark the end of their stay in Berlin.

Some of the domestic staff had already gone to Obersalzberg with instructions to get Hitler's house, the Berghof, ready for immediate occupation. Hitler's chauffeur had been told to prepare for the journey and a list of the entire motorcade — private cars, trucks, buses, armored vehicles — had been drawn up, along with the allocation of seats.

There was very little time left. The Americans had reached the River Elbe in the west. The Red Army was sweeping across the Oder and Neisse rivers in the east. When the Americans and Russians met, Germany would be cut in half and all overland connections with Obersalzberg would be severed. General Patton's tanks were advancing deep into Bavaria. The Ruhr and Rhine and the great ports of the north were occupied by the British. The French had taken Stuttgart and were sweeping southeast towards the Alps. For Hitler and his entourage in Berlin there was no longer any refuge in the east, west, or northwest, and the Russian encirclement of Berlin was almost complete. The need to move south was imperative. On 20 April, Himmler left Hitler's bunker for the last time and Reich Marshal Goering, together with various lesser Nazi officials and sections of the army and air force staffs, departed for Berchtesgaden, expecting Hitler to follow shortly.

On the afternoon of Hitler's birthday, Bormann intimated that the departure was scheduled for 22 April at the latest. He told the secretaries to start packing their bags. He advised Hitler's valet and cook to get the Führer's wardrobe and pantry ready for departure. In his notebook he wrote: "Ordered departure of advance party to Salzburg." With the Russians already shelling the southbound autobahn the only way out now was by air — and then only by flying at night.

But still Hitler would not budge and on 22 April he finally broke down in a paroxysm of anger which terrified all who witnessed it. The cause of Hitler's collapse was the failure of one of his generals, SS Lieutenant-General Steiner, to carry out his orders and utilize his combined forces (which were largely nonexistent) in a last-ditch knockout blow against the Russians. When Hitler learned that Steiner, instead of attacking the Russians, had abandoned Berlin to its fate and led his ragtag army westwards into American capitivity, Hitler began to scream. As his voice rose to a demonic shriek, utterly unnerving to all who were present, Hitler raged at the treachery all around him, at the deceit and corruption with which he was surrounded, at the desertion of his army and the doom of his mission. Lurching backwards and forwards on his feet, his right arm swinging wildly, his left arm flopping limply at his side, the demented Führer's face turned chalky white and his body shook as if smitten by a violent stroke.

No one had ever seen him lose his self-control so completely. For the first time he acknowledged that the end had come and the Third Reich was doomed. As Hitler's violent rage subsided he collapsed into a chair. In a trembling voice rent with anguish he declared: "The war is lost!" The Third Reich had ended in failure and there was nothing left for him to do but to die. He would stay in Berlin and meet the end when it came. Others could do what they wanted, those who wanted to leave the bunker could do so, the women could be flown to Berchtesgaden — but he would not go to the south.

Late on 22 April the majority of the Chancellery staff took off in ten aircraft from four different airfields in Berlin, and on Bormann's orders the heads of most government ministries and agencies also left Berlin that night. (One of these ten aircraft, a Junkers 352, its take-off from Berlin fatally delayed by airport workers, who were angry the the Party privileged were deserting the capital and threw their baggage off the plane, was still in the air at daybreak and was shot down by the Russians over Boernersdorf in Saxony, killing 16 of the 17 persons on board. It was this plane which was supposed to have been carrying Hitler's private diaries, first revealed to the world in April 1983 and proved to be fake by Federal German experts in the following month.)

Goebbels now announced in a broadcast: "The Führer will die in Berlin." When Himmler learned of Hitler's fateful decision he believed he was at last free of his oath of loyalty to the Führer. It seemed to be the signal for the rats to abandon the sinking ship. From that moment the SS began to grab whatever was its own, and whatever it felt was its due, before it was too late. In this final snatch the Reichsbank proved a convenient target. In Munich the 13 sacks of foreign currency brought back to the bank by Rosenberg-Lipinski, together with a number of parcels that may have contained Himmler's personal papers, were rudely seized by one of the leading SS generals under Himmler — SS General Gottlob Berger, Chief of the SS Main Office. Berger was Himmler's *éminence grise*, the architect of the Waffen-SS, and a war criminal who was to be sentenced to 25 years imprisonment at Nuremberg (and released after serving two). According to later testimony by General Berger, he was acting directly on Himmler's instructions, which were to take the money and hide it and burn his personal papers. In any event, the money ended up in ingenious obscurity under the floorboards of a small barn in the grounds of the residence of the Chief Forester of St. Johann, a village a few miles from Salzburg. A portion of the money was found after Berger led the Americans to the spot fol-

lowing his capture in May. According to a SHAEF report the sacks were
sealed with Himmler's stamp and contained his personal fortune estimated
at $2,000,000 in the currencies of 22 nations. The fortune was not intact,
however, for some of the sacks were missing and a later count revealed that
the recovery was short to the tune of at least $200,000 — or over a million
dollars by today's values. If the money was taken by Berger — and it is difficult to see who else might have taken it — it was never retrieved.

On 25 April the Munich bank was hit again by the SS, this time on the
rather more narrowly personal initiative of an unknown RSHA official accompanied by a gentleman by the name of Dr. Österreich, who removed
85,000 Swiss francs (worth nearly $20,000) from one of the bags of foreign
currency brought back by Rosenberg-Lipinski, and then vanished. But
the robberies from the Reichsbank in Munich, substantial though they
were, were dwarfed by the haul taken by the RSHA by force on 22 April
from what was left in the vaults of the Reichsbank back in Berlin.

On the orders of Ernst Kaltenbrunner, a party of SS troopers under
39-year-old SS Brigadier-General Josef Spacil, head of Office II, the
Budget Administration Section of the RSHA, carried out an audacious
robbery at the new Reichsbank headquarters in Berlin, removing at
gunpoint jewels, securities, and the last remaining foreign exchange assets
held in the vault, valued altogether at 23 million gold marks ($9,131,000).
This monumental snatch-and-grab of almost all that was left in the Third
Reich's coffers had to be carried out in great haste. Berlin was almost
surrounded. The Russians had penetrated the city's outer defensive ring.
The roads to the south were already cut, the airfields were under
bombardment, and artillery fire raked the city center. In one of the last
planes to leave the beleaguered city, General Spacil took off with his prodigious haul, aimed for a gap in the circle of artillery fire, and — like every
other Nazi chief who still believed he had a future — headed south for the
national redoubt, leaving the burning capital surrounded by a ring of steel
and fire.

Spacil's plane flew into Salzburg. There the loot was loaded onto a truck
and driven to the town of Burgwies. Here Spacil was met by an SS officer,
who reported that the Allies were now so close that further progress would
be impossible. Spacil hastily decided to bury the loot. With the help of two
reliable agents from nearby villages — a Volkssturm official and a Chief
Forester who was also a trusted Nazi official — the loot was buried under
the cover of trees on a steep slope barely a hundred yards from the road
leading from Taxenbach to the high Tyrolean town of Rauris. Later, more

treasure from the Berlin Reichsbank was packed in half a dozen jute sacks and a heavy iron chest and buried in a hole on a wooded mountainside near Rauris.

General Spacil still had a huge quantity of valuables in his possession for which he desperately needed to find a hiding place. Some of it was distributed among surviving Gestapo officers. To any high-standing SS officials he came across he handed out largesse on a grand scale. At Fischhorn Castle he lavished 500,000 Reichsmarks, 2,500 dollars, and 1,550 Swiss francs on a certain Franz Conrad, the SS man who had been responsible for requisitioning all the factories and Jewish property in the Warsaw Ghetto. A few days later Spacil handed out a further 500,000 Reichsmarks, 10,000 Swiss francs, 3,000 dollars, 200 Swedish crowns, and 40 English pounds — allegedly for back pay due to the 55 men under Conrad's command. On 26 April he arranged for the disposition of foreign securities and 5,000 carats of diamonds (valued at $450,000 at $90 per carat and worth $1,800,000 on the black market in 1945), and on the following day made a rendezvous with Captain Karl Radl, adjutant to the legendary SS Commando leader, Colonel Otto Skorzeny. Skorzeny was head of Office VI/5 of the Reich Security Head Office (RSHA) responsible for sabotage and subversion in western Europe and in charge of various paramilitary units engaged in sabotage, subversion, and political warfare in territories under German rule. In 1943 he had become a hero of the German people when, at the head of a band of parachute troops, he had rescued Mussolini from captivity in a remote mountain hotel in the Abruzzi. To Skorzeny's adjutant, Spacil handed over large sums of gold and securities, including 50,000 francs worth of gold coins, 10,000 Swedish crowns, 5,000 dollars, 5,000 Swiss francs, and 5 million Reichsmarks. On the following day Radl, Skorzeny, and a few SS officers, who up till now had been based in a special train in a siding at Radstadt in the Austrian Tyrol, left the train and took refuge up in the mountains. There, in an unknown hiding place, they concealed the huge quantity of valuables that had come into their possession.

Part of the loot hidden by Spacil was later recovered by the Americans. None of that taken by Skorzeny was ever found. Unlike Skorzeny, Spacil had always hoped that he could, in the event of his capture, barter his knowledge of the Reichsbank treasure in exchange for his freedom. When he was eventually picked up by the Americans and thrown into a POW cage near Munich he attempted to do just that. Disguised as an SS corporal named Gruber, he attempted to bribe a Military Intelligence/Counter-Intelligence Corps (CIC) screening team into giving him a discharge in return for information about the RSHA and the whereabouts of treasure and money "formerly belonging to German intelligence."

But some of Gruber's confidants at the camp informed American intelligence that he had not revealed everything. Gruber, they said, was in fact "a fanatical Nazi named Josef Spacil who was purported to have information that could lead to the discovery of Hitler's body and diary, the whereabouts of the gold crown and scepter of Charlemagne, and other riches. They said he had some poison and any open attempt to arrest him as a Nazi would result in his suicide." The Americans decided to play along with Spacil and mislead him into believing a discharge could be bought. Spacil was tricked into furnishing a password and a letter of authority enabling Lieutenant Nacke, of U.S. Army Intelligence, to contact accomplices of Spacil who knew where the treasure was hidden.

On 9 June 1945 Lieutenant Nacke and an SS Lieutenant in American custody went to Taxembach to contact one of Spacil's liaison men, a local forester, who knew where the valuables were hidden. Persuaded by the password and Spacil's letter that it was in order to show his visitors where the treasure was hidden, the forester led them up the mountain road to Rauris and the home of an individual called Urschunger. There, under the floor of a barn, they found a cache of 19 bags of gold coin and bullion, the latter subsequently found to weigh 23 pounds and worth $11,722. Behind a bricked-up enclosure in the attic of the house they then found a stash of paper currency which included 160,179 U.S. dollars and 96,614 English pounds (not counterfeit) in sacks sealed with Berlin Reichsbank seals, worth $389,838.

More valuables were found at another cache just off the Rauris road. These comprised a very odd job lot of loot—a cross-section of the SS's magpie scourings from Nazi-occupied Europe, including such handsome prizes as 4 watches, 9 rings, 2 boxes of counterfeit pound notes, 1 jeweled cross with diamond, 1 silver English florin, 1 silver English half-crown, 2 English silver sixpences, 9 English threepenny bits, 2 American silver quarters (worth all of half a dollar), and 2 dimes (worth all of 20 cents). In all, the valuables recovered from Spacil—those whose value could be in any way accurately determined—amounted to $550,857, which left some $8,580,143 (worth $47,190,786 in 1983) unaccounted for.

Whatever happened to that prodigious sum of missing funds, it was never revealed by Colonel Skorzeny, nor was he ever asked about it by U.S. Army intelligence. When he gave himself up to the Americans on 16 May, Skorzeny was immediately driven off to Salzburg so that he could discuss the surrender of his men with higher-ranking officers. The American sergeant who drove him there had never heard of the name Skorzeny, but when the German explained that it was he who had led the Mussolini rescue operation, the sergeant's interest was suddenly riveted.

"Then you must be the guy that led those Germans wearing our uniforms behind our lines during the Battle of the Bulge?"

Skorzeny admitted that he was indeed that man.

"Well, I'll be damned!" the sergeant exclaimed, pulling up in front of a *Weinhaus* in Berchtesgaden. "Buddy, I'm going to get you a bottle of wine so you'll enjoy the rest of the trip to Salzburg. When they get their hands on you at divisional headquarters they're going to string you up feet-first."

At Salzburg, Skorzeny was promptly arrested and escorted to a Counter-Intelligence Corps (CIC) headquarters in Augsburg for interrogation. He talked freely about professional business, about new sabotage techniques, "werewolf" training, and political insurrection against the Russians in the Ukraine and the Balkans. He complained that his agents had not been properly looked after by the *Wehrmacht*, were not given commissions, never given enough to live on, never had their expenses paid on time. He chatted happily on, the confident German hero and professional saboteur, assassin, and subverter, but not a word did he utter about the treasure Spacil had placed in his custody. He did not talk about it during the three years he was in captivity at Nuremberg and at Dachau internment camp, nor during his trial on war crimes charges (in which he was acquitted), nor after his former SS comrades had organized his escape from American custody. Only when Skorzeny resurfaced as a free man in Spain in 1950 did it become apparent that a substantial portion of the missing treasure had resurfaced with him. He was now a rich man, living in a large villa in Madrid, entertaining lavishly, married to a Countess, and actively engaged in lucrative arms sales and deals in railway stock worth more than $5 million. And as the organizer and operational director of the clandestine SS escape organization *Die Spinne*, which helped smuggle fugitive SS men out of Germany to comparative safety in South America and the Middle East, it was clear to American intelligence that Skorzeny now had large funds at his disposal. The SS assets snatched at gunpoint from the Reichsbank in war-torn Berlin in 1945 were being put to work again — and for the same old gang.

The SS robbery was not the last time the Berlin Reichsbank was to be ransacked by intruders. For after the SS came the Red Army. The military situation in the capital had deteriorated rapidly after Spacil's departure and by 24 April the encirclement of the city was complete. To the north and east the Russians were approaching the S-Bahn defense ring. In the west and south they had reached Spandau and Potsdam. In the days that followed, the Red Army advance continued irresistibly towards the dead center of the Nazi empire, the Reich Chancellery, from whose bunker the palsied and half-cracked Führer continued to direct his nonexistent troops. On 30 April, Adolf Hitler killed himself. On 2 May, Berlin fell to the Russians.

On 15 May, Reichsbank officials holding keys were summoned to the provisional Reichsbank building (not only the original Reichsbank but its successor had been totally destroyed by bombing) and were ordered by a Russian officer, Major Feodor Novikov of Red Army Intelligence, to open the vaults.

Before the final collapse there had been 90 gold bars worth $1,278,000 ($18,531,000 in 1983) and over four and a half million gold coins (dollars, sovereigns, guilders, francs) worth $2,156,625 ($31,271,062 in 1983), along with 400 million dollars worth of negotiable bonds technically payable in gold or dollars. Major Novikov examined the contents of the vaults, then ordered them to be locked up again and demanded the keys. Shortly afterwards the contents of the Reichsbank disappeared. Whether Novikov was acting under orders — the Supreme Soviet never pased any laws for the confiscation of enemy property during the war — or operating on his own account has never been established. The gold was never seen again. But the bonds (Weimar, Westphalia, Industrial) have turned up at long intervals in West Germany, Holland, Israel, the United States, Switzerland, Canada, and Great Britain.

The first known reappearance of the bonds was in 1951. On 13 August of that year a dubious private American banker, Herman William Brann, created a sensation at the U.S. Air Force's European Headquarters in Wiesbaden when he told officers an incredible story. A Russian agent called Churra Gorenstein, who ran a small business from a flat in Paris, had approached him with a request to sell back to the new German Federal Government $75,000,000 worth of dollar-denominated German bearer bonds (Weimar bonds). There were caches of these Weimar bonds in Paris and Liechtenstein, Brann said, with a face value of $275,000,000 and these were being sold on the black market with forged proofs of ownership. Brann believed the bonds had been seized by the Russians when they invaded East Germany, then smuggled out through Czechoslovakia and given to Gorenstein to sell in the West in return for much-needed Western currency. The incident was reported to Washington and a special agent from the U.S. Counter-Intelligence Office of Special Investigations was assigned to track down the bonds and their current owners. Over the next ten years the agent and his associates were able to sort out $240,000,000 worth of genuinely-held German Government bonds from the ones looted by the Russians. By then the German Federal Government had enacted legislation for validating the pre-war bonds so that they could either be redeemed for cash or exchanged for other securities or negotiable certificates. The bonds were payable to the bearer but under the new law the bearer had to establish proof of ownership of the bonds on 1 January 1945. By 1961 it seemed that the problem of the looted bonds was at an end. But in 1969 a new source of bonds appeared.

In October 1969 a London bank received a request from New York to sell £27,000,000 of the bonds. Scotland Yard, the German Federal Bank, Interpol, the FBI, and the American Department of Justice were called in and investigations revealed that the bonds had belonged to a branch of the now defunct Reichsbank and had been smuggled from East Germany to New York "probably to finance Russian intelligence activities in the West."

In spite of the German government's legislation the bonds have continued to surface right up to the present day. The Mafia are supposed to have a room full of them to subsidize their devious operations. In 1974, $2,500,000 of Westphalia bonds were deposited in a bank in Hamilton, Ontario. Subsequently the bonds began to appear all over the United States and approaches were made to financial institutions in Washington to redeem $10,000,000 in German gold bonds that were said to have matured. In March 1979, three men were tried and sentenced in Brantford, Ontario, for fraudulently attempting to obtain credit for Westphalia bonds with a face value of $1,000,000. As recently as the summer of 1982 a Gibraltar-based insurance company called Signal Life built up a substantial part of its portfolio with gilt bonds backed by Weimar Republic and other industrial bonds acquired from a convicted American securities swindler named Chester Gray.

All latter-day attempts to negotiate German gold and dollar bonds taken from the Berlin Reichsbank by the Red Army after the end of the war have ultimately foundered on the near-impossibility of establishing legal ownership on 1 January 1945. But one particular form of bond, the German industrial bearer bond, has proved more of a headache. German banks have admitted that they have to be careful about rejecting claims on these bonds because of the possibility that the original owners may have been Jews who disappeared in the concentration camps. It was not unusual during the war for Jews to try to buy their freedom by transferring jewelery and bonds to their captors in return for a promise to be allowed to escape.

While it is almost certain that most of the Westphalian and Weimar gold and dollar bonds in circulation were stolen by the Soviets, there are still about $20,000,000 of legitimately held bonds, though as time goes on it will become increasingly difficult to prove ownership of a bearer bond all the way back to 1 January 1945. Until that time the Reichsbank robbery, in a sense, still lives.

The theft of $400 million of gold bonds from the vaults of the Reichsbank in Berlin, the disappearance of $3,434,625 of gold bars and gold coins from the same vaults, the armed robbery from those vaults of $9,131,000 of foreign currency and other valuables by General Spacil on 22 April, the piecemeal theft by General Berger, Reichsbank Director Rosenberg-Lipinski, and others of immense amounts of foreign currency brought from the Berlin branch to the Munich branch for safekeeping—all these individual robberies combined to make the disappearance of a large portion of the Reichsbank reserves in the spring of 1945 the greatest monetary loss through grand larceny suffered by any organization in modern times. The Great Train Robbery of 1963, in which fifteen masked men stopped the Glasgow-to-London night express and robbed it of £2,500,000, is the Great Reichsbank Robbery's nearest rival in this century, but still falls far short in sums involved, while a comparison with other modern robberies on a similar scale—the value of their total takings greatly distorted by the worldwide inflation that has taken place since the early 1970s—is given at the end of Chapter 13. To find anything which compares in magnitude to the robbery of 1945 one must go back more than 260 years, to April 1721, when two pirates, Captain John Taylor and Captain Olivier La Buze, made their historic capture of the Portuguese East Indiaman *Nossa Senhora do Cabo* in the harbor of St. Denis in the Mauritius Island group, and robbed the retiring Viceroy of Goa (Portuguese India), the Count of Ericeira, of £500,000 worth of diamonds and a further £375,000 worth of Indian and Chinese silks, porcelain, and other precious goods from the East—a nice haul then and worth a king's ransom now.

The final inventory of the Great Reichsbank Robbery, however, was destined to grow even longer. For on the day that General Spacil lifted nearly ten million dollars of loot from the Berlin Reichsbank vaults, the surviving contents of that bank reached their journey's end. On 22 April the gold convoy from Berlin at last drew up outside the Officers' Mess of the Mountain Infantry Training School at Mittenwald with an estimated 15 million dollars in gold and currency loaded on board its Opel-Blitz trucks. From that date forward the fate of this prodigious hoard of treasure has been a matter of intense mystery and speculation which has defied every kind of investigative inquiry. The true story of that extraordinary consignment — of the robbery, murder, racketeering, corruption, scandal, and cover-up which it engendered, and which embarrassed an army and nearly shamed a nation — can now be told.

3

The Burial of the Treasure

The ancient frontier town of Mittenwald is one of the most attractive of the Alpine resorts of southern Bavaria. Strategically located at the head of the important Mittenwald pass through the mountains into the Austrian province of Tyrol, and superbly situated in the green valley of the Isar, the town is overlooked by towering Alps, densely forested on their lower slopes—Mittenwald literally means "middlewood" or "in the middle of the wood"—and in winter thickly covered with snow and heavily scored with ski slopes. The older quarter of the town presents an almost medieval appearance. The streets are lined by picturesque old houses with long, low-sweeping roofs and prominent eaves, and frescoed facades elaborately painted by local artists centuries ago. Dominating the middle of the town stands a candy-striped little baroque church of curiously Russian-looking design, with a tower vividly painted from top to bottom. Mittenwald is still, as Goethe once described it, "a living picture-book."

The income of Mittenwald was—and is—derived almost entirely from the manufacturing of violins and from tourism and winter sports. In the last spring of the war neither of these activities was much in evidence. For though the town bore no scars of battle, the war had not passed it by. Throughout the region hospitals and sanatoria provided convalescence and "R & R" for wounded soldiers from the front and exhausted U-boat crews in need of air. At Walchensee the Post Hotel had been leased by Nazi Party Secretary Martin Bormann, disguised as a hospital and turned into a refuge for SS officers and their wives. And only a few hundred yards from Mittenwald town center stood the principal military installation of the place—the *Kaserne*, the barracks of the Gebirgsjägerschule, the Mountain Infantry Training School, a modern, white-walled training establishment, pleasantly situated among meadows of the Isar Valley at the foot of the fir-covered slopes of the Karwendel Mountains.

The Mountain Infantry School for reserve officers and officer cadets at Mittenwald was one of several training establishments in the Bavarian Alps or the Tyrol where the *Wehrmacht* trained its troops in the special skills of mountain warfare. German mountain or Alpine troops—Gebirgstruppen or Gebirgsjäger—were an elite within the *Wehrmacht*. The German mountain soldiers, renowned for their skill, self-reliance, and exceptional stamina, had fought with great distinction on many fronts throughout the war, sometimes in theaters of operation where they could exercise their special training and experience, more often in an ordinary infantry role on the plains and steppes of the Russian Front—and even against the British in the sands of the North African desert. On the snow slopes and the thickly wooded heights around Mittenwald, Gebirgsjäger officer trainees were taught the esoteric arts of rock climbing, compass marching, mountain rescue and survival, shooting on skis, high-altitude combat, antipartisan operations, the use of special mountain weapons, and the handling of the usual Gebirgsjäger mode of transport—the pack mule. Such skills, needless to say, admirably suited the men of the Gebirgsjäher Training School—or more exactly, their instructors, the school's officers—for the crucial task with which they were now entrusted—the hiding and safekeeping of the gold and currency reserves of the Reich. And it is doubtful if Funk or his assistant Schwedler could have handed the responsibility for the Reichsbank treasure to a more suitably qualified man than the school's commanding officer, Colonel Franz Wilhelm Pfeiffer.

Colonel Pfeiffer looked every inch an honest and honorable soldier. He was 40 years old at this time, a tall, balding man of upright bearing and impeccable manners, with a highly developed sense of duty and responsibility to the men under his command. Unswervingly loyal to Hitler, Colonel Pfeiffer was a good German patriot and a distinguished front-line soldier who had won one of Germany's highest awards for bravery, the *Ritterkreuz* (Knight's Cross)—almost the equivalent of the British VC or the American Medal of Honor—in Greece in 1941. Pfeiffer had served in many theaters and fought and been wounded on many fronts. In Poland he had been shot through the leg by a dumdum bullet. After a disastrous encounter with the British at sea off Crete he had been hospitalized for many weeks. In Russia he had been shot through the spine during the siege of Leningrad and was lucky to be extricated from Russian encirclement with the remains of his regiment. Pfeiffer's reputation as a soldier stood high. A semiofficial history of the Brandenburg Regiments, one of which was commanded by Pfeiffer during the 1st Mountain Division's campaign in the Balkans, described him at this time: "Day after day, in countless battles and engagements in northern Greece, Albania, and especially Serbian territory, the 2nd Brandenburg Regiment under the prudent, energetic, and caring leadership of its commander, Colonel Pfeiffer, inflicted on the enemy the heaviest possible losses in men and materials." In the battle of Belgrade, Pfeiffer was wounded one last time, by a shot in the back of the head, during an engagement which virtually destroyed his whole regiment.

Colonel Pfeiffer's fighting days were done. Like many other wounded veterans, he was posted to the gentler backwaters of a training command. He had plenty of experience as a specialist instructor—at a military ski school near Salzburg, with an infantry division in Norway, with the Brandburg Regiment (one of the first commando formations in Germany). Now Colonel Pfeiffer was posted to the Mountain Infantry Training School in Mittenwald. He arrived there in December 1944, and it was there, on the night of 21/22 April, that he took on the most onerous responsibility of his entire military career.

Pfeiffer's first intimation of what was in store for him came from Colonel Rauch. He had first met Rauch during a duty visit to Berchtesgaden earlier in the war. Now, under very different circumstances, he unexpectedly met him again. Colonel Rauch arrived at the *Kaserne* in a truck from Berlin with news that a convoy bringing the Reichsbank treasure was at that very moment on its way to the *Kaserne* and that henceforth Pfeiffer's sacred duty would be to hide that treasure and guard it for the sake of the Reich for as long as there was a German nation in existence.

Pfeiffer, who was already shaping up for the impending prospect of a last-ditch battle to defend the district against the advancing Allies, could have done without this extra burden. But he was a soldier and a patriot. He would do what had to be done to the best of his ability.

During the evening of 20 April—Hitler's birthday—Colonel Pfeiffer summoned half a dozen or so of his most trusted officers into his simple, white-walled office in the *Kaserne*. Young, able, front-line veterans—most of them recovering, like their Colonel, from wounds incurred in the savage fighting on the Russian or Balkan fronts—they stood in a line opposite their Commanding Officer's desk, with a framed picture of the Führer looking down from the wall behind them, and listened in mounting astonishment as the Colonel briefed them about their forthcoming task—the last operational task, in all probability, that they would be called upon to perform in the war, and certainly the most bizarre.

"Gentlemen," Pfeiffer said gravely, "We are faced with a task of great national importance—a task you must take with the utmost seriousness."

A portion of the State treasure, he told them, representing a sum roughly equal to that which the Bavarian State had donated to the Reich in 1933, was at this moment on its way from Berlin—was expected in Mittenwald at any minute, in fact—and the immense responsibility for keeping this treasure out of the hands of the enemy had fallen on himself and his fellow officers.

"Our job now," Pfeiffer informed them, "is to ensure the safe custody of this treasure. We want to make such a thorough job of hiding it that finding it will be next to impossible."

Once a new Bavarian State had been formed, he went on, the treasure would be recovered and used to finance it. Until then the matter had to be treated with absolute secrecy. Colonel Pfeiffer then outlined his plan, and afterwards solemnly shook hands with each officer in turn and swore him to secrecy. A few hours later the Opel-Blitz trucks of the Berlin Police Department, with 15,000,000 dollars' worth of gold and foreign notes packed under their tightly-drawn gray awnings, drew up outside the Officers' Mess at the end of the nine-day journey from the capital.

With the Americans already on the point of overrunning Bavaria, the great need now was for speed. A space for the treasure had been cleared in the old bowling alley in the cellar of the Casino (the leisure area of the Officers' Mess). There were actually two bowling alleys in the cellar, with rough wooden runs of the traditional kind, with old worn and warped boards, lumpy bowls, and heavily loaded wooden skittles, all laid out in a room of dark, wood-paneled walls with chairs and scrubbed white tables grouped around them. This was where the remaining reserves of Hitler's Reich were brought from the trucks for temporary safekeeping before plans for their final concealment were worked out.

The unloading was carried out under cover of darkness. It was no mean task. Gold is one of the densest and heaviest metals, and though the gold bars were rather smaller than ordinary house bricks, each one weighed about 25 pounds—almost five times the weight of a house brick. By the time the gray gold bags—packed two bars to a bag, each bag tied and sealed with a lead seal—and the boxes of gold coins and bars, and bags of banknotes (nearly a hundred of them) had been laid out in the bowling alley, the sky was lightening over the gaunt peaks of the Karwendel Mountains and the camp bugler was trumpeting the call for *Appel* on the parade ground. The police escort, their duty done, were dismissed: the little line of Opel-Blitz trucks trundled out of the *Kaserne*, turned left onto the Mittenwald road and disappeared into the dawn and out of the story.

The Reichsbank officials who had come down from Berlin—Emil Jan-uszewski, along with George Netzeband and Friedrich Will, who had caught up with the convoy at Mittenwald after returning from Munich with the Reichsmark printing plates and banknote printing paper still in their possession—stayed behind. Though responsibility for the treasure now rested firmly on the capable shoulders of Colonel Pfeiffer, the bank officials remained at Mittenwald to represent the Reichsbank's interests. Their first act was to count the hoard of gold and currency now piled up in the bowling alley. To the consternation and embarrassment of at least two of the three officials involved, they discovered that one bag containing two gold bars had already been robbed, almost certainly on the jouney from Munich to Mittenwald. A recount failed to make up the number of gold bags to be the correct total of 365 and a hurried local search failed to locate the missing bars. Had the Berlin police escort made off with them? Or was there a thief—and a traitor—in their midst? For the moment there seemed no way of knowing and little time to find out.

Colonel Pfeiffer was now sitting on 364 bags of gold (making 728 bars all told and worth some $10,000,000), 94 sacks of foreign currency (includ-ing over $2,400,000 in U.S. dollars), and 12 other boxes and cases contain-ing miscellaneous gold and currency—and this was not to be the end of it. At the Mittenwald *Kaserne* the Colonel now considered his next move. The treasure had been gathered in, but the rapidly worsening military situation on the Bavarian front threatened at any moment to distract—or even pre-vent—its concealment.

The so-called national redoubt was proving to be less a fortress than a refuge and an escape route for privileged Nazis who had most to lose by capture and most to gain by flight. To the Supreme Allied Commander, General Eisenhower, however, all this was as yet far from clear. He knew that Hitler had elected to remain in Berlin and conduct his last stand from there, and he knew that the drive by Patton's Third Army down the Dan-ube valley into Czechoslovakia and Austria had cut the north-south link between the capital and the area of the redoubt. But he was taking no chances. In his view the redoubt should be attacked and taken before any Nazi resistance movement could man and organize its set defensive posi-tions. On his orders the advance into the redoubt—carried out by General Patch's Seventh Army, with elements of the Third Army on its left flank and of the French First Army on its right—assumed the highest military priority. On 22 April—the fateful date on which SS General Spacil had robbed the Reichsbank in Berlin and the Reichsbank gold convoy had fi-nally reached Mittenwald—Patch launched his attack.

Crossing the Danube and simultaneously advancing on Munich and on the Alpine redoubt, the Seventh Army swept all before it. "Push on and push hard," the U.S. VI Corps Commander, General Brooks, had exhorted. "This is a pursuit, not an attack."

At extraordinary speed—up to 40 mph on occasion—American armored units raced towards the mountains, the tanks festooned with infantrymen holding on to their helmets. German resistance melted away before the weight and speed of the American advance. Ulm (near Rommel's home town) and Landsberg (where Hitler wrote *Mein Kampf*) soon fell. Ingolstadt and Augsburg were threatened. The pursuit of the Germans, in the words of the Seventh Army's *After Action Report*, "seemed like a fantasy of violence and speed and extravagant incident." Rumor and counterrumor, order and counterorder reached the remoter German military outposts like ripples from a distant storm. In 23 April the 10th Armored Division, pointed like an arrow southwards towards Garmisch-Partenkirchen, captured 28 towns between sunrise and sunset.

On 24 April, Colonel Hörl, commander of the garrison at Garmisch-Partenkirchen, a famous Bavarian winter resort and the nearest sizeable town to Mittenwald, drove over to the Mittenwald *Kaserne* to discuss the deteriorating situation with Colonel Pfeiffer. They agreed that the German forces in the area were too weak and too poorly equpped to resist the full weight of the American Army. Only 75 percent of the men carried small arms of any kind, and of these only 33 percent had a full supply of ammunition, the rest having to make do with precisely six rounds apiece. The two colonels reached the conclusion that the best use they could put their forces to would be the protection of the civilian population and the numerous military hospitals in the area and the preservation of law and order. The next day Colonel Hörl (a secret member of the local German resistance) assumed overall command of the Garmisch area.

It was not only the front that was collapsing in Bavaria. Society itself seemed in a state of disintegration. Colonel Pfeiffer, the appointed guardian of the Third Reich's riches, was witness to the collapse of the very fabric of the Reich all round him. He was obliged to spare 20 of his officers for the undignified task of controlling the so-called *Bonzenflucht* (the flight of the Party favorites), the ever-increasing influx of Nazi Party officials, and government civil servants on the run, the continuous stream of demoralized *Wehrmacht* units and rear-echelon staffs rolling chaotically southwards from one mountain village to another. A motorized patrol which was sent out to intercept fleeing Nazis and recommandeer their vehicles found a huge bus packed with the furniture of a Nazi bigwig called Christian

Weber (a hulking ex-horse dealer and barroom bouncer who had been a close friend of Hitler in the old days) and an automobile laden with carpets belonging to Reich Marshal Goering. At nearby Oberammergau, scene of the world-renowned passion play every ten years, the 600-strong staff of SS General Hans Kammler (head of the V1 and V2 rocket programs and special representative of Adolf Hitler) were on the point of desertion. Colonel Pfeiffer is recorded as saying at this time: "The Party is finished. Its behavior is unworthy. It is not worth spilling the blood of a single mountain soldier for it." On that same day, 26 April, when the Colonel was overseeing the operation intended to conceal the Reichsbank treasure, another thought might well have occurred to him: if it was no longer worth fighting for the Third Reich, perhaps it was no longer worth preserving the Third Reich's treasure for the Third Reich alone.

For the moment at least, Colonel Pfeiffer was prepared to do his duty. The treasure clearly could not stay in the *Kaserne*. But where exactly, in all that tangled topography of Alpine ridges, valleys, passes, and woods, could it best be hidden? It had never been part of Funk's plan that the treasure should be buried. Nor was it what Pfeiffer had in mind at first either. His first thought was to store it in the headquarters of a local army engineer unit—possibly the 54th Engineer Battalion which was based in Mittenwald—suitably camouflaged as a pile of army stores. But that could only be a temporary solution. Somewhere a permanently secure hiding place had to be found.

Pfeiffer sought the advice of the best qualified people in the area—the foresters. The Head Forester of Mittenwald was a certain Otto Klotz, an ardent Nazi whom Pfeiffer had already approached with a request for help in hiding—should the occasion arise—the Economics Minister and Reichsbank President, Walther Funk, the Chancellery Secretary Lammers, and twenty other senior officers of the German High Command. Klotz had suggested two private hunting lodges high up on a part of the mountains called the Vereinsalm—one belonging to a prominent Munich banker by the name of August Baron von Finck, the other to a former Minister of Economics, Dr. Kurt Schmitt—both of them big enough and comfortable enough to accommodate such a large and distinguished company. He also recommended a guide, a local man called Josef Veit, a poacher turned gamekeeper who had been employed by the baron as a hunter and in the past had taken such Nazi luminaries as Goering, von Papen, and von Neurath on hunting expeditions in the surrounding forests and knew every inch of the Karwendel Mountains.

On 23 April Veit, now a medical orderly at the Reservists Hospital in

Mittenwald, received a visit from one of the members of the proposed party, a tall, swarthy, dark-haired, and rather menacing individual in civilian
clothes who spoke with a Bavarian accent and looked like a refugee, and
who turned out to be none other than Lieutenant-Colonel Friedrich
Rauch, late of the SS and Schutzpolizei in Berlin. Rauch, who had left the
capital at the same time as the gold convoy, had made his way to Berchtesgaden where he obtained his discharge papers in an attempt, presumably,
to dissociate himself from the SS (all membership of which, under Allied
occupation laws, fell into the Automatic Arrest category). Whatever it was
that Rauch was up to, he terrified the wits out of Veit. Rauch was bullying
and threatening. Veit was to conduct Funk, Lammers, and the twenty officers to the huts on the Vereinsalm, Rauch told him. If he did as he was told
he would be given his army discharge papers and be a free man. But Veit
stood his ground.

"I can lead you up to the Vereinsalm," he told Rauch. "But I can't hand
over the keys to the hunting lodges without written orders from Baron
Finck and Herr Reichsminister Schmitt."

Rauch's reply was a sharp and undeniable order. "Have provisions
ready at 3 o'clock," he snapped, "and take us to the huts!"

For poor Veit this presented an intolerable dilemma. If he did not do as
he was told he would probably be shot. But what if he *did* do as he was
told? What would the Americans do with a member of the German medical corps if they met him in uniform carrying a weapon in the company of
two Ministers of the Third Reich and twenty General Staff Officers of the
German High Command? They would probably shoot him too. In vain
he appealed to Klotz. Klotz could offer no sympathy and no alternative.
He turned to his chief medical officer at the hospital. If he didn't get lost
quick, the doctor advised him, he was done for. In the end Veit decided
that discretion was the better part of duty and took to the hills. He was not
seen again until some weeks after the Americans had occupied the area.

With Veit's disappearance the Funk escape plan fell apart. The Vereinsalm was under deep snow and without a guide there was little chance of
Funk's party finding their own way to the huts. Pfeiffer was free to concentrate his attention on the matter of the treasure alone. For advice about this
he now turned to the other chief forester in the region, Hans Neuhauser,
Sr., Chief Forester of Walchensee, who lived in the Forest House at Einsiedl, a tiny place some 12½ miles north of Mittenwald, at the southwest
edge of Lake Walchen. Pfeiffer had good reason to turn his eyes in that direction. For one of his officers was the chief forester's son—a connection
too good to ignore.

Captain Hans Neuhauser, the forester's 30-year-old son, had a war record every bit as remarkable as that of his superior officer, Colonel Pfeiffer. A graduate of Munich University and a member of the Nazi Party since 1938, he had served with distinction in the 1st Gebirgsjäger Division in campaigns in Poland, Yugoslavia, Russia, and the Balkans. For bravery under fire he had been decorated with the Close Combat Medal in Silver and the German Cross in Gold. Wounded at the front at the end of 1944, he was sent back to Germany in March 1945 and was still convalescing at his parents' house at Einsiedl when the Reichsbank reserves arrived in the area. Neuhauser was no longer on the active service list, and may not even have been on the official roll call of the Mountain Infantry School in Mittenwald, but this did not deter Colonel Pfeiffer from giving him his marching orders. On about 23 April the Colonel called at the Forest House to discuss with Neuhauser father and son a suitable spot in the locality in which to hide the Reichsbank reserves. Frau Neuhauser recalled later: "Colonel Pfeiffer came to see us and told us what was wanted. Of course, we all respected him as an honorable and courageous person at that time...." Then she added bitterly: "That gold caused the breaking up of my family. It was the death of my husband, and it sent both myself and my son to jail.... Yet we were guilty of nothing more serious than allowing it to be stored for 24 hours in our house."

It was finally agreed (against Colonel Pfeiffer's better judgment, it seems) that the Forest House itself would be ideal as an intermediate cache for the treasure before it was taken up into the mountains to its final resting place. Captain Neuhauser was ordered to report to the *Kaserne* in Mittenwald and there he was let into the old bowling alley and shown the great stack of boxes, cases, crates, and sacks containing Germany's precious nest egg. Neuhauser's job, Pfeiffer baldly informed him, was I/C burial party. Neuhauser was not overpleased to be burdened with the responsibility of interring the wealth of the Fatherland at the eleventh hour and made some demur. His complaint fell on deaf ears. In overall charge of the operation Pfeiffer appointed Major Rupert Braun. Other officers involved in what was to prove one of the most mysterious treasure burials since the golden age of piracy were Major Rott and Captains Otto Reindl, Walter Martl, Karl Lutz, Heinz Rüger, and Johann Rauter. It is possible that another convalescent Gebirgsjäger veteran, Captain Lüder von Blücher, who was to play a significant part in the subsequent fate of the Reichsbank treasure, was also involved, if only in an advisory capacity, on the recommendation of Pfeiffer's adjutant.

For the next few days the Forest House became the center of feverish activity. It was a picturesque place, constructed partly of wood in Bavarian chalet style, and after the local hotel and the nearby sawmill it was the biggest building in Einsiedl. Einsiedl in German means "hermitage" or "solitary retreat." In normal times it was a quiet spot for anglers and country ramblers. Its seclusion made it particularly suitable for the role it was called upon to perform now. There were few people around and next to no traffic passing by on the road. The gray waters of Lake Walchen lapped gently at the edge of the Forest House grounds. At the back rose a dark fir-clad ridge called the Steinriegel, and behind that the 3,500-foot-high Klausenkopf, one of several peaks stretching away to the east. The Forest House at Einsiedl, in short, was big enough to hold the considerable bulk of the Reichsbank treasure, remote enough for this to be done without attracting undue attention, and close enough to the sites selected for the burial — spots high among the dense woods of the Steinriegel — for the transfer to be accomplished with the utmost speed and secrecy.

The first delivery to arrive at the house was a truck carrying 11 mysterious oblong boxes. According to the driver, these had been dispatched from Berchtesgaden — near which Hitler, Bormann, and Goering had their private residences — on the orders of the fugitive Reichsbank President Walther Funk. Each of the 11 boxes weighed approximately 330 pounds and measured about 3 feet in length, 2 feet in width, and 1½ feet in depth. When Pfeiffer's driver, George Hempfling, took a peep into one of the boxes, all he could see was a row of wine bottles, but this, he thought, was probably just camouflage, for the boxes were so extraordinarily heavy that it seemed more likely they contained gold than wine. The boxes were followed by drills and bits and 66 pounds of dynamite which Hempfling had been told to bring over from the *Kaserne*.

Shortly afterwards another truckload of extra gold turned up at the *Kaserne*, again on Funk's orders. This consignment, which came from the Reichsbank in Munich but was not necessarily part of the Reichsbank reserves, consisted of 25 boxes of gold bars (four bars to each box) from the Konstanz branch which the Reichsbank official Rosenberg-Lipinski had collected and had tried to hand over to the Berlin gold convoy at the Peissenberg mine on 22 April. After missing the convoy by 24 hours Rosenberg-Lipinski had finally delivered the 25 boxes to the Munich Reichsbank for safekeeping. From there they were brought down to Mittenwald under the charge of another bank official by the name of Mielke. Mielke arrived with orders from Funk to extract $50,000 worth of foreign currency from the sacks now stored in the *Kaserne*. This he did by simply taking five whole sacks from the pile. (When he got back to Munich with them the next day, the five sacks were found to contain not $50,000 in foreign currency, but over $120,000 in U.S. currency. Later it was discovered that $5,000 of this was missing—stolen, it seems, by Mielke.)

On the afternoon of 25 April, a fatigue party of four Mountain Riflemen began to load up a civilian truck at the *Kaserne* with the first delivery of Reichbank treasure, consisting of between 50 and 75 bags of gold and the 25 boxes of gold bullion from Konstanz. One of the riflemen, Vitus Mayr, recalled the occasion well. "We were ordered to bring sacks up from the bowling alley and load them onto a truck," he related some years afterwards. "The sacks were gray with black printing. The tops were tied up and I think they even had lead seals attached. We soon learned that there were gold bars in the sacks. The gold was brought by the officers to the forester's lodge in Einsiedl." When the first load was ready the truck set off for Einsiedl, accompanied by Mielke, Captain Rüger, who was in charge of the transport arrangements, and the Reichsbank official George Netzeband, exhausted and nervy after many sleepless nights spent on the road from Berlin. Security does not seem to have been of the highest order. On the road to Einsiedl the gold truck encountered another truck driven by a local pig keeper called Josef Pinzl, a familiar figure who often called at the barracks to collect pig food from the soldiers' mess. The two drivers stopped briefly to exchange greetings and with bluff good humor the army driver called out: "I wouldn't mind swapping some of the gold in my truck for one of your pigs, Sepp—or even your pig food!" From that moment the presence of gold in the vicinity could have been no less than—at best—an open secret in Mittenwald. For this and many other blatant breaches of proper secutity, Colonel Pfeiffer, who was not present at the transportation or the subsequent burial of the Reichsbank reserves, blamed his deputy, Major Braun, the officer he had placed in overall charge of the operation.

There was a large, dark, stone-floored room at the back of the Forest House which used to serve as the stable, and this was where the gold was brought and neatly stacked against the walls. The operation not unnaturally caused a degree of excitement in the Neuhauser household and among their lodgers—a civilian refugee from Munich, Hans Forstreicher, and his family, and an attractive 30-year-old Serbian woman from Yugoslavia called Vera de Costra. Hans Neuhauser, Sr. and his wife were loyal Nazi Party members and considered it an honor to play a part in the salvation of the Third Reich's reserves. As Frau Neuhauser later admitted: "We were proud to have our house selected for such an important purpose." Nevertheless, they were all in a fever of nervous tension. The war had so far passed the Mittenwald area. But now every minute brought news of the

rapid advance of the American Army in their direction. The prospect of
the imminent arrival of foreign invaders, with their tanks and their flame-
throwers and (so the racist Propaganda Minister Dr. Goebbels threatened)
their black men, filled everyone with extreme apprehension which the
presence of the gold and other valuable only served to double.

When the first load of gold had been unloaded the army truck drove
back to the barracks in Mittenwald for more. A local driver called Willi
Hormann delivered 20 airtight boxes to Einsiedl. The final load, too, was
unloaded and methodically stacked in the Forest House storeroom, a cot
was moved in, and a 24-hour guard of officers and Reichsbank officials
was placed over the treasure. Then the Reichsbank officials made their
final inventories before departing the scene. Mielke made one list, and
Netzeband made another. Neither list agreed with the other and neither
conformed with the truth. The lists acknowledged the loss of two bars of
gold from the original Berlin consignment but did not record the requisitioning by Mielke of five sacks of currency, nor the recent addition of 11
boxes of what may have been gold, nor the 20 airtight boxes brought over
by Willi Hormann, nor any other assets or valuables from any other
source which could not be strictly described as Reichsbank property on a
Reichsbank inventory. As far as can be ascertained, what the treasure actually comprised on the eve of its burial was:

364 bags of gold, each containing 2 bars, making 728 bars in total
4 boxes thought to contain gold bullion
25 boxes of gold bars, each box weighing 110 pounds and containing 4 bars
2 bags of gold coins
6 cases thought to contain Danish coins
11 boxes, allegedly containing gold, weighing 330 pounds
20 airtight boxes, thought to contain gold coin
89 bags of foreign currency made up as follows:

U.S. dollars	2,430,000
English pounds	230,500
French francs	2,000,000
Swiss francs	500,000
Dutch guilders	1,000,000
Norwegian kroner	2,340,000
Swedish kroner	45,000
Italian lira	1,000,000
Portuguese escudos	69,000
Egyptian pounds	40,000
Turkish pounds	226,650
Palestinian pounds	1,700

The Reichsbank officials had always intended that Colonel Pfeiffer should sign an official receipt for the treasure now that it had been formally handed over to him. But to their consternation the Colonel refused to sign. "In actual fact," Pfeiffer explained later, "I had not seen the gold, the foreign currency, or the jewels. [Existing documentation does not indicate the presence of any jewels in the Reichsbank shipment.] The Reich treasure was certainly delivered by truck from Berlin to my barracks, but there was never any opportunity to count each individual gold bar."

The men from the Reichsbank were powerless to insist. In almost their last act in connection with the Reichsbank hoard they took a boat out on to Lake Walchen and tossed the banknote printing plates into its 600-foot-deep waters (where they have remained to this day). They then returned to the *Kaserne* in Mittenwald.

For 24 hours the Reichsbank treasure remained in the Forest House while Pfeiffer's officers prepared the mountain caches in which it would be hidden. Soil does not always lay deep on the steep slopes of the Alps. Only a little way down beneath the pine needles, ferns, and spongy black humus lie bedrock and rubble. To dig holes big enough to take the voluminous bulk of the Reichsbank reserves required a great deal of grinding physical labor with picks, shovels, and drills—and now and then the judicious application of a little dynamite. For reasons of security only the officers were involved in this work—all of them dressed as private soldiers. All through the night of 25/26 April they toiled away, trusting that any noises they made would be attributed to night exercises. By daylight, three or four large holes had been completed high on the Steinriegel and the Klausenkopf.

The exact locations of the caches do not appear to have been chosen by Colonel Pfeiffer himself but by his subordinate officers in conjunction with Reichsbank official Friedrich Will. Pfeiffer by now was more preoccupied with the deteriorating military situation in his sector than with the treasure and only possessed a very approximate knowledge of the caches in which it was to be buried. In fact, the sites for the gold caches were located on the north slope of the Steinriegel in an area heavily timbered with fir, larch, and beech, on the side of a forest track that ran west-east along the main axis of the ridge, some 300 or 400 feet above the level of the lake and some 30 minutes away on foot from the Forest House. There were at least two and possibly three separate holes. The first hole, some six feet to the left of the track, measured about six feet by four feet and was intended as a cache for provisions, medical supplies, and ammunition, which might prove necessary if the area came under attack. The second hole was some 30 yards further up the track and about 12 feet to the left. It was a more substantial hole than the first, measuring nine feet by five feet and deep enough for a man to stand up in. This was the main burial site where the 728 gold bullion bars were to be lodged. It was expertly constructed, with planks to line and reinforce the sides, but no roof. It is possible that there was another, smaller hole in the vicinity for the concealment of a separate and smaller consignment of gold.

Only the heavy valuables which were more difficult to transport into the mountains were to be buried on the Steinriegel, both close to Einsiedl and the road to Mittenwald. The currency, which was more voluminous but infinitely less weighty, was to be carried farther into the mountains to a big cache dug on the Klausenkopf, in the middle of a forest, between one and two hours climb from Einsiedl. This cache was more a bunker than a hole and was a relatively elaborate affair, some nine to 12 feet square, shored with logs and beams of timber, made watertight inside, with a timber roof and a small hatch for an entrance. Skillfully camouflaged with a covering of moss and grass, the currency cache was completely unrecognizable to anyone who did not know what was there. The earth excavated from it was carried to a spot 200 yards away and was also carefully disguised so as not to betray the presence of the main shaft. With the excavation completed, the next step was to bring up the Reichsbank treasure and other valuables that were to be concealed inside them.

The characteristic mode of transport for German mountain troops was the pack animal. The particular species depended on the terrain and the country. In Lapland, the Gebirgsjäger used reindeer; in the Caucasus, camels and small, frugal donkeys. In the Alps the favored beast of burden was the mule. The Gebirgsjäger barracks in Mittenwald had about 5,000 of these creatures during the war. Sure-footed on rough and precipitous terrain and sturdy enough to carry heavy loads in special wicker baskets up tiring slopes, mules were an obvious choice for humping the treasure, weighing well over 11 tons, up the mountainside to the gold and currency caches on the Steinriegel and Klausenkopf.

Late on the evening of 26 April, therefore—a dark and cloudy evening, highly suitable for such a clandestine operation—eight of these creatures were assembled outside the Forest House and loaded. Each mule could carry a maximum of four *Zentner*, or 400 pounds in the baskets slung from each side of the animal's wooden saddle. On this occasion each mule was laden with three bags of gold for each trip up into the hills. Just before midnight the heavily laden mules were led behind the Forest House and along the edge of the road at the back, until they reached a rough track that led off to the right into a thicket. Here eight dark figures—Gebirgsjäger from the Mittenwald *Kaserne*—emerged from the shadows and took over the bridles from the first team of drivers. The column then set off again, winding its way through thick forest as stealthily as the darkness and roughness of the track allowed, until it came to a narrow, stony path that led to the crest of the Steinriegel. With a clattering of hoofs, much panting of breath, and an occasional curse or word of encouragement, the mule train struggled up the steep incline until, just before the summit, the officers—each one now dressed in the dark-green uniform of a Gebirgsjäger private—took over the mules and their precious cargo and led them to the caches among the trees. So the gold from Berlin was carried up the mountain on the backs of beasts of burden—just three days before American spearhead units reached the valley.

All through the night the mule-shuttle continued, as a few bags and boxes at a time were borne into the darkness and through the woods to the four caches, where they were tidily stowed by the waiting officers. All concerned believed they were operating in total secrecy and unobserved. Indeed the area around the Forest House had been cordoned off by local Home Guard units on Colonel Pfeiffer's orders—though the cordon seems simply to have increased public speculation about the strange goings-on in the vicinity. In fact the entire operation was observed from the slopes on the opposite side of the valley by one of the lodgers at the Forest House, the civilian refugee, Hans Forstreicher. Forstreicher had slipped out of the house after the mules had departed and climbed to a vantage point overlooking the flanks of the Steinriegel, where he was able to see the direction in which the mules went and the mountain track which they would be climbing. Though it was a dark night, he had no difficulty in following the progress of the mule train into the woods. A low mountain mist and a settling frost made his watch temporary torture, however, and he was glad to return to the warmth of the fire in the Forest House.

For two more nights the mule-shuttle continued. By dawn on 28 April the gold and currency reserves of the Berlin Reichsbank lay snug in their watertight holes in the frost-rimmed ground of the Bavarian Alps, all trace of their burial artfully concealed with a cover of turf and grass.

That same day Colonel Pfeiffer traveled to Walther Funk's house at Bergerhof (near Bad Tölz) and reported the successful concealment of the Reichsbank reserves near Mittenwald. Funk was surprised to hear that the reserves were already buried and voiced the opinion that it was a pity that they were, since he would gladly have had them at his disposal later to prime-pump the economy. In that connection he told Pfeiffer that some

Swiss francs might still be particularly useful. Pfeiffer explained that it was not yet too late to retrieve banknotes from the currency cache — unlike the gold, the paper money was stored in a dry, roofed bunker with a proper entrance — and that he could arrange for Funk's assistant, Dr. Schwedler, to be escorted to the currency cache next morning to pick up the francs if Funk so wished.

The next morning Dr. Schwedler drove to Mittenwald, picked up Reichsbank official Netzeband and two of Pfeiffer's officers (including Major Braun), and went on to Einsiedl. In pouring rain the party climbed to the currency cache on the Klausenkopf. "It was really difficult," Schwedler recalled later. "We kept changing course this way and that across the terrain. The climb up took a different path from the one by which we later came down. The hiding place itself was extremely well camouflaged. I came upon it suddenly without noticing it. I was asked whether I could see anything unusual. When I said I could not, I was told that we had arrived. We were in the middle of a forest. The Reichsbank official, to whom I had given the Minister's [i.e., Funk's] instructions, went into the cache. Finding the items must have been a pretty laborious affair, because there was a long interval before the official emerged."

Netzeband hoisted three bags of banknotes through a hatch in the currency bunker. On subsequent examination these turned out to contain not Swiss francs but $87,000 American dollars and $40,000 worth of English pounds. Their subsequent fate was to prove a curious one.

Schwedler, Netzeband, and the two Gebirgsjäger officers climbed down the mountain with the three bags and returned to Mittenwald. At the *Kaserne*, Colonel Pfeiffer handed Schwedler the two missing bars of gold. These had been found at the Officers' Mess, seemingly by accident and much to everybody's surprise, during his absence on the mountain. It appears that while awaiting the return of Schwedler and Netzeband from the mountains, Will felt cold and decided to light the stove in the officers' mess. The wood was laid and the fire kindled, but instead of a cheerful crackling glow all that came out of the stove was choking blue smoke which seeped from the cracks and joints of the flue and filled the room. It was immediately obvious that the flue was obstructed and a quick search revealed a well-smoked canvas bag, stencilled with the words REICHSBANK HAUPTKASSE, and containing two gold bars numbered 41919 and 41920 and worth about $30,000 (or about $120,000 on the black market) at that time. Both Reichsbank officials Netzeband and Will suspected that their colleague, Emil Januszewski, was the culprit, for the two bars had disap-

peared on the journey between Munich and Mittenwald, when Januszewski was in charge of the consignment. Later, on 13 March 1946, the
unfortunate Januszewski—a respectable bank official of advancing years
who succumbed to temptation and opportunity in the hope of salting away
something against hard times that were coming—blew out his brains in
Munich.

Schwedler could not bear the thought of trailing up the mountain yet
again just to bury the two bars with the other 728, so he simply popped
them in his briefcase and took them with the three bags of banknotes to
Funk's house at the Bergerhof, where he placed them, as instructed, in the
bowling alley.

When Dr. Schwedler was questioned about these events during an investigation conducted into the Reichsbank affair by the Munich Police
Criminal Investigation Department in 1952, he had this pertinent remark
to make about Pfeiffer and Funk:

Colonel Pfeiffer made a remarkable impression on me. He was a holder of the
Knight's Cross and my feeling was that he had provided assistance for patriotic
reasons. I had the conviction then, and am of the firm opinion today—I would like
to emphasize this—that neither Colonel Pfeiffer nor the Minister had any thought
of enriching themselves personally. I think I can assert this very particularly of
Herr Funk. He was certainly sincere in his aim to put these assets at the disposal
of German industry at the appropriate time. I know that this happened with regard to other assets. I have myself heard how instructions were given to hold such
assets in readiness for the repriming of German industry if the need arose.

Schwedler's surprise visit to the Klausenkopf currency cache had an unnerving effect on Gebirgsjäger officers who had been responsible for the
burial of the money. They did not care who Schwedler was or what status
he had in the Reich—the fact was, the location of the currency was no
longer secret and would have to be changed. On Pfeiffer's orders three new
currency caches were therefore prepared in the mountains to replace the
original one. According to Captain Neuhauser the work was done in
broad daylight by three separate groups of officers dressed in civilian
clothes. Each group was responsible for its own cache and knew nothing
about the localities of the other two caches. Only Neuhauser seems to have
known the exact location of each cache. As a further precaution the new
caches seem to have been widely dispersed on three separate mountains—
the Klausenkopf, the Altlachberg, and the Simmetsberg. The currency
was transferred from the old cache (so Neuhauser reported later) in gas-
cans from the HKP (the *Heereskraftfahrpark* or GHQ motor pool), and up-

rooted tree stumps were placed on top of each new cache. This meant that there were now at least six or seven Reichsbank caches on the mountainsides above the Walchensee, including the ammunition and gold stashes on the Steinriegel, as well as the old currency stash.

Pfeiffer's men now dispersed, seeking the refuge of the surrounding villages—all, that is, except one. On the convalescent war veteran, Captain Hans Neuhauser, local boy and forester's son, fell the irksome duty of standing guard over the buried hoard, seemingly for an indefinite period. At night the captain slept in a cave or in the forest hut. In the day he climbed to the northern edge of the Steinriegel and from there kept watch on the Forest House and the mountain approaches through his binoculars. He had arranged some simple signals with his mother. When the coast was clear and no danger threatened she would hang a white sheet from her bedroom window. If there was any sign of the Americans in the vicinity she would change a red eiderdown for the sheet. Food was brought up to Neuhauser by a lodger at the house, the attractive Yugoslav woman, Vera de Costra, with whom he had formed a close friendship. Every day Vera would climb to a hollow tree and place a meal inside it. Every evening after dark Captain Neuhauser would creep down to the tree and collect his dinner. And so the days passed.

The Americans were not long in coming. While the Reichsbank treasure was being safely buried underground, tanks of the U.S. 10th Armored Division were at Schongau, only 30 miles up the road from Garmisch-Partenkirchen, and advancing rapidly. By the time the burial had been completed on 28 April, German troops manning the barricades at Peissenberg had fled, the SS garrison at Oberammergau had deserted, and the Bavarian Freedom Movement had taken over the Munich Broadcasting Station.

The following morning of 29 April, the Americans swept through Oberammergau and Oberau and bore down on Garmisch-Partenkirchen. Colonel Pfeiffer had been put in command of the sector of the Nordalpen front (stretching from Füssen all the way to Tegernsee) which included Garmisch, replacing Colonel Hörl, who was considered an unreliable anti-Nazi. From Army Headquarters he received a radio message: "The fate of the Alpine Fortress lies in your hands." From higher command in Innsbruck he received a telephone call: "Do all that is humanly possible to block the pass between Garmisch and the Tyrol." In reality the situation was hopeless. Everywhere there was chaos. Pfeiffer himself had next to no transport or communications, few officers, hardly any weapons or ammunition. His sector of the front stretched for miles and when his car, which drove on wood gas, gave out he had no alternative but to continue on foot. After the war he was to claim that he saw his main job as saving Garmisch—not from the enemy but from destruction. Thousands of refugees had sought sanctuary in Garmisch and some 10,000 wounded lay helpless in the many military hospitals and converted hotels in the area. Resistance would be futile and would lead inevitably to the deaths of many of these people and to the senseless destruction of a beautiful town.

From 19th Army Headquarters in Imst, Austria, Colonel Pfeiffer received one last order from a *Wehrmacht* general who warned him at Field Marshal Kesselring's direction that any failure to block the American advance on Garmisch would be dealt with with the utmost severity. Pfeiffer replied that as a long-serving officer he did not require anyone to tell him what his duty was. Nevertheless he did pass on the order to the Garmisch garrison, commanded by Colonel Luis Hörl: "By order of Field Marshal Kesselring, the Garmisch area must be defended at Farchant. I am sending 250 officers from the German High Command (OKH) Führer-Reserve at Mittenwald. [Signed] Colonel Pfeiffer." That message arrived at 5 o'clock on the evening of 29 April. But by then the defense of Garmisch was out of Pfeiffer's hands. Colonel Hörl and a group of veteran Gebirgsjäger officers in the Garmisch barracks, including Major Michael Pössinger, Captain Mucki Clausing, and Lieutenant Guntram Licht, had decided that to avoid the senseless destruction of the town, Garmisch should be surrendered to the Americans without a shot being fired. That morning 26-year-old Major Pössinger—holder of the Knight's Cross with Oak Leaves and the German Cross in Gold, and seven times wounded in six years of combat on the eastern and western fronts—headed a surrender delegation which went forward to meet the leading American tanks of the 10th Armored Division advancing on Garmisch.

Pössinger met the Americans at Oberammergau just in time. In support of their armored advance into the national redoubt the Americans had ordered a 200-bomber airstrike with the object of reducing every town and military target between Oberammergau and Innsbruck to ashes—including, of course, Garmisch-Partenkirchen. The American tank commander told Pössinger that it was too late to turn the bombers back—in two hours they would be overhead. Frantically Pössinger pleaded with him. *"Also bitte versuchen Sie es,"* he begged, *"das darf nicht unmöglich sein!"* Eventually the American relented. By radio and field telephone the word was passed to recall the bomber force. Then Major Pössinger and Lieutenant Licht were seized as hostages and tied to the turret of the leading tank. So the advance on Garmisch continued. At every tank barrier the German soldiers laid down their arms and at 6:45 in the evening the Americans rolled triumphantly into Garmisch in a long, squealing column, with Major Pössinger involuntarily at their head. Outside the City Hall the tanks halted and there Pössinger—the savior of Garmisch—was seized once more and thrown into the city jail. So Garmisch, the venue of many important events later in this story, fell without a shot, its pristine charm unravaged by war.

Colonel Pfeiffer had not gone forward to confront the Americans. (Indeed he learned later that he had been sentenced to death by Field Marshal Kesselring for his failure to hold Garmisch, but the German front collapsed before the sentence could be carried out.) Back in Mittenwald he was busy organizing the emergency evacuation of the barracks there, hustling his mountain riflemen up into the mountains where they could —if the need arose, if the order came—carry on the resistance, not as werewolves but as partisan regulars, the role for which they had been trained. But even this soon proved to be a futile gesture. On 30 April, Munich fell. All around the villages and townships were being turned into outposts of American military occupation. There was nowhere for Pfeiffer's mountain riflemen to go, nothing for them to do. Sitting on the bare mountainside, exposed to the sleet and the frost, achieving no object and serving no cause, it dawned on Pfeiffer and his men that for them the war was really over. Hitler was dead and Germany was defeated. They could go home. Rations and cash were shared out among them. In an emotional farewell Colonel Pfeiffer dismissed his troops for the last time, and with a parting valedictory, "God be with you!" sent them down the mountain, back to their homes and families and empty future.

But Colonel Pfeiffer himself did not go. He stayed in the hills, hiding in the sodden woods, wandering from hut to hut, with only the crows and the deer for company. And in his solitude he must have debated continually with his conscience. For he was still the custodian of the Reichsbank treasure, the wealth of Germany was still his responsibility and his alone. Down there in the valleys the enemies of the Fatherland would already be out and about, ferreting this way and that, prying into barns and farmyards, asking questions in their hunt for the missing Reichsbank reserves. What was the right course to take? In his eyes the Americans had no right to the treasure, of that he was sure. But who did? At a rough count, the number of people who knew the whereabouts of the treasure could be counted on the fingers of both hands. Sitting on 15 million dollars' worth of buried treasure, Colonel Pfeiffer considered his own and his country's cloudy future, and the best or the proper thing to do.

And in the valleys, coming fast behind the fighting vanguard, finding clues like cross-country paper-chasers, the American Gold Rush teams moved in.

4

In Quest of Gold, Silver, and Foreign Exchange

All through the last days of April a bright and unseasonably warm spring sun shone on the fighting men on the Alpine front. For a moment it seemed that the war in the national redoubt, far from erupting in the Armageddon of blood and steel which a few die-hard Nazis hoped and predicted, would draw to a limp conclusion in a vacationlike atmosphere of almost peacetime euphoria. The tracks of the Sherman tanks squealed and rattled along the roads, whose banks were bright with Alpine flowers, forced into bloom along the battle front by the premature summery weather. The doughboys of the American 10th Armored, advancing due south, were happy to feel the warm sun on their faces. For Gauleiter and stormtrooper, GI and DP (displaced person), tankman and civilian alike, the last balmy days of total war in the Third Reich induced a sense of unreality, a common desire to get this thing over, one way or another, as soon as possible. For Colonel Pfeiffer and Captain Neuhauser of the Mountain Infantry, custodian and sentinel over the Reich treasure, the weather made their fugitive existence in the high woods more bearable, but served also to prolong their grawing insecurity and doubt: where should they go from here, and what should they do with the treasure?

Then suddenly the springlike days of late April gave way to a return to winter weather. The temperature plummeted and it began to snow heavily. The sky was blanketed by thick gray snow clouds and dense mists rolled through the valleys and gorges of the mountains, concealing the opposing ground forces from each other and obscuring their gunlayers' targets. The high roads turned icy, the low roads turned to slush, and a raw dank wind from the Tyrol whipped across the highways of the American advance. Three thousand feet in the mountains above Mittenwald fresh snow covered the gold and currency caches, and the bleak weather forced Captain Neuhauser and Colonel Pfeiffer to look to their personal survival as their overriding priority. Perhaps it was this which promoted the Colonel's next move. Or perhaps it was his continuing responsibility for the military situation in the area under his command — or even the burden of the state treasure which still weighed heavily with him. At any rate he — or someone purporting to be him — seems to have felt compelled to try and make contact with the enemy advance units known to be bivouacked in Garmisch — possibly to discuss terms for the surrender of the town of Mittenwald, which controlled the narrow Mittenwald leading across the Austrian border to Innsbruck and (farther to the south) the Brenner Pass through the Tyrol into Italy.

To parley with the enemy, one of Pfeiffer's officers seems to have used a means which was relatively little employed on the German side — the public telephone. The Allies had been using the telephone to wage war against the Germans ever since they had first crossed the German frontiers and discovered that, no matter how ruined and depopulated the area might be, the telephone service was generally in working order — a technological idiosyncracy they put to good use to instruct, threaten, bully, or demoralize the German commander of their next objective along the line of advance. British and American field commanders fell into the habit of carrying a pocketful of German coins to put in the public pay-phones with which they communicated their instuctions to the *Burgermeister* or Army commanders of the towns or cities in their path: surrender and put out white flags or we will raze the place to the ground. Even the Russians sometimes used the phone. Only ten days previously, a Russian officer in an abandoned apartment in the Siemensstadt district of East Berlin had put a call through to Dr. Goebbels in the Führer's bunker and actually spoke to the Propaganda Minister long enough to ask him: "When and in what direction will you be running away from Berlin? Remember this, Herr Goebbels. We'll find you anywhere you run, and the scaffold is ready and waiting for you."

The phone was simple and cheap, it saved a lot of lives and property, and it often did the trick. But it was rare that it was used the other way around, for few Germans cared to call up the forces bearing down on them. Colonel Pfeiffer (or one of his officers, for Pfeiffer himself spoke no English) seems to have been one of the few exceptions. Quite what happened is not entirely clear. What is certain is that the telephone system be-

tween Mittenwald and Garmisch was still in working order when the
Americans took Garmisch and that at about 7 P.M. on the evening of 30
April, just as it was getting dark, one of Colonel Pfeiffer's English-speaking
officers, after consuming a considerable quantity of alcohol, put a call
through to Clausing's Post Hotel in Garmisch. Purporting to be Colonel
Pfeiffer, he spoke with a waiter and demanded to be put on to an "honorable American officer." Clausing's was — or had been until that morning —
the fashionable watering hole in Garmisch. When the town was surrendered without a fight the hotel was captured with its windows, cellar, and
chef intact and was promptly designated a temporary field headquarters
for the 10th Armored Division. When the frightened waiter made it
known to the American Headquarters staff that a call had come through
from somewhere in the enemy lines, the division's G-2 (Intelligence) staff
officer, Lieutenant-Colonel William E. Eckles, who had just that moment
arrived in Garmisch, was summoned to the phone. Eckles picked up the
handset and a crackly voice with a German accent announced in English:
"This is Colonel Pfeiffer, German Army, Mittenwald."

It is possible that at about this time Mittenwald was actually under
American artillery bombardment from guns sited near Garmisch-Partenkirchen, and that this may have had something to do with the telephone
call. The Americans regarded Mittenwald as the gateway to the national
redoubt and Colonel Pfeiffer's *Kaserne* as a real threat to their advance into
that legendary stronghold. So a few salvos were hurled in that direction as
a means of weakening German resolve. In the process some priceless old
houses in Goethestrasse were destroyed and three people killed, including
a 12-year-old boy.

Colonel Eckles later recollected his telephone conversation with the German quite clearly. "He stated that he wanted to talk with an 'honorable'
American officer and he believed that I was honorable and that I could
help him," Eckles recalled. "He further stated

that he knew of me and that I could remove a great burden from his mind. He
asked that I take his surrender and place him and his staff under my personal supervision. At that time I was very busy with operational considerations and this
call did not appeal to me as anything I should or could get involved with. Our job
was killing Germans if they refused to surrender or insisted on fighting. So I told
the Colonel that I could not accept his surrender and that our forces were coming
through Mittenwald next morning and he and his staff should surrender when
they arrived. He was upset, but I hung up the telephone on him. That was the last
I heard from him for about two weeks.

Nothing had been said of the 15 million dollars' worth of gold and currency buried in the hills near Mittenwald, and Eckles had certainly heard nothing about them.

The Americans entered Mittenwald the next morning after a *Wehrmacht* sergeant and the local baker waving a white flag surrendered the town to them. None of Pfeiffer's officers was there to greet them, let alone surrender. With his military sphere of responsibility at a virtual end, Colonel Pfeiffer had sent his adjutant to convene a last special meeting with a dozen or so of his officers at the old mountain hut on the Klausenkopf in order to issue his final instructions concerning his remaining responsibility—the Reichsbank treasure. It seems that not only Colonel Pfeiffer and the men who buried the gold (including perhaps Lüder von Blücher) were present at this meeting, but also Colonel Rauch, formerly of Hitler's Chancellery. The first thing to be decided at this last briefing was a cover story in case any of them were captured. It was agreed that in such an event their interrogators should simply be told that an SS unit had arrived, dug up the treasure and transported it lock, stock, and barrel to an unknown place farther into the national redoubt. Such a story would not only preserve the anonymity of the gold and currency caches, but absolve the Gebirgsjäger officers from further questioning.

According to a statement made later by Captain Neuhauser, who was also present at the meeting, a second matter cropped up in the discussion which seemed curiously at odds with the spirit of the first. In an interview with a German journalist in 1952 Neuhauser claimed that one of Pfeiffer's officers was asked to obtain travel passes (*Ausweise*) for Rauch and Pfeiffer and was told that the considerable sum required to bribe the American occupation authorities in Garmisch into providing them could be found from the U.S. paper currency stacked in abundance in one or other of the currency caches on the Klausenkopf. Needless to say, Neuhauser's statement is uncorroborated.

There, for the moment, the matter rested. The meeting in the mountain hut broke up and most of Pfeiffer's officers made their way back to wherever they called home. Pfeiffer, his adjutant, and Rauch, unobtrusively dressed as wood choppers or forestry workers to avoid drawing the attention of the Americans to themselves, vanished completely—exactly where is still a matter of conjecture. Neuhauser believed that Colonels Pfeiffer and Rauch had set off for Munich to report to the Bavarian government that the Reichsbank treasure was intact, safely concealed, and ready to be handed over when the time came. This may well have been their original intention—Colonel Pfeiffer was to declare subsequently that he tried no less than four times to make contact with the Bavarian government with this purpose in mind. But in the chaos immediately following the American occupation there was no Bavarian government in existence to report to, and the two colonels were obliged to make themselves as scarce as they could while they awaited developments in the intensely uncertain and volatile conditions that now prevailed in the towns and countryside of defeated Germany.

But they did not lose contact with the vast fortune that had been buried at their behest on the heights overlooking Lake Walchen. On Pfeiffer's orders Captain Neuhauser — equipped with binoculars, tent, blanket, backpack, sausages, meat, fat, and dry bread — continued to maintain his solitary vigil on the Klausenkopf, sometimes sleeping in the mountain hut, sometimes roaming about the area, but never losing sight of the treasure caches or the Forest House down in Einsiedl, where a red eiderdown hung from an upstairs window would warn him that the arrival of the Americans was imminent.

While the key figures in the concealment of the Reichsbank reserves succeeded in evading the enemy until the moment they voluntarily gave themselves up, a good many weeks later, their political and military superiors, who had authorized the dispersal of the contents of the Berlin Reichsbank in the first place, managed to evade arrest only briefly and were soon rounded up and incarcerated. Almost the last significant objective to be taken by the Allies in Germany in World War Two was the small Alpine resort of Berchtesgaden, set amongst some of the most magnificent scenery in the whole of southern Germany. On the heights of the Obersalzberg overlooking the town, Hitler had built his famous Alpine retreat, the Berghof, and established virtually a second capital for the Nazi elite of the Reich. Believing that the Berchtesgaden area was to form the command center and inner citadel of the national redoubt, the Allies had viewed the prize of Hitler's mountain sanctuary in the south as being almost as great as that of his capital, Berlin, in the north, and they took its capture seriously. On 25 April the British had bombed the cluster of top Nazi villas and SS bunker installations on the Obersalzberg, badly damaging not only Hitler's luxury Alpine domicile, but Goering's, Bormann's, and Albert Speer's as well. On 5 May the departing German guard force, in virtually the last scorched-earth action in the war, set fire to the Führer's home and damaged it still further. By the time the Americans finally stormed the place later that day, Obersalzberg had not only been bombed by the Allies and burned by the Nazis but looted by the local populace for good measure as well. Even so, the GIs found Hitler's knickknacks still on the mantelpiece, his favorite armchair by the fire and his nightgowns stored in the linen cupboard. Around the establishment they found vast stocks of arms, ammunition, wine, linen, chocolates, contraceptives, china, and phonograph records. The next day they found Hitler's top aides in the vicinity and his top generals on the road. The Americans seized everything and everybody, souvenirs and suspects alike.

Berchtesgaden was surrendered to the Americans by the only important local official left in the town — the *Landrat* (or Prefect), Karl Theodor Jacob. One of the first Nazi VIPs to be apprehended after the surrender was Walther Funk, the Economics Minister and Reichsbank President. Like many desperate top Nazis who were able to foresee the inevitable end of the war, Funk had been drunk for months. He had fled to Berchtesgaden from his home near Bad Tölz on 1 May, bringing with him the two bars of gold which had been found in the stove of the Officers' Mess at the Gebirgsjäger Training School at Mittenwald, and the three bags of foreign currency which his aide, Dr. Schwedler, had removed from the currency caches at the Klausenkopf shortly after the burial of the treasure. On Funk's arrival at Berchtesgaden, the two gold bars (worth $30,000 then) and the three bags of currency (containing U.S. $87,000 and $40,350 worth of pound sterling notes) were handed over to Karl Jacob, the *Landrat*. Jacob passed them on to the head of the Berchtesgaden Savings Bank, then took back one bag containing $60,000 and a total of $7,120 out of one of the other bags. This money was never recovered. It is possible that Funk had some of it, since $3,300 was found in his possession when he was arrested by the Americans a few days later, but suspicion falls most heavily on Karl Jacob. As a result of an investigation into this affair by the Munich Criminal Investigation Division the facts of Jacob's case were submitted to the Public Prosecutor's Office at the Bavarian Upper Regional Court, but no further enquiries could be made, since the police were advised that any possible criminal activities brought to light would fall under the statute of limitations. At that time Dr. Jacob was once again *Landrat* of Berchtesgaden and by the time of his death a few years ago had become President of the Savings Bank in Munich and one of Berchtesgaden's wealthiest land and property owners.

What was left of the money Funk brought to Berchtesgaden — the gold bars, the English pounds and 19,840 American dollars (see Chapter 13) — was handed over to the American military authorities when they took over the area on 5 May. This money, too, seems to have vanished, and official records confirm that the Foreign Exchange Depository in Frankfurt, to which all captured money and valuables were supposed to be forwarded, received neither the currency from Berchtesgaden, nor the gold. The gold does seem to have been shipped up the line to Munich, where it was stored in a bank vault under American control for some while, but it was always officially listed as missing by both the Foreign Exchange Depository and the Land Commission for Bavaria, and in the end seems to have disappeared altogether. One of the officers of the American Military Government detachment which was initially involved with the Reichsbank gold and currency in Berchtesgaden was a young captain by the name of Melvin W. Nitz, who was later Military Governor of Garmisch-Partenkirchen.

All this was largely unknown to Funk, however, who was taken prisoner near Berchtesgaden by the Seventh U.S. Army on 6 May as he was trying to get away from the place with the evacuating German troops. Funk was just one of the 2,000 important military and political prisoners held by the Americans at Berchtesgaden during and after the last days of the war. Of the Berchtesgaden Nazis only Goering succeeded in making a temporary getaway — he was not captured until 9 May when he was found stuck in a traffic jam in the Austrian Alps. Notable prisoners held with Funk included the Reich Chancellery Secretary, Dr. Lammers, who had been in Berchtesgaden on what he called "a brief vacation" and, according to his captors, "looked like a typical German tourist"; Hans Frank, former Governor-General of Poland; Julius Streicher, Hitler's leading Jew-baiter; Robert Ley, the alcoholic former Labor Minister; Hitler's sister-in-law, his stenographers, his cook, barber, private secretary, and personal physician, Dr. Morell; Himmler's wife and 15-year-old daughter, together with his mistress and her two children; the family of Albert Speer, the Minister of War Economy; Field Marshal Kesselring; SS General Gottlob Berger, Chief of the SS Main Office, who had seized 12 sacks of foreign currency from the Munich Reichsbank three weeks previously; and Ernst Kaltenbrunner, Chief of the Reich Security Head Office (RSHA), who had authorized SS General Spacil's gunpoint robbery of the Berlin Reichsbank vaults on 22 April.

Kaltenbrunner, the No. 2 man in the SS, and overall head of the much-dreaded secret police (Gestapo), security service (*Sicherheits-dienst* — SD) and military intelligence (*Abwehr*), was captured at his home at Alt Aussee, in the Tyrol, where he had sought refuge in the last days of the war. He had tried to disguise himself by shaving off his moustache. But he was an unmistakable figure — a huge man standing nearly seven feet tall, with massive shoulders, huge arms, a head like a crag, thick square chin, and a long scar from an old automobile accident prominently etched down one side of his face. An excitable alcoholic and chain smoker, this terrifying giant —

until a few days before the absolute boss of the world's most dreaded secret police force—was soon spotted and brought into custody. Positive identification of Kaltenbrunner was complete when his mistress, Countess Gisela von Westrop, ran up and impulsively kissed him as he was led into custody.

Kaltenbrunner had been caught with a great deal of weapons, ammunition, candy, and counterfeit American dollars in his possession, and in the gardens of the Villa Kerry, his headquarters at Alt Aussee, the Americans unearthed 165 pounds of gold coins and a number of gold bars. Kaltenbrunner would have had access to far more valuables than this, of course. As Chief of the RSHA he would have been one of a handful of men who knew the true state of the accounts of the very substantial but nonaccountable funds (what the British Secret Service termed "unvouchered funds" for which no details are given) of the SS secret intelligence serivce, the *Abwehr*, and their present whereabouts—including the loot snatched by Spacil from the Berlin Reichsbank and flown to Salzburg a few weeks previously. But Kaltenbrunner's interrogation at the hands of the Allies never went into this area and whatever knowledge he had about it died with him on the gallows at Nuremberg in the following year.

While the men ultimately responsible for the former contents of the Reichsbank in Berlin—the President of the Reichsbank, Funk, and the Chief of the RSHA, Kaltenbrunner—were securely under lock and key the custodians of the Reichsbank treasure in Bavaria had effectively gone underground and disappeared almost without a trace. But only a day after Funk's arrest a hue and cry was raised at SHAEF (which was destined to track the treasure down to within a mile of its hiding place) and, for the moment, Colonel Pfeiffer was posted temporarily as one of the most wanted men in Germany.

During the planning for the Allied invasion of Europe, SHAEF planners in England had foreseen a future need for teams of experts in a variety of fields to execute special investigations in Germany immediately behind the vanguard of the fighting troops. In February 1945, on the eve of the main advance into Germany, SHAEF's G-2 (Intelligence) Division created a Special Sections Sub-Division to coordinate the operations of these specialist teams, which had been grouped under G-2's control.

These teams—known as T (Target) Forces—were many and various. Some were composed of scientists in uniform whose mission was to comb German plants and laboratories for scientific and industrial secrets on anything from plastics to shipbuilding, V-weapons to poison gas, synthetic oil, supersonic wind tunnels, and patents on research and development projects likely to be of value to the world in general and to the Allies in particular. There was the Enemy Personnel Exploitation Section, whose task was to pick the brains of German scientists and economic and industrial experts, including the 450 experts from the rocket development program (Werner von Braun among them) who had been captured and brought to Garmisch for interrogation before being shipped to the United States. There was the Top Secret Alsos Mission, charged with investigating German progress in the production of a German atomic bomb. There were the Goldcup teams, whose task was to uncover any intact parts of the German government and archives. There were groups of psychologists, sociologists, anthropologists, and poets who had been sent to examine the German mind and German society for clues to the cause of the German phenomenon of Nazism. There were the Strategic Bombing Survey teams investigating the effects on the German war economy of the Allied strategic bombing campaign (which was soon seen to have been a disastrous failure and one of the great miscalculations of the war).

Parallel with the scientific and technical agencies were others scouring the ruins of the Reich for prozed of a different kind. The Allied Monuments, Fine Arts, and Archeology Commission, composed entirely of officers who were art historians, museum curators, or archaeologists in civilian life, searched cellars, caves, dungeons, bunkers, and flak towers for works of art looted by the Nazis from all over occupied Europe. The Decartelization Branch sent businessmen and fiscal experts to burrow through countless tons of files and unravel the intricate business dealings of the big banks and the giant industrial and financial combines such as I. G. Farben, the House of Krupp, and United Steel which had subsidized Hitler and the Nazi military machine. Finally, the Gold Rush teams, under the direction of the Deputy Chief of the financial Branch of SHAEF, Colonel Bernard Bernstein, traveled the length and breadth of Germany tracking down leads to the real Nazi treasure — all the SS loot and Reichsbank gold, silver, foreign currency, and other valuables that had *not* been captured by the Americans in the Merkers mine in April.

The closing balances of the Berlin Reichsbank's Precious Metals Department prior to the German collapse showed that their official gold reserves totaled $255.96 million. Of this $238.49 million (93.17 percent of the German State gold reserves) had been captured by the Americans at Merkers on 6 April. Of the $17.47 million still left, $3.5 million had been retained in Berlin, and the remaining $14 million was known to have been kept in special storage in various provincial branches of the Reichsbank in central and southern Germany. These special storage points were the principal targets of the Gold Rush teams.

The Gold Rush had begun on 19 April and proceeded at full tilt for the rest of the month and into May. In two weeks the Gold Rush teams covered 1,900 miles checking Reichsbanks all over American-occupied Germany and following up every clue and rumor as to the previous whereabouts of the gold and its subsequent movement. The main reconnaissance party was headed by Colonel Bernstein himself and included Commander Joel H. Fisher and Lieutenant Herbert DuBois. They were aided in this whirlwind task by a man named Albert Thoms, the Chief of the Precious Metals Department at the Reichsbank in Berlin and former deputy to Emil Puhl, the Reichsbank's Vice-President and *de facto* head. Thoms was taken along by the Gold Rush people to help identify the hiding places in their searches and force necessary information from provincial Reichsbank employees.

The Gold Rush teams found all sorts of treasure hoards, including at least a small amount of gold. At the Halle branch on 20 April, 64 bars of non-Reichsbank gold and 65 bags of foreign currency, which included $1 million in U.S. currency, were found. At Plauen the vaults of the local branch were found to be buried under the rubble of the bombed-out bank building and one of the keys to the multiple lock was interred with the body of the cashier under the debris of his ruined apartment. Since it would take several days to find his body and retrieve the key, the Gold Rush team was forced to resort to dynamite to blast their way into the vaults of the Plauen bank. They were rewarded by the discovery of 35 bags of gold coins (including a million Swiss francs and a quarter million U.S. gold dollars) deposited by the SD security service for the Reichsführer SS, Heinrich Himmler. On 27 April the team learned of the location of 82 bars of gold bullion in the branch at Aue, still in German hands and heavily defended, and at the Magdeburg branch the next day they turned up over 6,000 bars of silver and nearly 500 cases of silver bars weighing a total of 99 tons, belonging to the Magyar National Bank of Hungary and representing Hungary's entire silver reserves. At Eschwege on 29 April they found 82 gold bars and at Coburg on 30 April they dug up another 82 gold bars from under a chicken coop, a manure heap, and a back garden where they had been buried by the bank's director. In the Nuremberg branch on 1 May they found more gold — 34 cases and two bags of non-Reichsbank gold weighing 2,200 pounds.

All these valuables were shipped up to Frankfurt, where they were stored in the vaults of the Reichsbank building serving as the Foreign Exchange Depository (FED), the strong point of all valuables recovered by the Allies in the territories of the former great German Reich. Throughout the last two weeks of the war armored convoys carring recovered loot and Reichsbank gold located by Gold Rush teams and combat troops alike—including a prodigious 32 million dollars worth of gold belonging to the National Bank of Hungary found in a freight train in a moutain siding at Spital am Pyhrn in the Austrian Tyrol—streamed back to Frankfurt from places as far away as the Czechoslovak border."With something tangible like looted gold to take in hand," reported one eyewitness, the Chief of the Decartelization Branch, James Stewart Martin, whose office was next door to the FED in Frankfurt, "the combat commanders were doing a job that would make the Brinks Express Company turn green. A truckful of bullion would arrive, not in an armored car with some armed men but escorted by half tracks with machine guns and one or two light tanks.... The half-billion dollars or so of valuable accumulating in the vaults downstairs were secure from burglars. The entire block around the Reichsbank was behind barbed wire and sandbagged machine gun nests. There were anticraft emplacements on the roof and a Sherman tank and crew sitting in front of our door."

Of all the big buildings of Frankfurt—a city which before the war had boasted a remarkable number of very big buildings—only two had escaped the bombing intact. One was the Frankfurt Reichsbank. The other was I. G. Farben in the industrial suburb of Hoechst, comprising the administrative headquarters and the chemical plant of one of the largest chemical combines in the world—the manufacturers, among other means of destruction, of the Zyklon-B poison gas used in the gas chambers of the Nazi death camps, and the super poison Tabun and the super-super poison Sarin, a tiny droplet of which meant instant death. Many people expressed surprise that these prominent targets, representing the biggest bank and the biggest business in the city, should have escaped destruction during the 20 air raids on Frankfurt in which over half of the city center was destroyed and the rest of the city flattened into mile upon mile of utter desolation. The cathedral where the kings of the Holy Roman Empire had once been crowned, the little inns with their carvings and paintings, the old quarter and most of the other monuments to the old times before Bismarck, the Kaiser, and Hitler had been burned or obliterated. The ruins of Frankfurt were now so vast that the U.S. Army-issue street maps served as little more than compass directories. In these ruins the inhabitants lived like troglodytes in cellars and caverns hollowed out of the rubble, without water, sewers, electricity, gas, telephones, mail, or any form of transport, not even bikes. And yet the colossal steel and stone Farben main building—a Nazi edifice of the new Order, a giant filing cabinet loaded with hundreds of tons of papers and records of the Farben empire, one of the largest buildings in the world and one of the single most important bombing targets in Germany—was unscathed. Not a single bomb had fallen on it and hardly a window had been cracked or a file or a shelf disturbed in the two-day battle that had raged around the building before the city fell.

Many people believed that the Farben building had been spared, not because of a miraculous accident or the inherent inaccuracy of saturation bombing, but as a result of deliberate policy—to preserve this monolith for the postwar advantage of Germany's conquerors, perhaps, or to unravel the secrets of Farben's suspescted wartime connection with American business and banking interests. Whatever the reason, the strange survival of the great Farben edifice was a manifold blessing for the Allies. Into its six wings and seven stories moved all the departments and agencies for the promulgation of Occupation rule in the U.S. Zone of Germany—Eisenhower's office, SHAEF's headquarters, the Office of Military Government of the United States (later transferred to Berlin), UNRAA, the T Forces, everyone and everything. At the same time the Farben files were moved from the parent building with the assistance of 500 prisoners-of-war and Farben employees and unloaded next door to the other surviving edifice, the Reichsbank, the new headquarters of the FED.

The FED was now the ultimate authority for financial affairs in postwar Germany. The huge underground vaults of this three-floor building housed all the rapidly swelling accumulation of valuables—the national reserves, SS loot, private hoards, European art treasures, and the wealth of foreign states—seized by the Allied military authorities and brought back from caches all over Germany.

A lot of work had been done on the Reichsbank building since the Americans took it over the month before. New glass had been put in the windows, fresh plaster on the walls, iron bars on the doors, and an emergency tarpaper roof over the south wing. Order and system had been introduced by the new owners. "In case of fire," one notice in the bank declared, "ring the German field telephone in front of the main vault and report to the person answering at Frankfurt Civilian Fire Department: 'FIRE REICHSBANK.' Note: There is no one at the Civilian Fire Department who speaks English."

So large was the inflow of treasure that the bank's existing underground vaults had to be considerably enlarged. The main basis of the treasure trove in the FED vaults was the huge cache found at Merkers and brought to Frankfurt in 11,750 containers on 15 April. As further shipments followed — over a hundred all told, most of them from the U.S. Zone of Germany — these vaults filled almost to the ceilings and overflowed into secondary strongrooms that had formerly been used as air-raid shelters.

The pressure of space was so great that currencies and other valuables recovered between mid-July and early September 1945 had to be held in other Reichsbanks in the U.S. Zone until room could be found for them in the FED. The total value of all the assets held in the FED vaults was thought to be well in excess of $500,000,000. Up to October 1946 Allied investigations had discovered and confiscated some 220 tons of Nazi gold in Germany and located a further 50 tons in Switzerland and 7 tons in Sweden. By then the concentration of treasure held at the FED was said to be the largest single collection of wealth in the world, with the possible exception of Fort Knox — no one seemed quite sure which was the greater. The gold holdings alone, valued at approximately $350,000,000, were second only to those at Fort Knox.

Among the more spectacular sights in the FED vaults were the rooms filled with gold bars stacked three deep from wall to wall, each bar weighing 25 pounds and worth $15,000. In one cage there was a gold nugget the size of a grapefruit, the biggest nugget ever seen. In another was some of the gold of the German Foreign Office, a portion of the so-called Ribbentrop Gold hoard, and in another virtually the entire Hungarian gold reserves. Serveral compartments in the vaults were filled with the gold coins of a number of nations. One large room contained 200 suitcases and trunks full of the infamous SS loot which included 600 pounds of gold fillings extracted from the mouths of murder camp victims. Two other rooms in the air-raid-shelter vaults were stacked to the ceilings with another kind of SS loot — boxes and boxes of cheap alarm clocks. There were compartments housing boxes of cut diamonds (17,000 carats worth $10,000,000); precious metals such as platinum, iridium, palladium, and rhodium; the crown jewels of the Hungarian and Hohenzollern dynasties; and eight million dollars worth of counterfeit English pound notes in denominations from £5 to £100, all neatly stacked and bill-strapped as if they had just come from the printing press, and almost indistinguishable (according to Bank of England experts who examined them) from genuine ones.

Just how much all the stuff in the FED vaults was worth nobody knew because nobody knew exactly what was in the FED vaults anyway. Initially, the FED served simply as a storehouse. The task of producing an evaluated inventory of the mountainous assets of the FED was daunting in the extreme and beyond the limited resources of the FED's staff at the end of the war. To describe and catalogue the treasure in its entirety was work for experts, and there were simply not enough of them and probably never could be. Many of the items were very small but immensely valuable, and these alone could involve experts in gemstones and jewelry laboring for months on an inventory without making any appreciable progress towards the completion of their work. The problem was compounded into a kind of Catch-22 situation by the fact that such work could only be accomplished under strict security controls designed to prevent loss — "not a simple problem," as one FED official commented, "when it is considered that no one knows what is in the depository now." In other words, work on the inventory of the FED could ideally only begin when it was known what the depository contained, but no one could know what the depository contained until work on the inventory had begun. This fact was of crucial significance in the development of this story, for it entailed a fatal delay before the discovery that a considerable portion of the Reichsbank reserves had gone astray.

Inventoried or not, the FED treasure at the Frankfurt Reichsbank clearly demanded the most elaborate security system possible. To ensure the external security of the bank premises, barbed-wire barriers and floodlights were flung up around the outside of the building and the single entrance to the bank and the approaches to the vaults were guarded by a company of the 29th Infantry Division. The internal security system was based on that used in the U.S. mints. Only persons possessing passes signed by the Chief of the Currency Branch were allowed to approach the vault entrances. There was a triple control over the main vaults and a dual control over all the other strongrooms. The door to the main vault had a combination lock known only to three officers, each of whom carried keys to dual locks under his exclusive control, and no person could enter any vault or strongroom unless two of the three officers were present.

In spite of these stringent precautions, two thefts did subsequently occur inside the FED vaults — once when a DP (displaced person) laborer palmed a small bag of ten Austrian gold crowns (worth $6,200) while some boxes of coins were being inventoried, and again when four other DPs stole 197,200 Allied military marks while the supervising officers' attention was distracted during the transfer of currency from one strongroom to another. But the principal preoccupation of the FED staff was not with what might go out of their overburdened vaults but what ought to be coming in. And this, it was already becoming clear by early May of 1945, was not entirely sufficient.

The interrogation of arrested Reichsbank officials and the perusal of captured Reichsbank documents indicated to Colonel Bernstein and his

Gold Rush officers that of the Reichsbank branches which had previously stored more than 17 million dollars worth of Reichsbank gold only three had actually yielded recoveries—246 gold bars, to be exact, and worth some $3,000,000. That still left over $14,000,000 of gold unaccounted for. Subsequently, $500,000 worth was reported in Regensburg and nearly $3,500,000 worth (comprising 90 bars of bullion worth $1,278,000 and 147 bags of coin worth $2,156,375) was in Russian hands in Berlin. The Reichsbank records captured at Magdeburg indicated that in the first half of April most of the remainder of the gold, totaling $10,000,000, had been hastily evacuated to Berlin from six branches in central Germany and then shipped south on a trail which, according to reliable Reichsbank officials, led deep into the mountains somewhere in southern Germany.

The next step was to follow that trail into the Alps. By now, Colonel Bernstein was deeply preoccupied with the complex decartelization investigation of German heavy industry, which came under the wing of his Financial Branch, and he was shortly off to Washington for discussions with President Truman on this subject. He therefore relinquished responsibility of tracking the Reichsbank treasure to its final resting placae to the junior member of his original Gold Rush party, Lieutenant Herbert G. DuBois, a young officer who was to occupy a prominent position on the stage in the next two weeks and thereafter vanish almost without trace into total obscurity, for almost nothing can be discovered about him. It is known that at the time he followed the treasure trail down to Bavaria he was working for Supreme Headquarters Allied Expeditionary Forces (SHAEF) Financial Intelligence Section (in the subsection designated Foreign Exchange, Blocking, and Property Control). It is thought that he spoke fluent German (and wrote fluent English) and it was said that he came from Paris— which could either mean that he was French (like his surname) or merely that he had previously worked in Paris at SHAEF headquarters (which is in any case likely). Judging by his junior rank he was presumably young and presumably had some sort of fiscal background—perhaps in banking, like some of his colleagues. He was obviously highly competent and very conscientious and hardworking. But where he came from before he briefly stepped into the spotlight to play out his part in the Reichsbank mystery is as obscure a matter as where he went to afterwards. The curiously unworldly nature of his mission seems to have engaged his fancy at any rate. When he had completed his fairy-tale task he gave his official report a fairy-tale title: "In Quest of Gold, Silver, and Foreign Exchange." This report seems to have been Herbert DuBois' only permanent bequest to posterity—if a secret document remained hidden in the archives for the next thirty-five years could be described in this way.

Lieutenant DuBois set out on his quest on 8 May 1945. Frankfurt had been in American hands for over a month, Munich and Mittenwald for a week—and the President of the Reichsbank, Walther Funk, for two days. Though he makes absolutely no mention of the fact, the day DuBois chose to set off was a momentous day for the American Army, a dreadful one for the German people, and a milestone in the history of the world. May 8th was V-E Day. At General Eisenhower's headquarters at Reims on the previous morning the German forces in the west had surrendered unconditionally to the Allies, effective from midnight that night. The first stage of DuBois' quest, therefore, entailed driving from one euphoric American military post to another through a conquered populace plunged into the most abject melancholy and despair. In the major garrison towns there were full-dress parades and victory marches, salutes, flags, and fine food. For Lieutenant DuBois there were K rations (one labeled Breakfast, one Lunch, one Dinner, complete with cigarettes, gum, and toilet paper), chlorinated water, makeshift quarters, and the first of many onerous interviews in the pursuit of his difficult mission. On V-E Day he got no further than Heidelberg, where he was to discuss his plans with the Finance Officer at 6th Army Group Headquarters. The next morning he departed for Munich and the south.

DuBois traveled in a U.S. Army staff car, a sedan, with a driver, an armed GI guard, a German-speaking fellow officer, and the Gold Rush team's peripatetic German companion, Albert Thoms, the gold and precious-metal expert from Berlin. Driving a car around Germany once the war was over was an exhilarating and adventurous business and there were many difficulties along the road.

Germany in that first summer of peace—and for a long time afterwards—was a civilization in torment. In the moment of hiatus that followed the German surrender—that absolute rock-bottom moment of nothingness the Germans were to call "die Stunde Null," zero hour—Germany presented a scene without precedent in modern times, a surrealist tableau of disaster. It was a land of ruins peopled by ghosts, a land without government, order, or purpose, without industry, communications, or proper means of existence, a nation that had entirely forfeited its nationhood and lay entirely at the beck and call of foreign armies. Hardly any of the great cities of Germany had escaped the destruction of the air raids or the land fighting. An estimated 400 million cubic feet of rubble covered the devastated areas. Many of the great public buildings and much of the infrastructure of a once-great industrial nation had been erased as well. The almost complete cessation of the means of communication — mail, telephone, railways, motor transport — seemed to have brought civilized life itself to a halt.

And yet, paradoxically, the rolling German countryside looked spring-like, beautiful, and untouched by war in the warm, summery weather of V-E plus one. The autobahn down to Munich ran through a pastoral setting — all vineyards and orchards and pine forests, wayside crucifixes, milk cows pulling carts, medieval villages with smoke curling gently from the chimneys. The only reminders of battle were the one-legged men and the trucks full of ragged DPs, a few burnt-out tanks dotted the meadows, and an occasional plane was pancaked at the edge of the freeway. In sunlight even the ruins of the cities — Stuttgart, Ulm, Augsburg — seemed less oppressive to the spirit, and the stink from the rotting corpses buried beneath the rubble grew less with each day, although some streets were still labeled "Gruesome." And now it was peacetime — no more killing, no more blackout, no more curfew for troops. All signs of Germany's recent past had already miraculously vanished — there were no more Nazi slogans to be seen, no more portraits of Hitler hanging in rooms, no more "Adolf Hitler Strasse" plaques on the walls of streets.

The American occupation was still in its infancy but already a visitor from some other part of Germany — from the British Zone, for example — would have notices the burgeoning idiosyncrasies of the U.S. military style. Billboards were already going up beside the two-lane concrete autobahns along which DuBois and his party headed, pumping road sense and courtesies in curious rhyming couplets. "BRING IN YOUR JEEP," drivers running out of gas were advised, "WE NEVER SLEEP"; and "WE'VE GOT OIL AND GAS, SO PLEASE DON'T PASS." "DON'T BE A SAP — PULL IN AND NAP. SAVE WEAR AND TEAR — LET'S CHECK YOUR AIR." Sometimes the tenor of the billboards changed. "SOLDIERS WISE DON'T FRATERNIZE!" declared some, warning the troops against forming friendships with Germans, and especially German girls. Under one a GI intent on sowing a few oats had scribbled: "THIS DON'T MEAN ME, BUDDY." Every few miles the sign "BRIDGE OUT" forced military traffic off the autobahn and on to complicated detours around blown bridges which had not yet been repaired, along corduroy roads, mud tracks, and open fields, or over makeshift Bailey bridges across creeks and rivers, double-tracked affairs resting on rubber pontoons that billowed slowly up and down in the waves.

The road was full of people — people on foot, people on bikes, people driving horse carts, people pulling boxes on wheels, scruffy, liberation-happy DPs going home after years of slave labor; weary German civilians on the great trek from the east, their faces blank and unresponsive; long columns of surrendered German soldiers trudging towards some vast open-air prisoner-of-war cage in their disheveled *Feldgrau*; American transport convoys of jeeps, trucks, 6 × 6's, and half-tracks grinding ceaselessly along in both directions, loaded with soldiers, stores, and secreted Fräuleins. At the end of the war all Europe was on the move. Sixty million people had been uprooted from their homes in a displacement of peoples without parallel in the history of the human race. Now they were going home. Germany became the arena for refugees of all kinds — including millions of former slave laborers and concentration camp survivors and countless million homeless German evacuees, returning prisoners of war, refugees, and expellees from the East — made their various ways north, south, east, and west across the land. To the visitor, this vast ragged army of people on the move was one of the most unforgettable impressions of Germany in defeat. Men collected cigarette ends in gutters. Children begged for candy from the occupation troops. Girls slowly cruised the pavements trying to catch a soldier's eye, hoping for food in exchange for sex. Filthy and tattered ex-*Wehrmacht* men, many minus a leg or arm, their eyes blank, empty food tins tied to the strings that girt their waist, their feet bound with sacking, hobbled around the ruins in a desperate search for their families, work, and shelter.

Lieutenant DuBois and his party neared Munich in late afternoon. Munich was in Third Army territory and Third Army was known to have the snappiest Military Police in the European Theater. Huge new signs bearing the Third Army emblem now appeared at the roadside: "YOU ARE NOW ENTERING 3RD ARMY TERRITORY. TRAFFIC LAWS STRICTLY IN FORCE." Then smaller signs spaced at 100-yard intervals, like Burma Shave signs back in the States: "MOTOR CYCLES, ¼ TONS, SEDANS." "40 MILES." With the signs came the military police (MPs), hunting for traffic violators and German Army deserters, forever prying into vehicles and checking papers — above all, papers. "Paper is a passport to anywhere," noted a visiting British T-Force Colonel. "If you want a meal, a billet, or a car in the American Zone they merely say 'Have you got orders?' and you brandish a bundle and they say 'OK' and fix you up. My bundle (maps, travel booklets, and spare notepaper) is much more impressive than my T-Force pass since the latter merely authorized me to obtain 'papers' from God knows where—and it is 'papers' that matter."

DuBois' papers from SHAEF and 6th Army Group headquarters were of impeccable pedigree. But they did not spare him from the angst every traveling serviceman felt when he was overtaken by night in former enemy territory: fear of missing a decent place to sleep and a square meal, fear of being stranded homeless in the ruins, the umbilical cord to the military system severed till morning. It was dark when DuBois got to Munich. Like Frankfurt and Stuttgart and just about everywhere else, Munich had been flattened by air raids—74 of them in all—and 50 percent of the city, the historic home of the Nazi Party and the venue of Hitler's earliest meetings and political battles, now lay in ruins. "The devastation of Munich was different from that of other cities," recalled one visitor at this time, the writer James Stern. "Munich's ruins looked like a million overturned garbage carts multiplied in size as many times." There was no street lighting and the black, rubble-lined streets of gutted shells and tottering walls bore no names. At nightfall an eerie silence fell over this wasteland. The only sounds that could be heard were the gnawing of rats emerging from the sewers. Great and fine buidings stood still like fossils in the moonlight as if they had fallen into ruin during millennia of time. During the daylight hours Army MP signboards pointed out unit locations in a hundred different directions, but it was easy to get lost in the back streets and arrive late to be told: "All available billets are full. Red Cross—or bivouac in the station yard." DuBois and his party were lucky to squeeze in—the Financial Officer in the Munich Military Government had not been expecting them until next morning.

On 10 May the hard questioning began. Twenty-eight Reichsbank officials who had reached Munich from Berlin on board the special trains *Adler* and *Dohle* had been held under guard by T (Target) Forces. Among them was one man who knew a great deal more about the disposition of the missing Reichsbank treasure than he was initially capable of revealing to his interrogators. This was Mielke, who had actually been down to Mittenwald when he brought an extra 25 boxes of gold bullion to the *Kaserne* and afterwards listed all the treasure as it lay in the Forest House at Einsiedl waiting to be taken to the mountains for burial. "Mielke," DuBois reported after the interrogation, "was very uncertain about the facts and it was necessary to repeat some questions a number of times before he could give a clear statement. He appeared to have been shell-shocked. He was not certain whether the other gold at Mittenwald was 50 or 75 bags or perhaps there was even more."

Mielke's condition was a familiar one at that time. Half the streets in Germany were full of such people — mostly middle-aged, with dazed, apathetic faces, a past that was dead within them and a future for which they had no thought whatsoever. Mielke's confusion may also have been aggravated by the state of his conscience, for he knew only too well that of the $120,000 he had brought back to Munich from Einsiedl on Funk's instructions, $5,000 had gone astray — and only he knew where. But in spite of his pathetic condition, Mielke had revealed enough. From him Lieutenant DeBois had learned the crucial names — Mittenwald, Einsiedl, Pfeiffer. His next step was obvious. That afternoon he set out for Garmisch *en route* to the *Kaserne* and the Forest House — and hopefully the tracks of the Gebirgsjäger colonel who seemed to lie at the heart of this mysterious matter.

The next morning DuBois found himself in Mittenwald. The Casino at the *Kaserne* where the treasure had first been stored was now being used as a hospital for German officers, but an old man who had worked there for years recalled that boxes and bags had indeed been stored there until about eight days before the Americans arrived, when they were transported by truck on two trips to Einsiedl. At the Forest House DuBois confronted the forester, Hans Neuhauser, and his wife and lodger, the Serbian girl Vera de Costra. They all agreed the treasure had been brought there, they all agreed that it had been stacked in the storeroom at the back, and they all agreed that it had been taken away again. But by whom? And to where? Neuhauser senior trotted out the well-rehearsed line that had been agreed by Pfeiffer's men up at the Klausenkopf hut for just such an emergency. Neuhauser attributed the disappearance of the Reichsbank treasure to the action of everybody's universal bogeymen, the SS. The SS took the stuff away (without Colonel Pfeiffer's permission), he said, when the Americans occupied Wallgau, which was only four miles away down the Mittenwald road. "Neuhauser professed to have little knowledge of the bags and boxes," DuBois noted in his report, "because he did not like to butt in wherever he thought the SS were concerned."

Having successfully drawn one red herring across the trail, Neuhauser proceeded to draw another. Since the road to the north of Einsiedl, like the road to the south, was in American hands, the SS trucks must have driven down the only other road still open, a dirt road skirting round Lake Walchen eastwards towards Jachenau. "Lt. DuBois hesitated to continue the reconnaissance to Jachenau," DuBois wrote in his report, referring to himself, like Julius Caesar in his war memoirs, in the third person, "because a number of German soldiers had already been seen in the woods near the lake and it was thought desirable to secure additional guards before proceeding." Henriette von Schirach (the wife of Hitler's former Youth Leader and Lord Mayor of Vienna), who moved into Jachenau subsequently, confirmed the fact. "The forest was infested with hungry soldiers," she remembered, "who had fed on nothing but brandy." These soldiers almost certainly included some of the men from the Gebirgsjäger Training School whom Colonel Pfeiffer had dismissed in that area a week or so previously. Fourteen German soldiers and two mules had been seen recently on a mountain summit near the Klausenkopf, along with eight others on a neighboring mountain pasture. Probably they were waiting for the military situation to settle down after the ceasefire before making their bid for home. Whoever they were, they were not entirely harmless. Only a few days previously a mother and her thirteen-year-old daughter had been gunned down in cold blood on the Jachenau road by a group of soldiers lurking in the woods. "Werewolf" partisans were still thought to be a real threat to the Allies in the first weeks following the end of the war, and Lieutenant DuBois was not serving in the role of a combat soldier. He returned to Munich, all in one piece but empty-handed, having located neither the treasure's hiding place nor the men who had been responsible for hiding it.

DuBois made a breakthrough when he got back to Munich, however. The bomb-happy Mielke had collected his wits somewhat while the Lieutenant was away and, rummaging around, had come up with an inventory that he had made of the gold and currency that had been stored in the Forest House at Einsiedl while he was there. The gold came to over ten million dollars worth and the currency to over five million dollars worth, including more than two millions in actual U.S. dollar bills. Lieutenant DuBois now knew that the object of his quest was the equivalent of a king's ransom—a treasure trove worth by today's valuation a colossal $170,000,000. That alone made further pursuit of the target worthwhile. On 13 May the Lieutenant set off to the south again, this time in search of the bigger game, and with a task force comfortingly augmented by an extra truck and an additional three armed guards to accompany him.

By lunchtime DuBois was in Bad Tölz, enquiring for the whereabouts of Dr. Walther Funk, who until recently had been living at his luxurious 22-room home, the Bergerhof, on his rich farming estate at Hechenberg, five miles out of town. Funk, DuBois felt sure, could help solve the puzzle. But Funk was not there—the Bergerhof was shortly to be requisitioned by General Patton—and nobody knew where he was. They knew where his wife was, though—she was living with the *Bürgermeister* in Bad Tölz. DuBois wasted no time. He banged on the *Bürgermeister's* door and demanded to see Frau Funk. Where, he demanded of the startled lady, was the Reichsbank President, her husband, Funk? The lady did not know where the treasure was; in fact, she had never heard of it, so she claimed. But she knew where her husband was. She had just heard on Radio Munich (the Military Government radio station that had only started broadcasting the previous day). He had been taken prisoner by the Seventh Army at Berchtesgaden and was locked up in an American prison somewhere.

Liaison between the myriad units composing the huge complex that made up the U.S. Army in Germany was not always very swift or very sure. Though Funk was now a prisoner of the Americans it could prove a formidable task for DuBois to discover exactly which Americans had him in their custody. Now approaching the three-thousandth mile of his quest, the lieutenant immediately turned his little T-Force convoy eastward and headed for the Austrian border and the town of Salzburg, where he hoped that G-2 at 15 Corps, which had its headquarters in the town, could provide a clue to the Reichsbank President's whereabouts within the corps area. G-2 did indeed know where Funk was. He was being held in the Seventh Army Interrogation Center at Augsburg, a city 40 miles to the northwest of Munich and in exactly the direction from which DuBois and his party had just come. Undaunted, the party retraced their steps. They were to cover more than 190 miles before the day's work was done.

At 9 o'clock on the morning of 14 May the Junior Lieutenant at last confronted the former Nazi Minister on the subject of Nazi gold. Funk had not been in custody long enough to lose much weight and he was still chubby and round—a small, ugly, bald, gnomelike little man with a drooping lower lip and the melancholy eyes of a clown. He was less of a clown than a juggler, however—a financial juggler of some talent who had negotiated the great industrialists' sponsorship of the Nazi Party before the war and helped finance the German war machine during it. Within the year he was to stand trial in Nuremberg accused of hoarding in the Reichsbank vaults tons of tooth gold torn from the mouths of the concentration camp dead. Funk's health was already beginning to deteriorate when DuBois saw him that morning. He had contracted a venereal disease when he was thirteen and had endured bad health ever since—nervous disorders, diabetes, cardiac trouble, bad migraines. He was already heading for a nervous collapse, yet he proved a fearful, compliant, and willing interviewee. He told DuBois all about the Reichsbank shipment from Berlin, the attempt to hide the treasure in a lead mine and the delivery of the gold and currency to Colonel Pfeiffer at the Mittenwald *Kaserne*. What he could not tell the American lieutenant was where the treasure was now. Perhaps it was in another lead mine near Mittenwald, he suggested, but he did not really know. DuBois was dubious. "It should be stated," he recorded in his report, "that no pressure was exerted on Funk whatsoever and it is quite possible that he knew more than what he stated."

The encounter with Funk produced one tangible result. A notebook had been found in Funk's possesssion with the name and address of one Josef Veit scribbled in it. Veit was the professional hunter who towards the end of April had been approached by Colonel Rauch with a view to finding a forest hideaway for Funk and other Nazi VIPs. Clearly, he was a man who might throw more light on the Reichsbank treasure. So shortly afterwards Veit was rudely awakened by a loud banging on the front door of his house in Mittenwald. It was nearly midnight and when he opened the door he found an American Counter-Intelligence Corps (CIC) officer standing there. The officer wore no badges of rank and spoke fluent German with a thick Bavarian accent.

"Sagen sie die Wahrheit, sonst..." said the American threateningly. "You tell the truth—or else...Do you know Funk?"

"Nein."

"Have you been in contact with him?"

"Nein."

In a sharper tone the American warned Veit to tell the truth. The American strode into the house. Veit told him all he knew about his encounter with Colonel Rauch and his plan to hide Funk in the mountains.

"Wissen Sie was vom Gold" the American asked. "Do you know anything about the gold?"

"Only from a comrade who drove two loads of gold, first to the Officers' Mess, then to the barracaks and then to Einsiedl."

"That's where I've come from."

"Where is the gold?" Veit was naturally curious to know.

"In the lake," the American told him.

"Where did you get my name from?" Veit asked.

"Out of Funk's diary. I interrogated him tonight."

Funk was interviewed twice again about the Reichsbank reserves. At both interviews Funk was joined by Hermann Goering, who as head of the German Four-Year Plan, which directed Nazi financial strategy, had been nominally Funk's superior in the sphere of economics in the Third Reich.

Like Funk, Goering was also held in detention at the Seventh Army Interrogation Center in Augsburg. He was quartered in a working-class block in the suburbs of the city where he had a primitive living room, an adequate bedroom and an extremely small kitchen, but no lavatory or bath — a deliberate humilation. By now the former Reich Marshal, Chief of the German Air Force, Hitler's one-time nominated successor, and war criminal No. 1, had been stripped not only of his decorations — his *Pour le Mérite* (the German First World War equivalent of the Congressional Medal of Honor) and his Grand Cross of the Iron Cross with Swords and Diamonds — but also of his Field Marshal's baton, his gold shoulder tabs and even his diamond ring. The Americans had originally kept him at Augsburg to interrogate him about his huge collection of looted art treasures, and they had been very quickly impressed by the intelligence, wit, and cunning of this normally slothful, drug-addicted Nazi leader. On the last day of his confinement at Augsburg, a week after DuBois' visit there, Goering was brought along to Funk's second interrogation in the hope that he might shed some further light on what was now known as the matter of "gold bullion hidden the Alps." But at any event the ex-Reich Marshal, who was undergoing cold turkey greatment for his codeine addiction and was more preoccupied with his own withdrawal symptoms than someone else's treasure, contributed little, and it was Funk who did most of the talking.

"I am convinced," Funk told his interrogator, "that they have hidden the gold in a cave."

"Was it bullion?" the interrogator asked him.

"Only gold bullion...there was also some foreign currency. I do not believe Pfeiffer knows anything about the location. I would stake my right hand on it that the gold was not stolen. They have dug it in so well — I do not know where. They told me that it was in a lime pit, and all you have to do is take it out. At first there was no intention of digging it in; they were only to guard it."

"How much gold was there — ten million?" the interrogator asked Funk.

"Ten tons," Funk corrected him.

"How heavy is such an ingot?"

"Usually 44 pounds, but there are also smaller ones — 22 pounds." Then suddenly Funk's exasperation — with the gold, with his own predicament, with life in general — seemed to boil over. "To think," he exploded, "that this bank manager handed these things over to the *Wehrmacht!*"

For the first time Goering spoke. "It is not surprising," he said soothingly but unhelpfully, "in times like these."

"Is it in Mittenwald?" the interrogator persisted.

"It must be down there," Funk answered.

"In a cave?"

"Yes," pontificated Goering, who had no means of knowing. "Schwedler must know about it."

That day Goering and Funk were transported as prisoners of war to Camp Ashcan, the internment center reserved for topmost Nazis, including those to be tried as major war criminals at Nuremberg. Ashcan was then housed in the 90-room Palace Hotel at Bad Mondorf in Luxembourg. The Palace was a long, low, white, once modestly fashionable resort hotel, now totally surrounded by a high-banked wire fence covered from top to bottom with a greenish-yellow camouflage cloth and guarded everywhere by sentries with machine guns. It was an unusual prison in that it was much easier to get out than to get in. Vistors seeking admission would be told by the Sergeant of the Guard that they would need "a pass from God and someone to verify the signature." Ashcan was run by a rather overbearing U.S. Army jailer, Colonel Bertram C. Andrus, who was to serve as chief warden at Nuremberg from August onwards. There was also a British counterpart of Ashcan, called Camp Dustbin, near Frankfurt, which was reserved for more technical prisoners; some of the accused men, like Speer, Schacht, and Funk, were candidates for both places.

In Ashcan Funk and Goering joined all the other surviving dignitaries of the late great German Reich. They were fed on prisoner-of-war rations, usually U.S. Army C and K rations, and each given a room which possessed one hard chair and one canvas cot with two blankets but no pillow. Because of his great girth, Goering was given the special privilege of a double mattress to cover his single cot and he spent much of his time lying on it, his vast body sagging over the edges, while he endured the torment of drug withdrawal. He was not a very helpful source of information about the matters he was supposed to have been responsible for, such as Luftwaffe operations, let alone the esoteric matter of the Reichsbank gold, and he gave whatever answers he thought would be most likely to please his interrogators and to end the interview as speedily as possible. Nor was Funk much better. He too was suffering from withdrawal symptoms—from alcohol addiction, in his case—and like Goering displayed an astonishing ignorance of his own special subjects, such as the German economy and the business of the Reichsbank. In exasperation, their interrogator was forced to resort to sarcastic abuse, no doubt echoing the disillusion of one astonished Allied visitor to Ashcan, who said on leaving: "Who'd have thought we were fighting the war against a bunch of jerks?"

"Our investigation of foreign exchange can be explained only in terms of the complete panic and stupidity of the German personnel," berated the American interrogator of Funk and Goering. "The chief personnel were concerned with finding comfortable billets in mountain resorts and watering places and did not seem to give a damn about the records and activities of the Ministry. We found that the Party left Berlin and went to Bad Salzungen but they left their records behind, and moved back towards Berlin. Then they scattered north and south. In the north they stayed in the finest hotels of Hamburg and didn't do anything. Those that went south went to Bad Wiessee, a very beautiful place on the Tegernsee, and did nothing. Some of them landed up in a small town of about 250, where they are tending pigs. Is that the way that the evacuation of the Department of Foreign Exchange was planned?"

"Certainly not!" retorted an affronted Funk.

The American interrogators were obviously well briefed, because they were very specific in cross-examining Funk about the movement of gold in Bavaria.

"Did you ever send gold from Berchtesgaden to Mittenwald?" one of them asked Funk.

"No."

"What was in the eleven cases you sent from Berchtesgaden to Mittenwald? You know that you sent these boxes. The driver said that he was ordered by Dr. Funk."

"I don't know anything about these boxes," Funk replied. "I never had any boxes sent from Berchtesgaden. There must be some error. There has been no gold in Berchtesgaden."

Funk had already conveniently forgotten that with his own hands he had brought 50 pounds of gold bullion from his home at the Bergerhof to Berchtesgaden at the beginning of May.

Lieutenant DuBois, meanwhile, had been getting little farther forward, and by 17 May his quest for the missing Reichsbank treasure was drawing to an end. He had followed up Funk's suggestion that the treasure might be cached in lead mines in the Lake Walchen area, but it proved a fruitless and tiresome undertaking. North of Wallgau the reconnaissance party discovered that four bridges along the road had been blown and this necessitated a walk of four miles before they reached the only likely mine. There was nothing in the mine buildings and the mine itself could be reached only by a narrow and hair-raising catwalk across the swirling River Isar. Du Bois declined to cross over the river by such a precarious contraption.

In his view it was most improbable that heavy loads of gold could have been manhandled across the river in that direction and he turned back to Mittenwald and the comforts of the Post Hotel.

Herbert DuBois appeared to have drawn a blank. Somewhere in this region of mountains, valleys, caves, and mines lay 15 million dollars worth of gold and currency. And somewhere about lurked men who knew exactly where. DuBois had done his utmost, but he had tracked down neither treasure nor treasurers. From Mittenwald he tried to make a phone call back to base at Sixth Army Group in Heidelberg. But the line was down and he was advised to drive on to Innsbruck and make the call from there. The line was out of order there too and DuBois had no choice but to send a cable asking for further instructions from SHAEF. In the meantime he pondered the crucial question. If there was one man who could provide the answers he wanted, it was Colonel Pfeiffer. But neither the intelligence officer with the 10th Armored detachment in Mittenwald nor G-2 at 10th Armored headquarters in Garmisch had any record of any prisoner of war of that name in their custody. Nor was there any trace of him in Innsbruck or Salzburg.

So where *was* Colonel Pfeiffer?

5

The House on the Hill

Colonel Pfeiffer, it will be remembered, had dismissesd his troops with the words *"Gott behüte euch!"* (God be with you) soon after the Americans had entered Mittenwald, and then sent his officers home after a final meeting at the forest hut on the Klausenkopf near Lake Walchen. After that he had simply disappeared. For most of a month his whereabouts were unknown to all but a handful of individuals, and accounts of his movements are contradictory and suggest that at times he seemed to be in two places at once.

This is hardly surprising. It was a chaotic period. There was no proper government and no fully established order. Colonel Pfeiffer was a fugitive intent on avoiding the usual fate of the German Officer Corps at this time — internment as a prisoner of war. He left no tracks and kept no records of his movements. Perhaps this is why his memory, which was able to recall in minute detail his bloody experiences during the last five years of war, grew so vague when it came to the first month or two of peace. Perhaps, like half the German race, he lived through this period of defeat and disintegration in a state of traumatic shock. "I don't like to remember those bad times," he was to explain later. "I had all sorts of things to worry about. The world was collapsing all around me. I didn't know what the next day would bring, or the day after that, or the day after that. As German soldiers, we were despised and hated by everybody — even by our own people. I slept under the trees. I didn't know what was happening or where I was going."

According to Pfeiffer's own account, the first few weeks saw him living the life of a partisan, wandering in the woods from place to place, like many other German soldiers in the region of the national redoubt at this time. Possibly it was during this period that Pfeiffer and Rauch, who were still in touch with one another, tried to report to the Bavarian authorities in Munich concerning the matter of the Reichsbank reserves—the dates cannot now be exactly determined.

Sometime in May, Colonel Pfeiffer abandoned the partisan life and shook the mud of the Bavarian Alps from his feet. There has been some speculation as to where exactly he directed his steps next. According to one statement made later by Pfeiffer himself, he set off for the Austrian Tyrol on his own after dismissing his troops at Walchensee. According to a subsequent statement he went to stay at his mother's home near Schliersee. According to another statement, he eventually made his way by bicycle to Bad Reichenhall, near Berchtesgaden in Eastern Bavaria, using a fake American pass, and there rejoined his wife in their family home.

It is unlikely that Colonel Pfeiffer went far during the first few weeks of May. In the conditions then prevailing it would have made little sense to have attempted to do so. Bad Reichenhall was a long way away, situated about 187 miles away by Alpine road at the far eastern end of the Bavarian Alps. For a German in 1945 a motor vehicle and gas were virtually unattainable commodities—unless the person concerned was especially privileged for one reason or another (as Colonel Pfeiffer was later to be). Travel over any distance along open roads was a dangerous undertaking for Germans at the end of the war, and they ventured forth at their own peril. Everyone in uniform or of arms-bearing age was being rounded up by the occupation troops and thrown into prisoner-of-war cages to await screening. The Allied soldiers in the early stages of this operation were for the most part the front-line tactical troops for whom the SS and the concentration camp at Dachau were still fresh memories, and in the first half of May these soldiers were not fond of Germans and could still be trigger-happy when the occasion demanded. Moreover, the road to Bad Reichenhall was particularly menacing, for it led past the U.S. Third Army headquarters at Bad Tölz and other Army posts bristling with jeeps, half-tracks, and armed GIs. To avoid them by traveling at night and off the beaten track over such a distance was a formidable proposition and it did not make much sense to try it if there was somewhere more convenient to go.

Colonel Pfeiffer himself is as vague about time as he is about place. On different occasions he has said he left the Walchensee at the beginning of May, almost immediately after he had dismissed his troops, spend several weeks of May wandering around the mountains before being released by the French. It is possible that these apparently conflicting activities are in fact all different stages of a continuous process, dismembered and scrambled by the quirks of a fading memory.

As already noted, it is most unlikely that Pfeiffer strayed far during the

first week of May. The shooting war was not yet over and the entire region
was streaming with American combat units fanning out along the highways and byways as they consolidated their physical occupation of the surrounding territory. To have broken cover under those circumstances
would have invited inevitable captivity, or worse. Nor is it likely that Pfeiffer, if he had any sense, would have ventured far in the second week in
May, the mopping-up and settling-down period immediately following
V-E Day, for then the U.S. occupation administration would have been in
a state of some flux and confusion as combat formations adjusted to peacetime duties. Civil affairs staffs moved in and the multifarious units of a
vast and complex army were redeployed to new roles in new stations. It
was a logical and recognized procedure among certian high-ranking Germans—those who had goods and services to offer and deals to strike with
the occupation forces—to allow time for the first wave of front-line troops
to move on and the second and third waves of rear-echelon divisional and
army staffs to come and establish more permanent administrative headquarters. Major-General Reinhard Gehlen, for example, the former head
of the Soviet intelligence section of the German General Staff, remained in
hiding in the Bavarian Alps until 20 May before making contact with the
Americans and handing over his priceless intelligence archives on the
Soviet Union and its armed forces—the original basis of postwar U.S. secret intelligence about the USSR. It could be argued that Colonel Pfeiffer,
who as custodian of the Reichsbank reserves had been dealt a trump card
almost as precious as General Gehlen's, might have been tempted to play
his hand along much the same lines. The confusion in the days following
the cessation of hostilities was no time to strike a bargain with the enemy
over the matter of Nazi gold and other treasure.

In the immediate posthostilities period Austria, though regarded in a
more friendly light by the Allies as a liberated rather than an occupied nation, was not much more tempting than Germany as a place in which to
surrender one's freedom to the enemy. If anything, the confusion of the
Austrian side of the Mittenwald pass was even greater than on the German side. Like Germany, Austria had been divided into four zones, one
for each of the invading Allied armies. Unlike Germany, the occupation of
these zones by the armies allocated to them proved a chaotic and uncoordinated process. The Russians overran part of the British Zone in the
southeast and were reluctant to budge from it. The Americans, instead of
entering Austria from Italy to the south, entered it from Germany to the
north and began the occupation of their zone (the provinces of Salzburg
and Upper Austria) with military government personnel trained for the

wrong country—Germany instead of Austria. The French, invading the country from the direction of Lake Konstanze in the west, found the Americans already ensconced in the Tyrol, which was meant to be part of the French Zone. It took time for this confusion to be sorted out and for the right armies to take up their right positions in the right places. For a short while, therefore, Innsbruck and other townships in the Tyrol remained in the hands of the Americans, who continued with their usual practice of throwing all officials and soldiers, whether in uniform or out of it, into the nearest prisoner-of-war pen.

This would have been Colonel Pfeiffer's fate if he had strayed over the mountains into the Innsbruck district. Indeed, in one of his various testimonies Pfeiffer claimed that this is exactly what happened. But there were people of his acquaintance who were to claim that at this time, around the middle of May, Colonel Pfeiffer was actually still in Bavaria—to be precise, in the home of one of his officers in the attractive and well-to-do Alpine resort of Garmisch-Partenkirchen.

The house in question was the Haus Hohe Halde, No. 38 Gsteigstrasse (Hill Rise would be the equivalent English name), a leafy, quiet, and secluded road rising steeply at the extreme southeast edge of Partenkirchen in the direction of Mittenwald and the Walchensee. The houses in Gsteigstrasse, solid, detached structures put up in the prewar years within ample and secluded gardens, exuded an air of discreet, almost rural exclusivity appropriate to the standing and prosperity of their owners. No. 38, situated on the crest of the road as it rose from the town, enjoyed magnificent views south over a green valley and forested slopes towards the jagged ridges and smowy peaks of the Wetterstein mountains. The house was less a mansion than a villa: two floors and an attic under a broad Bavarian roof, approached from the road through a splendid hand-carved wooden gateway; a small porched entrance beneath a white-walled front pierced by four unusual little decorated oval windows, like ornamental niches or holy shrines high on a street wall; a swimming pool on the lawn at the back, facing south and catching the sun and the breathtaking views. A nice place, worth a not very small fortune now, and in the summer of 1945 especially desirable and entirely suitable as an ark of refuge from the swirling turbulence of war and defeat.

For a number of years this house on the hill had been in the possession of one of Garmisch-Partenkirchen's most distinguished and respected families, the von Blüchers, whose celebrated antecedent was Field Marshal Gebhard von Blücher, a career soldier who had established the family's estates in Silesia and as commander of the Prussian Army had contributed decisively to the British victory at Waterloo and the overthrow of Napoleon. In 1945 the head of the Blücher family, Ambassador Wipert von Blücher, was a career diplomat who had formerly been German ambassador in Sweden and then occupied a key diplomatic post in the Nazi hegemony in Europe—that of German ambassador in Finland. At the end of the war von Blücher senior had taken refuge with his wife and daughter in the family home in Garmisch-Partenkirchen, where he was in due course arrested on charges of having conspired to prolong the war between Finland and the Soviet Union. As it happened, the vagaries of war had also brought both of the ambassador's young sons to the family home in Garmisch as the end of the hostilities drew near—a fortunate turn of events at a time when millions of their countrymen were homeless, lost, imprisoned, or vagrant. As the sons of a senior German diplomat and godsons of a famous Swedish explorer, Sven Hedin, both brothers were cosmopolitan young men, experienced and knowledgeable beyond their years. They were to play leading roles in both the story of the Reichsbank treasure and the drama surrounding the U.S. occupation of Garmisch and of southern Bavaria.

The eldest son was Captain Lüder von Blücher, until recently on the nominal roll of officers at the Mountain Infantry Training School at Mittenwald. Lüder was twenty-six at this time, a much-decorated Gebirgsjäger officer who had been seriously wounded at the fighting around the Kuban bridgehead (near the Sea of Azov in southern Russia) in November 1944. Flown back to Germany in the belly of a Gigant glider transport plane, in which he half bled to death and from which he had to be cut out with a knife, Lüder ended up in the military hospital near the *Kaserne* at Mittenwald. In view of his wounds he was not required to stay in the garrison town at Mittenwald and was allowed home to convalesce at his family house in nearby Garmisch-Partenkirchen instead. Later his advice was enlisted in the matter of the burial of the Reichsbank treasure. That was virtually his last act of duty as a serving *Wehrmacht* officer. In civilian clothes, Lüder remained in the house in Gsteigstrasse, where he was shortly joined by his younger brother, Hubert, another fugitive from the cataclysm engulfilng Germany, and like his brother an anti-Nazi.

Hubert von Blücher was a truly remarkable young man—a quick wit, a *petit esprit malin* who thought very fast on his feet. He was only twenty-one but he had many of the qualities of an infinitely more mature man. He was over six feet tall and slim, dignified, and aristocratic in bearing, handsome and elegant in appearance, charming and impulsively generous in manner, picaresque in character, and imbued with a self-confidence which sus-

tained him in any situation and a self-sufficiency that precluded any need
for close friendship or dependence on others. For all his flamboyance, his
wild exuberance, his love of the grand gesture — and of women — he was
abstemious in his habits, did not smoke and drank almost not at all,
though he could stay up all night at a party and give his guests the impression that he was on the same terms with them throughout. Very bright and
witty, and passionately fond of intelligent conversation, his aptitude for
foreign languages was considerable and the range and depth of his knowledge on many subjects was unusual in one so young.

Hubert von Blücher had been born in Sweden, where his father was
then the German ambassador. As a result, he was entitled to dual nationality and two passports — a German one and a Swedish Red Cross one — a
dispensation which was to prove of the gretest possible use in the postwar
period. By his own account his wartime career seemed to have been as
manifold and bewildering as his own personality. It has often been assumed that he had spent the latter part of the war working for the *Abwehr*
(German Military Intelligence) in Berlin, a job for which his quick mind,
linguistic ability, and cosmopolitan background would have eminently
suited him. Hubert himself was supposed to have claimed at one time that
he actually finished his training at the *Abwehr* training school in Hamburg — though he was barely in his twenties, and still ostensibly a civilian.
According to his brother, however, at the end of the war Hubert was a civilian employee of the German Newsreel Company, UFA. When questioned about this period recently, Hubert von Blücher hinted at someting
faintly devious and unorthodox in his youthful wartime past. The interview had its comic moments, but at the same time illuminated the more
chameleonlike side of the man's personality:

> Q: Your military records say that you entered the German Service in
>   December 1942 in Munich and that you were invalided out in May
>   1944.
> von B: '43.
> Q: Sorry, '43. Is that correct?
> von B: No.
> Q: That's what your Army records show.
> von B: I know. I have three.
> Q: Three what?
> von B: Army records.
> Q: Ah...what do the other two say?
> von B: No comment.
> Q: Why should you have three Army records? It's a remarkable thing to
>   have.

von B: No comment on that.

Q: I mean, these documents are fairly clear. They indicate that you
        entered the Service, that you were invalided out, that you went into
        hospital with a heart complaint and that you were then
        recommended for discharge from the Army a few months later.
        There's no record of you having any further military service.

von B: I tell you there's a second record, and that says I was assistant to the
        military attaché at the German Embassy in Helsinki. That's the
        second.

Q: When was that?

von B: From 1942 to 1944.

Q: Well, there's no record of your being in the Air Force.

von B: OK. There is.

Q: Well, it's not traceable, put it like that.

von B: It is.

Q: Why should you have three records?

von B: I've told you—there's no comment on that.

Q: I mean it's not normal. You said German records are very good and
        very reliable and very correct. German officials don't make mistakes.

In fact, available records show that Hubert served in the German Army
in the 2nd Battalion of the 7th Reconnaissance Unit and that by the spring
of 1944, after leaving the forces on medical grounds, he was working as a
probationary assistant film director for Berlin-Film on a production entitled *Eines Tages...(One Day...)*. He seems to have had a talent for cinema
(to blossom after the war in Bavaria and America), for Berlin-Film informed the Reich Film Board that the director "would like to work again
in the future with Herr von Blücher, since he was very pleased with the latter's performance." Perhaps it was as a filmmaker that he subsequently
came to fly with the Luftwaffe, for it is to the third of his wartime careers
to which Hubert von Blücker referred in his own account of how he came
to Garmisch-Partenkirchen at the end of the war. This account, too, gives
a good idea of the flavor of the man, his raciness, humor—and perhaps in-
ventiveness:

I turned up in Garmisch from Berlin [he recalled]. I was traveling in an Opel
Admiral automobile belonging to a Japanese general who at that time was Japanese ambassador in Berlin. The Opel Admiral had a *laissez-passer* and we brought
the Japanese general's two German secretaries with us. I had left my flat at 49
Hagenstrasse in the Grünewald area of Berlin, which had been completely destroyed in the bombing. I possessed nothing in the world. Everything was burned
to a cinder. The Japanese general lived in a house four doors away from my flat
and on the other side lived SS General (Obergruppenfüher) Lorenz, whom I shall

never forget because he had two of the loveliest daughters I have ever seen. He's the only SS general whose house I tried to save from burning down. One of the girls, Jutti, married a Count Kinkelbusch, who owned one of the biggest wine businesses in Germany, and the other daughter, Rosemarie, married Axel Springer, the newspaper publisher. I was in the German Air Force then, the Luftwaffe. I was flying bombers, Junkers 88. It is a period I do not like talking about. My heart had a fault that made me black out, my eyes did not register certain colors in a turn at 4Gs. (I am still a keen pilot and until six months ago I was still flying Lear jets and helicopters and T33s with the Bundeswehr.)

When I turned up during the night at Garmisch, Pfeiffer and Rauch were both sitting together upstairs in the house in Gsteigstrasse. They had been discussing the situation for a couple of hours. It was all news to me. They asked a question. What would *I* do about the shipment—the Reichsbank reserves from Berlin?

According to Hubert, he is referring here to the time immediately preceding the burial of the reserves in the mountains abouve the Walchensee in late April. Three weeks later, in mid-May, the same question was as urgent and problematic as ever. Fifteen million dollars in gold and currency still lay undetected on the slopes of the Steinriegel and Klausenkopf. It could not remain there, unused and useless, until the end of time. Nor could it be allowed to fall into the hands of the enemy, the Americans. Or rather, it would be a tragic waste if it did. But what should be done with it? The government to which most of it belonged, the Third Reich, no longer existed. There was no other German government to replace it and no prospect of one for decades to come, or so it seemed. When the shipment had first arrived in Mittenwald it had been said the treasure was to be kept safe for a future government of Bavaria. But where was that government? Colonel Pfeiffer was later to claim that he and Colonel Rauch had tried no less than four times to make contact with such a body, but in vain.

It was evident that by mid-May Pfeiffer was having a difficult time living in the open, sleeping under trees, supplies and morale running low, nerves on edge, the future as aimless as his present solitary wandering. In his fortieth year, Pfeiffer was no longer in the prime of youth; and with his war wounds and his rheumatism he was no longer in the best of health. In the day, the sun and the rain beat down on him. At night the Alpine cold chilled him to the marrow. Pfeiffer himself called it the life of the partisan. With the war over, it was more like the life of the outlaw. His name had been posted and the Americans were looking for him everywhere. Lieutenant DuBois had been checking all his old haunts—the *Kaserne*, the Forest House, the Bergerhof, even as far away as Salzburg. Informants had disclosed the whereabouts of his next of kin—his wife at 10 Riedelstrasse in Bad Reichenhall, his mother at Neuhaus, near the Schliersee.

His was a desperate life and one which could not be continued indefi-
nitely. Almost immediately after Lieutenant DuBois had abandoned his
preliminary reconnaissance in the quest of Nazi gold, silver, and foreign
exchange—the timing was probably coincidence—Pfeiffer decided to
emerge from hiding and seek help from the only sources available to him:
the von Blücher family. Lüder von Blücher was recontacted and his offer
of assistance was gratefully accepted. Once again the Colonel pushed
through the wooden portico at 38 Gsteigstrasse and stepped into the security of a safe house and the warmth and comfort of a civilized household.
Almost immediately afterwards he was asked to step out again.

For 38 Gsteigstrasse was bursting at the seams. Bedrooms and day
rooms alike had been turned into dormitories, and there were people
sleeping in the bath, under the kitchen table and at the top of the stairs,
outside in the wood shed and in the summer house, anywhere where a human being could curl up in a little space he could call his own. It was the
time of the great flight from the east. The mass exodus of German civilians
from the eastern provinces had begun as soon as the Red Army had
crossed Germany's eastern border in the new year and continued ever
since. The Germans in the east had fled in the thousands, millions, to escape the vengeful Soviet invaders. Young and old, rich and poor, they
struggled into an already torn and blasted wartime western Germany carrying what they could salvage of their worldly goods by whatever means
they had at their disposal—horse cart, wheelbarrow, bicycle, human back.
Many had nowhere to go and were wiped out *en masse* when they were
caught in the open streets in the great air raids on Berlin, Dresden, and
other cities. A fortunate few from the better-connected stratum of society
had friends and relatives in the west. The Blücher tribe was one such
group. The land-owning members of the family had begun arriving with
their households at the house in Gsteigstrasse as the Red Army began its
onslaught in Silesia. They had been given hospitality and by May, according to Hubert, 70 of these family refugees had taken shelter there. Under
the circumstances, there was precious little room in which to accomodate
Colonel Pfeiffer, who was not family, whatever else he might be. On 20
May the von Blücher brothers decided to enlist the help of their next-door
neighbor, Mathias Stinnes, who now lived at No. 40 Gsteigstrasse.

Mathias Stinnes, a member of one of Germany's richest families,
was—according to Hubert von Blücher—the product of a left-handed
marriage by Hugo Stinnes, Sr., one of Germany's leading prewar industrialists, head of the vast Stinnes Combine which included the Rhine-West-

phalian Coal Syndicate and the other Stinnes coal, steel, shipping, newspaper, and hotel interests in Germany, as well as two industrial corporations in the United States. Mathias' father had been the prototype of a
Ruhr business tycoon who regarded the State as an appendage of his interests and saw politics as an extension of economics by other means. Extremely right-wing, Hugo Stinnes had been one of Hitler's main sup-
porters in his earliest days and one of the earliest financial backers of the
Nazi Party. After his death in 1934 his business ran into financial difficulties and was liquidated in the following year. A new company was formed
under his eldest son, Hugo Stinnes, Jr. — Mathias' elder brother — with the
Stinnes family retaining forty percent of the shares. During the Second
World War, Mathias' brother, an outspoken opportunist, controlled a vast
industrial complex which became one of the most important components
of the armaments and engineering industries that built the war machine of
the Third Reich.

Mathias Stinnes was, therefore, born into a world of almost limitless
wealth and power, Yet despite this privilege, there was evidently something
odd about the man which prevented him from capitalizing on his advantages. In spite of the vast wealth he had inherited through his family, the
considerable financial contribution he had personally made to the funds of
the SS, his wide-ranging social connections, his personal talents and high-
minded patriotism and loyalty to the Hitler regime, he never participated
in the running of the Stinnes business and never rose above the rank of private soldier throughout the war. This was not for want of trying. As early
as 10 October 1939, when the Second World War was little more than a
month old, the 29-year-old Stinnes had sent an extraordinary letter to the
SS Central Chancellery in Prinz Albrechtstrasse in Berlin in which he put
forward a plan, based on his own first-hand knowledge of English geography, to assist in a future German invasion of Britain. In his letter Stinnes
wrote:

If consideration were to be given to attempting a landing in England, I should like
to draw attention to the following.

North of London, the River Ouse flows into the bay called "The Wash." In a
section of the Ouse Valley, the land is lower than the water level of the river and
canals. This is the area of the so-called Downs.

In the event of a landing attempt, the area north and south of The Wash could
well come under consideration, if any thought were being given to the east coast
being a possibility. A force of parachutists would be sufficient to destroy the dykes
and put this region under water.

Stinnes then contributed a second idea for the furthering of the German war effort — the establishment of a pro-Hitler regime in Great Britain.

As we know [he wrote] the British Government gives as one of its war aims the destruction of the "Hitler-regime." It would perhaps be advantageous for us to turn the tables on them and from our side demand a change of government in Britain. I might mention that the Duke of Windsor still enjoys a great popularity in Britain even today, and a propaganda effort in that direction would have all the more chance of success in that there exists in Britain organized opposition parties which are dissatisfied about his resignation.

I should add that I am pretty well acquainted with British conditions, since I studied for two years at Oxford, worked for two years in a British firm [in Berlin], and have often visited the country in the meanwhile, as well as meeting officers of the British Navy practically every summer in the Mediterranean.

I hope I have been of use to you with these suggestions.

Heil Hitler! `

The SS were uncharacteristically inefficient in responding to Mathias Stinnes' war-winning plans. It was seven months before the letter eventually got to the Reichsführer SS Heinrich Himmler's desk, by which time the Luftwaffe was gearing itself up for its air assault in the skies over England and plans for the German invasion that Stinnes had foreseen were reaching an advanced stage. Himmler would have been well aware of the debt which his own SS and the Nazi Party and war machine owed to the lavish backing of the Stinnes industrial complex. On 17 May 1940, Himmler's personal staff acknowledged receipt of Stinnes' letter. At the same time the Reich Security Police and the *Sicherheitdienst* (SD) headquarters in Berlin were asked to check out Mathias Stinnes' credentials.

It seemed that the rigidly conformist bureaucrats of the SS oligarchy had difficulty making heads or tails of Stinnes' faintly eccentric and dilettante upper-class individualism. In 1934 he had joined the motorized SS in Berlin, then joined the Mittenwald Company of the SS as a Senior Private. From 1935 to 1938 he worked for the local SD headquarters in Garmisch-Partenkirchen, and contined to contribute substantial sums of money to the SS central funds. He was not a member of the Nazi Party but in the company of foreigners, particularly the British, he always presented himself as a Nationalist Socialist. He also voluntarily placed himself at the disposal of the German Intelligence Services on several occasions. In 1935, for example, he traveled to Moscow to attend a medical conference with a cousin, a well-known physiologist in Britain, and subsequently toured the Soviet Union with him. "From this journey," reported the Berlin SD, "he brought back a mass of photographs of, *inter alia*, military items, which on his own initiative he duly put at the disposal of the Intelligence Ser-

vices." During the 1936 Winter Olympics, held in Garmisch-Partenkirchen, Stinnes again made himself available to the Intelligence Services "for
tasks where his knowledge of several foreign languages made him useful."

Stinnes had traveled widely in Europe, made geological expeditions to
Germany's former colonies in Africa, and studied at the universities of
Munich, Berlin, and Oxford. But nothing he attempted ever seemed to
succeed. He never completed his university studies, because the deaths of
both his parents, which provided him with a considerable independent fortune, obviated the need to do so. He bought and managed a big farming
estate at Hachtsee, on which he invested considerable financial resources,
but as the SD noted, "it is not expected that it will produce a profit, so
Stinnes may soon have to turn his mind to other projects." Stinnes toyed
with a literary career and tried to write a travel book about a journey
through Yugoslavia in a canoe, but he got nowhere with it. "He occupies
himself in the field of technical inventions," the security police noted, "but
seems so far not to have produced any positive results." (Subsequently
Stinnes was to produce a grandiose scheme for irrigating the Sahara and
claimed to have discovered the cure for cancer.)

The Berlin SD summed Stinnes up thus: "We have no knowledge of
anything prejudicial to him in a political sense." On the other hand they
noted that "he may be designated as a 'Phantast' [a dreamer, an oddball]."
After the war acquaintances of Stinnes were to confide the opinion that he
was actually mentally disturbed. "He was a very fine man," recalled
Hubert von Blücher, "but he was a neurotic chap; he had a complex, a persecution mania."

Mathias Stinnes' correspondence with the SS was the nearest he ever got
to the higher conduct of the war in Germany. By the time he returned
home to 40 Gsteigstrasse more than five years later, this rather odd and
disappointed millionaire had still not risen above the rank of private and
had seen no more of the conflict than the inside of the American and British prisoner-of-war camps in which he had worked as an interpreter. Only
for two brief periods as a student in the *Abwehr* and the Brandenburg Division (the German equivalent of the British Special Operations Executive)
did Stinnes brush briefly with the cloak-and-dagger world to which his talents and inclinations might have ideally suited him if the military establishment had but perceived them. Unlike some five million of his fellow
citizens, however, Mathias was still alive. After a few days' captivity as a
prisoner-of-war at the end of the war, he was allowed to return home to his
villa in Garmisch-Partenkirchen.

He was no longer the very rich man he had once been. The Nazis had taken his farm and the Allies had blocked his bank account. Reichsmarks were almost valueless anyway, and as a German he was not allowed to possess foreign currency, gold, or other valuables. He was, therefore, as needy and as open to opportunities as the next man. His only asset was an attractive and talented wife, by the name of Tucki. Of his return to Garmisch, Stinnes was to recall later: "When I arrived back at Gsteigstrasse, the 'Gold Affair' had just started. Lüder von Blücher asked me if his former driver might sleep in my house for a few days. Some days later the so-called driver turned out to be Colonel Franz Pfeiffer."

With the return of Pfeiffer, incognito, to the world of men, and the reunion of the leading *dramatis personae* now living under two adjacent roofs, the fate of the Reichsbank treasure became a matter for even more urgent debate. Everyone contributed his own suggestions, some dotty, most of them honorable, some apparently even philanthropic. "Up to this day," Mathias Stinnes wrote in a signed statement some years later, "I believe in the sincerity of most of the participants." The overriding motivation was to keep the German treasure out of the hands of the Americans. Hubert von Blücher remembered some of the idealistic proposals put forward:

The first scenario was Rauch's who wanted to set up a new Bavarian state with Colonel Pfeiffer. A crackpot idea. The second idea came from a man with whom I have to be a bit careful, because he is still alive and has an important job. This man was among the German organizational elite in wartime, not with Speer, not with the *Wehrmacht*, but with the *Organisation Todt*. He approached my brother and said, "Listen, we'll do something else. We'll open up a factory in the Black Forest for making artificial limbs for the German war wounded, using local skilled labor. All these wounded will need artificial limbs and no one will be interested in financing such an operation." This idea fascinated my brother and he tried to get Pfeiffer interested in it too.

But Pfeiffer had ideas of his own. Mathias Stinnes remembered one. "Colonel Pfeiffer took me into his confidence," he recalled. "Vast sums of foreign currency and gold, he said, and been hidden. We should try to get this treasure secretly to the Vatican so that the Church, when things have quieted down, would be able to distribute it among war orphans and cripples. I had no doubt that these intentions were serious and honest." Pfeiffer's idea was to rebury the treasure and wait until the general situation in the area settled down before contacting the Pope via Cardinal Faulhaber, a respected German member of the Vatican.

Another idea put forward by Pfeiffer—Hubert von Blücher believes it was passed on to him by the Bavarian industrialist, Arnold Reichberg—was that as the gold and the money was German capital it should be preserved and turned over to a big German refugee welfare organization. But Hubert himself was dubious about such notions. "I heard all this," he recollected later, "while going in and out and looking after our relatives staying in the house. With my ingrained sense of realism it all seemed utterly unrealistic, and also a bore. I was sure that all the money was registered and accounted for somewhere in the Reichsbank records and, therefore, the whole notion was nonsense. It was, as I saw it, hot money. The more selfless and vague the whole thing became the more attraction it seemed to have. Probably it was some way of unloading the guilt feelings that had filtered over from the past, some form of self-purification process. But these people were bear hunters who simply did not have the bear..."

Hubert's contribution to the debate was to go after the bear. One wild idea attributed to him during this period involved landing an American flying boat on Lake Walchen, loading it with the currency and gold, and flying it to Switzerland under the pretext of being part of a geological expedition. Mathias Stinnes was convinced that most of the people involved had no intention of using the treasure for their own purposes. Pfeiffer himself had complete trust in the von Blücher brothers, for he knew that they came from an absolutely honorable and trustworthy family with an impeccable pedigree.

Then, after a few days, a scheme began to take shape.

6

The Money Baggers

The scheme was simple in conception but arduous in execution. It involved walking at night all the way to the Walchensee, which was 16 miles away; climbing up the Klausenkopf, which was over 1,000 feet above the level of the lake; digging up the currency in the holes, which were six feet deep; sorting out the foreign currency, which was stuffed into a total of 89 bank bags; selecting the more desirable banknotes (e.g., American dollars and English pounds) from the less desirable (e.g., Italian lira and Egyptian pounds) out of the countless thousands contained in the sacks; repacking the selected notes into backpacks and reburying the rejected notes in the caches; then trudging the 16 miles back to Garmisch-Partenkirchen while still under the cover of darkness. The whole operation had to be carried out in the utmost secrecy and extra care taken to avoid mobile American Army patrols on the country roads and prying German neighbors in the streets of the town. In case the two ex-Colonels, Rauch and Pfeiffer, met anyone on the way they agreed to pass themselves off as a former corporal and a lorry driver. But though there was a strict sunset-to-sunrise curfew in force at the time, they walked the long distance to the Klausenkopf several nights without being challenged. In this respect it helped enormously, of course, that the von Blücher villa was such a safe house, ideally situated on the very edge of Garmisch — and on the Walchensee side at that — thus obviating any need to walk through the streets of the town, with its busy concentration of American garrison troops.

The final report of the Munich Criminal Investigation Division (CID) confirms the nature of this operation, while limiting its scope. "The former head of the Gebirgsjäger School in Mittenwald, Colonel Pfeiffer," ran the report, "and the former Adjutant of the Reichsminister, Lammers, Storm Troop leader of the SS and First Lieutenant of the City Police Force,

Rauch, in about the middle of May 1945 handed to Lüder von Blücher, latterly an officer in the Gebirgsjäger School, Mittenwald, and who lived with his brother and parents in Garmisch-Partenkirchen, two backpacks full of American dollars and English pound notes." Mathias Stinnes, unlike the detectives of the Munich CID, was actually in Gesteigstrasse at this time and recalled that the operation was carried out on a much larger scale. "Every night," he related afterwards, "Pfeiffer and Rauch used to walk from Gsteigstrasse to the Clausenberg [Klausenkopf] and back, returning with sometimes two backpacks each, filled with pound notes and dollar bills. We used to call them the Two Mules."

The backpacks were brought into the kitchen at 38 Gsteigstrasse, where their contents—dollar and sterling notes from one to a hundred—were emptied on to the floor and sorted. "We would start counting the money. Hubert von Blücher soon became seriously ill with trenchmouth, caused through moistening his fingers with saliva while counting the bills. We then invented another method of counting. We used to weigh the bills and pack them into parcels of 2 pounds each. When dealing in these sums it certainly did not matter if the parcels differed by 10 or 20 dollars." In fact, Lüder von Blücher later confirmed that neither he nor Hubert knew the exact amount of dollar bills that had been brought into the house. There were thought to have been millions of thems, but the brothers never had the time or the opportunity to count such a quantity preciesely. Many of the greenbacks, they noted, were very old and very used.

After the notes had been stacked and roughly counted in the kitchen they were systematically repacked into every kind of nonmetallic container that came to hand—culinary vessels, for the most part, including earthenware jars, casseroles, jugs, pickling jars, and pots of every description. These containers were then wrapped in waterproof material to preserve the contents from the damp and buried in the garden—a few in the small garden at the front of the house, most in the vegetable plots in the large expanse out in back of the house. Hubert von Blücher's recollection of this operation was somewhat different. He contends that only one large parcel of notes containing about half a million dollars, wrapped in rubber insulation taken from the Mountain Infantry Traning School and tied up by Pfeiffer and Rauch, was buried in his garden at Gsteigstrasse—in the tomato bed, to be precise. But he concedes that similar parcels were also buried elsewhere. One way or the other, the reburial of the notes was carefully thought out. As Mathias Stinnes commented: "No mine detector would ever have found them."

It was decided that sufficient money was buried in the garden at No. 38

to buy an army and that the rest should be dispersed to other hiding places. Between Garmisch and the village of Oberau, 6 miles north of Garmisch, lay the broad, flat, grassy valley of the Loisach. Thickly dotted over this valley were numerous diminutive log cabins, with inward sloping walls and roofs weighed down with rocks, which were used to store hay for cattle feed in winter. Under these hay barns along the Oberau road were hidden a number of currency bags. One day the von Blüchers approached a local acquaintance of theirs, a former German officer by the name of Klaus Bremme, a 32-year-old Berliner. A tall, good-looking, well-mannered, and intelligent man, fluent in languages, Bremme had taken up residence with his Argentinian-born wife, Chiquita, at a large farm at Oberau.

The von Blücher brothers [Bremme related subsequently] asked me if I could provide a good hiding place for a hoard of dollars on a farm, called Gut Buchwies, at Oberau, where I was staying at that time. Their argument [that these dollars would later be used for helping wounded soldiers] struck me as being both good and honest, so I agreed to help them. I indicated a little hut, about 500 meters from the main house, which was used only by a seventy-year-old laborer for his small tools or for hay.

One day the von Blucher brothers came to the main house at "Gut Buchwies" and informed me that they had that morning hidden a portion of the dollars, packed in wooden cases, in the hut I had shown them. Another portion of the dollars, they said, had already been concealed in the garden of their own house. (They never mentioned gold or any other cash to me.) We went together to inspect the hut, and I still remember pointing out that anyone entering the place would be bound to notice the freshly turned earth. So the spot was covered over with grass, etc., in a way that no one could find it accidentally. The von Blüchers never told me how many dollars were contained in the wooden cases, nor did I ever personally set eyes on them.

To deter any inconvenient American intrusion, Bremme posted an OFF LIMITS sign he had "borrowed" from the U.S. Army at the front of the house and draped a large Argentinian flag from the top of it.

According to a statement made by Bremme in 1978 he was also required to assist the von Blücher in the physical transportation of the currency to Gsteigstrasse. Though he never actually counted the amount of dollars he transported by bicycle and automobile from Oberau, some sources estimate that the total amounted to some four to five million dollars. The fact that Klaus Bremme was married to an Argentinian lady was a distant advantage here. Because Sweden was then the consular representative for Argentina in Germany, the couple were able to obtain Swedish registration plates for the car Bremme had brought to Oberau. These plates bestowed a rare privilege on Bremme as a German citizen in those days, for he was permitted by the American authorities not only to own a car but to drive about and above all to purchase the necessary gas—a priceless commodity. One day Hubert von Blücher approached Klaus Bremme to ask another favor: could he give a tow to a brown, two-door DKW car (of the type known as Reichsklasse) that had broken down in the woods near the Walchensee and bring it back to 38 Gsteigstrasse? Bremme obliged. Several times along the road to Garmisch they were stopped by American military patrols, but every time the Swedish number plates on Bremme's car and his own excellent command of English got them through. Bremme left the DKW on the grounds of Hubert's house. A week later he was furious to learn that the truck of the car had allegedly been stuffed full of pound notes and dollar bills. (Hubert von Blücher, it should be noted, does not concur with this account. He believes that the car was not a DKW but an Opel Kapitän which belonged to Bremme himself and that it contained not foreign currency but a submachine gun and a large quantity of ammunition which Bremme had carried with him on a drive back to Bavaria through partisan country in Italy. Such a cargo would have been an even more risky one to transport, for the possession of firearms was strictly forbidden under Occupation law, and the penalty would have been severe indeed.)

So for a number of nights the fraught and exhausting shuttle continued as the treasure stashes on the Klausenkopf were systematically plumbed for the foreign currency reserves of the Reich. It was inevitably a bizarre and equivocal time in the lives of those who were involved. Moving from shadow to shadow through the Alpine summer night, the two fugitive colonels in their civilian Bavarian green shuffled stealthily through the sleeping landscape of the Mittenwald valley, where the only sounds in the stillness were the clanging of cow bells in the darkened meadows, the barking of dogs in the shuttered villages along the road, the odd American jeep changing gear on a distant hill; then up through the woods where only the solitary owl and *Wehrmacht* deserter—and the ever-loyal Captain Neuhauser—kept lonely vigil among the beech and firs; to the holes in the soft pine-needled mountain earth, where a flashlight revealed the nestling gray sacks. It was a difficult time to forget but an unbearable one to remember: Colonel Pfeiffer claims to have no recollection of it whatsoever, and Colonel Rauch, who was finally traced to a smart apartment block in Graz, Austria, in October 1982, refuses to speak about it at all.

The Gsteigstrasse-Klausenkopf shuttle was rudely interrupted on 22 May by news that sent shivers of apprehension down several German

12 April 1945. Part of the huge hoard of German gold and currency reserves captured in a 2,000-foot deep salt mine at Merkers in Thuringia by the US Third Army is examined by American military leaders, including (centre) General Dwight D. Eisenhower, Supreme Allied Commander; Lt-General George S. Patton, commanding the Third Army (left); General Omar Bradley, commanding the US 12th Army Group (second from left); and Colonel Bernard Bernstein (right), then in charge of the American Gold Rush teams. The reserves, valued at $315,000,000, were later removed to Frankfurt for safekeeping.

The largest concentration of treasure in the world is shown to visitors by Colonel Bernstein in Frankfurt in the summer of 1945. Some $500,000,000 worth of gold, silver, diamonds, jewellery, foreign currency and other valuables captured throughout Germany were stored by the Allies in deep underground vaults beneath the Reichsbank building. Here visitors finger bars from an 88-ton pile of silver bars comprising the entire Hungarian silver reserves.

400 tons of priceless art treasures, 2 million rare books and 30 railroad car loads of German patent records were also captured in the Merkers mine, along with part of the Reichsbank gold and currency reserves. Here GIs remove a case of historic engravings from a mine vault.

Art treasures hidden in Merkers included paintings by Rembrandt, Titian, Van Dyck, Raphael and Dürer. Here an American soldier from the 90th US Division examines a Dürer engraving from the Berlin Museum in a tunnel deep in the mine.

Four men who helped decide the fate of the remaining Reichsbank reserves in the last days of the Third Reich. *Top left*: Dr Walther Funk, Hitler's Economic Minister and President of the German Reichsbank, who persuaded the Führer to authorize the shipment of the reserves to Bavaria after the Berlin Reichsbank HQ was bombed out in an air raid. *Top right*: SS Brigadier-General Josef Spacil, who at gunpoint removed all that was left in the Third Reich's coffers in Berlin, including money and jewels worth nearly $10,000,000. *Bottom left*: Lt-Colonel Friedrich Josef Rauch, adjutant to Hitler's Chancellery Secretary and officer in charge of the Führer's security at the Chancellery, who first dreamed up the idea of shipping the gold and currency reserves to the Alpine Fortress. *Bottom right*: Colonel Franz Pfeiffer, Eastern Front veteran and holder of the Knight's Cross (the German VC), who as commander of the Mountain Infantry Training School at Mittenwald assumed responsibility for the Reichsbank treasure in Bavaria.

The last weeks of the war and the first weeks of the peace were crucial ones in the story of the Reichsbank treasure. *Right*: A stream of German soldiers on their way to surrender to the American Seventh Army in Garmisch-Partenkirchen, the famous winter sports resort in the Bavarian Alps, soon to become notorious as the 'Dodge City' of the American Zone. *Below*: In nearby Mittenwald DPs (Displaced Persons) outside the barracks of the former German Mountain Infantry Training School, where the Reichsbank treasure from Berlin was stored prior to burial, move off at the start of the long road home.

backs, not least that of Colonel Pfeiffer. The Americans had not let up in their search for the missing Reichsbank reserves following Lieutenant DuBois' inconclusive report of 17 May, and both the U.S. Army Counter-Intelligence Corps (CIC) and the Financial Branch of SHAEF had persisted with their enquiries. They had been greatly helped by a remarkable little local organization called Turicum based at Mittenwald.

Turicum had been formed towards the end of the war as an anti-Nazi underground resistance movement. Its leading light was German journalist, Dr. Hans-Georg Bentz, who had been Deputy Editor in Chief of the *Berliner Morgenpost* and was later to gain fame as an author of popular storybooks. Bentz was an unusual and highly individualistic character. During the war he had worked as a secret agent for the Allies in Potsdam. By the time he was removed from his post in Berlin on account of his all too discernible lack of enthusiasm for the Hitlerian regime, he had become a convert to Buddhism. Exiled to Mittenwald (where he seems to have adopted the alias of George Hilt) he had set about forming a resistance cell of likeminded spirits and forging links with similar cells in neighboring towns. One of his undercover comrades at that time was a Swiss journalist, J. C. Meyer, who had been an accredited correspondent in Berlin until 1944 and came from Zurich, which the Romans had called Turicum, hence the code name of the Mittenwald cell.

There is no record that Turicum actually achieved anything of great consequence during the war but it impressed the Americans enormously after it. Actually to be anti-Nazi was amazing enough, but Bentz claimed that he had run a resistance movement in Mittenwald and Garmisch-Partenkirchen as well, and that he had connections with the British Secret Service and even with Churchill himself. The Americans were inclined to turn Turicum to their own advantage as a pro-Allied intelligence-gathering organization in Upper Bavaria—a kind of grassroots operation deep inside German society at a level the Americans themselves could not hope to reach. In due course, Bentz and his wife and associates were to be installed in some style in Munich at American expense and set to work as informers reporting on shifts of opinion among the various political movements then finding their feet in the nascent Bavaria. But at the beginning Turicum, operating out of the local CIC office and from the bar of the Alpenrose Hotel, was given to solve more specifically local problems, almost the first of which was the whereabouts of the Reichsbank reserves and of the men who had been in charge of them.

Lieutenant DuBois had first encountered Turicum in Mittenwald at the very end of his preliminary quest. His meeting was brief but useful. Turicum came up with the address of Pfeiffer's wife and mother—clues which were to lead nowhere, as it happened—but DuBois was duly impressed. He had no hesitation in recommending the organization to military intelligence for further spying. In a memo to Captain Walter R. Dee, G-2 (Intelligence) Section at 10th Armored Division Headquarters in Garmisch-Partenkirchen, DuBois wrote:

1.   Am returning to SHAEF today and enclose a report of developments in connection with the gold and foreign notes presumably secreted in this area.

2.   Suggest that you consider this as a high priority target in view of the fact the treasure presumably includes over ten tons of gold and over two million U.S. dollars.

3.   Also suggest that Turicum in Mittenwald be contacted as they are producing information that I do not have time to follow up.

4.   In the event treasure should be located recommend strong guard be posted and request made through channels to SHAEF for appropriate instructions as to removal.

By 22 May 1945, Turicum had prepared a complete report on the events that took place between the arrival of the Reichsbank reserves in the *Kaserne* at Mittenwald and its burial in the mountains above the Walchensee. The report was addressed to Lieutenant DuBois at G-5 Financial SHAEF, and copied to DuBois' successor on the spot, a Lieutenant Kurt Meyer, commanding Military Intelligence Team 474. With the help of evidence from soldiers from the *Kaserne* who were still resident in Mittenwald (including Pfeiffer's driver, George Hempfling) and the civililan refugees lodging at the Forest House at Einsiedl (including Herr Forstreicher, the man who had watched the mule train set off into the mountains), Turicum was able to confirm that the Reichsbank reserves (together with other valuables, including a consignment allegedly consisting of gold from Berchtesgaden) had been carried into the mountains by mules and buried there and that most of the Gebirgsjäger offices and Reichsbank officials involved in the operation—with the exceptions of Colonel Pfeiffer and Captain Neuhauser—were still living in the vicinity. Turicum added the rider that the *Wehrmacht* officers implicated in the gold affair were not Nazis but "pure militarists." For this reason, Turicum warned, they were probably more dangerous than Nazi officers, who were "often cowards." The *Wehrmacht* officers were "discreet men" who would have to be "put under heavy pressure" if further details about the gold operation were to be wrung from them. The one exception could be Colonel Pfeiffer, Turicum added. Pfeiffer, who knew most about the gold, might be persuaded to talk more easily.

The effect of the Turicum investigation was instant. Three American

Counter-Intelligence Corps (CIC) officers arrived at the Forest House to interrogate the refugee guest, Hans Forstreicher, who was bitterly criticized by local inhabitants for the help he gave the Americans. He later explained what had happened. "I had no wish to conceal anything from them," he related. "There was no question of a reward. I told them what I had seen from the mountain, so they asked me to take them up and show them the route the mules had followed. I had no alternative but to guide them. So we went up together to have a look. First, we found a cache full of pistols, binoculars, and ammunition. Then we came to a large area where the earth was all churned up. The hoof marks of mules were still visible..." According to one of the Americans, all around there were signs of dynamiting and other activities.

Soon afterwards six of Pfeiffer's officers were arrested by the CIC and thrown into the Military Government jail or the city jail in Garmisch for questioning—Major Rupert Braun, who had been in charge of the mule transport; Captain Heinz Rüger, who had been in charge of the motor transport; Captain Otto Reindl, Captain Walter Martl, Captain Karl Lutz, and Captain Johann Rauter. On the same day Captain Neuhauser's father, Hans Neuhauser, Sr., the Chief Forester of Walchensee, in whose house at Einsiedl the treasure had been stored prior to burial, was taken into custody. Two days later, the 61st Armored Infantry Battalion recorded in its After Action Report: "24 May 1945—Sent patrol to search the Military *Kaserne* Hospital near Mittenwald for weapons, ammunition, and a German officer named Col. Pfeiffer, connected with hidden gold. Found no weapons or ammunition. Colonel Pfeiffer was not in the hospital." A few days later the fervently Nazi mayor and the equally fervent Nazi Chief Forester of Mittenwald—who had been involved in earlier plans to conceal the Reichsbank bullion and such Nazi *Parteibonzen* as Funk—were arrested by the CIC as threats to security, the latter as a result of his denunciation by the population of Mittenwald.

More heads were yet to roll as the Americans, acting on Turicum's tip-offs, pulled in everyone they could lay hands on who had been embroiled in the Reichsbank operation. In the last week of May, Reichsbank officials George Netzeband, Friedrich Will, and Emil Januszewski, who had been involved in the affair since they left Berlin with the gold convoy, finally came to the attention of the CIC detachment in Mittenwald. The three officials had been living quietly in Mittenwald ever since they discovered that the speed of the Allied advance had cut off their return route to Berlin and that they could not return to the capital either by air or overland. Netzeband and Will were staying in a guesthouse where Netzeband had often spent holidays in the past. Januszewski—ostracized, perhaps, because of his colleagues' suspicions about his role in the disappearanace of two gold bars—had had to find separate accomodation where he lived apart. Inevitably all three bank officials became the object of curiosity, if not suspicion, after the American occupation of the town. "After some while I had the impression that we were being shadowed," Will later testified to the Munich CID.

Various attempts were made by plainclothes police to find out something about us. When these efforts produced no results, a member of the Secret Service, a Dr. Bentz, turned up one day. Despite our protests a search of our rooms was carried out, after Herr Netzeband and I had been subjected to an interrogation lasting several hours. When this produced no results either, Dr. Bentz confronted us with Herr Januszewski. He had been interrogated likewise, but in his case—strange to say—no search was carried out. In pouring rain we were than taken to the mountains, where we were supposed to reveal the place where the assets were buried. This foray was fruitless, too, since we "could not locate" the spot.

In fact, Will *did* know where the cache was situated, but like Pfeiffer he was determined not to reveal the German reserves to the American conquerors. With Netzeband he had written an account of the Reichsbank treasure affair on pieces of old newspaper which they had hidden under a pile of coal in the cellar of their guesthouse. This, too, he kept from the investigators. Back in Mittenwald the Reichsbank officials were placed under local arrest pending further interrogation and for the time being the investigators rturned their attentions elsewhere.

The occupants of No. 38 Gsteigstrasse had already experienced several close encounters with the U.S. Army of Occupation. In an extensive search and arrest operation about the middle of May, virtually every house and apartment in Garmisch-Partenkirchen had been raided by squads of American soldiers, and the upper-class homes in Gsteigstrasse were not exempt from this process. By the time the search party knocked on the door of No. 38 the von Blücher brothers were ready for them. From an upstairs window a rope ladder reached down to the ground to provide a quick getaway. Bank notes that had not yet been buried in the ground were rolled in a saddle blanket and hung out of an attic window. When the Americans combed through the house, they found nothing and departed empty-handed. When they returned, it was under very different circumstances indeed.

Hubert's behavior must have become a matter of growing concern for Colonel Pfeiffer, and perhaps also for Colonel Rauch and Mathias Stinnes. He was a young man of great intelligence and exceeding charm and vivacity. The trouble was not just that he sailed very close to the wind—everyone in postwar Germany did to some extent; it was a necessary requisite of survival. But he also flew very close to the sun. He had a nose for the main chance, a talent for organizing that was exceptional even by the standards of Germany in 1945. He quickly perceived that for the deprived citizens of occupied Germany the American military was for the foreseeable future the source of all privilege, wealth, and power. With his cosmopolitan upbringing and his realistic view of human nature, he also very quickly perceived that the American military were not objects of awe, godlike creatures dispensing Democracy, Justice, and other high-minded abstractions among the abject survivors of totalitarian tyranny, but men like other men.

Even while he was salting away the foreign exchange of the Third Reich in his tomato beds, Hubert von Blücher was taking the first tentative step towards cooperation with the American Army of occupation in areas of mutual interest. He began to collect unused headed notepaper and blank official printed forms wherever he could find them—from individuals, military government departments, and companies—and these he would use to apply for travel permits, gasoline, curfew passes, and other privileges. Less than two weeks after the German surrender he did something even more remarkable. On 21 May, the very day that Turicum completed its secret report on the gold and currency affair, Hubert set off from No. 38 bound for Austria with an American convoy.

It seemed that Hubert von Blücher or one of his friends was still the proprietor of a deposit of wine and Italian grappa in the South Tyrol, Austria. The only way to capitalize on this asset was to bring it across the border to Garmisch—and the only way to do that was to enlist the aid of the only organization running any kind of trucking service at that time, namely the U.S. Army. With the help of Mathias Stinnes, Hubert established contact with a certain 1st Lieutenant Folke R. Anderson, Third Army. At 8:30 on the evening of 21 May, a Monday, the G-2 of the 21st Tank Battalion phoned Corps G-2 to tell them that Anderson would be reporting for instructions to Divisional Headquarters in Garmisch with four trucks that were being made available for the transportation of documents. The trucks duly set off, with Hubert von Blücher on board as guide, but what they brought back was not documents but a number of barrels of wine and eight barrels of grappa, 26 gallons to each barrel, from the Tyrolean depository.

Back in Garmisch the deal was completed: six barrels of grappa for Lieutenant Anderson, the remaining two barrels and all the wine to von

Blücher and Stinnes for resale. The grappa was then decanted into bottles and put on sale to soldiers at the U.S. garrison at a big *Schnappsnacht* party held in one of the villas. "Never in my life have I been so tight," Mathias Stinnes recalled of that occasion. "On a hot summer morning I was sitting in Gsteigstrasse filling bottles. Only sucking the rubber pipe to make the liquor run was sufficient to do me in. That night you could not have found a single soldier in Garmisch who had not drunk his fill. A single werewolf (thank God there weren't any) could have killed the lot." According to Stinnes they alledgedly made tens of thousands of marks and dollars out of the *Schnappsnacht* grappa transaction.

Hubert von Blücher had returned to Garmisch-Partenkirchen from the Tyrol on 22 May, the same day that his brother's fellow officers in the Reichsbank treasure burial were arrested. The events of 22 May and the week following sent considerable alarm through the busy household of dollar-diggers and money-baggers at 38 Gsteigstrasse and contrived to put a sudden and permanent brake on their self-appointed task of exhuming the Reichsbank foreign currency reserves. It was bad enough that an American Army intelligence officer had climbed up the mule track on the Steinriegel and stared down into the gaping, albeit empty, burial hole in which the currency had first been stashed. But it was pure disaster when three of the officials who had delivered it and six of the dozen or so men who had buried it were arrested by the Americans for interrogation. For the former knew how much was put in the holes and the latter knew where the holes it was put in were. Between them they knew all and could reveal all. At 38 Gsteigstrasse it was considered not beyond the wits of American Army Intelligence to put two and two together and come up with an answer that was, for all practical purposes, approximately four. For Colonel Pfeiffer it must have been pressingly obvious that the time had come to show a pair of heels that were as clean as circumstances would allow. To linger would be to court imminent arrest. The clear air and the free life of Austria beckoned from the other side of the mountain ridges dividing occupied Germany from liberated Austria. But first there was some unfinished business to settle. The good colonel bade a hasty farewell and slipped down the hill and was quickly gone. Ever a resourceful man, he was to return before long as a French army advisor—and according to a few local gossips, dressed in the uniform of an officer of the Chasseurs Alpins.

7

Finders Keepers

The leading tracker of the posse of international fiscal detectives who now began to hound Colonel Pfeiffer up and down boggy Alpine trails and craggy woods, in and out of spa towns and lakeside resorts, bank vaults and military police cells, prisoner-of-war compounds, and the homes of relatives and friends across the length and breadth of Bavaria, was a 39-year-old British staff officer from London with an ill-fitting uniform and impeccable manners, Brigadier Michael Henry Frank Waring.

The product of an English establishment background which included Winchester School, the Royal Military Academy at Woolwich, the Royal Artillery, and the Indian Army Staff College at Quetta, Brigadier Waring was everything every German expected an Englishman to be. In the first place, his trousers were amazingly baggy. In the second place, he was tall and reserved. In the third place, he was a gentleman — a typical, downright, old-fashioned English gentleman. His correctness and unfailing courtesy commanded the respect of almost every German with whom he came in contact. Captain Neuhauser's mother was to recall that he was the only Allied officer ever to have shown her any manners or courtesy. The well-connected Hubert von Blücher remembered him as "a highly cultivated man, with perfect manners." Only the unfortunate Colonel Pfeiffer was destined to form a starkly contrary impression of this totally English brigadier.

Because of his unfamiliar uniform, his red collar patches and red staff officer's cap band, the Germans sometimes mistook Waring for a general and sometimes for a colonel. The confusion was understandable, for British Army staff officers were not a common sight in the American Zone of Germany. Whatever brought Brigadier Waring to Bavaria in the first place has never been disclosed. During the last months of the war he had

served as the War Office representative on a committee of the European
Advisory Commission — an inter-Allied policy and planning body responsible for advising on postwar European problems and for working out the
Occupation administration of postwar Germany. At the end of the war
Waring was appointed as one of the liaison officers at Supreme Headquarters Allied Expeditionary Foreces (SHAEF) engaged in setting up what
was to become the Control Commission for the British Zone of Germany.
It was a somewhat vague appointment and Waring was to confess later
that at the time of the Reichsbank affair he did not really know what he
was supposed to be doing. When he was contacted by telephone at his
home in Zimbabwe a few weeks before his death in September 1978, Brigadier Waring stated that he had become involved in the Reichsbank investigation solely by chance and on a purely informal *ad hoc* basis. "I had been
down in the Garmisch and Mittenwald area on quite different business,"
he explained, "when I received instructions to switch my inquiries to the
matter of the missing Reichsbank funds, acting in collaboration with
American Army Intelligence. It proved to be a very odd business indeed."

Waring's appointment to the case may have been a chance one but it was
certainly not an inappropriate one. He had spent the entire war in intelligence work, first in Burma, then in Africa, Italy, and northwest Europe,
and was thus thoroughly conversant with the ways and means of conducting an intelligence investigation on foreign ground. Nor was he working
alone. He formed the British — and senior — element of an *ad hoc* tripartite
Allied team which also included American and French representatives,
among whom were an American colonel, a Third Army intelligence captain called Neumann, and a Captain Hugues Sauteau from the French
Deuxième Bureau, who was based at Seefeld in the Austrian Tyrol and
acted as French liaison officer with the American Counter-Intelligence
Corps in Bavaria. By the last week of May 1945, the prolonged mystery of
the missing Reichsbank reserves had become so urgent and so vexing that
this high-powered investigative team was especially put together with the
purpose of taking over where Lieutenant DuBois' preliminary reconnaissance had left off and directed to find the solution to the mystery once and
for all. The problem was to preoccupy the team for more than three
months and in the end the solution was to elude them.

Word that Brigadier Waring was looking for him in due course reached
Colonel Pfeiffer by word of mouth along the ex-*Wehrmacht* grapevine. By
now the Colonel was a deeply troubled man. The responsibility for the
Reichsbank treasure weighed heavily on his sense of duty and plagued his
conscience. The life of the fugitive exhausted his constitution and frayed

his nerves. When he received news that he was once again the object of a special search, not by a mere American lieutenant this time, but by a British brigadier whom some called a general, and a whole team of jabbering Frenchmen and Americans, Pfeiffer seems to have come to a decision: he would come in from the cold, make a clean breast of things, and reveal to the Allies all—or, within reason, nearly all—that he knew about the affair of the Reichsbank reserves. Obviously there would have to be a deal. Some advantages would have to be forthcoming—at the very least his own liberty and that of his fellow officers—in return for his revelations. But in this way he could discharge his duty, allay his conscience, and perhaps reap some reward. The Reichsbank treasure would be off his back and he would be a free man, in more than one sense.

At the very end of May or the beginning of June 1945, Colonel Pfeiffer began looking for a means of getting in touch with the enemy in the person of Brigadier Waring, a devious process which required some careful arranging. While he did so, Brigadier Waring himself moved his center of operations to Mittenwald, where he and his team set up headquarters in the pleasant surroundings at the comfortable and quaint Post Hotel, one of the oldest coaching inns in Europe.

Eight days after the Reichsbank officials George Netzeband and Friedrich Will were picked up at their guesthouse in Mittenwald and interrogated by Hans Georg Bentz of Turicum, they were sent for again and brought before two Allied officers in a private room at the Post Hotel—one an American officer who spoke fluent German (possibly Captain Neumann), the other a British "colonel" (probably Brigadier Waring). For seven to eight hours the two officials were subjected to an intensive interrogation by these two officers, the American doing the talking, the Britisher making copious notes. In order to check whether their stories tallied, each bank official was interrogated individually, and each was required to write a detailed statement concerning the quantities of bullion and currency involved, the circumstances relating to the handover to Colonel Pfeiffer's jurisdiction, and the areas where the treasure had been concealed. Netzeband and Will had been in the employ of the Reichsbank for 32 and 35 years, respectively, and were still determined to protect the interests of their bank and their nation in the face of the enemy. They declined to reveal the whereabouts of the reserves (though only Will knew the exact location of some of the caches) and resisted the grilling as best they could. In the evening they were allowed to return to their lodgings, but they still had to hold themselves at the disposal of the interrogating officers and two days later, on about 1 June, they were picked up again.

This time they were driven once again to the Forest House at Einsiedl. With the forester under arrest and his son still in hiding, the house was now almost empty of its original occupants. Once again Netzeband and Will were escorted up the mule track on the Steinriegel. Once again they went through the motions of looking for the caches, wandering aimlessly through the dense thickets of trees, vaguely kicking at last winter's leaves and the bumps and hollows in the uneven ground. "The search once again looked like proving a great waste of time," Friedrich Will stated later, "since we *nichts mehr wüssten* (had no further information). However, chance would have it that the British Colonel [Waring] came near to the hiding place, and suddenly we were standing in front of the camouflaged shaft." They had reached the original currency cache and Will for one was dumbfounded at what he saw. "It had been opened," he recorded, "and its contents had disappeared. In my opinion the removal of the reserves must have been the work of specialists, otherwise torn labels — and there were about 450 bags — or bits of packing material would have been found lying about. It is still not clear to me today how it was possible for this hiding place to have been betrayed."

What Will did not know, of course, was that the original currency cache had been emptied by the Mountain Infantry officers following Schwedler's visit to it on 29 April, and its contents reburied in three fresh caches elsewhere in the neighboring hills. "When I stood in amazement in front of the excavated shaft above the Forest House," Will continued, "the British colonel suddenly asked me whether there might not be other caches and 'whether Dr. Schwedler had also taken something with him.' From these questions it was clear that the Americans must have gained information from the small circle of people who had taken part in the burial operation. But the six officers who had actually excavated the shaft had long since disappeared; and they might well have fallen in battle. As far as I can see the only explanation lies in the possibility that some forest ranger with ambitions of becoming Chief Forester at Walchensee had watched the excavation of the shaft and subsequently reported it to the Americans."

Further search of the Steinriegel proved fruitless and Netzeband and Will, now almost as mystified about the fate of the Reichsbank treasure as their interrogators, were allowed to return to Mittenwald. They were still under town arrest, but a month later Will succeeded in making his getaway and headed north for Hesse, where he planned to stay at his daughter's home. On route to Hesse he tried twice to hand over to the appropriate Reichsbank authorities the rough outline of the story of the Reichsbank shipment he had prepared with Netzeband and hidden in the coal cellar in

Mittenwald. On both occasions the Reichsbank branches refused to accept the document, owing to the tricky and potentially troublesome nature of its contents. In September, Will set off from Hesse to rejoin his family, who were living in the Russian Zone. He had no papers of any kind and consequently was soon apprehended by the Russians and interned. He was released after eight days, however, and allowed to resume his journey to his family home. Not until 1952, at the time of the Munich Criminal Investigation Division inquiry into this case, was he able to make public his account of events, and never at any time did he discover the full truth of the mystery which baffled even him.

In fact, contrary to Will's stated belief, the Gebirgsjäger officers who had buried the Reichsbank treasure had not fallen in battle but into the hands of the Americans. Arrested in Mittenwald on 22 May, shortly before Will and his colleague, they had undergone interrogation by Waring and his team at about the same time, and in the end it was the officer in charge of the gold transport between Mittenwald and Einsiedl, Captain Heinz Rüger, who had cracked and talked.

At first Rüger had protested that he knew nothing about the Reichsbank gold. Perhaps, he suggested, Major Braun could help. *"Er weiss auch nichts,"* the skeptical interrogator replied. "He knows nothing either." Like the Reichsbank officials and like Pfeiffer and the von Blüchers, the Gebirgsjäger officers, acting out of the finest motives of duty and patriotism, could not easily bring themselves to betray their country's national treasure to the enemy, even though the war was now over. But persistent interrogation in the military government jail in Garmisch wore down the young captain's resolve. By 5 June he had told the Americans all he knew. He had even gone so far as to offer to lead them right to the gold stash itself.

Although there is no doubt that it was Rüger who pinpointed the gold cache for the Americans, the local populace always blamed Hans Forstreicher, the lodger at the Forest House who had watched the mule train climb the mountainside with the gold, for betraying the whereabouts of the Reichsbank bullion. Frau Neuhauser, for one, always spoke of Forstreicher with unrestrained contempt and bitterness as a man who had betrayed both his country and his people. "Of course," she said, "it is generally assumed that Forstreicher sold the information to the Americans and received a substantial reward in return." The reward, Frau Neuhauser claimed, was sufficient to enable Forstreicher to buy a bar — a rather shabby bar in a rather shabby district of Munich along the Pariserstrasse, but a bar of his own nonetheless. Hans Forstreicher himself denied this. "The only thing I got out of it all was a load of hay for my horses," he was to claim. "I used to keep a few trotters in those days and they were practically starving, so I asked the Americans for some fodder. They very kindly gave me as much as I needed."

The Americans were now ready to pounce. In Mittenwald on 6 June, Josef Veit (the local hunter who back in April had fled to the hills when he was ordered by Colonel Rauch to prepare a hideout for Funk, Lammers, and other top-ranking Nazis) was told by the Americans to report at the Post Hotel at 6 A.M. the next morning and to bring from Captain Rüger's wife, who lived in the town, shoes, socks, and warm clothing for her husband. Early on the following morning, 7 June, another well-known Mittenwald local, Josef Pinzl (the 57-year-old pig keeper who had encountered the gold convoy on its way from the *Kaserne* to the Forest House) was rudely wakened by a loud banging on his front door.

Pinzl was not in the best of shape. He had been in bed some weeks recovering from a poisoning caused — so he said — by accidentally drinking methylated spirits in mistake for schnapps. When he opened the door he found an American officer standing there and saw an American Army jeep with Captain Rüger and Josef Veit in it parked outside on the road. The officer, who spoke fluent German, ordered Pinzl to get dressed and come with them to Einsiedl. The pig keeper's knowledge of the local terrain, and his chance encounter with the gold, had persuaded the Americans that he might be of some use to the gold recovery operation. Moreover, he was now a paid informer of U.S. Army Intelligence. He put on his clothes, shut the front door behind him, and got into the jeep. Then they set off, bouncing along the valley road towards Einsiedl, past the Gebirgsjäger barracks where the gold had first been delivered, up and around the snaking forest-lined bends beyond Wallgau, until they came to the Forest House at Einsiedl. Here, by prior arrangement, they met a platoon of C Company, 55th Armored Engineering Battalion, 10th Armored Division, who had arrived from Garmisch equipped, on Veit's advice, with mine detectors — ostensibly as a precaution in case the area around the cache had been mined rather than as a means of locating the gold. Captain George Garwood was the commanding officer of C Company, which supplied the work detail. The operation itself was under the overall command of Major Wilⅼliam R. Geiler, Divisional Engineer (now a judge of the Supreme Court of the State of New York). With them was Captain Walter Dee, Intelligence Officer for 10th Armored G-2, the section which had masterminded the recovery. One of the Americans told Veit that the matter was now almost finished, the German officers had confessed everything, and one of them would lead them to the gold.

The jeep with Rüger, Veit, and Pinzl led the way. They headed back down the road till they came to the Jachenau turn, a few hundred yards beyond the Forest House. They turned left there, then almost immediately right again, up a rough forestry track that ascended in a southerly direction through thick forest, then took a left fork that led eastwards and climbed steeply towards the summit of the Steinriegel, some 300 to 400 feet above the level of the road below. The jeep crawled up the incline till it could carry its burden no farther. Then the occupants got out and plodded towards the summit on foot. The lighter jeep followed behind. Near the summit they met again with the platoon of soldiers and the officers in charge.

Fifteen minutes after they had reached the target area, just at one side of the track, Captain Rüger gave the order for the mine detectors to be switched on. In a short while one of the detectors emitted a warning whistle and the soldiers began to dig gingerly down into the soft mountain earth. But there was no mine and no gold; all they uncovered was a moss-covered stone buried some way down. Something had triggered off the detectors, however. Mine detectors cannot detect absolutely pure gold, but most gold contains a little iron ore and it was this infinitesimal quantity of iron that was now picked up by the sensitive detectors. Inching forward very slowly, step by step, the soldiers moved the mine detectors over the forest floor between the ferns and sapling trees and rocky outcrops, and the whistle persisted and intensified as they approached a large tree stump some 30 feet away. The cause of the whistle seemed to come from beneath the stump, and the soldiers began to scoop away at the roots with their spades in an effort to dig the stump out of the ground. To their astonishment they found that the stump was not rooted at all and it only required the application of muscle power to heave it out of the way. The soil underneath was loose and yielding and the soldiers began to dig into it with mounting excitement until one of them uncovered a soggy gray burlap bag with the words REICHSBANK HAUPTKASSE stencilled on it.

It was more than one man could manage to lift the bag out of the earth, for it weighed over fifty pounds. Inside were two 25-pound bars of gold, gleaming with a bright burnished luster in the dappled woodland sunshine. With whoops of joy the GIs of C Company dug away at the Reichsbank gold cache on the Steinriegel until they had uncovered a hole measuring six foot deep and square—a hole which Major Geiler in his subsequent report was to describe as "expertly camouflaged....a hasty but efficient job." In due course all 364 bags containing a total of 728 bars of gold bullion weighing 9 tons and worth $10,000,000 had been exhumed and lay in an untidy heap at the side of the forest track.

It is not often that a group of young men are given the opportunity to act out their boyhood dreams and dig up a genuine treasure hoard. That warm idyllic June on the wooded slopes above Lake Walchen, the American Armored Engineers, with the war behind them and most of their adult life still to come, whooped and danced around the treasure hole like children on a picnic outing, their cries and laughter echoing among the trees as the solemn Germans looked on. Someone produced a camera and they all posed, grinning and carefree, with bullion bars worth $15,000 apiece in their hands and not a thought in their heads. They moved out of the shade of the trees into the brighter light beside the track and bunched together for a group photograph to commemorate the occasion: Major Geiler, Divisional Engineer, beaming hugely; Captain Garwood, Company Commander, smoking a Lucky Strike; Captain Dee, Intelligence Officer, taking the weight of a bullion bar on his right shoulder; GIs in steel helmets and forage caps and sunglasses; moustachioed Josef Veit, poacher turned gamekeeper, in a Bavarian trilby; burly Josef Pinzl, pig keeper, from his sickbed and well-wrapped in convalescent garb of a Bavarian jacket, waistcoat, and button-up cardigan. Only Captain Rüger was missing. Perhaps the shame of it all was too much for him. Perhaps it was he who took the photographs.

After recovery, the gold was formally handed over to Major Geiler and Captain Dee. Jeeps were summoned and the gold loaded and driven down the Steinriegel to the road. There was so much gold it required a number of round trips before all 728 bars had been brought down the mountain. the gold was reloaded onto two-and-a-half-ton trucks, covered with tarpaulins, and guarded by GIs armed with carbines sitting up top. One of the guards was Private First Class Vahn Berberian. As he posed for a last photograph in the back of one of the trucks, holding in his hands a bullion bar worth $15,000, he was heard to comment: "I'd sure like to have just a little of it." Then the convoy drove back to Mittenwald, dropped off Pinzl and Veit—who received a thank-you note and an empty gold bag as a souvenir—and disappeared in the direction of Garmisch.

For obvious reasons the mission was now shrouded in the profoundest secrecy. Nine tons of gold was a target for anybody and everybody. That night and the following day the gold remained under guard in Divisional Headquarters at Garmisch. Then, on Saturday, 9 June, it was hauled from Garmisch to 7th Army Headquarters in Munich, using several two-and-a-half-ton trucks. Years later one of the convoy escorts, Louis J.

Graziano, 55th Armored Engineer Battalion, remembered: "The operation took one complete day. The intersections along the way were guarded
by tanks and half-tracks. We deposited the gold in a jailhouse, this I remember well, because there were three sets of gates which we had to go
through, and we were all frisked on the way out. The gold was in sacks,
two gold bars in each sack. Then we left to go back to our outfits."

Before returning to Garmisch, the two 10th Armored officers were
given a receipt for handover of their precious consignment. It read:

G-5 7th Army. 9 June 1945

Received of Major William R. Geiler, 55th Armd Engr Bn and Captain Walter
R. Dee, G-2 sec. seven hundred and twenty eight bars (364 bags) of gold bullion.
Total value unknown.

Signed Robert P. Rowe
Lt. Col. FD
G-5, HQ 7th Army

The next day the gold was driven up to Augsburg. There it was loaded
on a convoy together with a haul of non-Reichsbank gold and an assort-
ment of foreign paper currency and driven to the Foreign Exchange Depository (FED) in the Reichsbank building in Frankfurt, where it arrived
on the evening of 10 June. The convoy was unloaded, an inventory taken,
and each item painstakingly checked into the Currency Section. The 728
bars of Reichsbank gold dug up on the Steinriegel had thus ended up
exactly where they should have — in the main strong room of the FED in
Frankfurt.

And yet it was on the hillside near Einsiedl that, as the 728 bars passed
into history, a myth was born. The myth, thriving on rumor, speculation,
and ignorance, persisted and grew until, in the absence of any official
denial, it came to be rooted as an apparent fact — a fact which was finally
perserved in the *Guinness Book of Records* in 1957 under the heading
"ROBBERY: Biggest Unsolved."

The greatest robbery on record was of the German National Gold Reserves in
Bavaria by a combine of U.S. military personnel and German civilians in June
1945. A total of 730 gold bars valued at $14,235,400 together with six sacks of
bank notes and 25 boxes of platinum bars and precious stones disappeared in
transit but none of those responsible has been brought to trial.

In fact, a monumental robbery did indeed take place, *but it did not include
the 728 gold bars.* Though no official denial was ever issued, the evidence for
a refutation had always existed in the official records. In 1976 this evidence
came to light. It took the form of a Secret Report in the Washington ar-

chives entitled *Register of Valuables in the Custody of the Foreign Exchange Depository, Frankfurt A/M, Germany*. Under shipment 27G was an entry which read "7th U.S. Army—10th June 1945—Wallgau—364." And in the margin someone had appended a handwritten comment which simply noted: "728 gold bars."

The consequence of the false legend surrounding the fate of these 728 bars cannot be underestimated. It served both as a diversionary smoke-screen for the perpetration of robberies of other valuables hardly less substantial in the same area at about this time, and it acted as a red herring which lured subsequent investigators off the right track into a blind alley. These belated investigations overlooked the crime that *had* taken place and instead attempted to solve a crime that had not. It is probably for this reason that no one has ever been arrested, charged, or tried in connection with the real robbery of the Reichsbank reserves—the greatest unsolved robbery in history.

For security reasons news of the recovery of the Reichsbank gold from the Steinriegel on 7 June was not released until more than a fortnight later. On 23 June the 10th Armored division's weekly newspaper *Tiger's Tales*, published in Garmisch-Partenkirchen, carried a three-quarter-page column and two photos concerning the incident. The Army news story was substantially accurate but contained one glaring and significant anomaly. This was in a paragraph which read: "Discovery of the bullion followed a tip given by an SS Lieutenant-General who told interrogators that 25 boxes of gold had been moved between 25 April and 2 May from the Reichsbank at Munich to Mittenwald where it had been stored briefly in the Casino. Subsequently, he said, the gold was moved into the mountains by trucks and mules. He did not know the exact location of the cache."

It is quite true that 25 boxes of gold *had* been moved from the Munich Reichsbank to Mittenwald on 25 April. These were the 25 boxes which on 22 April had been brought by Reichsbank director Rosenberg-Lipinski from the Konstanz Reichsbank to Munich and from there taken on to Mittenwald by Reichsbank official Mielke. Like the rest of the gold stored in the Casino at Mittenwald, these 25 boxes, consisting of 100 bars weighing a total of nearly one and a quarter tons and worth $1,500,000, were brought to the Forest House at Einsiedl prior to burial. But though they had been held for safekeeping by the Reichsbank, the 25 boxes did not form part of the Reichsbank national gold reserves and were not listed as such in the final inventory of precious metals drawn up in Reichsbank headquarters in Berlin towards the end of the war. The SS general quoted in the *Tiger's Tales* report—all German generals were SS to the Allied press corps in Germany at that time—was quite right in stating that these 25 boxes had been moved into the mountains by mules and cached. But *Tiger's Tales*, or its U.S. Army informant, was wrong in assuming that these 25 boxes represented the gold that had been recovered by the 55th AEB on 7 June, for the 25 boxes had been buried in a separate cache and were not recovered when the 728 bars were dug up.

In other words, *Tiger's Tales*, and presumably certain elements in the U.S. Army, had confused two separate and substantial gold hoards as one and the same. This confusion may go some way towards explaining the mystery surrounding the next gold recovery and the almost impossible problems confronting Army intelligence and other investigators when they were eventually required to look into the Reichsbank gold affair. As far as can be determined the second gold recovery took place a week or two after the 7 June recovery in much the same area. In the absence of any documentation either at the time or afterwards, it seems evident that the second recovery remained unknown—and uninvestigated—for the next 32 years.

The first mention ever made of the second retrieval came in response to a request for information about the discovery of the Reichsbank gold—the 728 bars—which appeared in the 10th Armored Association's newsletter in August 1976. A reply was received from Albert Singleton, the busy and prospering president of the Albert Singleton Corporation, an industrial metal-plating concern based in Cleveland, Ohio. Singleton, who at the time shared the same confusion as *Tiger's Tales*, the U.S. Army, and everyone else and believed that the operation he had been involved in was the 7 June retrieval of the Reichsbank gold reserves, wrote in to say:

Regarding the "Ten Tons of Gold" which was returned to the Munich Bank, it was cached in a bunker on the side of a mountain near Krün, northeast of Mittenwald.

I was acting Provost Marshal of the 61st AIB [Armored Infantry Battalion] and was in charge of picking up the gold under two intelligence officers. It was done without fanfare one damned hot day using the services of the German officers who put it there and were supposed to be guarding it. I have photos of the whole operation. Everyone was instructed not to talk about it.

At first it was assumed that Albert Singleton's assumption was correct. But in the course of two lengthy interviews, at both of which Singleton's story remained in all significant details unchanged, it became increasingly clear that what he had been involved in was a totally different incident which had culminated in the commission of major crime. Albert Singleton's story in his own words, is as follows.

In about June 1945 I was serving in A Company, 61st Armored Infantry Battalion,* 10th Armored Division, when I was made acting Provost Marshal for Mittenwald. I was the only Provost Marshal in the U.S. Army in Europe that was not a commissioned officer. I'd been in the Air Corps before World War Two, and when the war came and I went back in I was offered a commission. But though there were quite a few times when I ended up with officer duties I never was commissioned. You see, I was a perfect foul-up; I was in trouble more often than you can ever possible imagine. Anyway, some officers and myself were interviewed for Provost Marshal and because I am three-quarters German — even though I've got an English name — I was the only one who got the job. I understand these people, you see. As Provost Marshal I was responsible not just for Mittenwald, but for Wallgau and Krün and a couple of other little towns around there, and I reported directly to Captain Craig, who was the S-2 officer.

One afternoon about six weeks after the end of the war Captain Craig told me that he had had orders from Divisional Headquarters up in Garmisch-Partenkirchen to detail myself, as Provost Marshal of the area, and a couple of guards and a half-track to go up in the mountains with five German officers who lived in Mittenwald and get a load of gold that was reported to have been buried there. The five German officers were a colonel and four captains from the 54th Mountain Engineer Battalion which had been based in Mittenwald near the *Kaserne*. I can't remember these officers' names now, but they were the same men who had buried the gold in the first place on the instructions of a General Strack. [In fact, the "Colonel" was probably 39-year-old Major Adolf ("Adi") Weiss, who lived at Ferchenseestrasse No. 7, Mittenwald. Weiss died in Garmisch in 1979 before he could be questioned about the gold incident.] The officers were supposed to go up and guard the gold from time to time, but they only did it for a week and then they quit. They figured that someone might tip someone else off about where the gold was hidden and then they would be killed, just for knowing. They weren't in the Wehrmacht now, of course. Their homes were in Mittenwald and they just went around in civilian clothes, *Lederhosen*, and stayed with their wives and families at night. For two weeks or so I had them working for me clearing up the area. Whenever I had a cleanup detail I called them out. Every day I used to collect them to work for me. The colonel loathed my guts. See, being basically German myself, I knew that if you make the top man work for you you've got control, and the other Germans, the captains, enjoyed it because the superior officer was made to work along with them. Oh, he and I used to get into some pretty good debates, me being only a sergeant and all. He could speak very good English. They all could.

Well, the next morning we went up to pick up the gold. We met up on the road leading out of Mittenwald with two American intelligence officers from the OSS, or something similar, that had come down to Mittenwald with a couple of trucks — stakebodies, you know, six by six, the regular Army two-and-a-half tonners — and a couple of drivers from Garmisch. So with the five Germans and myself and

---

* At that time Spiro Agnew — later Vice-President of the United States of America under President Nixon — was a captain in the same battalion in Mittenwald.

my half-track driver and my two guards, that made twelve of us altogether. We followed the intelligence officers' trucks and they led us back through the mountain heading north in the direction of Krün and eventually we came to a creek maybe 5 or 6 feet wide on our right and not more than 15 feet from the side of the road. We got out of the trucks and went down into the creek, across the creek and up the side of a mountain at an incline of about — oh — 30 degrees for about 600 feet upwards. Then there was a level spot.

You wouldn't know for looking around right there that there was anything there at all. The cache had been disturbed before we got there. In fact I was standing right on it without knowing it and German officers were all laughing. They walked right over to the spot, kicked the leaves and other covering aside and revealed a square hole, like a trap door that led down into the bunker. We pulled the trap door off and then we went down into a hole in the ground about 10 to 12 foot square, about 9 foot deep, with logs over the top, and an opening about 2½ foot square. Inside, to guard the gold, were six full-size Mauser rifles, four carbines — I still have one of the rifles and one of the carbines — and four Schmeisser machine pistols (submachine guns). In the center of this pit, this bunker, the gold was stacked about 3 feet wide and 3 foot high and it was in the very center of the bunker stacked up crisscrossed like bricks, not in boxes and not in sacks.

Well, we passed the gold up, and took it to the edge. We were supposed to carry it down that incline, but a couple of my men fell down trying to carry the gold down the side of the mountain, it was so heavy. So I told them: "Now look, we are going to divide this up. I want you fellers lifting the gold out of the hole here, and the rest of you fellers down at the foot of the hill 'cos we gonna slide the gold down that incline into the creek. Then you fellers pick it up and put it into the trucks."

My men carried the gold through the creek and put it on the trucks as I had told them. It was a very hot day and hard work but by about noon we were done. The last time I saw the gold it was in the two trucks with the two drivers and the two intelligence officers. They did at least put the gold in burlap bags, but I remember making the comment: "Well, you sure as hell don't have many guards to guard this!" And they said: "Look we don't want to attract any attention." Then they drove away and I never saw them or the gold again.

While the gold trucks were driving away I had to go back with the Germans and pick up the rifles and submachine guns from the mountain and put them in the half-track. As we were driving back to Mittenwald, the German colonel, the one who hated my guts, said to me:

"Singleton, you know, those rifles are loaded."

I said: "I know. I didn't say anything about unloading 'em when we came up here to move the gold."

He said: "Well, you know, we could start a war right here."

"Yeah? Just about right — with five of you and three of us."

He looked at me and he said: "You ready?"

"I'm always ready for a fight."

Then he said to me: "You know, you're an arrogant son-of-a-bitch."

"You know what? I've got the same respect for you."

"What makes you so damn sure why the American soldiers won the war?"

"Because we could outfight yer."

"Well, you know, I've heard you talking. How good are you?"

I picked up one of the German rifles and I said, "Driver, stop the half-track." Then I turned to the German colonel and I said: "Look, none of your drivers were ever trained to shoot, were they?"

"No."

I told the colonel to carry a pop bottle down the road and put it on a post. He did that and then he came back to the half-track, and I said; "Now, driver, shoot that bottle off that post."

The colonel said: "He's not going to hit that, that's too long a range."

"Look, he doesn't even know the rifle. That's a German rifle, right?"

The kid shot the bottle off the post.

"Now give me the rifle," I said.

There was still a part of the bottle on the post and I shot that off. "Here," I said to the German colonel, "*you* do that."

"Oh, we can't shoot like that."

"All right, now," I said to him. "I'm ready for yer any time you're ready."

Well, when we got back to headquarers, my colonel, Colonel Hankins [Lieutenant-Colonel Curtis L. Hankins, OC 61st AIB, 10th Armored Division] heard about it all afterwards.

He said: "Out of the whole damned American Army we got the one man who would throw gold around like kindling wood. I don't know of anybody that would slide gold down a mountain."

So I said to the colonel: "Look, what the hell, it wasn't even mine. I just didn't want the men to get hurt."

The very next day, I was told to go to General Strack's home in Mittenwald, where he was living with his daughter and his wife, and pick him up and take him to the internment camp in Garmisch-Partenkirchen. The reason they hadn't touched General Strack previously, so I was told, was because he was the man who'd been responsible for putting the gold up in the mountain and it was through him that they found out where the gold was at. He was the senior officer over the colonel and the captains who had put the gold there just before the end of the war. I remember this very vividly—the American officers, including Captain Craig, had piled up all the silverware in the middle of General Strack's living-room floor. That pile was at least three feet high and six feet in diameter and it was laid out on a bedspread. They were starting to sort through it, so I reached over and said: "What the hell, I'll take a silver pitcher as a souvenir." Then the officers told me: "Hey. You put that back. We're not really taking this. This belongs to the family." Over along the wall was the Alpenstock—you know, a climbing stick—so I reached over and said: "By God, this isn't anybody else's, I'm taking this as a souvenir." (I have it at home now.)* So I loaded General Strack into the half-track to take up to Garmisch, and his daughter—oh, his daughter called me everything but a white man. She went back into my ancestry and everything else. She was a little cat, about 25, 27 years old.

That same day I got a telegram from Divisional Headquarters in Garmisch-Partenkirchen saying that all of the gold was back in the right spot in Munich. Not one bar was missing. I had just taken it as an Army operation. We did it and that was it. As far as I'm concerned it was just one of those duties I performed and forgot—and that was it.

A few weeks later, on 29 July 1945, Singleton sent home to his wife some of the photographs he had taken at the gold location, and wrote in a covering letter:

Here are more negatives. 2 through 10 is going up to the gold hole a few weeks ago after the weapons that were left there. Three of the men helped put the gold here from the Casino. One colonel and two captains from the 54th German Engineers stationed at the camp before the surrender. 11 and 12 are of coming down the last steep hill with the weapons.

Both the letter and the photographs indicate that Singleton's memory of the gold incident more than 35 years before was essentially accurate.

It is already clear that in many respects Singleton's account of his gold recovery differed substantially from that of the 7 June recovery. The location, the weather, the description of the burial site, the army unit detailed for the job, the numbers and nationality of the personnel involved, the vehicles, and the method employed to retrieve the gold—all were different. As an acid test, Singleton was sent prints of the photos taken during the 7 June operation and in return he sent the photos he had himself taken of his burial site and of the German officers involved in his own operation. His response was quite positive.

I'll be honest with you. I can't connect up anything with the gold that I picked up—either in the description of the gold hole or anything else—with that other gold find the local hunter was involved with. It just doesn't make sense. There are those men holding bars of gold and I don't recognize any one of them and I know damn well who was up there on the mountain with me. I don't recognize any of the Americans in that photograph, not a one. I never saw 'em before, and I couldn't recognize the spot. And there wasn't nearly that number of men on the operation I was on, and there was no German like that hunter.

---

*This kind of thing was pretty normal in Germany shortly after the end of the war. In Mittenwald Major L. Stautner, a Wehrmacht officer and a holder of the Knight's Cross (like Colonel Pfeiffer), had his prized decoration stolen by the invading Americans. "When the Americans marched into Mittenwald they plundered my house there," he wrote to the authors, "and even carried off the children's toys back to America. At that time—the beginning of May 1945—I was on the southern front. In all probability I should have been no worse off if the Russians had come there. I myself took part in both world wars, on every front there was, but I have never taken, or allowed my soldiers to take, the very smallest trifle. I *have* to tell you that."

The June 7 pictures do not relate to the same incident. The only thing I can think of is that there *must* have been two caches of gold.

I feel stupid now. Patton had real strict orders that we were not to loot any of the cathedrals or anything in our area. I mean, he was strict as hell, and I never gave it a thought that anybody with an officer's uniform on would even think of such a thing. And there were so many people involved! I mean, the order had to go to Captain Craig to tell me to provide guards and Germans. There must be records in Munich to show the gold got there safely or not. And there must be records in 10th Armored, otherwise how the hell did they get in there with the authority? Mind you, the orders were not in writing — and I never got a receipt [apart from the telegram, that is].

The circumstantial evidence that the gold recovered by Major Geiler of the 55th Armored Engineering Battalion and the gold recovered by Sergeant Singleton of the 61st Armored Infantry Battalion were from two separate caches is overwhelming. Even if the general *locality* was the same, the particular *location* of Singleton's burial site simply was not the same as Geiler's. Singleton, 32 years after the event, was under the impression that his gold stash was located in the mountains not far past the *Kaserne* at Mittenwald, perhaps in the vicinity of Krün. Actually the valley widens at Krün and the terrain there is flat. But just north of Krün's twin village of Wallgau the land begins to rise steeply to form the southern slopes of the mountains whose several summits and ridges include the Klausenkopf and Steinriegel where virtually all the gold and currency brought to Mittenwald in the Reichsbanks shipment was buried. Quite possibly Singleton's gold had been buried in this area too, but the approach to his gold stash was quite different from the approach to the Geiler's burial site. Geiler's men drove most of the way up to their hold by jeep on a firm, serviceable, forest track. They did not have to cross a creek to get there, as Singleton's men did, nor were they ever on a slope so steep that they ran the risk of falling and injuring themselves, as Singleton's men apparently did when they tried to carry the bullion down on foot. Singleton found the ground so steep that he had to instruct his party to slide the gold bars down the hill to the creek at the bottom. It is difficult to imagine how this could possibly be done at the Geiler gold site, or why anyone should want to do it. Even if there were not jeeps to carry the gold down (as in Singleton's case), it would be simple enough to bring the gold down on foot by just following the track. That Singleton and his party were able to follow a proper track at least some of the way up to their site is clear from his photos. In some of the photos the track quite closely resembled the one that leads up to the Steinriegel, and one must presume the reason was because the path was too narrow for his half-track and the two-and-a-half tonners, and he had no jeeps. However, a closer examination of his photos, taken in bright sunshine around the middle of a summer's day, makes clear from the shadows cast by the sun that the track followed by Singleton led in a completely different direction from the one on the Steinriegel. To reach the gold hole where Geiler's men disinterred 728 bars of bullion you must first ascend from north to south and then, after bearing sharply left at a fork, continue to ascend west to east. The men in Singleton's photographs were ascending from east to west. This means that in order to reach the same spot as the one where 728 bars were buried they would have to come along a different track from the opposite direction; but the lay of the land and a glance at a map would immediately indicate that approach to be nonsense.

Nor was the burial trench itself the same. Singleton's was a proper bunker, like a weapon pit — a substantial affair measuring 10 to 12 feet square, deep enough for a man to go down into, with a trap door and a log roof. By comparison the cache containing the 728 bars on the Steinriegel was merely a hole in the ground, only six feet square, and filled in with earth. In fact, in size and construction Singelton's burial site most closely resembled the original currency stash on the Steinriegel, but this had been emptied more than six weeks previously and its contents reburied elsewhere. From a comparison of photographs it is clear that the Singleton gold stash was located on steeply shelving ground and that the men standing by the hole had to brace their legs to remain upright. The Geiler site, on the other hand, was situated on relatively flat ground, where a man could stand up straight in a perfectly normal way. The Geiler site, too, had been covered with a tree stump. Singleton recalled no such object at his cache. Nor did he use mine detectors to find the gold or jeeps to transport it; nor was the gold he found wrapped in bags, as it had been at the Geiler cache.

Finally, there was the decisive matter of the people involved in the two recoveries. The gold from the Geiler cache was loaded by a platoon of American GIs from the 55th Armored Engineering Battalion. The gold from the Singleton cache was loaded by a handful of German officers from the 54th Mountain Engineer Battalion. There was only one German officer at the Geiler recovery, and he was from a different unit, the Mountain Infantry School. There were no German civilians at the Singleton hole, but there were two at the Geiler one. Singleton himself does not recognize the names or the faces of any of the Americans or Germans in the Geiler recovery. Nor do any of the Americans in those photos taken at his recovery — and neither, for that matter, do Colonel Pfeiffer or Captain Neuhauser.

If the circumstantial evidence for the existence of two separate gold caches is overwhelming, the documentary evidence that the contents of one of the caches reached its right destination and the other did not is conclusive. The 728 bullion bars exhumed by Major Geiler were duly included on the inventory of the FED at Frankfurt. The bullion bars exhumed by Sergeant Singleton were not.

There is no reason to doubt Albert Singleton's word when he says that the gold he dug was safely delivered to Munich and that not a bar was missing. As far as he and the 10th Armored Division were concerned, that was the end of the matter. But the gold never made the next leg of its journey to its proper destination. Though it was possibly non-Reichsbank gold it was still bound by occupation law to be forwarded for depositing at the FED vaults in the Frankfurt Reichsbank building, where it would be entered, with its relevant shipment identification number, on the inventory of gold held by the FED. But Singleton's gold was never entered on any inventory. It was never entered because it never reached Frankfurt. It never reached Frankfurt because all of it—worth many millions of dollars by today's standards—was in all probability stolen.

The theft of the gold bullion recovered by Albert Singleton in June 1945 is not an entirely open-and-shut case. There are curious features—the absence of guards on the trucks, the informality of the recovery, the unusual telegram from divisional headquarters to a relatively lowly sergeant confirming that the gold had reached Munich safely. And there remain a number of unanswered questions. What exactly did Singleton's gold hoard consist of? What was its origin? Who was the SS general who tipped off the Americans about the 25 boxes? Was it—as it might seem logical to assume—the same General Strack whom Sergeant Singleton arrested in Mittenwald and carted off to the internment camp in Garmisch once the general had finally divulged the whereabouts of the hoard which was allegedly his responsibility? If, as Singleton says, the gold reached the Munich Bank—how, and through whose hands, did this immensely valuable consignment of exceedingly heavy metal disappear into thin air?

It would seem reasonable to suppose that the 25 boxes of gold bullion whose existence was revealed to U.S. Army interrogators by an SS Lieutenant-General were the same 25 boxes of gold bullion that were brought down from Konstanz (which was in imminent danger of falling to the French Army) to Munich and from there to Mittenwald for concealment in the mountains above Lake Walchen. Since there is no record that the 25 boxes of gold bullion were ever recovered intact from the mountains by the U.S. authorities, it seems equally reasonable to assume either that they were never found or that they never reached their proper destination.

But was this the gold that Singleton found? His gold was not in boxes or any other kind of container. The 100 bars contained in the 25 boxes would not have formed a pile as large as the one Singleton found, which measured three foot by three foot by three foot (if his memory is correct). Nor would 100 bars weighing 1.25 tons need two two-and-a-half ton trucks to carry them away.

A plausible answer to these questions was alluded to in an article published in the magazine *Wochenend*, titled "Wo bleib das Gold der Reichsbank?," written by one Henrietta Hoffman, formerly Henrietta von Schirach, wife of Hitler's Youth Leader, which raised the possibility of yet another convoy of gold and valuables originating in Berlin and sent to Munich. The shipment she told of, however, proceeded to Mittenwald by a route completely different from that of the well-documented convoy of official Reichsbank reserves. This little-known shipment went from Munich through Holzkirchen, Bad Tolz, Kodel and Urfeld, arriving at its Mittenwald destination in March, a full month before the convoy received by Colonel Pfeiffer of the Gebirgsjägerschule.

As far as can be ascertained this first convoy carried 72 sacks totaling 144 gold bars weighing 1.8 tons and worth about $2,000,000, together with a quantity of foreign currency, diamonds, and mercury. This shipment was delivered to the German army engineering batallion in Mittenwald commanded by a shadowy "General H.," who in turn delegated the job of its burial near the Steinriegel.

Several informants presently living in Garmisch have indicatead the possibility of two separate treasure convoys. One of them claimed that the earliler convoy (the one in March) was led by a "Colonel H.," who had only one arm. Further, a U.S. Army CID officer in charge of the investigation of disappearing gold, who was murdered in 1948, also believed that there were two separate gold convoys to Mittenwald. Finally, Colonel Pfeiffer, when he was interviewed, said that he had wanted to give the gold and currency in his charge to the army engineering battalion located near Mittenwald.

If this theory were correct, it would account for Singleton's gold and for the unaccounted-for dollars in the Blücher story as well as the dollars found by Rawley and handed over to McIntyre. All of this would of course be in addition to the as yet unpublicized "Ribbentrop-Foreign Office" gold shipments.

Perhaps another clue to the riddle lies in the figure of General Strack. It would be tempting to assume that this general, who appears to have been responsible for the gold hoard which was recovered by Albert Singleton, was the same general who tipped off the Americans about the 25 boxes of bullion hidden in the same area. It is clear, however, that no such person was in command of the Reichsbank treasure operation over the heads of Colonel Pfeiffer and Colonel Rauch. There was indeed a General Strack — Karl Strack — though he seems to have been *Wehrmacht* (Panzer Grenadier), not SS. There was also a Nazi Foreign Office official by the name of Dr. Hans Strack, former head of Section Pol II in the Political Department of the Ribbentrop Bureau and from 1943 German Consul-General in Klausenburg, Hungary. By a curious coincidence, this individual was picked up in Kohlgrub on the same day as Major Braun and the other Mountain Infantry officers involved in the Reichsbank treasure affair. On the same day previous to Dr. Strack's arrest, 24 boxes of gold bars and coins worth some $1,893,680 were turned in to VI Corps and deposited at the Reichsbank in Innsbruck. These boxes had been found by the Americans at Füssen, a town in the Allgäu to the west of Garmisch, and on being opened were found to be marked "Foreign Office, Berlin." If Consul-General Strack was in fact Singleton's "General" Strack, the possibility exists that the gold found by Singleton was of a similar origin to the Füssen gold and was not Reichsbank gold and not SS gold but Foreign Office gold, part of the huge gold stock known to have been in the possession of Ribbentrop's Ministry before the end of the war.

At the time of Singleton's gold recovery next to nothing was known about the disposition of German Foreign Office gold stocks and nothing at all about a special gold fund called the "Ribbentrop Gold Fund," a secret gold hoard in the German Foreign Ministry in Berlin, over which Reichs Foreign Minister von Ribbentrop had retained personal control. The "Ribbentrop Gold" consisted initially of Belgian gold bullion of the same origin as the Reichsbank gold, supplemented later by several tons of gold coin from the Banco d'Italia. The first that was heard about this was during the course of the trial of the Nazi "diplomats" at Nuremberg — the so-called *Wilhelmstrassen-Prozess* — in 1948. Among the accused who were tried and sentenced were several who have already featured in the Reichsbank story, including Colonel Rauch's former boss, Chancellery Secretary Hans-Heinrich Lammers (who got 20 years); SS General Gottlob Berger, who had snatched 11 sacks of foreign exchange from the Berlin Reichsbank shipment in April 1945 (25 years); and Reichsbank Vice-President Emil Puhl (5 years). The chief American prosecutor at this trial was Dr. Robert M. W. Kempner, who had established his reputation at the trial of the major Nazi war criminals (Goering, Hess, Ribbentrop, and other surviving leaders of the Third Reich) which had ended in Nuremberg in October

1946. From the Office of Chief of Counsel for War Crimes in Nuremberg
on 28 December 1948, Kempner wrote a highly significant letter to Mr.
Perry Lankhuff of the Political Division of OMGUS (Office of Military
Government, United States) in Berlin:

In the course of our trial against Nazi diplomats which has just been concluded,
it was brought to light that the German Foreign Office had — besides other gold
funds — a special Ribbentrop gold fund, in gold bullion, weighing approximately
fifteen tons.

Leads and newspaper accounts from various countries in the Western Hemi-
sphere indicate that unrecovered Foreign Office gold probably in the hands of former German Foreign Office officials is still at work for anti-American purposes.

Large numbers of former German diplomats who had to do with the Foreign
Office gold are still in foreign countries, e.g., Spain, Italy, Ireland, Argentina,
Sweden, and Switzerland, living well from unknown resources.

It should be noted that besides other former German diplomats, a brother-in-
law of Ribbentrop is living in Switzerland and at least two other German Foreign
Office officials who dealt with German gold matters.

Out of the fifteen tons, about eleven tons of Ribbentrop's Foreign Office gold
was hurriedly removed from Berlin in 1945:

1.   6.5 tons to Ribbentrop's Castle Fuschl in Austria (now American Zone of
     Austria). The larger part of this consignment was allegedly turned over to
     American troops in the neighborhood of Fuschl. However German Foreign
     Office officials stated here in Nürenberg that *the amount allegedly turned over
     was less than the amount which was shipped to Fuschl.*
2.   2 tons to Schleswig-Holstein in the British Zone, allegedly turned over to
     the British.
3.   *3 tons to the South of Germany on the shores of Lake Konstanze,* an area at that time
     in American hands. Out of the last amount, two-thirds of a ton were
     brought over to Berne, Switzerland, in the closing days of the war. This
     was done in the presence of the son of the former German Minister of For-
     eign Affairs, von Neurath, who, according to newspaper reports, arrived
     a short time ago in the Argentine.

About four tons were sent between 1943 and 1945 to German embasssies, not-
ably to Madrid, Spain (one ton), to Stockholm, Sweden (one-half ton), to Berne,
Switzerland (three-fourths ton), to Ankara, Turkey (about one ton), to Lisbon,
Portugal (an unknown quantity).

Since I interviewed several hundred German diplomats, including ambassa-
dors, ministers, and fiscal and personnel administrators, I know that the summa-
tion which I made above is highly reliable.

But so far as I know *there was never any check made whether gold of this amount was ever
recovered or whether the amount of Foreign Office gold turned over by German foreign service people to Allied authorities at the end of the war was identical with sums indicated by my investigation.*

In the course of the trial, I have from time to time pointed out the danger and the problem of this missing gold, but nobody as yet tackled the problem, and with my heavy trial work in Nürnberg, I could not devote much time to it, since no war crime was involved. I feel very strongly that this gold project should not be neglected further in these critical times, in which a large amount of uncontrolled gold constitutes a force for evil and mischief in the hands of unscrupulous opportunists working closely together and located in many countries all over the world.

Robert Kempner's query was forwarded to the Foreign Exchange Depository (FED), and on 3 May 1949 the Acting Chief of the FED, Frank J. Roberts, responded with a statement about the German Foreign Office gold as reflected in the records of the FED. According to Roberts, it was not possible to distinguish the Ribbentrop gold from other Foreign Office gold as far as the FED records were concerned. All that could be stated with complete confidence was that only three recoveries of Foreign Office gold had ever ended up in the vaults of the FED. These were all part of the same shipment, brought down to the Lake Konstanz area from Berlin on Ribbentrop's personal orders by Hans Schroeder, Chief of the Personal and Finance Section of the Foreign Ministry, on about 20 April 1945. The first recovery (listed as Shipment 27A at the FED) consisted of 1.45 tons of gold bars and coins which had been stored at the home of a Protestant minister in Füssen, southern Bavaria. The second recovery (Shipment 27B) consisted of just under one ton of gold bars hidden in the house of a farmer near Isny, 18 miles from Lake Konstanz. The third recovery (Shipment 27C) consisted of 1.60 tons of gold bars found in the home of a woman living in Lindau, on the shores of Lake Konstanz. These three shipments to the Lake Konstanz area totaled a little over four tons, rather than three tons specified in Robert Kempner's letter, and comprised the entire amount of Foreign Office or Ribbentrop gold that ended up in the proper place after the end of the war—the gold vaults of the FED in Frankfurt. Of the 6.5 tons of gold allegedly recovered in part from Ribbentrop's castle, Schloss Fuschl, near Salzburg in Austria, there was no trace in the FED records. All that was known was that $5,000,000 worth of gold had been seized from Martin Bormann's former aide, Dr. von Hummel, as he tried to get away. According to the proceedings of the Wilhelmstrasse trial at Nuremberg a large part of this gold had been turned over to American troops of the Third or Seventh Army on 15 June 1945. But had it? If so, what had happened to it? As far as the books of the Allied occupation administration are concerned this gold—$108,000,000 today—appeared to have utterly vanished. This case would seem to have some alarming similarities with the case of the *Goldzug*, or Gold Train, which also entailed the mysterious disappearance of recovered valuables apparently while in

American hands. The Gold Train, was found at Bad Ischl, Austria, where it had arrived from Budapest, Hungary, laden with some $3,000,000 of gold, jewels, and other valuables which Hungarian Jews had given to an SS lieutenant-colonel, Kurt Becher, in exchange for their freedom (or so they had hoped). The contents of the Gold Train were handed over to the Counter-Intelligence Corps who made a full inventory and then passed them on to officers of U.S. Military Government Property Control in Salzburg. Only $30,000 of the estimated $3,000,000 was ever handed over to the proper recipients — the Jewish Agency — and in spite of postwar Jewish protests no trace of the remainder was ever found.

Kempner did not let the matter of the missing Ribbentrop gold rest, and in 1950 he decided to lobby the U.S. Congress on this subject. On 12 June 1950 at his behest, Congressman Lindley Beckworth again raised the question of the 6.5 tons of Ribbentrop gold missing from Schloss Fuschl with the Interstate and Foreign Commerce Committee of the House of Representatives, and then demanded to know whether this, or any other of the Ribbentrop and Reichsbank funds secreted in Switzerland and elsewhere, had been accounted for. But no new information was forthcoming and the matter lapsed into obscurity. As Sir Ronald Wingate, the British Gold Commissioner on the Tripartite Commission for the Restitution of Monetary Gold, pointed out in 1959, "There may be more gold still hidden in the mountains and undiscovered, and quite a lot of novels have been written on this theme. But the trite saying 'Truth is stranger than fiction' seems in the case of the treasure of the Nazis to have some validity."

Whether Sergeant Singleton recovered the contents of 25 boxes which had contained 100 bars of gold, or an even bigger gold hoard from a different source, must forever be a matter of speculation. But the fact still remains that 25 boxes of bullion weighing one-and-a-quarter tons did disappear. And it seems that a further six-and-a-half tons (unconnected with the Reichsbank reserves) were never accounted for.

The 25 boxes of gold bullion were not the only part of the treasure to disappear without trace from the region of Walchensee that first summer of peace. More gold and a prodigious quantity of paper money was also to find its way into hands other than those for whom it was intended — not always the same hands. To clarify the other parts of the huge collective robbery of the Reichsbank reserves that was perpetrated between the beginning of June and the end of August 1945, we must return to Colonel Pfeiffer, the custodian of the Reichsbank treasure, and a man now sorely tried by the contradictions involved in doing his duty, protecting his brother officers, and salvaging his own life from the ruins.

8

Losers Weepers

Colonel Pfeiffer had not been idle while Major Geiler's Americans and Sergeant Singleton's Germans were digging up their gold hoards in the mountains south of Lake Walchen. Almost at the exact time of their gold recovery operations, Pfeiffer was, on his own initiative, beginning a currency retrieval which would yield a treasure in dollar bills almost equal to half the value of the huge Reichsbank gold cache dug up by the Americans on 7 June — dollars which were to disappear under mysterious circumstances exactly like Singleton's gold.

Pfeiffer believed that establishing contact with the American military authorities was now a matter of extreme urgency. "The crucial problem in the first month," he recalled later, "was to make contact with Military Government. I can't remember what the hurry was but I knew that an English General — General Waring — was looking for the gold, and I knew I was on the wanted list and that he was after me." Pfeiffer had few options left open to him. In his own mind — and apparently in the minds of the Allied investigators — he was the man who was above all responsible for the safekeeping of the Reichsbank reserves. But the steady erosion of the gold and currency caches by private enterprise and official endeavor was not likely to help Pfeiffer's case when the time came for him to be called to account for the assets in his charge. Nor would he be in any position to use his knowledge of the whereabouts of the reserves to strike a bargain with the new rulers of Germany — for his personal freedom, perhaps, and that of his officers — if there were no reserves left to bargain with. His fears that one or another of his officers in American hands might sooner or later talk were confirmed when Captain Rüger revealed the location of the cache on the Steinriegel containing the 728 gold bars. In any case, the original burial of the Reichsbank reserves had been carried out so hurriedly and so careless-

ly that it had become common knowledge all around the district that there
was treasure in the hills above the Walchensee. "I was amazed how many
people knew about it," Pfeiffer admitted later. I thought the whole thing
had been a confidential matter but it turned out that it was a complete air
bubble. It wasn't just carelessness. It was more than carelessness. It was
betrayal. It was treason against our country." Pfeiffer's highest priority was
to preempt any major heist of the Reichsbank reserves still hidden in the
mountains. There was not a moment to lose.

Though Colonel Pfeiffer's ultimate goal was to go to Austria, he does not
seem to have established himself there immediately. It is possible that his
first port of call after leaving Garmisch was the nearest friendly house
along his route—the home of Colonel Rauch at 38 Wallbergstrasse, Bad
Wiessee. It is also possible that he stayed at his mother's house at Schliersee, a few miles to the east. It does seem that very early in June he suddenly popped up in the heart of the enemy camp—the nearby Third Army
headquarters town of Bad Tölz. The voluntary arrival of this anxious and
troubled *Wehrmacht* colonel in General Patton's bristling garrison required
commendable courage. Pfeiffer was in a bad way and appeared to have no
official connections or accreditation. His purpose was absolutely clear,
however, and when the Americans finally picked him off the streets, he
quickly made it known to them. Colonel William E. Eckles, the 10th
Armored Division's Intelligence Officer in Garmisch—the same officer
who on the day the Division had occupied Garmisch had taken the telephone call from a German purporting to be Colonel Pfeiffer in Mittenwald—remembered the occasion well:

I received a call from Colonel Oscar Koch, G-2 of Third Army, at about 8 P.M.
in the evening. Oscar and I had been very close throughout the war and we had
worked together almost on an hourly basis through combat stages. Oscar told me
that the MPs of the Third Army had arrested Colonel Pfeiffer while he was walking around the streets of Bad Tölz. When he was interrogated, Pfeiffer had the
audacity to tell Oscar Koch that I was a friend of his and that he had been given
the mission of hiding all the monetary reserves of the Munich bank to prevent it
being captured by the Americans. The interrogators laughed at him, but he insisted, so Oscar sent him out under guard and to everyone's surprise he brought
in a large amount of dollars and threw it on the table at Army Headquarters. That
is when Oscar called me in. Oscar asked me to take over Colonel Pfeiffer and get
him to show us where all the money was hidden.

Eckles' recollection of Pfeiffer's state of mind is particularly clear. "Colonel
Pfeiffer was a nervous wreck," he recalled. "The responsibility of having
hidden the money preyed on his mind and his particular fear was that the

Russians were closing in on him and his money." The nearest Russian troops at this time were over 110 miles away and their lines were static — the war had, after all, been over for the best part of a month. At any rate, the Americans were sufficiently convinced by his anxiety and sense of urgency — not to mention his trick of producing large sums of money out of nowhere — that they assigned an officer, Major Roger Rawley (Colonel Eckles' assistant and subsequent successor at G-2) and a squad of soldiers to go and bring back the rest of it.

"My impression then and now," Eckles recalled, " is that the hiding places were in the rock fences and under the many hay sheds that are along both sides of the road between Garmisch and Oberau. Later Major Rawley pointed out some of the spots where he had gotten the money along this road. He told me that Colonel Pfeiffer seemed to be confused and had difficulty in being certain just where to look for the money. They were out all night and came in after daylight with a two-and-a-half-ton truck full of United States currency."

Colonel Pfeiffer had been very careful not to betray to the Americans any of his compatriots involved with the Reichsbank currency. Though he had revealed the whereabouts of dollar caches all along the Garmisch-Oberau road he had not led the Americans to the large cache concealed at either end of it — one at Klaus Bremme's farm at Gut Buchwies, in Oberau, the other at the von Blüchers' house at 38 Gsteigstrasse in Garmisch. Nevertheless, the amount of money that had been picked up that night was prodigious.

"Several million dollars were recovered, I was informed at the time," Eckles stated. "I cannot remember the exact amount now. The money was all paper bills, all denominations of United States currency. Some of it was old, large-sized paper money that had been replaced by our government with smaller bills several years before. The back of the truck was piled high with paper currency."

Although Colonel Eckles could not recall the total value of his haul, his assistant, Major Rawley,who actually picked up the stuff, when contacted in California in 1978 not only confirmed Eckles' account of the recovery but estimated that it totaled in the region of seven to eight million dollars.

Since handling money — especially money in such huge quantities — was outside Colonel Eckles' sphere of responsibility, he was very anxious to get rid of the project. This was not as easy as he had expected. "In the morning, after the recovery of the money, it never occurred to me that we would have a problem disposing of it. I had known our Division Finance Officer, Lieutenant-Colonel Raymond St. Clair, for several years and was certain that he would take it off our hands. Imagine my shock when he informed me in no uncertain terms that the recovered money had nothing to do with the United States Army and that he would not touch it with a ten-foot pole!"

Bill Eckles was in a dilemma. If the American Army would not accept the money, who would? There was only the Military Government. Military Government was a curiously amorphous organization which, while being military (as its name suggested), was somehow not Army, in that it concerned itself with civil affairs rather than tactical tasks. Eckles trundled his truckload of dollars over to the *Bürgermeister*'s office at the city hall in Garmisch-Partenkirchen, which was the office of the local Military Government Officer. There he tried his luck with the Town Major, a certain Major Kenneth McIntyre, one of the more extraordinary members of that extraordinary cast of latter-day proconsuls and eccentrics of Military Government which ruled the U.S. Zone of Germany, fitfully but absolutely, in the immediate postwar period.

Kenneth Asa McIntyre, 37, a former diesel engineer from Wisconsin, had been transferred from the 132nd Ordnance Maintenance Battalion to the 10th Armored Divison's Provisional Military Goverment Detachment on 5 May. Now, barely a month later, he was in the unforeseen position of having thrust upon him a quantity of dollar bills that filled the back of an Army truck and would today be worth in the region of up to $45,000,000. McIntyre made an indelible impression on Colonel Eckles.

"He was a likeable guy," he remembered, "but very naive and stupid. I am sure there was skullduggery in Garmisch in those days and I am afraid that McIntyre was weak as water and he probably succumbed to some of the temptations that came his way."

I recall [Eckles continued] that he had a tremendous set of flat silver [tableware] which he said he had gotten from some home in Garmisch and belonged to the Nazi Bormann. No telling what this silver service was worth. He told me that he planned to keep it as a souvenir and asked me what I thought about it. I advised him to get rid of the set without delay and to get a receipt for it from whomever he turned it over to. Everyone in Garmisch knew he had the silver.

Another reason I remember McIntyre is that he asked me several times to submit recommendations to our G-1 (Personnel Officer) for him to receive the Silver Star and the Bronze Star for heroic deeds he had done. I couldn't imagine how he could have done anything like this as he was always in the Divison rear echelon. I was not a witness to the heroic acts and therefore could not sign the descriptive write-ups. Later, I heard that he had written-up the so-called events, signed them himself, and submitted them through channels. He received the medals, I guess in July.

McIntyre's German secretary, Sieglinde Odorfer, in 1976 was located in Munich, where she was livng with her husband, the first postwar president of Bavaria, Dr. Hans Ehard. She recalled that Major McIntyre was (in her opinion) very intelligent but also possessed of a weak character. She recollected very clearly that one day a large quantity of dollars, some of which had been dug up, were indeed brought into her boss's office. They were contained in a single sack and when they were counted under guard they totaled "no more than a million dollars." But this was just one sack. If the dollars recovered by Major Rawley and Colonel Pfeiffer filled the back of a truck, as Colonel Eckles claimed, they would not have amounted to a single sack-load worth a great deal more.

So at the beginning of June 1945 a very large number of U.S. dollars were turned over to a man who had already acquired a large hoard of looted silverware and forged his own citations for bravery medals. At the end of July, by which time the dollars had vanished from sight for good, this man was charged with soliciting and receiving an award for an heroic deed which did not take place. "The accused is charged with the 95th Article of War," the Division Judge Advocate declared, "with wrongfully procuring an Oak-Leaf Cluster to the Bronze Star Medal on the basis of a citation not founded on fact and also of wrongfully procuring a Purple Heart Medal on the basis of a personal certification of fact known by him to be false." In August, in lieu of trial by court-martial, McIntyre tendered his resignation from the Army "for the good of the service...and under other than honorable conditions."

On 30 August McIntyre's immediate superior officer wrote to the Commanding General of the 10th Armored Division of Gamisch with a somewhat ambivalent announcement: "Major Kenneth A. McIntyre is not accountable or responsible for any public property or funds in this organization."

This should have been the finish of McIntyre in Bavaria. But oddly enough it was not. When the 10th Armored Division sailed home to the States in early September 1945, the disgraced McIntyre did not sail home with it. Instead, the day after his duties with the Military Goverment Section terminated, he was appointed as Chief Machinery and Equipment Officer, first to the G-5 Section of General Patton's Third Army and then to Military Government Detachment in Munich under the command of Colonel Roy Dalferes. This same Dalferes, as Acting Chief of Staff, G-5 Section of Third Army, was the officer who arranged for millions of dollars' worth of foreign exchange recovered from the Third Army area near Einsiedl to be transported to the Currency Section for Germany located at

Frankfurt. The records show that the millions of dollars handed over to McIntyre in his office in Garmisch were not among those that had been transported and were never checked into the vaults of the Foreign Exchange Depository in the Frankfurt Reichsbank building

It was extraordinary enough that McIntyre should remain in the employ of the U.S. Army in Germany until December 1945, five months after he had been required to resign the service. It is even more extraordinary that McIntyre should, after being returned to the United States, be recalled to service in the U.S. Army in Germany the following March — by which time, up to his old tricks again, he had thought fit to inquire whether or not the Army authorities had received orders for his promotion to the rank of Lieutenant-Colonel! Once again Major McIntyre took up the position of Chief Machinery and Equipment Officer, this time at the headquarters of the 3rd Military Government Regiment, Office of Military Government for Bavaria. Not until July 1946 — more than a year since he had taken delivery of up to eight million dollars in U.S. notes which later vanished, and nearly a year after he had tendered his resignation from the Army — was Kenneth McIntyre finally relieved from active duty. Then he was booted home, without terminal leave, mustering-out pay, or travel expenses.

The recovery of the great dollar caches along the Oberau road benefited neither the Americans nor Colonel Pfeiffer as much as either party had hoped. For the former never actually managed to hold on to the money and the latter never totally succeeded in getting his name scratched from the wanted list or the gold and currency investigators off his back. But considering that Waring and his team were still trying to track him down at the very time he was in the hands of Third Army intelligence, it was extraordinary that Pfeiffer came out of the episode with anything at all. "With the Yanks at that time," he explained later, "the right hand often did not know what the left hand was doing."

Third Army kept to their side of the bargain and let Pfeiffer keep his freedom in return for the currency he had located for them. A *laissez-passer*, valid for the French Zone of Austria and prepared in conjunction with the French Army of Occupation, was issued to him via a Captain Fred Neumann, a member of Third Army Counter-Intelligence Branch (CIB) and Patton's personal interpreter, of whom Pfeiffer was to see more in the near future. For the moment it seemed that Pfeiffer's troubles over the Reichsbank reserves were at an end. Armed with his *laissez-passer* he set off unmolested for Austria. In mid-June 1945 he found accommodation for himself and his wife in a house in Seefeld, a small town on the Mittenwald road a few miles north of Innsbruck in the Tyrol, where he was soon very thick with the French, the only one of the Allies to treat Colonel Pfeiffer with the respect to which he felt entitled.

Tyrol province in June 1945 was an occupation zone in a state of considerable confusion. It had been assigned to the French but conquered by the Americans. Now the Americans were preparing to pull out and hand the territory over to the French. Though the transfer did not officially take place until 13 July, the change of command had begun some weeks before and the second half of June saw an interim period of mixed American-French administration. It was during this period that Franz Pfeiffer's more soldierly virtues as a distinguished field commander of mountain troops came to the attention of one of the Allies' senior mountain warfare specialists — General Antoine Béthouart.

General Béthouart had graduated from the same class at the French Military Academy as General de Gaulle. Before the war he had studied mountain warfare techniques in Norway and commanded a brigade of Chasseurs Alpins during the ill-fated Norway campaign in 1940. Later he served as head of the French Military Mission to the United States and as a Corps Commander in the Allied campaign in Germany. At the end of the war Béthouart was Commander-in-Chief of the French forces in the French-occupied Zone of Austria, and it was in this capacity that his attention was drawn to the former Gebirgsjäger commander, Colonel Pfeiffer.

One of the innumerable problems confronting General Béthouart in postwar Austria was the presence on Austrian soil of a vast number of foreign nationals, many of them former members of the *Wehrmacht*. Half a million refugees from many different countries milled aimlessly about the towns and DP camps in a ceaseless quest for food and shelter. Many thousands of German soldiers had been thrown into prisoner-of-war pens by the Americans, only to be released as soon as the French arrived. Their numbers were added to the great tide of the displaced human beings sweeping through Austria in every direction. There were, also, thousands of German soldiers who had not been made captive at the end of the war who, armed and increasingly desperate, still roamed at large through the region. Remnants of disorganized and isolated German units that had been cut off in the mountains and forests while the towns and valleys below were being occupied by Allied forces, they had abandoned their vehicles and scattered into the wilds, finding shelter in mountain huts, on the *alpages*, or in the forest. Anxious and uncertain about what was happening in their own country, they did not dare to go down into the valleys for fear of being taken prisoner. The local populace supplied them with food, either by theft or by force. They were not werewolves, merely fugitives. Their presence gave rise to the rumor of werewolves, a source of fear among the local population and a great nuisance to the occupation forces.

To have searched the thickly forested and mountainous terrain would have required a massive operation and might have led to a renewed outbreak of fighting—especially since the French would have had to use French Moroccan troops, who had a reputation for brutality in the early days of the occupation. Then a simple and convenient solution presented itself. General Béthouart, in his account of the French occupation, *La Bataille pour L'Autriche*, takes up the story.

Certain officers of my staff established contact with the former commandant of the German Mountain Training School at Mittenwald, on the borders of Tyrol—a Colonel Pfeiffer—and it occurred to us that we could use this man to sort out the situation for us. Although his training school had been disbanded following the German surrender, he was still able to enlist the services of some of his former officers and noncommissioned officers to help him. He knew the region like the back of his hand and was in a better position than anyone to make contact with the *Wehrmacht* fugitives and communicate our instructions to them.

A joint paramilitary operation between the soldiers of hitherto opposing armies was unusual, and raised special problems. "My officers and I discussed the proposal," Colonel Pfeiffer recalled, "and we knew it was going to be a tricky and dangerous operation. The dispersed German troops whom we were to seek out and approach personally would inevitably suspect us of acting on behalf of Allies in order to have them taken prisoner, and this meant that the whole operation was going to be extremely dangerous until the word finally got around as to what it was all about. I don't know how the thing was cleared by the French at their headquarters in Innsbruck."

In fact, not only the French Army in the Tyrol but the American Third Army in southern Bavaria would be involved, since the majority of the troops demobilized in the operation would have to be repatriated into Germany through Third Army territory. To work with Colonel Pfeiffer and work out the necessary details, the French Army sent one of their headquarter staff officers, Captain Sauteau, the French agent of the Deuxième Bureau, who had been attached to the American Counter-Intelligence Corps as a Joint Liaison officer since the early days of the U.S. Forces in England, and who spoke perfect American English as well as fluent German. Through Sauteau the Third Army was informed about the proposed operation. Not long afterwards, Sauteau sent Captain Neumann, the

Third Army Counter-Intelligence Branch (CIB) officer whom Pfeiffer had already met concerning his *laissez-passer*, to establish contact with Pfeiffer.

The details did not take long. "I agreed to cooperate," Pfeiffer stated afterwards, "to make things easier for the soldiers in the mountains to come down from their hideouts. The overriding condition was an immediate and legally correct demobilization of the troops without their having to enter a prisoner-of-war camp." The French accepted this condition. Only men who were wanted for war crimes or were known to be die-hard Nazis were to be taken into custody. Colonel Pfeiffer would receive no payment for his services, but the French would provide him with vehicles and gasoline — his own personal car was a commandeered DKW — together with ID card, ration card, and other official documents. He was now an officially accredited auxiliary of the Allied Occupation forces, and free to come and go in Germany and Austria as he pleased.

After the intrigue and ethical ambivalence of the Reichsbank business, Colonel Pfeiffer must have returned with relief to straightforward soldiering. Once more he was back in the hills with his old comrades-in-arms, doing the sort of job for which he was trained. No longer a man on the run but a respected expert in his field with a significant role to play in affairs of government, Colonel Pfeiffer carried out his duties in the service of the French Army of Occupation in Austria for a period of several weeks. He must have enjoyed himself. He was certainly highly successful. Under his overall direction, groups of two or three German or Austrian ex-army officers, selected from those who had a good knowledge of the area and personal contacts among the inhabitants, set off into the Tyrol and the Vorarlberg. Zone by zone they made contact with the fugitive soldiers, generally through intermediaries in the local populace.

"It was all done by word of mouth," Colonel Pfeiffer explained later. "A sort of whispering propaganda campaign. The local *Bürgermeisters* helped to pass the word around. The men were dispersed all over the area. In Tyrol and the Vorarlberg." At first Pfeiffer's efforts were treated with great suspicion by the soldiers, who feared they were being lured into a trap. But they were sick of their futile existence in the wilds, and were gradually persuaded to surrender. "They came down individually from the mountains to Innsbruck," Pfeiffer explained. "It was quite a job. I undertook to produce a short biography of each man, his name, personal details, who he was, what he had done, and so on. On the basis of that, the French would then judge whether the man could be demobilized immediately or not. If not, then I would tell the soldier he was on his own from then on. The French Deuxième Bureau had set up an office for the purpose. A French

Army medical officer examined the men and then they were given their discharge papers and enough money to get home."

The whole operation was remarkably successful. In his memoirs the French Commander-in-Chief General Béthouart, described it in glowing terms. "After a period of some weeks," he wrote, "6,000 to 7,000 men were demobilized in this way, many tons of arms and ammunition were recovered and the whole situation completely cleared up. An atmosphere of friendship and cooperation was established between my officers and Colonel Pfeiffer's team, which not only enabled us to bring the operation to a satisfactory conclusion but augured well for the future. It was one of the first operations carried out jointly by the French, Austrian, and German military. Because of it an alliance of an entirely new nature was born."

The Americans were not included in the lists of credits. Though the French observed their agreement with Pfeiffer to the letter, the Americans did not. At first they had said they would agree to go along with the French plans, but later they decided to back out. "This accounts for my dislike of the Americans," Pfeiffer declared years afterwards. "They nearly caused me to betray my comrades, which would have been disgraceful and would have pursued me for the rest of my life." After the French had demobilized a batch of German troops from the mountains and assembled them in readiness for repatriation—some of them had already crossed the border into Germany—the Americans announced that the whole operation had been vetoed by the Supreme Headquarters Allied Expeditionary Forces in Frankfurt. "Fortunately I was able to disperse the German soldiers again," Pfeiffer related afterwards, "or they might have been locked up in camps by the Americans and I would have been responsible. We got around it by giving the soldiers private addresses to report to in the French Zone of Austria, without reference to the Americans."

In the meantime, while Colonel Pfeiffer's operation in Austria was still in its early days, two of his former colleagues on the German side of the Tyrol decided to make a move. By now they doubtless knew that the Americans had discovered the main gold cache and had hauled off a large quantity of dollars following Pfeiffer's direction in Bad Tölz. These incidents left Captain Neuhauser and Colonel Rauch in a somewhat precarious position. If they still had any cards to play, it was time to play them now.

9

Opportunists of the Worst Order

First to creep out of hiding was Captain Neuhauser. After six weeks of living alone among the trees, the young Gebirgsjäger officer must have begun to wonder what purpose he was now serving in life. The Serbian girl, Vera de Costra, evidently wondered the same thing and had finally drifted away to join the great stream of human flotsam bobbing this way and that across the wasteland of defeated Germany (it is thought she later emigrated to Argentina). American Counter-Intelligence Corps men kept calling at the Forest House, looking for his father. Day after day they had come to question his mother and the evacuee family Forstreicher. But now the captain's home was abandoned and its hearth grown cold. His father languished in a prison camp and his mother had sought refuge with relatives in a distant town. The plank floors of the Forest House echoed to the boots of foreign soldiers — Brigadier Waring in his baggy pants, and rowdy GIs forever chewing wads of gum.

Captain Neuhauser's appointed task was supposedly to stand guard over the official reserves of the German state, the surviving wealth of the nation. The task did not generate much satisfaction. From time to time, in the day or the night, on foot or in jeeps, a group of Americans or a group of Germans would come up the mountainside and probe around with sticks or mine detectors and dig up a load of gold or banknotes and then disappear back to civilization with their haul. There was little Neuhauser could do about it. He could hardly shoot them. The caches were so widely dispersed it was not possible to keep an eye on all of them all of the time. Holes would appear in the ground, like oblong bomb craters, as yet another cache vanished behind the captain's back. It was all very unsatisfactory. In his hut on the Klausenkopf Hans Neuhauser munched his way through his *knackwurst*, or sat in a sunbeam, whittling sticks and contemplating a dismal future.

As the days passed the opposition began to draw closer. The Americans sent out patrols to scour the mountainsides and search the huts. One day they came to Neuhauser's hut on the Klausenkopf when he was out. Thereafter he kept away from the hut as much as possible and took to sleeping in his little army bivouac tent, or in the undergrowth, or in make-shift beds made out of hay. There were moments of excitement, close encounters of the wrong kind, to break the monotony of his simple life. Once he came face to face with two strangers in the woods, a swineherd and a farmer's son. Though they were fellow Germans he was frightened they might betray him, but he acted as normally as the circumstances allowed and neither of the men gave him away. On another occasion he was horrified to see a dog lead an American, who was stalking deer in the woods, to his backpack concealed in the undergrowth; but the American showed little curiosity in the find, and left it where it was and moved on. Then one day Captain Neuhauser had a vistor. Toiling up the track to the prearranged rendezvous spot, the Klausenkopf hut, came the perspiring figure of a former fellow-officer in the shape of Colonel Pfeiffer's one-time adjutant, who had come to give the loyal Neuhauser his last orders. He was to give himself up.

The adjutant's role in the Reichsbank treasure affair has always been underrated. In fact, he seems to have served as a link between the scattered members of the syndicate of officers who maintained an interest in the Reichsbank treasure after the American occupation: Pfeiffer, Rauch, Braun, Neuhauser, the von Blüchers. Pfeiffer has always contended that he made a special point of keeping himself properly informed about any developments to do with the Reichsbank reserves and was constantly in touch with the principals. To this end, the adjutant moved with impunity about the country, still acting as Colonel Pfeiffer's *de facto* adjutant even though the war was over, and serving as a vital go-between purveying information and passing on orders between the interested parties.

According to Neuhauser, Pfeiffer's adjutant came to tell him that the gold had been dug up, Colonels Pfeiffer and Rauch were in American custody, and he might as well move on. In reality, not all the gold *had* been dug up and Pfeiffer and Rauch were *not* in American custody. The adjutant almost certainly had a different message to deliver. The cause of the message — the reasoning behind it — we can only guess at, but the effect of it was self-evident.

Neuhauser and Rauch were to give themselves up to the Americans, as simultaneously as circumstances could permit. They were to give the same preagreed statement to the Americans, relate the same cover story, divulge the same information about the treasure — 350 bags and 20 boxes of gold — and strike the same deal: their personal freedom in return for revealing the location of the caches. It is not difficult to deduce the reasoning behind this move. If they were to use their knowledge of the Reichsbank treasure in order to reach an accommodation with the American authorities, they would need to act swiftly before the Americans stumbled on the treasure on their own. It was now two months since the treasure had been buried. If they left it much longer the time would come when they would seem in Allied eyes to be more culpable than cooperative in the matter. And since some of the reserves had already been removed there was doubtless an element of fear behind their joint move.

Neuhauser's surrender was the easiest to arrange. He had merely to report to the nearest American unit, whereas Rauch proposed to contact General Patton's Third Army headquarters some distance away at Bad Tölz, a more difficult thing to arrange. Neuhauser was, therefore, the first to give himself up. In his own words he *"türmte über Berg und Tal"* (scampered over hill and dale) in the direction of Fall, a tiny hamlet on a minor road some 12 miles east of Wallgau. Neuhauser chose Fall "because I happened to be in the mountains near there." At Fall he surrendered to the 574th AAA Battalion. The report of the battalion's own intelligence officer provides the clearest narrative of the incident:

On 23 June 1945 Lt. Chatel of B Btry. was contacted at Fall by a German Captain, who stated that he wished to surrender to the American authorities, and that he had certain information that he wished to give to the Americans. It was arranged by Lt. Chatel to meet this officer at Fall in the office of the *Bürgermeister* at 1330 hours on 24 June. The meeting took place and through a German interpreter the Captain stated that he wished to advise an American Colonel of the whereabouts of some gold or other stuff of value which had been cached at a place known to him. It appeared from the Captain's talk that he wished to contact the Colonel of some American Unit which he had last heard of as being stationed at Garmisch-Partenkirchen, at a POW camp or enclosure there. He appeared not willing at that time to give his information directly to Lt. Chatel. So at about 1400 or 1500 hours on the 24th the German Captain, Lt. Chatel, T/4 McDonald, and Pfc. Zuberg (the last named acting as interpreter) in one jeep followed by Captain Thayer, T/Sgt. Nightingale and Cpl. Fumagalli in another jeep, drove down to Garmisch-Partenkirchen. There at the POW enclosure it was learned that the particular officer whom the German Captain had in mind had left that location, if he had ever been there. In order to expedite the matter it was suggested that the German Captain be asked to disclose the location of the cache to Lt. Chatel and Capt. Thayer. This he consented to do, asking at the same time whether he would be held at a POW enclosure for long. It was his desire, he said, to get back home as soon as possible, and so he said he would appreciate anything that Captain

Thayer and Lt. Chatel could do to assist him in getting an American clearance as quickly as possible. The request was met by the statement that everything that could be done through the proper channels would be done for him, that the POW screening authorities would be told of whatever help or cooperation that he gave, that they would also be told that he, the Captain, had surrendered himself to the Americans, through Lt. Chatel. This was actually the case. It might be stated here that the German Captain had no American Army Discharge, and had only his *SOLDBUCH.*

On returning from Gramisch-Partenkirchen just before reaching the Walchensee, and very near to the German Captain's home, he gave directions to turn off the main road. This was done and the two jeeps and their occupants climbed the hill south of the main road and reached a spot where the Captain directed (WD 685918). After alighting from the jeeps it was seen that there were two rather large holes beside the path. Some gas cape pouches (German) and papers (apparently envelopes) with Deutsche Reichsbank on them were near the holes. It appeared that some American troops had been in the area... After about 45 minutes searching through the area the German Captain finally located the place where he said the stuff had been buried. He stated that it was hard to find because when he was last at the spot there had been show on the ground.

After some digging the first wooden box appeared. These boxes were twenty (20) in number, all the same size, all about 13 × 11½ × 7 inches. Each box had a flat metal band crossed around it on two sides and the metal bands were sealed. Each box had black letters on it, DRB, and a number, such as 45, also each box had Kg on it with blue pencilled numerals opposite such as 41.4 etc. Some of these blue pencilled marks had been obliterated, perhaps from the damp or earth in which they were buried. These boxes were carried to the jeeps and loaded. The German Captain helped not only with the carrying of the boxes to the jeeps, but in digging for them.

Driving slowly the boxes were delivered to Bn. Hq. of this Unit and stored under guard inside the S-2 office overnight. Nothing was touched in the way of breaking the seals or tampering with the boxes. The Captain was left with Lt. Chatel for the night. And was brought back to Bn. Hq. for questioning briefly on the morning of 25 June.

These 20 boxes turned out to be something of an enigma. In a statement to the Munich Criminal Investigation Division in 1952 Neuhauser recalled that among the Reichsbank assets buried above Walchensee were 100 bars of gold bullion. He would have been referring here to the 25 boxes (containing four bars each) brought from Konstanz just before the burial. But the 20 boxes he revealed to the Americans turned out to contain not gold bullion but gold coins weighing 1,575 pounds and worth $805,684 at the official rate of the time (and $4,431,262 today). The confusion between the 20 boxes and the 25 boxes, the bullion and the coin, was significant, and the focal point of a continuing mystery.

There was nothing in Neuhauser's past which could put him at inordinate risk in Allied hands. Like many of his generation he had been an obligatory member of the Hitler Youth and the National Socialist *Studentenbund*. He had joined the National Socialist German Workers Party (NSDAP) in 1938 but he was little more than a Nazi in name only and he was no war criminal. He did not fall into the SHAEF Automatic Arrest category and, it seemed, should have expected no more than a few days or weeks at most in American hands while they interrogated him about the Reichsbank gold and currency.

Colonel Rauch's position, by contrast, was very different. As an Obersturmbannführer of the Allgemeine SS, a Hauptsturmführer of the Waffen-SS, and Oberstleutnant of the Schutzpolizei, adjutant to Hitler's Chancellery secretary, and a member of Hitler's personal security staff in Berlin, Friedrich Josef Rauch could expect to be thrown into the nearest jail promptly upon arrest. Rauch had done well to evade detection and interrogation so far. But to approach Patton's Third Army headquarters directly required caution. If he poked his own head into the lion's den it would undoubtedly be bitten off. His overture to the Americans would have to be made from a safe distance, at one or two stages removed, through go-betweens who could plead his case and pass on the Americans' response without compromising his own freedom. To achieve this delicate maneuver Rauch engaged the services of a chain of friends and friends of friends to intervene on his behalf: Karl Warth, Helmut Schreiber, and Helmut Groeger. Perhaps it is a measure of the man's cleverness that in the event it was not he who ended up in American captivity but the relatively ingenuous Captain Neuhauser.

Rauch's chain of friends were a mixed bunch. The 38-year-old Karl Warth, like his friend Rauch, also fell into the SHAEF Automatic Arrest category as a Captain (Hauptsturmführer) in the Waffen-SS, a member of the SS Führungshauptamt (Amt VI) and a member of the Allgemeine SS since 1934. Like Rauch, Warth had so far succeeded in evading arrest and in the summer of 1945 seemed to be able to come and go as he pleased. His role in the affair seems to have been that of contact man between Rauch and the next man in the chain, an acquaintance called Helmut Schreiber. Schreiber was also a former Nazi but he was not on the wanted list and was ensconced close to American headquarters in Munich.

Schreiber was a talented man. His occupation was described as actor, but between 1935 and 1945 he had been actively involved in film production and until 1939 he had been film production chief of Fox Films and

Tobis Films. On the intercession of both Hitler and the Bavarian Minister of State, Adolf Wagner, he was transferred to propaganda work at the Bavarian Film Company (Bavaria Filmkunst GmbH) — "a firm of importance," he boasted in a letter to a friend, "to the war effort." Schreiber was also a professional magician of some distinction, well known in Germany and abroad under the stage name of Kalanag. As President of the Magic Circle of Germany he had had many high-ranking Nazis as friends, including Hermann Goering and Martin Bormann, and for two days in 1942 he had stayed as a guest of Adolf Hitler at the Berghof, the Führer's mountain home on the Obersalzberg, where he performed several beguiling tricks to divert the Führer from more pressing concerns like genocide and the colonization of the Slavs. Schreiber was evidently a very good conjuror. Years later his opposite number in England, the President of the Magic Circle of Great Britain, described his talent in glowing terms. "Kalanag had one of the finest magical shows I have seen," he wrote, "and was regarded as a master showman."

Schreiber was more than that. A Counter-Intelligence Corps (CIC) Special Agent who interviewed him in Zurich in 1952 described him thus: "Approximately five feet, eight inches tall, stout but very energetic, distinguished in dress and appearance, a sharp, quick mind, speaks several languages, possesses a keen sense of humor, enjoys looking after himself as a cultured dramatic artist smilingly bowing to an enthusiastic audience and accepting the hospitality of aristocracy and wealthy friends throughout Europe." It is not surprising that such a man, with his aptitude for languages and his talent for ingratiating himself in influential circles, should have soon found profitable employment with the posthostilities regime in Bavaria — as interpreter with a Third Army detachment, the 512th Military Police Battalion.

Schreiber was to claim that there was nothing in his background to disbar him from such employment. Though he had made the acquaintance of many top Nazi officials, he protested that he had never belonged to the NSDAP, and was opposed to its philosophy and the cruel treatment of the Jews under its administration. In fact, his Party number was 7-040-625 and the date of his induction 1 May 1939. There was more to Helmut Schreiber than met the eye, another side not entirely irrelevant to the course of this story. In a later reassessment of Schreiber's status, the Director of the Intelligence Division of OMGB (Office of Military Government for Bavaria, Munich) wrote to the Director of Intelligence OMGUS (Office of Military Government, United States, Berlin):

During the investigation of his background, subject has repeatedly given wrong information concerning his past activities and maintained in his Military Government *Fragebogen* that he was only an applicant to the NSDAP although documentary evidence from the *Reichskulturkammer* show that the subject has been a full-fledged member of the Party. Subject must be considered an opportunist of the worst order who has no convictions whatsoever and does not hesitate to use any method available in order to make himself acceptable to whatever persons are in power at a given time. Files of this division contain proof that subject person handed names of his competitors over to the Gestapo in order to assure his own position. Subject person has consistently refused to face a German Denazification Tribunal in Bavaria although his case should have been tried in Munich under the provisions of the Law for the Liberation from National Socialism and Militarism. Subject person was therefore declared unacceptable for any position in the Information Media Field during the time that Military Government exercised control over such position.

We shall hear more of this "opportunist of the worst order" again before long. The fourth and final member of this quartet of ex-Nazis was a 42-year-old Berlin-born SS man by the name of Helmut Groeger. Groeger had traveled in the United States before the war, and spoke fluent English (and French). He joined the SS in 1932, rose to the rank of sergeant, and in 1934 served as a construction official in the German occupation government of Lithuania, one of the Baltic states which had previously been annexed by the Soviet Union. In the summer of 1944, just before the start of the Soviet offensive, Groeger formed a special unit for the construction of houses and other buildings and allowed many Lithuanians to register as volunteers in this unit. The panic caused by the Red Army advance led many more Lithuanians to register with Groeger's unit in order to escape a second Soviet reign of terror and flee to the Reich with the retreating Germans. When Groeger's unit came to rest in Austria, Groeger himself turned the adverse military situation to a profitable personal advantage by selling releases to Lithuanian workers for a bribe of 1,000 marks at a time. When the Austrian front in its turn collapsed, Groeger fled with his money and his wife to Rottach on the Tegernsee where, soon after the end of the war, he was employed for a time as the manager of an American recreational center.

Not long afterwards Groeger was stopped at a checkpoint by an officer of the Texas Division, Third U.S. Army; and when it was discovered that he spoke fluent English he was commandeered to serve as an interpreter for Third Army, Bad Tölz. By the end of June 1945, Helmut Groeger was working in this capacity for the Commanding Officer of the 512th Military Police Battalion. This was the same outfit for which Helmut Schreiber worked as interpreter. But whereas Schreiber was employed in Munich, Groeger was employed at Bad Tölz. He was thus very close to the heart of Third Army and it was he who was chosen to act as Rauch's ultimate contact with the Americans.

Shortly after Captain Neuhauser gave himself up to the Americans, Colonel Rauch set in motion the elaborate process of turning himself in — though unlike Neuhauser, this much more subtle character made sure he would do so only on conditions that would be favorable to him. On or after 23 June, Rauch gave the word to his friend Karl Warth, who passed the word on to Helmut Schreiber, who passed it on to Helmut Groeger, who passed it on to 2nd Lieutenant James F. Niederpreum of B Company, 512th Military Police Battalion in Bad Tölz, who passed it on to Lieutenant Jack Murphy, who passed it on to his Company Commander Captain Russell C. Rockwell, who on 27 June finally passed it on to *his* Commanding Officer, Major Robert M. Allgeier, at the end of the chain. In his report on the incident written a few days later, Major Allgeier described the scenario which Rauch had contrived:

Captain Rockwell came to me with a report to the effect that Groeger was in contact with German civilians who knew the location, within 100 miles south of Munich, of a buried cache of gold and currency reserve, quantity unknown. These civilians desired certain favors in return. They were informed that this could be taken up with proper authorities later. Groeger requested transportation and escort to bring back proof of existence of the cache and an inventory of same. Desiring such proof, I arranged for the request to be granted. It was my intention to place the evidence, if available, in the hands of the proper authorities for recovery.

During the course of the day the four members of the German chain were rounded up. At his interrogation Rauch was asked why he had not reported to the U.S. authorities about the Reichsbank treasure sooner. His reply was duly noted down by his interrogator, Major Lionel C. Perera, Chief of Military Government Finance Office at Third Army:

He declared that he had considered it for some time and was waiting for the political situation to clear, and, also, he wished to turn it over to the proper authorities without endangering his own position. Further questioning revealed that Rauch wished to relieve himself of responsibility in the matter, to preserve the treasure for the German government, and to provide funds in the event of conflict with Russia. Rauch wishes to record that he was only a middleman obeying the orders of higher authority, that he was not responsible for the allocation of the treasure, and was not a party to plans to use these resources to fight the Russians.

That same night Rauch and his associates were sent off on an extraordinary expedition. Accompanied only by two American guards and with no officers present, the four Germans—Hitler's former policeman, his one-time magician, an ex-member of the Führungshauptamt of the SS, and a notorious racketeer, each and every one of them a candidate for immediate arrest for one reason or another—were taken to Garmisch-Partenkirchen and there waited while Colonel Rauch drove to the Walchensee by himself in a civilian car to carry out an investigation of the remaining gold and currency caches. It was a bizarre situation and one in which the American authorities were undoubteadly at fault. For here was a prominent member of the SS, aide-de-camp to one of the top twenty Nazis of the Third Reich, a man close to Adolf Hitler and responsible for the Führer's personal secur-ity, driving a civilian car to an area where, at his instigation, millions and millions of dollars worth of treasure had been buried, while the only two American guards were waiting in a town some twenty miles away. Rauch should have been under arrest and in a prisoner-of-war enclosure. Instead he was rummaging around alone in the woods under cover of darkness, among bags and boxes whose contents were so valuable that only a single one, conveniently mislaid anywhere Rauch cared to choose, would have set a man up for life. As it was, the contents of the caches were already con-siderably depleted, of course, because of the currency was dug up by him-self and Pfeiffer in May and reburied in the von Blüchers' garden and on Klaus Bremme's farm.

According to Rauch's subsequent interrogation report, he visited all six gold and currency caches known to exist on the mountains above Wal-chensee during the night of 27 June. "He found that two of the gold caches had been uncovered and the gold removed," the report stated; "that the smallest cache remained untouched; and that there was no sign of interfer-ence with the caches of foreign paper currency. Rauch then dug up one of the caches of paper currency, loaded it into his car, and returned with it to Garmisch-Partenkirchen."

Dawn had not yet broken over the sharp ridges of the surrounding mountains as Rauch drove his cargo of currency bags to Helmut Schrei-ber's house in Garmisch. It was barely light when Major Allgeier was called to the house by Lieutenant Niederpreum around 5 o'clock on 28 June. Rauch does not appear to have been at the house when Allgeier ar-rived, but Groeger was there with Schreiber and they had in their posses-sion 23 bags of currency which they had already opened in order to check the contents. Some of the bags had been sealed, others merely tied loosely with string. All the bags were immediately placed under guard at the Schreiber house.

For some unknown reason Groeger and Schreiber now claimed that it was they who had recovered the currency, and they gave Allgeier an account of the state of the caches which was in direct contradiction of the one which Rauch was to make in his interrogation report. Rauch was to claim that there was no sign of interference with the currency caches, which was nonsense — as he, of all people, well knew. Schreiber and Groeger not only provided more accurate descriptions but a conveniently misleading explaination as well. "Civilians Groeger and Schreiber," wrote Major Allgeier in his report on the incident to the Third Army Provost Marshal, "informed me that they had brought back as much as possible because some of the cache had already been hauled away and urged that immediate action be taken before the balance disappeared. They assumed the 'partisans' in the hills were moving the cache to another location. They further stated that to the best of their knowledge there were twenty 110-pound boxes of gold bullion and an unknown quantity of bags of currency. Some gold bullion and currency bags had already been removed."

The young major now made a decision that almost blighted his career as a professional soldier. Instead of going through the usual channels of command, Allgeier took on himself the responsibility of securing the caches and guarding against possible "partisan" activity while on the mission. "I was chagrined at my poor decision," he was to admit years later. "My Adjutant, carelessly or on purpose, had failed to circulate to me a Third Army directive expressly forbidding unit commanders from taking action to recover such funds except in cases of extreme emergency. Otherwise information was to be passed to the nearest Military Government Unit for further action." If Major Allgeier was going to take things into his own hands, he might have saved himself some future embarrassment if he had at least gone out on a single mission under his own command to complete the recovery, instead of first sending out a verification party under the command of his subordinates. "That would have saved me many interrogations in the days that followed," he said ruefully later. "Generals Patton and Gay were kind enough to overlook any possible transgression on my part. The CIC and the FBI were not quite so generous."

While Captain Rockwell — a rancher and miner in civilian life, and a loner who "never wanted to see or hear of war or soldiers again in his lifetime" — and a squad of soldiers from the 512th MP Battalion were sent up the mountain with Colonel Rauch as guide on the morning of 28 June to check the state of the caches for themselves, Major Allgeier was hauled in front of Patton's veteran Chief of Staff, General Hobert ("Hap") Gay, and asked to explain the reasons why he had not gone through channels. "I hope you realize, Major," Gay reprimanded him, "that your procedure was quite *unusual*, to say the least. What you should have done was to go yourself, Major, inventory this currency right where it was, and bring it, together with the gold, to this headquarters where it could have been put under heavy guard."

Meanwhile Captain Rockwell and his men had located the remaining gold stash but found only four boxes and two bags of gold, not the 20 boxes they had been led to expect, and the Germans expressed the opinion, based on irrefutable arithmetic but ultimately refutable fact, that sixteen boxes of gold were missing. Rauch then led Captain Rockwell and his men to the two remaining currency caches. These were reported as lying "in the hills south of Walchensee, a little more than six miles east of Highway 11 (the Mittenwald-Walchensee road) and approximately on the Army Corps boundary." If this was true it placed the curency caches not only to the south of the Walchensee but well to the east of it, some considerable distance from the original burial holes on the Steinriegel and Klausenkopf. The exact location will never be known. In his official report Major Allgeier noted that owing to the lack of identification points on the map it was difficult to determine whether the caches had been uncovered in either Corps or Army zone of responsibility. But the caches found by Rockwell were so remote from the original scene of operations that the possibility exists that the currency had been reburied not once but twice and the second burial would have required motor transport to shift so many currency bags so far. At any rate 47 bags and six boxes of foreign currency turned up and the German civilians were again quick to point out that in their view some of the foreign currency was missing too. They were in a good position to know. Major Allgeier was inclined to the same view. "I suspect the two German informants, Schreiber and Groeger, had already secured a portion of the cache for their own use," he wrote later, "before they became frightened and came to Captain Rockwell for protection, turning in the remainder of the cache rather than see others secure a share and involve them if caught." Indeed, when the gold and currency recovered by Captain Rockwell was finally handed in at 8:30 on the evening of 28 June at Foward Echelon Command Post, Third Army, it seemed that as many as 19 currency bags had gone astray, since out of the 89 bags that had been buried in April, only 23 had been recovered by Rauch on the night of 27/28 June and 47 during the course of the following day.

In fact, much to Major Allgeier's acute embarrassment, two more bags of currency had been recovered, but they had been held back and not handed in with the rest of the bags. Allgeier later explained: "Actually one of my better officers and one better noncommissioned officer became greedy and planned to attempt to send the U.S. currency home for personal use. Because of their previous good records and because they came to me and confessed their temptation I chose to minimize the situation, a Commander's obligation to his good soldiers."

Allgeier was forced to add a hurried postscript to his official report and blur the truth for the sake of his men. "Due to loose handling by the civilians, two bags of currency overlooked in the unloading were delivered to Lt. Niederpreum at 0900 hours, 29 June and are in the hands of the Provost Marshal as of 1400 hours, 29 June 1945." It looked bad and it was bad. "That was what got the Investigative Units on my back," Allgeier confessed afterwards. If two of his men had tried to palm a couple of bags, perhaps some of the other missing bags might have disappeared in the same way, too. "I discussed the matter with General Gay," Allgeier recalled, "who then went to the open door to General Patton's adjacent office and related my explanation of the events. Patton told Gay that I was a damned good soldier and was not to be hurt for making an honest error which was the first one I had made in Third Army." Nevertheless, the Major remained under suspicion. "A combination of CIC (Counter-Intelligence Corps) and FBI people interrogated me and other members of the 512th at some length," Allgeier recalled. "The investigation must have been quite thorough since the FBI checked on my financial status regularly every month between 1945 and 1951 — and on my wife's finances and my parents'."

Four boxes and two bags of gold and 49 bags of currency were now stacked under a round-the-clock guard in the office of the third Army Provost Marshal, Colonel Philip C. Clayton, on the third floor of the Flint *Kaserne* at Bad Tölz. Sixteen boxes of gold were allegedly missing, and 17 bags of currency undoubtedly were. The consignment of treasure caused some considerable commotion among the Third Army brass. When the Provost Marshal rang General Gay to tell him that the consignment had been safely gathered in, Gay could not restrain his excitement. According to an account based on General Gay's personal diary, the following dialogue ensued:

"Is *it* there?" he asked Colonel Clayton.

"What do you mean?" replied the Provost Marshal, puzzled by Gay's veiled reference.

"Dammit, Phil, the gold! Have they brought it with them?"

"Well," the Provost Marshal answered, "I really don't know. The currency has been brought over and it's now in my office. And Niederpreum did bring back a number of boxes which are quite heavy. But I don't know what's in them."

"Is the guard heavy?"

"Well," said Clayton, "it depends on what you regard as heavy. I consider it adequate."

"Make sure," General Gay admonished his Provost Marshal tartly, "that your orders to them are also adequate." Gay took the matter of the treasure very seriously in all its ramifications.

"Now listen, Phil, listen carefully," he told Clayton. "The newspaper people must not be notified of this. No leaks, hear me, or you'll be dead! This is an incident that has serious international implications. It's a delicate matter and its got to be handled at the *highest* echelon."*

The following morning General Gay, Colonel Clayton, General Halley G. Maddox (Third Army G-3), and Lieutenant-Colonel John J. Edwards (Provost Executive Officer representing the Finance Officer) went to the room where the gold and currency were being stored. Security was so tight that at first the guard refused to let them in and they had to send for the duty officer of the day to give them security clearances. Once they were in the room Gay asked Edwards to open some of the bags and boxes. Some of the bags contained neatly tied bundles of foreign currency including U.S., British, Swedish, Swiss, and even Turkish banknotes. Two of the bags were so heavy that Colonel Edwards needed someone to help him lift them onto the table. When their necks were untied these bags were found to contain gold coins of 20 Reichsmarks each. Four of the boxes also con-contained gold coins, not the bullion that was expected. "I was unable to estimate the value of this paper money and gold coins," General Gay recorded in his diary. "My rough guess was that it amounted to something over a million bucks."

In fact, the dollar bills alone amounted to $1,261,717 and the gold coins (weighing 258 pounds) to $199,395. Without taking into consideration the nondollar currency, the total value of the bags and boxes brought into the

---

* This was to avoid any repetition of the unfortunate incident which occurred after the discovery of the Merkers treasure. A few days after the contents of the mine had been transferred to Frankfurt, Patton had involved himself in controversy for firing a SHAEF censor over whom he had no jurisdiction whatsoever—allegedly for leaking the story of the Merkers find to the press without his permission. For this, according to Eisenhower's aide, "Ike had taken Patton's hide off." The indident marked the beginning of a deterioration in Patton's relationship with Eisenhower and the decline of his reputation in the highest levels of the American Army.

Provost Marshal's office in the Flint *Kaserne*, Bad Tölz, at the instigation of Colonel Rauch, came to almost one and a half million dollars—a huge sum which today would be worth over eight million dollars.

It was at this point that General Patton was introduced to the haul which had so unexpectedly landed in his headquarters, for the ultimate decision as to what should be done with it fell on his shoulders. According to his Chief of Staff, General Gay, this larger-than-life Army Commander, who had already had the bulk of the Reichsbank reserves fall in his lap in the Merkers mine in early April, approached his second treasure windfall in a typically blunt and forthright manner.

"Okay, Hap," Patton ordered Gay. "Gimme the sta-goddamn-tistics! How much is this hoard worth all told?"

Gay told him what he thought.

"Does the press know about this?" Patton asked.

"No, sir."

"How many people do!"

"Well, sir," said Gay, "Major Allgeier is cognizant, of course, as is Lieutenant Murphy, and Captain Niederpreum, and..."

"Don't ackack, Hap!" barked Patton. "You esti-goddamn-mate, General Gay! *How many people know about this fuckin' hoard?*"

"I'd say a hundred, maybe more."

"You mean the entire Third Army. That's about a hundred too many, Hap. Tell Milliken [Divisional Finance Officer] to pack up this fuckin' find, all of it, and order Conway to send it to Frankfurt, right away. I want the padre to go along to pray all the way that it gets there safely, and Colonel Cheever [Divisional Judge Advocate] should also go to see to it that the receipt we get is legal."

As Gay turned to leave, Patton had another thought.

"And hear this, Hap, I want those civilian bastards handed over to the Criminal Investigation Department, and see to it, Hap, that an investigation is started to find out what happened to the rest of this hoard. I don't want anybody ever to say that sonuvabitch Patton had stole any part of it.

"Peanuts, Hap," grinned Patton as they went out. "A million bucks won't buy thirty seconds of war in the black market."

Nine days later the gold and currency were shipped by Third Army from Bad Tölz to the Foreign Exchange Depository (FED) in Frankfurt. The 72 bags and boxes of foreign currency and the four boxes and two bags of gold coin, revealed by Colonel Rauch, were listed as Shipment 52A. The 20 boxes of gold coin revealed by Captain Neuhauser were listed as Shipment 52B. Third Army had always assumed that both shipments represented parts of the same original German consignment and this is what the Third Army memo accompanying the shipments to Frankfurt suggested: "Documents attached represent available information concerning origin of these shipments. In the opinion of this headquarters, shipments 1 and 2 (52A and 52B) are part of the same cache uncovered by the 10th Armored Division and shipped to you on 10 June." (This referred to the 728 bars recovered on the Steinriegel on 7 June.) However, an examination of this documentation at the FED pointed to a completely different interpretation. On 10 July the Deputy Chief of the Currency Section at the FED sent a memo to the Assistant Director, Financial Division, U.S. Group Control Council, stating that he was unable to find "any indication in the papers supporting the shipment of the 20 boxes that they are connected with the 72 bags and 6 boxes of foreign currency or the 4 boxes and 2 bags of gold coin recovered in the same area."

This was very astute of the FED official, for the 20 boxes of gold coin undoubtedly were *not* connected with the original consignment of Reichsbank gold reserves from Berlin and Munich to Mittenwald. But for various reasons — by accident, or design, or both — those 20 boxes utterly confused the Americans' perception of what they had and had not recovered from the Walchensee hills. And this confusion in turn permitted them to overlook a major shortfall in their gold recoveries from that area.

By July 1945 the FED would undoubtedly have had in their possession the inventory of gold and currency assets prepared by Reichsbank official Mielke at the Forest House, Einsiedl, shortly before their burial by the officers of the Mittenwald Mountain Infantry School. This inventory listed the following ostensibly gold items:

364 bags containing 728 bars of gold
  6 cases of Danish coins
 25 boxes of bullion

Of these items the 728 bars had been recovered on 7 June and safely received intact at the FED shortly afterwards. The six cases of Danish coins recovered on 28 June turned out to contain not Danish coins but Danish currency, which was itemized as such on arrival at the FED. That left 25 boxes of gold bullion, containing four bars to each box, weighing nearly 1.25 tons and worth over $1,400,000 ($20,300,000 today). These 25 boxes of bullion had been described as such when they were taken from the Konstanz Reichsbank on 22 April and added to the main Mittenwald consignment; they had been signed for as such on the receipt given by the scrupulously conscientious Reichsbank official George Netzeband when they were delivered to the Forest House at Einsiedl; they were inventoried as such by Mielke before he returned with his list to Munich; and they were buried as such by the officers from the Mittenwald *Kaserne*. It was these same 25 boxes of gold bullion which *Tiger's Tales* reported to have been made known to the American authorities by a German general in early June.

However, it was not 25 boxes of gold bullion that were recovered from the caches at the end of the month but 20 boxes of gold coin from one cache and four boxes and two bags from another. Though the FED doubted that these two caches were in any way connected, the temptation to balance the books by identifying the 25 boxes of gold bullion on the Reichsbank officials' list with the 24 boxes and two bags of gold coin on the Third Army's list was apparently irresistible. After the 24 boxes and two bags had been received at the FED the contents of the two bags were re-sacked in one bag during processing by bullion experts, thereby producing the figure of 25 containers of gold. Magically, the books now appeared, after a fashion, to balance. The Germans had buried 25 containers of gold and the Americans had recovered 25 containers of gold. No matter that one lot of containers contained coins when they were supposed to contain bars. That could be put down to an error of nomenclature on the part of the banking bureaucracy of the defunct Third Reich. The important thing from the point of view of the Americans' bank ledger was that there were 25 of them. They could thus be said to have been accounted for. But in fact, of course, 25 boxes containing 100 bars of gold bullion were still missing.

That more gold and currency had been buried in the Walchensee hills than was officially acknowledged by the Reichsbank officials and *Wehrmacht* officers responsible seems practically certain. For example, in addition to the 25 boxes of gold bullion delivered to the Forest House by Mielke — which were put on the official Reichsbank inventory — a further 20 boxes were taken there from the Casino by Willi Hormann, but were not put on the inventory. It was in all probability these same 20 boxes which were (according to Neuhauser's testimony) dug up and reburied by a Reichsbank official and an SS officer on the night of 28 April and subsequently recovered by the Americans and found to be full of gold coins.

Moreover, in addition to six boxes officially listed on the Reichsbank inventory as containing Danish gold coins, there were four boxes and two bags which were not listed. Yet it was the latter which contained the gold coins, the former only Danish paper currency, a source of understandable confusion and potential exploitation.

Finally there were the 11 oblong wooden boxes which were delivered to the Forest House from Berchtesgaden, which according to Pfeiffer's driver were so heavy they could only have contained gold (though all he could see when he peeped inside was a layer of wine bottles at the top). These too never appeared on any official inventory and were never heard of again. Did they contain gold, or the weapons and ammunition later found in the caches, or even wine for Funk (who had a drinking problem) when he still planned to find refuge in one of the mountain huts in the area? We shall never know. The point is that the 11 boxes were never listed—but they *did* exist.

As for the paper currency, more U.S. dollars had been picked up by Major Rawley in early June on the Oberau road alone than were listed on the inventory of Reichsbank currency drawn up by Netzeband and Will in the Forest House on the day before the burial. For years afterwards the rumor persisted that *Abwehr*, Brandenburg Division, and other nonaccountable funds and secret assets had been brought down to Mittenwald along with the Reichsbank reserves. It is therefore possible that while Reichsbank assets and holdings appeared on the Reichsbank inventory, other funds did not, because they could not or need not be so registered.

The possibility that the Germans had buried more gold and currency than they had listed in the official Reichsbank inventory does not seem to have crossed the minds of the American fiscal authorities in Germany, or at any rate left no abiding questions. They were extremely persistent in rounding up assets which they knew existed and knew to be missing—as their remorseless hounding of Neuhauser, Pfeiffer, Netzeband, Will, and Rüger had shown. But they were less enthusiastic when it came to sorting out leads to assets whose existence was not definitely proven by documentation or could only be suspected, if not detected, as a result of painstaking cross-referencing of known facts in a high-caliber fiscal intelligence operation.

One handicap for the American finance experts was the absence of a *complete* inventory giving full details of *exactly* what had been hidden. Another was the lack of coordination and exchange of information between the various tactical units and investigataive bodies who were involved in each of the three different recovery operations. Another was a crippling lack of staff at the FED. So grievous was this shortage that the currency recovered from Walchensee (known as Shipment 52A) had to wait a whole year in a corner of the FED vaults before anyone actually got around to counting it. Not until 18 July 1946 was the Head of the Depository Section at the FED, Edwin P. Keller, able to send a progress report to his immediate superior. "The currency in Shipment 52A," he wrote, "includes a considerable amount of U.S. dollars, including many old bills. A one-dollar note of the series 1875 and a silver dollar note of the series 1896 are attached for your information. Count of currency in Shipment 52A is currently in progress (72 bags and six boxes). The section is operating at increasing tempo as additional personnel is gradually secured. Inventory is being confined to currency pending the securing of technical experts on jewelery, precious metals, and precious stones."

Not until March 1947, nearly two years after the Reichsbank currency had first been put in the ground at Walchensee, did the FED wake up to the shock that there was huge discrepancy in the contents of Shipment 52A. This inordinate time gap between digging up the Reichsbank reserves and counting them was to prove a fourth and fatal handicap for the financial authorities in Frankfurt. For it could have enabled certain highly placed persons at a certain strategic point in the financial transmission line to make use of their key position and inside information to plunder parts of the recovered funds at their leisure — and gave them ample time to cover their tracks and throw any bloodhounds off the scent. By the time official investigators began to probe what came to be known as the "gold affair" many of those responsible for the robbery of the Reichsbank reserves (and associated funds) had left the scene and many of the trails had long gone cold.

One thing the Americans *were* sure of, though, even in the summer of 1945 — 17 bags of foreign currency were unaccounted for. Eighty-nine bags had been put in the ground, they knew; but only 72 had been taken out. So where were the missing bags? The brunt of the Americans' not inconsiderable curiosity in this matter fell on the man who had spent the longest time at the currency caches but probably had the least idea of what had ultimately befallen their contents — Hans Neuhauser. Amazingly, Colonel Rauch — whom the Americans *knew* had dug up some of the currency on the night of 28 June — went scot free, even though his Nazi past should have ensured his automatic arrest. The same was true for his associate, Karl Warth, and for Schreiber and Groeger, who had been allowed to handle the currency in the privacy of Schreiber's home in Garmisch in the early hours of 29 June. Did Rauch come to an arrangement with the Americans on behalf of himself and his colleagues? If so, it seems to have been honoured in deed if not in word. Poor Neuhauser was to enjoy no such privilege.

By his own account, Neuhauser was given a rough time by the Allied investigators working on the case, even *after* he had led them to the 20 boxes of gold cached on the mountains. The first of his many interrogations began at Einsiedl. In the Forest House he was confronted by two American officers, Major Clarence A. Brown (Public Safety Officer of the

Munich Military Detachment) and Lieutenant Peter I. Pollack of the
Counter-Intelligence Corps (CIC), alias Wasyl Maldo, Peter Malko, Peter
Lukawskij, and "Pete the Polack." Lieutenant Pollack, an Austrian Jew by
birth, spoke fluent German.

"You were in the HJ, the Hitler Youth!" he accused Neuhauser.

"*Ja.*"

"You were in the SS!"

"*Nein!*"

"*Doch*, you were!"

"*Nein!*"

"You were an officer. You know what will happen to you if you tell lies.
Where is the gold?"

"The Americans took it away," Neuhauser replied, apparently puzzled
that they should ask such a question, since as far as he could see the Americans had located all the gold caches.

"Where is the currency?"

"In the Tyrol." He was going to stick to the agreed cover story — that the
SS had come and taken the stuff farther into the national redoubt.

They left the villa and drove up the Steinriegel to the main gold stash
where the 728 bars had been hidden. The hole was empty, of course. So
was the original currency cache, 220 yards away.

"There, you can see for yourselves," Neuhauser said to the Americans
by way of confirmation. "Can you let me go now?"

Lieutenant Pollack, who took every opportunity to let it be known that
he hated all Germans, gave a noncommittal reply. "Tomorrow," he told
Neuhauser. Tomorrow was to last the better part of two months.

From Walchensee, Hans Neuhauser was driven to Garmisch and
thrown in the police prison, where he was searched and his stomach pills
taken from him in case they were poison. Neuhauser's three-man cell contained 20 inmates, stacked like herrings, under the charge of a former corporal. Here Neuhauser was confined off and on for six weeks.

The following Sunday Neuhauser was taken out for further interrogation by Pollack. This time there was also a colonel and two interpreters
(one of them a woman) present. All the names of the people involved in
the Reichsbank business were read out to him but he remained evasive
and uncooperative, and continued to maintain that the remaining treasure
had been taken into the Tyrol. The investigators were obviously dissatisfied with his answers and returned him to the prison.

Two weeks later he was ordered by an American lieutenant who spoke
fluent German to pack his things and he was then taken from the police

cells in Garmisch to the Post Hotel in Mittenwald, then being used as a Special Incident Interrogation Center. Neuhauser noticed that an English General (Brigadier Waring) of the "Royal Army" was a member of this unit. To Neuhauser he seemed typically English—lean and lanky and with baggy trousers. Remorselessly, day after day, this "general" and his American colleagues, a colonel and a lieutenant, subjected Neuhauser to a ceaseless grilling. He was questined about Lammers. He was confronted with Major Braun and Friedrich Will, all to no avail. He had nothing further to say.

Neuhauser was now taken to the Hotel Ertl and confined in the cellar for two days with nothing to eat and only water to drink and with armed guards outside the door day and night. He was interrogated again, and then taken with the "general" to the Klausenkopf, where he had to wander around pushing a stick into the ground to find any soft spots which might indicate the presence of a treasure cache. "Are you going to run off from here?" the "general" asked him. "*Nein*," Neuhauser replied, and added: "I have shown good will." Needless to say, he was unable to oblige the "general" with any new caches of Reichsbank treasure and the party returned empty-handed to Mittenwald.

After this tough approach at the Hotel Ertl, Neuhauser's interrogators tried the soft touch in the Hotel Wetterstein. This time Neuhauser was confined not in the cellar but in a decent room on the second floor. He was given good food to eat and kept in this cozy environment for two days. It was probably the first comfortable lodging he had known since his convalescent leave at the Forest House had been brusquely interrupted three months before when he was sent up the mountain to keep watch over the Reichsbank reserves. Since then he had slept in the undergrowth, been packed in a prison, and holed up in a cellar. The guest room in the Hotel Wetterstein in Dekan-Karl-Platz was a profound change. He began to feel almost human again. His interrogators clearly hoped that they might catch him off guard. According to Neuhauser, they failed. On the third day he was led before the inquisition again. This time there was a little blonde to translate for him, but her presence made no difference, he still wouldn't talk. The interrogators decided that he was a hopeless case and that he would have to be thrown back in the jail in Garmisch and put back on bread and water again.

For the last time Brigadier Waring, Major Braun, and another CIC officer whom Neuhauser had not seen before tried to break him down. There was really only one thing Neuhauser knew which his interrogators did not: the fate of the missing bags of currency. Almost certainly Neuhauser knew very well that Colonel Pfeiffer and Colonel Rauch had exhumed some of the bags in May and taken them off to hide elsewhere. Indeed, since neither Pfeiffer nor Rauch had been present when the currency had been buried on the Klausenkopf, they could only have found the currency with Neuhauser's help. Neuhauser claims he told his interrogators nothing. But somebody did. For by the beginning of August 1945 a significant change had taken place in the progress of the investigation. Though no more gold was ever found, more currency from the Reichsbank treasure was soon to come to light, and in impressive abundance.

10

The Men from the Villa Ostler

While Hans Neuhauser was being alternately fattened and starved in various prewar holiday hotels in Mittenwald, or left to twiddle his thumbs in unison with 20 other prisoners in the police cells of Garmisch-Partenkirchen, the tireless Brigadier Waring, who was as assiduous as he was courteous, had still not given up the hunt for Colonel Pfeiffer. The dollar pickups on the Oberau road had left many questions unanswered. It was clear that much of the currency and perhaps some of the gold was still missing. Waring was anxious to interview Pfeiffer about this and the American Counter-Intelligence Corps (CIC) lent a hand in the chase.

One day officers from the CIC Detachment Headquarters in Miesbach, near Schliersee, broke into the house of Pfeiffer's mother, a lady in her sixties, ransacked the place, and took her off to be interrogated about her son's movements and any gold or currency he might have brought into the house. When Pfeiffer got to hear of this he drove at high speed up the hill to the CIC headquarters and in a fury banged on the door to protest at his mother's arrest. At first the Americans would not open the door, but simply closed the shutters. So Pfeiffer banged again and this time the CIC men opened up, grabbed Pfeiffer, took away his car keys, and led him off to the cells. But he got no farther than a cell door. At that point he pulled out his trump card—his official accreditation with the French Army. "I told them to check it out with Third Army," he recounted later, "and they let me go again. Next day they released my mother as well."

A more serious confrontation was to come. Some time towards the end of July, when the Tyrol demobilization operation was at its height, Waring tried a ruse. He arrestd three more of Pfeiffer's former officers, and hoped that Pfeiffer, with his deeply ingrained sense of loyalty and responsibility towards his men, would rise like a trout to the fly. Pfeiffer did. With a con-

fidence born of his good status among the French military, Pfeiffer decided
to confront the English brigadier and argue his case for the release of his
men. Through Captain Sauteau of the French Army, he reestablished contact with Captain Neumann of the Third Army, and Captain Neumann
in turn sounded out Brigadier Waring. Not long afterwards Waring arranged a meeting with Pfeiffer in Innsbruck. The discussion centered on
the question of a safe conduct for Pfeiffer into the American Zone and the
release of his officers in return for certain favors. It seems that at least the
safe conduct was promised by Waring—if not actually forthcoming.

Pfeiffer had had no reason to love the British any more than the Americans. To him they were simply two sides of the same coin. He had seen
many of his comrades blown out of the sea by the Royal Navy at Suda Bay
during the Battle of Crete and narrowly escaped death himself at British
hands. But it was perhaps in the serene and beautiful surroundings of
peacetime Garmisch-Partenkirchen that the Colonel's aversion for the
British took a distinct turn for the worse. Not even two world wars had entirely dimmed the stereotype of the English officer and gentleman which
had been so carefully instilled in the German populace for the best part of
the century. In spite of all evidence to the contrary, Colonel Pfeiffer, like
most of his fellow countrymen, still believed that an Englishman's word
was his bond and that fair play was the order of an Englishman's day. As
a former member of the German Officer Corps, Colonel Pfeiffer had a
great respect for the concepts of duty and honor, and expected other officers, even enemy ones, and undoubtedly English ones, to respect the same
virtues. In Innsbruck, Waring had agreed to give Pfeiffer a safe conduct
into the American Zone of Germany. So Pfeiffer's shock when Brigadier
Waring threatened to have him arrested was severe indeed. Even 37 years
later, his outrage when he recalls Waring's perfidiousness and unfair play
is barely restrained.

"General Waring broke his word to me," Pfeiffer was to recall with considerable vehemence. "He had locked up three of my officers, including
my adjutant, in the cellar of his villa in Garmisch. I wanted to explain to
him that the men he had arrested had nothing to do with the gold business
so I went there to get them released. To be on the safe side I asked for a
safe conduct and to make sure I asked Captain Sauteau to come with me."

Waring was at the Villa Ostler, formerly the large and sumptuous residence of the Chief Architect of Bavaria, a Herr Ostler, but now in the
hands of the American intelligence community in Garmisch-Partenkirchen. When Pfeiffer arrived there he walked straight into the trap which
Waring had set for him.

"Waring straightaway began to ask about gold—had I hidden any gold anywhere? Then an American brought in an empty old suitcase which I had left in the Forest House before the gold was buried. I was asked, 'How had that got there?' Then I was asked, 'What about the documents?' The American produced an old map of the Russian campaign I had brought back as a souvenir and which was found in the suitcase. Perhaps they thought it was a map of the gold holes."

Waring, it seemed, was dissatisfied with Pfeiffer's answers under inter-rogation—as well he might be, for at this stage the Allied recoveries from the Reichsbank reserves bore little relationship to the Reichsbank gold and currency inventories in Waring's possession.

"General Waring told me I had to stay, that I was under custodial ar-rest," Pfeiffer continued. "This was in complete breach of his agreement not to arrest me. Captain Sauteau was so angry when he heard him say this that he took his revolver from its holster and threw it into the corner of the room. He demanded that if I was going to be arrested then he should be arrested as well, and then he demanded to be put in touch with Third Army so that he could lodge a protest."

Colonel Pfeiffer was clearly under considerable pressure at this junc-ture. The Special Interrogation Unit at long last had this elusive figure in their grasp after three months of searching for him. They were unlikely to let him go again before they had wrung from him every drop of informa-tion he possessed about the fate of the missing Reichsbank treasure. It is true that Pfeiffer had already led the Americans to a substantial hoard of dollars along the Oberau road in early June. But the investigators knew that a great deal more was still unaccounted for—Rauch's testimony alone was sufficient to indicate that. It was therefore necessary to threaten Pfeif-fer in order to force him to cooperate a second time. That is why Waring and his team refused to release Pfeiffer's fellow officers and threatened to imprison Pfeiffer himself. Pfeiffer was to complain that this was a breach of Waring's word of honor. He obviously did not sufficiently appreciate the power of life and death which the Allied authorities then possessed over the citizens of occupied Germany and in particular over the former officers of the *Wehrmacht*. And he clearly overestimated the extent to which he, a Ger-man colonel, could hold out against the representatives of victorious armies who had almost limitless freedom to do almost anything they liked with him.

"I suffered a lot of disappointment in human beings as a result of all those events to do with the Reichsbank treasure," Colonel Pfeiffer was to complain later. "The whole thing is *ein bischen peinlich*—it hurts me to think about it." For all his French passes and American *laissez-passers* the German colonel was completely at the mercy of the Allied investigators.

One eyewitness has left an account of a final meeting at the Villa Ostler which provides a clue to the outcome of Pfeiffer's uncomfortable encounter with Waring. This eyewitness was one of Pfeiffer's former brother officers from the Gebirgsjäger, Captain Hans Neuhauser.

Hans Neuhauser, it will be remembered, had been incarcerated in the police cells at Garmisch after prolonged interrogation at the hands of the special investigators. Then, six weeks after he had given himself up to the Americans—which would make it about 7 August if his calculations were correct—Neuhauser was hauled from the cells for the last time by the little blonde interpreter he had met at a previous interrogation in Mittenwald.

"Wohin jetzt?" Neuhauser asked her as he emerged blinking and down-at-heel into the streets of Garmisch. "Where to now?"

"You'll soon see," snapped the little blonde.

Together they drove to the prison of the *Amtsgericht* (the District Court) where they collected Colonel Pfeiffer's former second-in-command, Major Rupert Braun (who had been in U.S. Army custody ever since May on account of his participation in the Reichsbank treasure burial). Then they continued on to the Villa Ostler.

In a room of this large and well-appointed residence were gathered all the old familiar faces. Besides Neuhauser and Braun there was Colonel Pfeiffer—looking very prosperous, Neuhauser thought, and boasting a car—along with his adjutant, and the mysterious Colonel Rauch, the scraggy English "general" (Waring), the *"Ami-Oberst"* (the American colonel), Peter the Polack of the Counter-Intelligence Corps (CIC), an interpreter, and others. It was clear to Neuhauser that this was not to be another interrogation. Something had happened since he had been thrown into the cells the last time. The confrontation over the Reichsbank business appeared to have been resolved in some way. Colonel Pfeiffer, sitting hatless with the light gleaming on his broad, balding head, acted as spokesman on the German side. He explained that the gold and currency had been handed over to the Americans and that in return the Americans had agreed to treat all the men who had been up on the Klausenkopf and were at present in custody as prisoners of war and not werewolves, and to set all the people involved in the Reichsbank affair free.

In other words, Pfeiffer had made a deal.

When Colonel Pfeiffer had accompanied Major Rawley on the search for dollar caches along the road between Garmisch and Oberau in early June he had been careful not to lead the Americans to the large caches at each end of the road, one at Klaus Bremme's farm in Oberau and the other at the von Blücher house in Garmisch-Partenkirchen. For two months Pfeiffer managed to preserve both the anonymity of his friends and colleagues and the security of the Reichsbank foreign exchange which he had placed, in a manner of speaking, in their charge. But the Villa Ostler meeting had changed all that. Under the pressure of the simple equation which the Brigadier had presented to him — tell all or endure indeterminate confinement — Pfeiffer had cracked.

Colonel Pfeiffer has always maintained that his knowledge of the Reichsbank treasure was very limited. He claims that he never knew the contents of all the boxes and bags of gold, currency, and (possibly) jewels that were brought to his Mountain Infantry School from Berlin and that for this reason he never signed an official receipt for them. He also claims that he never knew exactly where the treasure was buried and that he left this side of things to his subordinate officers while he busied himself with the more pressing matter of defending his section of the Alpine redoubt against the rapidly advancing Americans. All this is very possibly true. It is more than likely that the only treasure cache whose whereabouts was personally known to him was the one whose contents he helped to carry to Gsteigstrasse when he was staying at Mathias Stinnes' house in May. At any event, it was the remainder of this currency which Pfeiffer chose to reveal to Waring and the Americans at the beginning of August 1945, a few days before the final meeting at the Villa Ostler which was attended by Captain Neuhauser.

When the time came for Pfeiffer to point a finger, he pointed it unerringly and unequivocally in the dirction of 38 Gsteigstrasse and the two enterprising young men who dwelt there, Captain Lüder and Hubert von Blücher. So it was on 1 August 1945 that, in the army parlance of the time, the balloon went up — or as Mathias Stinnes preferred to put it, the bomb went off. "Colonel Pfeiffer, I was told, had gone to the CIC and told them everything," Stinnes wrote later. "He had been questioned and ordered to hand the money over."

Pfeiffer's denunciation produced a shock wave that stretched all the way from Garmisch to Oberau. The repercussions at Haus Hohe Halde were dramatic, in retrospect even comic opera. Lüder von Blücher was so incensed with Colonel Pfeiffer that he threatened he would "punch him on the nose if he ever met him in the street." Hubert von Blücher remembered the events of 1 August vividly:

A very funny thing happened. A jeep arrived and stopped in front of our house.

We were already occupied by the Americans. A General Baer was our house guest, everything was marvellous. (A lot of American brass were there later— General Truscott, General Patton from Bad Tölz, General Bradley on an inspection—they just came to see Baer, but they sat around our fireplace, it was very interesting.) Well, the jeep stopped. We had a splendid wooden entrance gateway to our property, and I was accustomed to people ringing the bell when they came to the house, or making some kind of noise—I would have understood if they had loosed off a few rounds, Texas-style, and we would have opened the gate. But what happened was that a tank rolled up off the roadway and simply overran and flattened our lovely wooden gateway, a completely senseless operation. And this made me angry. Nothing else had made me angry, not even the fact that we had lost the war; but that a beautiful handcarved wooden gateway that was centuries old should simply be mowed down by a tank just for the fun of it, that made me very mad. Then all the men from the jeep appeared at the house. To start with, they brought in an electric power plant. For me that was utterly incomprehensible, because of course we had electricity on the mains. They brought in their infrastructure, a generator, before they had asked a simple question. They didn't even know they would be staying and they brought a generator. Typical U.S. Army.

And then a second jeep turned up. In it was an English colonel from the Treasury in London [Brigadier Waring]. He was a sort of emergency colonel who had only just put on a uniform. A highly cultivated man with perfect manners. We had no problem as we found we had mutual acquaintances.

To Hubert von Blücher it seemed that Waring and his colleagues knew all there was to know about the Reichsbank shipment. This was still some way from the truth, but they knew enough to impress the youthful Hubert, for they had been working on the case for nearly three months now and had the advantage of Colonel Pfeiffer's most recent confession.

They knew everything [Hubert continued]. It was exactly what I had foreseen. When Berlin was captured the entire documentation was found in the Reichsbank, all neatly drawn up by an orderly German bookkeeper: how many lorries had been loaded, their registration numbers, names of the people who had taken over the stuff, in which direction, and with what destination they had left Berlin, the progress reports on the journey, what the weight of the load was, and how it was packed. Everything very correctly noted. This nice Englishman had all the documents with him. It was the simplest thing in the world to follow up.

Brigadier Waring naturally insisted on total cooperation from the von Blücher brothers and their associates. He knew all about the foreign exchange reburied at Oberau and in the garden of their house and he insisted on their help to locate the various caches and to dig them up. For reasons of secrecy the recovery would have to be carried out under cover of darkness, the sooner the better—he could see no reason for delaying beyond the coming night. Any information the brothers could give him to facilitate his investigation would count in their favor. Lüder gave Waring a military map of the locality with the caches marked on it—probably those which Pfeiffer had shown to the Americans along the Oberau road in June. Everyone was very nervous and tense.

Present throughout Waring's discussion with the von Blüchers was an American intelligence captain who had become closely connected with Waring's team and had been instrumental in bringing Colonel Pfeiffer to Garmisch to help with the investigation over the last few days. This was Captain Fred S. Neumann (a German name pronounced in the English way—Newman), Patton's interpreter and a member of the Third Army CIB (Counter-Intelligence Branch). In all previous efforts to unravel the mystery surrounding the Reichsbank affair, including those conducted by the FBI, the Criminal Investigation Division and the U.S. Army's own investigative intelligence units, the name of Captain Neumann has always loomed very large in the list of people suspected of complicity in the theft of large quantities of Reichsbank/U.S. government funds and other crimes. Indeed, he is the only suspect who was actively investigated for suspected misappropriation of funds—in other words, the robbery of part of the Reichsbank treasure. Some people believed that he had simply got away with it, others that he did not actually exist and that the name Neumann was a pseudonym for someone else who was never identified. In fact, Neumann *did* exist, though he exists no more. He *was* closely involved with a large portion of the Reichsbank treasure which *did* vanish and *was* stolen—to be exact, the portion dug up in the von Blüchers' garden—and the investigation into the extent of his complicity eventually extended all the way from southern Bavaria to the western seaboard of the United States. So who was this Captain Neumann, chatting volubly in perfect German in von Blücher's parlor that frantic August morning, and what was he really about?

Frederick Siegfried Neumann was a German Jew by origin and an American citizen by adoption. Born in Hersfeld, Germany, in January 1912, he had emigrated to the United States in 1930, was naturalized in 1937, and married an American girl in 1942. When he was 31 he was commissioned as a lieutenant in the U.S. Army Field Artillery and at the end of 1943 was interviewed by Military Intelligence with a view to a transfer to some other branch of the Service in which his knowledge of Germany and the German language could be better utilized. The intelligence officer who interviewed him at Camp Shelby, Mississippi, afterwards wrote this assessment of Neumann:

Subject made an excellent impression on this officer because of his intelligence and education. He is healthy-looking, serious, well mannered and philosophical, and earnestly desires to be transferred to MIS, Office of Strategic Services, or any other branch of the service where his knowledge of the European terrain and the German language can be quickly used. He is willing to volunteer for any type of assignment, no matter how dangerous it may be.

Neumann was accepted for intelligence work. He served for a period as a Prisoner-of-War Interrogation Officer, obtained a "Secret" clearance with Sixth Army, and from D-Day to the end of September 1945 served with Third Army as a special counter-intelligence officer, though his principal duty was interpreter for the Third Army Commander, General Patton. Three weeks before his arrival at the Haus Hohe Halde in Garmisch his immediate superior, Colonel Oscar W. Koch, Patton's intelligence chief, had given him an efficiency rating of 5.7 out of 7 (numerical rating) and "superior" (the maximum adjectival rating) in his periodic Efficency Report, and made this overall assessment of him:

Officer is well suited for interrogation of high-ranking prisoners of war, in which endeavor he has obtained good results. An able, conscientious officer capable of independent action in his specialized field.

Captain Neumann made a remarkable impression on the observant Hubert von Blücher.

He went about everywhere with a dog whip [von Blücher recalled]. And at this time he had no dog. I think he carried it because he had inner neurotic fears. It was nothing like a normal officer's cane. It was a plaited whip which had a sort of psycho association with it. Very remarkable indeed. He also had two pistols and was generally excessively armed.

I could tell at once that he was, how shall I say, quite clearly a Jew. One can't say Israeli, because Israel didn't exist at that time. I would say he was a classic Jew. I don't mean in his outward appearance. I mean intellectually. Highly intelligent, a very gentle man, a very educated man, athletically intellectual, a gentle intellectual. And he was an Israeli even then in the sense that he was a man with ideas of a Jewish state.

One evening he came to see us, privately. All of us were there — me, my brother, Klaus Bremme, and Mathias Stinnes. We talked a lot about various religious persuasions and very soon the conversation got a lot more relaxed. And now we come to the only story I have never told anyone in all these thirty or forty years since it happened. That is why I asked Mr. Löwernstern, my legal representative, to be present and to record the whole conversation on tape. Captain Neumann had an idea for which he tried to gain my support. He said that so much injustice had been done to the Jewish people that they were going to be given their own Jewish state in Palestine. His idea was to send the Reichsbank money in our garden in

The Forest House at Einsiedl overlooking the Walchensee, today. The Reichsbank reserves were stored in the stable, then carried on mules up the Steinriegel, the timber-clad hill at the back, where they were buried.

A tree stump which marked one of the secret treasure caches on the mountains overlooking the Walchensee.

The main gold hole on the Steinriegel as it was in 1974, nearly 30 years after nine tons of Nazi gold (worth $145,000,000 today) were buried here by Colonel Pfeiffer's men at the end of World War Two.

7 June 1945. Officers from the 10th Armored Division which retrieved 728 bars of Reichsbank gold from the Steinriegel cache pose for a shapshot carrying a $15,000 bar apiece. From left to right: Major William Geiler (Divisional Engineer in command of the retrieval), Captain George Garwood (Company Commander from the 55th Armored Engineering Battalion which supplied the work detail) and Captain Walter Dee (Divisional Intelligence Officer).

On the forestry track beside the gold hole: the American soldiers who dug up the gold with their local German guides – Josef Pinzl, pig-keeper from Mittenwald (back row, extreme right), and Josef Veit, poacher turned gamekeeper, who knew the neighbouring mountains (middle row, extreme right).

Three ex-officers of the former German Army recover weapons from the bunker in the mountains outside Mittenwald where a large bullion cache ('Singleton's gold') was recovered earlier on the same 'damned hot day' in July 1945.

Shortly after the gold had been driven off, never to be seen again, Sgt Singleton photographed the three German officers bringing the weapons down the mountainside from the gold bunker.

Top: Hitler's Chancellery Secretary, Hans-Heinrich Lammers, who passed on to the Führer the plan of his adjutant, Fritz Rauch, to hide the Reichsbank treasure in the Bavarian Alps.

Two Nazis who helped Friedrich Rauch dig up the Reichsbank currency. *Right*: Helmut Groeger in wartime SS uniform. *Below*: Helmut Schreiber as Kalanag the Magician in a postwar London theatre programme. Both worked as interpreters for American Military Police at the time of the currency pick-up. Only Groeger was ever investigated for illegal possession of foreign currency suspected to have been stolen.

Garmisch as a donation towards this new State. He said that nothing would be more just than that this money should be used to build up this new State. It was all to be done on a grand scale. A flying boat from the International Red Cross in Switzerland was to land on Lake Walchen and from there fly with the money to Palestine where it could be handed over to the Zionist leaders.

In a sort of way we found it no bad solution, though not a very practicable one. What the International Red Cross had to do with the foundation of Israel I simply could not comprehend. But the scheme appealed to my young mind. I considered it a productive new start. My brother was quite different from me. His reaction was, "Let's get rid of the stuff, we must start to build up again, get the factories working." He was impatient. But I was not at all interested in what you might call the Bavarian solution.

It never occurred to me for a second that Neumann might perhaps have put up this idea in order to keep the money for himself. The last six months had been so filled with realities that were so utterly improbable that there was really nothing improbable left that could happen. Personal property meant survival. But capital, the idea of financial capital as a concept when everything in our world had been lost, or disappeared, simply had no meaning any more.

Looking back, Neumann's scheme was probably intended as the right sort of medicine for us "Prussians" — a sort of foretaste of what was to come. There was a lot of Jewish *Schmonzes* [bullshit] about it. But it was very persuasive at that time — we were all starved for anything that had any real meaning.

Neumann's alleged scheme was, of course, fantastical. But it was, perhaps, a typical product of the peculiar circumstances of that time. The captain's first priority, however, was to help see to it that the treasure was actually got out of the ground — what was to be done with it was another matter. So, on the very first night after the meeting at 38 Gsteigstrasse, as soon as the late-setting summer sun had gone down behind the high peaks, the treasure retrieval operation swung into action.

During the night of 1/2 August a squad of American soldiers of the 10th Armored Division, accompanied by Hubert von Blücher, raided Klaus Bremme's farm, Gut Buchwies, at Oberau where he and his brother had buried a cache of dollars from the Klausenkopf currency stash in May. More than two months had passed since then and to Hubert's acute embarrassment he now found that in the darkness of the night he was unable to identify the particular haybarn in which the dollars had been concealed.

The grotesqueness of the situation only struck me when I came to dig the stuff up [Hubert recalled]. There were six haybarns in the vicinity and I didn't know in which one the stuff was buried. I searched for a long time but I could see the hopelessness of the situation. To make matters worse I had what you could call a whole opera cast with me — CIC, CCC, CIO, COP, and heaven knows what else, plus a couple of Englishmen from the Treasury and a couple of Frenchmen from the

Sûreté. Since it was filthy cold weather, cold and rainy, I could not make too heavy demands on everybody's patience, so I suggested they should fetch my brother, who was sitting at home upstairs practicing getting his fingers working again. My brother knew where it was; he had been given a better description than I had and as an infantryman he knew better how to pinpoint things on the ground —tree here, house there, and so on. So he came and joined up with me and I asked him, "Listen, where is all the stuff? and he told us, "It must be here, and here—now, if we take a bearing…" And so we found it.

The Americans tore the hut down and beneath the floorboards discovered a cache of wooden boxes containing a total of $400,000 in dollar bills (worth $2,200,000 now). From Oberau the money was transported to the Divisional Headquarters in Garmisch, where it was turned over to Captain Noel Hinrichs and Captain James H. Knight for processing and delivery to the "proper authorities" (as they were euphemistically called). The event was considered sufficiently noteworthy for an official photographer to be sent to record the scene. The resulting photograph reveals the two officers and a sergeant checking through piles of dollar bills stacked by denominations on an ordinary kitchen table in an extremely untidy room. In the background are two big steel safes, one surmounted by a tin hat, the other by a cheap alarm clock pointing to ten to one. Outside it is still dark and the streets of Garmisch are unlit. A week later an official acknowledgement of the retrieval was contained in a Third Army Secret Intelligence Report. Yet in spite of the official photograph and the official report, the $400,000 recovered from Klaus Bremme's farm never did reach the "proper authorities." Nor did most of the other foreign exchange recovered during the days that followed in the region of Garmisch-Partenkirchen.

The first that Klaus Bremme knew about the midnight raid on his farm was the sudden appearance of Brigadier Waring and friends on his doorstep during the course of the morning. Waring, whom Bremme remembered only as a "British general," brought with him another officer in British uniform, the little blonde interpreter who had helped interrogate Neuhauser, and a military map of the locality which had been taken from Lüder von Blücher the day before. Waring believed that certain spots marked on this map had some special significance to do with the Reichsbank treasure but wanted to check with Bremme whether they perhaps had some other meaning which he did not know about. In a letter written from Buenos Aires in 1956, Klaus Bremme recalled his encounter with the indefatigable "General" Waring very clearly:

The general stayed for about two hours, while we had a most interesting talk. Evidently he wanted to collect impressions of people who had lived through the war on the other side. I still remember that, while the woman officer was very short tempered and anti-German, the General calmed her down on various occasions and continued the conversation in a very gentlemanly way. I do want to make a special mention of this, because I never met another Allied officer who behaved in such a fine and straight way as this general, whose name I unfortunately do not remember.

The same afternoon, after Waring and his team had left, Bremme bicycled over to the von Blücher house in Garmisch. There he was informed that the American CIC knew all about the Reichsbank consignment and about the dollars hidden by the von Blüchers in Gsteigstrasse and Oberau, and they had come and collected it all. In fact, the Americans had not collected all of it, only a part. What happened was this. At four or five in the morning of 2 August, only a few hours after they had led the Americans to the currency cache at Oberau, the von Blücher brothers took Captain Neumann into the garden at 38 Gsteigstrasse and showed him the tomato bed where back in May they had hidden a guttapercha bag full of dollars.

It was still dark and the brothers were obliged to disinter the money by the light of candles — batteries for flashlights were then unobtainable. "It was just as if you were digging up an Easter egg you had buried in the yard for your son," Hubert recalled. "There was hardly any earth covering it. A few scrapes with the spade and there it was. Captain Neumann picked it up and carried it into the house and into the room where the fireplace was. Six of our Silesian relatives were sleeping on the floor there. Captain Neumann placed the bag in front of the fire and said he would have it picked up by the Military Police the next day." Next morning two jeeps, with four MPs in the first one and Captain Neumann in the second, came and fetched the money.

This first recovery from 38 Gsteigstrasse is officially documented in the Garmisch-Partenkirchen Military Government Annual Report (for the year ending June 1946) prepared by the then Military Governor, Major Melvin Nitz, as follows:

On Friday, 3 August 1945 the 10th Armored Division reported the finding of a bag containing U.S. $251,374 in currency, which bag was handed to this detachment by which it was transferred to Detachment F1H2 at Munich. These funds had been brought into the Landkreis by the former German Army. [This recovery at Garmisch was actually on the same day as the Oberau recovery — 2 August. The report of the recovery was made on 3 August, as stated.]

A few days later another bag, containing about $50,000 was found in the von Blüchers' garden and similarly transferred to the Military Government Detachment in Munich. But panic set in when Captain Neumann later returned to the house and claimed that the dollars so far recovered —

totalling over $1,650,000 by today's values — still fell short of the stipulated target and that the von Blücher brothers would be given a few days' grace to find the missing money, failing which they would be arrested and sent to prison.

The most fantastic search of the von Blücher garden then started [recalled Klaus Bremme, who had been asked by the von Blüchers to help in the search for the missing dollars]. Neither of them could remember where in the world they had hidden all the dollars in pots and cases, and after a whole day of fruitless searching we decided to dig systematically, yard by yard, right across the garden. And so, from morning till night, we continued for a few days and found a few pots. But still some money was missing. Then, at last, there came a day when one of the von Blüchers found yet another pot crammed full of 100-dollar bills, and the whole missing sum came together.

The total money found during those days was kept in a room in the von Blücher villa, where all three of us slept in order to keep guard over it. I was astonished that the CIC Captain Neumann did not put any armed guards at the villa or over the von Blüchers, as anyone could easily have disappeared with all the money.

Bremme's surprise is understandable. That the Americans should have left the recovery of the currency to a bunch of former SS or *Wehrmacht* men over an extended period of time without imposing a round-the-clock guard was quite extraordinary, especially considering that every one of the Germans was palpably suspect of an indictable offence under occupation law — the illegal possession of a foreign currency — for which they should now have been under arrest. Yet they were allowed to continue on in their own haphazard, unsupervised way, while Captain Neumann visited the villa from time to time to check how the recovery operation was progressing.

By 23 August 1945 enough pots and pickling jars of dollars had been found in the von Blücher garden to make a presentable total to give to Captain Neumann. The next day he came to collect them. August 24 was a red-letter day in the story of the Reichsbank treasure. On that day the principal German confederates (Colonel Franz Pfeiffer, Colonel Fritz Rauch, Captain Lüder von Blücher, Hubert von Blücher, Mathias Stinnes, and Klaus Bremme) assembled under the same roof — the steep-pitched Bavarian chalet roof of Haus Hohe Halde — with one of the principal Allied investigators and a great pile of American dollars ($104,956 to be precise, worth $577,258 today) on the table between them. On that day, too, these same seven men produced the only document detailing a Reichsbank treasure transaction ever to come to light — a receipt, hastily and badly typed on a piece of flimsy paper, for the total amount recovered from the von Blüchers' garden, and bearing the signatures of four of the men present. This receipt was to become a famous document in the story of the Reichsbank robbery. It was the one piece of evidence which gave the names, a sum, and a date to a quantity of foreign exchange, formerly belonging to the Deutsche Reichsbank and now the property of the United States government, which could be proved to have disappeared. It was the one firm starting point for every paper-chase investigation — military, governmental, or journalistic — that set off, in the years that followed, in the illusory hope of solving the unsolved mystery of the great Reichsbank robbery. The receipt (typing errors included) read:

24% August 145

TO WHOM IT MAY CONCERN

Lüder von BLUECHER and Hubert von BLUECHER have turned over to the U.S. Army the following sums of money entrusted to them by Colonel Franz PFEIFFER, former Commandant of the Gebirgsjagerschule Mittenwald Germany. This constitutes the entire amount originally entrusted into them.

$404,840.00
405.00   English Pounds

The undersigned acknoledges the receipt of the above stated amount.
(Signature)
FRED S. NEUMANN

Capt FA CIB
THIRD UNITED STATES ARMY

Signatures of witnesses present during the transaction appear below.

Signatures of witnesses:

FRANZ PFEIFFER   (Signature)
FRITZ RAUCH   (Signature)
CLAUS BREMME   (Signature)

It seems fairly likely that this receipt was typed at the last minute on the von Blüchers' typewriter in the von Blüchers' house — probably at the insistence of Colonel Pfeiffer to protect his own interests and those of his associates. Otherwise the document would have been typed on official Third Army notepaper and the spelling mistakes would have been corrected. Indeed, it is such a sloppy document, and its command of English so imperfect, that some have cast doubt on its authenticity and claimed it was

178   NAZI GOLD

forged by the Germans present to cover themselves against any possible
criminal charges in the future. Some have even doubted the existence of
Captain Neumann himself. It was a common custom in the early free-
wheeling days of the American occupation for U.S. officers to sign receipts
for valuables handed over by German subjects with fictitious names, many
of them as outrageously implausible as Paul Revere, Davy Crockett,
Mickey Rooney, and Robert E. Lee. Captain Neumann, it was believed,
was a similar such pseudonym of convenience, concocted to disguise the
signatory's real identity and give the officer in question a chance to get
away with a little opportunist embezzlement.

Colonel Pfeiffer never doubted the existence of Captain Neumann, of
course, but he has always looked rather blank when confronted with a
copy of the Neumann receipt. Pfeiffer has always attempted to distance
himself from the events surrounding the Reichsbank reserves. He has consistently denied that he was in the von Blücher house on 24 August (or any
other time), professed ignorance of the receipt, and maintained that his
signature could have been a forgery. The motives behind this attitude are
not difficult to understand. When it became known that the $404,840 and
about $1,635 worth of English pound notes handed over during the course
of August had disappeared, Pfeiffer was put in an unexpectedly harmful
position. In view of his previous close involvement with the Reichsband
funds the finger of suspicion, rightly or wrongly, now pointed in his direction, and his signature on the receipt, far from clearing him, now seemed
to implicate him in the disappearance of the currency, if only by association. In the absence of any available evidence with which to exonerate
himself, Pfeiffer's only course was to evade the issue, plead poor memory,
and deny all knowledge of the matter. If he could not be the attorney, he
would play the ostrich. And this he has done to this day.

Klaus Bremme, by contrast, displayed no such diffidence about his signature on the receipt. "My signature was refused by Captain Neumann,
as I was not implicated," he wrote later. "But I insisted to sign at least as
a witness, because I wanted to be able to prove in the future that I had
been present when the total missing sum of dollars had been handed over
and could not, therefore, have enriched myself from this source."

There is no doubt that the receipt *was* genuine, that the better part of
half a million dollars was handed over to Captain Neumann at 38 Gsteigstrasse, that the money was loaded into the back of his car and driven off
in the direction of Garmisch-Partenkirchen, and that it was never seen
again.

So what happened to it?

11

A Hole in the Bucket

When Captain Neumann of the Third United States Army disappeared down the road with the last portion of the $404,000 dug up from the von Blüchers' vegetable beds, it was still high summer in Garmisch-Partenkirchen, the sun burned down from an Alpine blue sky, and the shortages and austerity of the first winter of the peace—the much-dreaded *Hungerwinter*—were still some months away. The sense of urgency, the drastic measures for survival, would overtake the inhabitants of the area soon enough. For the moment the von Blücher brothers, on the orders of Captain Neumann, were confined to the house for 48 hours. Hubert von Blücher still remembers the occasion. "Of course, saying we were confined to the house on our own property was like saying don't leave Miami. The sun was shining, we went down to the swimming pool on the estate and lay in the sun, our friends came to see us—you know how it was. After two or three days we went into town again. Everything was forgotten."

One of Hubert's first tasks after leaving the house was to take Captain Neumann's receipt for the dollars down to the local chemist, who it seems was also an amateur photographer, and have a number of copies made of it. According to one account, Hubert then distributed these copies for safekeeping among his friends and acquaintances in Garmisch, so that he could be doubly sure, in the event of future interrogation by the Americans, of certain proof that he had handed the dollars over to the proper authorities and could no longer be held responsible for them.

The von Blüchers' most pressing problem now was survival. The Blücher family was distinguished but not rich. For the father and his sons regular employment had terminated with the German collapse. There was no income of any kind. Bank accounts were frozen. In any case, Reichsmarks did not buy many of the essentials of life in the cigarette economy of postwar Germany. It did not help matters that the father was in American custody, first at Nuremberg, later in the American internment camp at the former Gebirgsjäger barracks in Garmisch. The responsibility for looking after the extended family in the Haus Hohe Halde in Gsteigstrasse—for the mother, the sister, the interned father, the host of destitute and dependent refugee relatives from Silesia—thus fell squarely on the shoulders of the two young brothers. Like every German at that time the brothers were forced to resort to every possible means, legal or illegal, to keep their ship afloat. With hindsight, from the vantage point of the prosperous and respectable Germany of nearly 40 years later, some of the means of survival now appear embarassingly unrespectable, as Hubert von Blücher would be the first to admit. But that was not the vantage point of 1945 or 1946. Given the near-apocalyptic circumstances of those years, it is difficult to see how else people might have behaved when life was a matter of survival and the only resources available were the windfalls that came one's way, the native talents that one was born with, and like-minded friends.

Everything [Hubert recalled of that period] was black market. It was considered most dishonorable to abstain from the black market as long as members of one's family were starving. Not to join because of some code of honor or other, to exercise forbearance, was not good. My brother did some pretty extensive blackmarket business and I can tell you that the majority of the people in the Jäger barracks were fed in this way. Locked up in the Jäger barracks were the internees, including my father. The cooking was done in our home in Garmisch, in big cooking pots that had belonged to the German Army, proper cooking vats, and soups, thick soups, were cooked in them. And my brother had acquired—it was the most important possible acquisition at that time—in exchange for Persian pottery a chain saw. And with the chain saw he had managed to get a contract with the forestry office for cutting down trees and sawing them up. He cut down the trees and the ex-officers and ex-barons from Silesia cut up the wood and it was sold—and swapped, naturally—in large quantitites. In return he got macaroni, foodstuffs, and the devil knows what, for making the soup. It all went via the black market. And all the lads were mixed up in it. So one had to be very careful about getting moral issues mixed up with something that was, at that time, a most honorable business.

As the year of 1945 advanced so the struggle for survival grew more urgent. By the last half of October the leaves of the deciduous trees in the valleys and on the lower slopes of the mountains had turned a brilliant golden-yellow. By the last half of November the trees were bare and the sun was a cool, pale disc that barely cleared the rim of the surrounding peaks. By Christmas the frost had seized Garmisch in a grip of iron and the snow fell abundantly on the upper slopes. A trick of meteorology enabled Garmisch-Partenkirchen to flourish as a winter ski resort, even though it stood no higher than 2300 feet in altitude. In January the snow lies nearly two feet deep in the town and up to six feet deep on the surrounding slopes. At Haus Hohe Halde in Gsteigstrasse, on a cold northward hill opposite the snowy ramparts of the Wetterstein range, icicles hung from the steep, low-pitched roof like sugar walking sticks, humpbacked snow dunes filled the garden, and the roof groaned and strained under the weight of the snow. In the day the wind howled through the valley and at night the von Blücher house stood alone among the leafless trees in sharp relief against a sky full of stars "so frostbitten," one visitor recollected, "that they flashed slowly and intermittently like the revolving lamp of a lighthouse." It was no weather for cold hearths and empty larders. But by the New Year of 1946, the von Blücher brothers could be said to have done outstandingly well for the extended family. Indeed, they had not only gotten by, they had even gotten on in the world.

In this they were helped in some degree by their friends. Never was there a time when a man (or a woman) had greater need for a supportive circle of friends. The von Blücher brothers, largely through the charm and initiative of Hubert, enjoyed the benefit of an unusually extensive network of acquaintances and a very tight inner circle of close allies—old school friends from the prewar days in Garmisch, drifting back from the warfronts and prison camps, or refugees from the Russian-occupied territories of the former Reich, looking for a quiet corner in which to hole up till the shouting died down. There were perhaps no more than seven of them. But it seemed inevitable that they should gravitate towards one another's company. They had a lot in common. Young, bright, energetic, and resourceful, adventurers and opportunists with the same interests and the same background, keen and accomplished winter sportsmen who shared the same ski slopes and were members of the same exclusive sporting club—the Riessersee Ice Hockey Club in Garmisch—these men of mixed German and Polish nationality were determined to turn disadvantage to advantage, to use their wits to exploit the chance of windfalls of those postwar havoc days to the full, and not only survive but prosper and grow rich by any means available to them.

A leading member of this inner circle had been Mathias Stinnes, who lived next door. In October poor Mathias was carted off to an internment camp by the Americans and not cleared and released until May 1946. His place in the circle was taken by a young man called Walter ("Mucki") Clausing, the elder son of the owner of the Post Hotel in Garmisch, a former Gebirgsjäger officer and war veteran, and a former European ski champion now employed as a chief ski instructor for American forces personnel.* Others in the group included two brothers, Ardo and Roman Rousselle, members of a wealthy family in southern Bavaria. Ardo, described as "an extremely correct and honest man," had recently returned from a prisoner-of-war camp in Albania. Roman, a tall, strong, international playboy type, had deserted from the German Army just before the end of the war and remained in hiding in the cellar of a friend's house in Garmisch until the Americans occupied the town. Formerly married to the daughter of the mistress of King Alfonso of Spain, he had a passion for speed, owned a white Hispano Suiza cabriolet, and was a European bobsled champion who often crewed with Lüder von Blücher on the Garmisch bob run. Another member of this group, with his brother Erhard, was a remarkable Polish DP by the name of Ivar Buxell, a former member of the *Abwehr* in Warsaw, who appears again later in the story.

It was in and around this group in Garmisch that strange rumors began to circulate as the months went by. The rumors differed in detail but agreed in their main purport, which was that something strange had happened to the money that had been dug up in Gsteigstrasse, and that it had never reached the hands of the proper authorities. There were really only two possible suspects. One was the man to whom the $404,000 had been handed over, Captain Fred Neumann. The other was the man who had handed it over, Hubert von Blücher. The Americans tended to believe in the authenticity of the von Blücher receipt and to regard with corresponding disfavor the role played by Captain Neumann in this curious affair. Certain Germans, by contrast, unsure whether Captain Neumann really existed or whether the name was merely a pseudonym, considered the receipt a forgery, and expressed the view that Hubert von Blücher was responsible for any Reichsbank currency that might have disappeared. As if to corroborate their suspicions they related stories about dollar bills that poured out of the drainpipes at Haus Hohe Halde when it rained or that fluttered out of books in the von Blüchers' library when the pages were turned; about extravagant gifts and lavish parties thrown by the von

---

* Former Garmisch MG Legal Officer Captain Edward Bird, who as a one-time member of the U.S. Army Special Services had been responsible for skiing facilities for military personnel in Garmisch, became a very good friend of Clausing. "I knew him very well," he recalled. "I didn't distrust him. He was very intelligent man and a very likeable fellow. I put him on his feet. He worked for me as ski instructor. He was a hell of a good skier and if it had not been for the war he would have been Olympic material. Believe me, he was that good."

Blücher brothers in a style reminiscent of more opulent prewar days, and about Hubert riding around in a huge supercharged Mercedes with a movie camera stuffed with concealed dollars. The inference was that the von Blücher brothers had somehow hung on to the dollar hoard buried in their garden and overnight had become rich in consequence.

In an interview conducted in German in the prestigious Industrie Club in Düsseldorf in April 1982, Hubert von Blücher, then a distinguished captain of industry of 58 years of age, gave a characteristically energetic and disarming account of the matter of the $404,000 dug up in the garden at 38 Gsteigstrasse and what happened to it.

Q: Were you ever told later that the money was supposed to have got into the wrong hands?

von B: A hundred times. Most people think I had it.

Q: They still do.

von B: Now I will tell you exactly. I am chief shareholder of Pan American Airways. I am the best friend of Howard Hughes. The Beach Hotel in Las Vegas is 45 percent financed by me. I am thus the biggest financier ever to appear in the Arabian Nights tales dreamed up by these people over their second bottle of brandy.

Q: Maybe that explains those stories.

von B: Of course what I just said was persiflage, irony I must tell you honestly, I am disappointed. The last thing I heard was about $400,000,000. Now it's going down. That's a bad sign. And things will get difficult when they say $30,000, for that could be true.

Q: It is reported that some of the stuff might still be on your property.

von B: That is always being asserted. You know, I am thinking of selling the house and if I sell it I shall say that about 800 millions are still lying there. (In English: "You sell a castle with a ghost.") I must honestly say I consider all this virtually impossible. Guttapercha wrappings, I can tell you as a physicist, have a maximum lifespan under the ground, in a moist Central European climate, buried half a meter down, of five to six years before they rot away completely. And if the banknotes were then exposed to damp for another three to five years, in a Central European climate with frost to ten degrees below freezing, which you have in Garmisch, and then in the summer up to 17 or 18 degrees Centigrade, I would say if anything was lying there it would now have deterioriated completely. But it is utterly improbable.

What, in the end, is one to make of this crop of drolleries? What, indeed, was Hubert von Blücher to make of them? The question was put to him in Düsseldorf:

Q: You were with the American newsreel company at that time?

von B: Yes, correct. U.S. newsreel.

Q: I only mention it because it is alleged that you refused to open the
        film and camera boxes because you had...

von B: Secreted a million dollars?

Q: Perhaps not quite that much.

von B: All that is perfectly correct, only there was nothing in the contain-
        ers, and the entire newsreel period lasted nine or ten days. I will tell
        you how it all started. It happened because the Americans wanted
        to turn Garmisch into a recreational center within ten minutes —
        hardly had they arrived and it had become a recreational center.
        And my brother Lüder was made driver for General Truscott, not
        driving a car but a bobsled. Because he was a very expert bobsled
        driver. And so he drove generals and colonels on the bobsled, down
        the bobsled track. It was our own personal bobsled. Now the U.S.
        newsreel wanted to get film material of the recreational center. And
        in this connection I applied for a job. (Curt Jürgens, the German
        film star, was also involved with the newsreel and used to come to
        our house. His manager had a gorgeous blonde girlfriend, a won-
        derful woman, a sort of blonde bombshell. And in the spring of that
        year she wore a wonderful raccoon coat and nothing underneath
        and with this she managed to pass through all the checkpoints.)
        Anyway, my job was to film for the unit newsreel when General
        Truscott rode on the bobsled with my brother. To do this I was
        given a Bell and Howell reporter's movie camera, plus four cans of
        film, and I had to travel from Garmisch in a jeep of the U.S. news-
        reel and pass through six roadblocks. And they always told me to
        [speaking English] "Open these boxes." And I told them: "No." The
        film of General Truscott on the bobsled track exists, but I fell into
        disgrace afterwards because I filmed a second story on the same
        day, in which a fortuneteller called La Colona (she was ghastly, with
        a huge wart on her nose) read out of General Truscott's palm that
        "Future peace treaties are being negotiated here," between the for-
        tuneteller La Colona and General Truscott in the recreational cen-
        ter in Garmisch-Partenkirchen. He thought it was very funny, but
        the newsreel editorial department didn't think it at all funny. So
        they chucked me out of the newsreel.

It was during his period with the Allied newsreels that Hubert first realized
he had fallen under the surveillance of the U.S. Army investigators. One
of the stories he had worked out for the newsreel was about the work of the
local Alpine Rescue Service (*Hochbergrettungsdienst*) in Garmisch. He dictated his outline over the telephone to the unit's secretary — a simple story
about how an American officer got lost in the high mountains and died in
the ice of the Höllstal (Hell's Valley) and how the rescue people climbed up

and brought his body down. "About two hours later," Hubert recounted, "some jeeps came up and the Americans said to me: 'OK, where's the body of this officer?' And from then on I knew the phone was tapped. They had a wax record of the whole thing."

So what about the parties — those lavish and extravagant parties at the Haus Hohe Halde where the wine flowed and the buffet table groaned under the weight of dishes beyond the dreams of ordinary deprived Germans in the bleak aftermath of the war? Those too, it seems, were empty soufflés.

These parties were the most harmless things compared with what goes on today. Just to have drinks and cigarettes and army candles, don't forget the candles, you set up the candles, candles that actually burned, and you had a drink and cigarettes and you said [in English]: "Roll me over, Yankee soldier..." Now that was a party.

The most exciting party I went to in Garmisch, which is quite unforgettable for me, was given by an American major — a huge man, he once knocked down an American girl, a WAC, very bloody. Imagine a room this size, five meters by five meters, in a requisitioned house with a table like this one — a real Nazi table, oak and all that sort of thing. This table was laden with everything in the PX at that time, everything you see in a Welfare State food advertisement today was lying on that table. Unimaginable. I said to myself, that is what California must look like. That day with the major was the most unforgettable beanfeast I had ever experienced. And it was all ghastly tinned food, tuna fish, and so on.

The parties at that time did not have the elegance of the Twenties, where cocaine was part of the chic scene. They were just get-togethers without a blackout. Without blackout — that in itself was absolutely sensational. You arrive at a house and you can see through the windows and they are not covered with paper. That break with the past — it was like celebrating Christmas.

All these stories, Hubert explained, emanated from the "story kitchen" of his old friends. "It's all out of the envy kitchen. I have all the newspaper clippings, masses of them from England, these stories which they sold. They simply sat around with a bottle of brandy in Garmisch, all six of them, with the journalists, and invented these stories. And it was never the same story. And of course you would have to put on your dark glasses, otherwise you would be dazzled by the light reflected off the pure gold."

Unfortunately, as far as the $404,000 dug up from the von Blücher's garden is concerned, the suspicion persisted among the investigating authorities that either Captain Neumann or the von Blücher brothers — or conceivably all three together — had some part in its disappearance, but the matter was never resolved and with the demise of Military Government in 1949 it died a natural death. Only now, with the advantage of documents recently released from the Washington archives for the first time, it is possible to take an informed overview of the whole affair. From these documents it would seem (as related more fully in Chapter 13) that the $404,000 did indeed disappear, but under circumstances rather more curious than originally supposed. It would also seem that neither Captain Fred Neumann nor Hubert or Lüder von Blücher had anything to do with the disappearance of this large item of currency from the Reichsbank reserves.

So far this chapter has been concerned only with the mystery surrounding the disappearance of sums of Reichsbank foreign *currency*, mainly U.S. dollars, which it was alleged was not recovered by the proper authorities. But there was also the related matter of the gold. Among the bevies of U.S. Army investigators who eventually moved in on Garmisch-Partenkirchen between 1946 and 1948 there seems to have persisted a vague, nagging, unwritten question mark about missing Nazi gold. The investigators had no precise knowledge of what they were looking for or where they could find it. Certainly there had been no directive about gold from the Foreign Exchange Depository in Frankfurt. Perhaps the inconclusive quest for missing gold was a repercussion from the mystery surrounding the fate of the gold bullion recovered by Sergeant Singleton near Mittenwald in June 1945. Or perhaps it was a preliminary gust preceding the storm raised in 1948 by Robert Kempner, at the Nuremberg Prosecutor's Office, over the apparent disappearance of the so-called "Ribbentrop Gold."

The question is: what gold? There is one possible explanation. When the Reichsbank treasure was originally buried at Walchensee, a consignment of 25 boxes of gold—stated to be bullion—was buried with it, but only 20 boxes, containing not gold bullion but gold coins, were recovered. If the 25 boxes had, in fact, contained not bullion but coins, it followed that 5 boxes of gold were missing—though in the confusion surrounding the Reichsbank gold and currency recoveries this is difficult to determine exactly. Whatever the grounds for suspicion, they seem to have been sufficient to impel the Americans to launch an intensive investigation into the matter of the missing Reichsbank reserves.

12

The Boys from the CID

It was an extraordinary quirk of fate that General Patton, commander of the Third United States army and one of America's most acclaimed military leaders, should be burdened with the responsibility for the Reichsbank treasure twice in the space of three months. It was Patton's army that had first stumbled on the main part of the Reichsbank hoard at the Merkers mine in April 1945, and Patton himself had been one of the first Americans to set eyes on this prodigious wealth. It was again Patton's army, after fighting its way across Germany from one side to the other, that came across a second hoard of Reichsbank treasure — or what was left of it — in the area of Mittenwald in June, and Patton himself who initiated the investigation into the mysterious circumstances surrounding its recovery and disappearance. In an earlier chapter we have seen how the gold and foreign currency located in the hills above Lake Walchen by Hitler's former security officer, Colonel Friedrich Rauch, was brought to Patton's headquarters at Bad Tölz on 29 June 1945 by a squad of Third Army Military Police and how the general, in the salty and unequivocal language that was so characteristic of him, outlined his proposals for future action in that connection: "I want those civilian bastards handed over to the Criminal Investigation Department, and see to it that an investigation is started to find out what happened to the rest of this hoard. I don't want anybody ever to say that sonuvabitch Patton had stolen any part of it."

It was thus in Patton's office, in an order bawled through an open door in a former SS barracks, that the long, tortuous, baffling American investigation into the Reichsbank affair had its origins. The series of successive and overlapping enquiries was to take the best part of four years and involve just about every investigative agency that the Americans could bring to bear on the case — the Criminal Investigation Division (CID), Counter-

Intelligence Corps (CIC), Civil Censorship Division (CCD), FBI, Inspector General's Department, Public Safety Branch, Military Government Special Branch, and Theater Provost Marshal. They were to focus on Garmisch and gold and spill over into Munich and narcotics. They were to use the whole weight of the Army and every trick in the book, and yet by the time they had finished Patton would be long dead, the treasure would have vanished, the thieves would have fled, and the Pentagon would be sweeping the records under the carpet. The whole sorry saga could be seen as a farce, were it not for the extent of the crime, corruption, and incompetence that were laid bare in the process, and the impermeability of the mystery that has survived to the very end.

Many of the problems that confronted the investigators were inherent in the nature of the American occupation. At the end of the war the Allies had envisaged that for an indeterminate period — perhaps for 20, perhaps for 50 years — Germany would be ruled as an occupied enemy country until such time as it was fit to rejoin the community of nations. Germany was roughly quartered, each zone occupied by the forces of one of the victorious Allied Powers — the Russians in the east, the British in the northwest, the French in the southwest and the Americans in the south. Initially the Commander-in-Chief and Military Government on the American side was General Eisenhower, but in reality he was more of a prestigious figurehead, who had won his spurs in war rather than government, and the effective day-to-day running of the American Zone of Germany fell on the shoulders of his Deputy Military Governor (who later became Military Governor and later still Commander-in-Chief as well), General Lucius D. Clay — the dominant Allied arbiter of western Germany's destiny in the hiatus periods between the death of the Third Reich in 1945 and the birth of the autonomous Federal German Republic in 1949, more or less the period covered by this book.

In the first year and a half after the war the American presence in Germany — which bore the generic title of United States Forces, European Theater (or USFET for short) — was divided in two; the U.S. Army and the U.S. Military Government, known as OMGUS (Office of Military Government, United States). Under OMGUS headquarters in Berlin came the Military Government of the three southern provinces of Bavaria, Hesse and North Würtemburg-Baden and the northern port enclave of Bremen which made up the American Zone and generated three-quarters of its problems — was usually known as OMGB, which stood for Office of Military Government, Bavaria, and was run by a succession of Military Governors with varying degrees of talent and success. The entire occupation was an improvisation and the people who ran it were an improvised bureaucracy. In this respect the American Zone resembled the British, French, and Soviet Zones. There simply was no precedent in history for four civilized nations governing a fifth as absolute rulers. Given such unique circumstances, it is not greatly surprising that the new rulers of Germany—certainly those in the U.S. Zone—were unable to devise in advance a system of government that was adequate to cope with the unimaginable difficulties confronting it at the end of the war. "The apparently unanimous judgment of contemporary critics," one American academic historian of the Occupation wrote recently, "is that the Occupation suffered mightily from defects of organization, from beginning to end and from top to botton. The most obvious defect was the abyss between Military Government and the Army."

Military Government was supposed to rule through German agencies, while the Army was intended merely to provide troops as enforcers. In reality the Army got in the way of both Military Government and the fledgling German civil service. The tactical army units continued to behave as if they owned their areas and the conflicts that sprang up between the two sets of Americans in uniform—the Military Government and the Army proper—threatened to undermine the authority of the Occupation.

American investigative units were not exempt from this jealousy and estrangement. Thus the Criminal Investigative Division (CID), which was responsible for investigating major crimes committed by or against members of the United States Army, was part of the Army's Corps of Military Police under the command of the Theater Provost Marshal. On the other hand, the Counter-Intelligence Corps (CIC), whose primary function was the protection of the U.S. occupation against espionage, sabotage, and subversion within the boundaries of the U.S. Zone, was largely responsible to Military Government, though in practice it was often involved in the same cases as the CID.

There was not only jealousy between Army and Military Government agencies but a severe lack of coordination between them. These two broad compartments of the American occupation were vertically structured, with few lateral connections from one to the other. Many local Military Government commanders considered themselves perfectly free agents, ignored directives from above and (in the words of one contemporary critic) operated in "a variety of feudal kingdoms in which they ruled supreme." They were not entirely to blame. The channel of communication between the people at the bottom of the hierarchical pyramid and their peers at the top was a clogged and faltering one. Policy and plans tended not to filter down to the men in the field. The action and intelligence reports from the men in the field jammed somewhere in the bottlenecks on the way to headquarters in Frankfurt and Berlin. In other words, it was as difficult to cooperate within one chain of command as it was between one chain of command and another.

No wonder the numerous agencies that investigated the Reichsbank robbery (and other matters) found themselves either working in ignorance of one another's findings or trampling over one another's evidence. Conflicts led to poor intelligence. "Germany was deluged with intelligence teams and commissions of inquiry of every possible description," wrote one former intelligence officer. "In this general melee and struggle for information, organized intelligence work became impossible. Various groups worked at cross-purposes, information was not exchanged." Even General Clay, the Governor of the U.S. Zone, was forced to accept the criticism that the intelligence agencies were not functioning well. Intelligence from both the Army and the CID was not satisfactory, since it was largely the product of men who were simply good at languages and hated Germans — many of them Jews of German origin or East Europeans from countries which had suffered under Nazism. Military Government intelligence was little better because it came mostly from German sources, was often faulty, and could not be checked by the Americans themselves.

Human factors complicated the competence of the American occupation as a whole and the success of the investigative agencies in particular. There was a high rotation of personnel, a constant reshuffling of officials as new men took over who were unfamiliar with the local situation, did not know what had happened under their predecessors, and would themselves be replaced as soon as they had mastered their jobs. A French historian of postwar Germany wrote of OMGUS: "With very few exceptions, they lacked really first-class men." Most Americans were reluctant to serve overseas. Few saw the occupation as a long-term career prospect. The most experienced and best qualified men were usually the ones with the most "points" and among the first to return to the States for demobilization. Military Government was only allowed to offer one-year contracts and a top salary of $10,000 per annum; many of the more able men in the occupation felt they could not afford such short-term and relatively low-paid work, and returned to America as soon as they could to establish themselves in more permanent careers with brighter prospects. Those that were left were either men from the regular Army or career employees from federal departments and agencies who were obliged to serve wherever they were ordered; or else they were men who had volunteered to stay on because they doubted their competence to obtain as good a job at home and had vested interest in the German scene, with its lucrative black market and sex on tap—"the wine, women, and song boys," as one OMGUS political advisor once decribed them.

The CID, who bore the initial responsibility for investigating the Reichsbank robbery, had its full share of Occupation types. A provisional wartime organization of screened and trained men drawn mainly from Military Police organizations, the CID at the end of the war consisted mostly of men counting the days until they could go home—preferably before Christmas, or sooner. Replacements were recruited from available military personnel and even from civilian life. "The background checks of some of the people who had slipped in via overseas recruiting was interesting," wrote one CID permanent employee. "Several had criminal records, while others were discredited police officers, etc. Naturally these people were kicked out, but what did they get away with while they had the badge?" The same source has provided, with others, a series of pen portraits of some of his colleagues from that time, a rich gallery of Occupation types, some good, some bad, all of them only too human. Here is a cross-section (with their names omitted for obvious reasons):

In my opinion he would have done the Nazis real credit. Corrupt.

A real jerk. Was a former Ohio state trooper and thought in terms of uniformed patrols. Had no idea of investigations of anything more complicated than a traffic accident or a hold-up.

Formerly a Lieutenant in the Nazi Gestapo, later a Master Sergeant in the U.S. Army CID. Before the war he had to flee for his life following a quarrel with Gestapo Chief Reinhard Heydrich. After internment in England, he emigrated to the United States, renounced his hereditary Prussian titles of Baron and Count, and was drafted into the American Army. As he was fluent in German, French, and Russian, incredibly well connected with the German nobility and with many Nazi widows, including Frau Goering, he proved a very valuable CID agent. He was used exclusively for high-level cases and was outstandingly successful.

A fine man. Honorable and supportive of his men. He had studied for the priesthood at one time. Later went to the air force and was killed in a plane crash in Alaska.

An odd character, a real funny guy. He was a sapper in the British Army in World War Two, and joined the American Army CID in Algeria in 1943. An orthodox Jew, he spoke seven languages, including fluent Arabic, but in English spoke only in the third person. He had many friends in high places and seemed to play a lone hand most of the time. There was a rumor that he was an agent of the Zionist underground. His sister's first name was Tel and his was Aviv—allegedly because he was the very first Jewish male child to be born in that town after its creation.

One of the fair-haired boys. A handsome man who created a good first impression, but he was all facade. A compulsive drinker and gambler. Had been a policeman in Miami, Florida.

Was only 23 years old, but mature beyond his years. Very able and diplomatic. Later became a full colonel.

Such was the range of individual types within the organization that from the fall of 1945 was burdened with the task of solving the mystery of the Reichsbank treasure. But in eccentricity no CID man in Germany came anywhere near a particular Command Provost Marshal, who had the ultimate authority over the CID. A former CID agent recalled this controversial personality, who seemed to have stepped straight out of a novel by Evelyn Waugh:

Brigadier-General George H. "Pappy" Weems was a West Point officer. His basic branch of service was the horse cavalry. He was supposed to have been a brilliant young officer in that branch, but apparently he was unable to keep up with changing times and thus was not absorbed into the armored force. As a senior officer he was given staff assignment and prior to being assigned to Germany he had been head of the military mission to Hungary. He had no background in police work whatsoever and even less of CID. In fact, he never seemed to be able to comprehend why he had soldiers who weren't wearing uniforms and living in barracks.
    It seemed apparent that Weems had had some kind of stroke. He walked with a cane, had a faulty memory, seemed to have trouble comprehending anything of a complex nature, and was given to issuing outrageous orders. (Oh, yes, I almost forgot—he was hard of hearing!) He was obsessed with the idea that there was some sort of international conspiracy to steal typewriters and any case involving the theft of a typewriter had to be brought to his attention. He had me confused with an agent named Zeron and used to refer to me by that name. However, he didn't like to be corrected. Colonel Karp told me, on one occasion when I had to brief Weems on a case, that Weems would call me Zeron. He said not to pay any attention, because if I interrupted Weems' train of thought he would go into a tantrum. In other words, he was prematurely senile, probably as a result of a stroke. I doubt that he was dishonest, and any meddling he did was as a result of befuddlement. [Lieutenant-Colonel William A. Karp, on military leave from the U.S. Secret Services, took command of the CID in September 1947.]

Just because a man was a provost marshal or commander of a Military Police battalion or an agent of the CID was no guarantee that he had any capability or expertise in the field of police operations, much less that of complex investigations. So often what may have seemed dishonesty was actually incompetence, though there were some arrogant types who felt that because in essence they were the law, they were above the law and could do as they pleased.

The best that could be said about the CID's problems was that at least they were all-American. The problems with the CIC, the other main investigative body concerned with the Reichsbank robbery, and the scandals of Garmisch were far more exotic. The CIC was in a constant state of internal feud. Many of its agents were German-born and most of these were Jewish. There were two main categories of Jews in Germany and in the CIC: the western-oriented and the eastern-oriented. Broadly, the western sect viewed their Jewishness as a matter of religion and cultural heritage and considered Germany as their home, notwithstanding the holocaust brought about by the Nazis in that country during the Hitler years. The main concern of these western Jews was to root out the Nazis and see Germany become a democratic state to which they could one day return as their rightful homeland. The eastern Jews, by contrast, had their roots in in Poland and Russia and were mostly Zionist and saw the future state of Israel as their ultimate home. These eastern Jews considered themselves to be little more than temporary birds-of-passage in Germany and hoped to see that country crushed forever. The presence of feuding Jewish sects within the ranks of the CIC in Germany, and of first-generation Poles, Czechs, and other agents of east and central European origin, led not only to divided loyalties and internal stresses inside the Corps but to opportunistic and illegal alliances outside of it. The CID, a rather more professional outfit, tended to look askance at the CIC. "I tried to stay away from the CIC," confirmed one CID agent, "because they were a bunch of bums as far as I was concerned. They were a bunch of hooligans." Another CID agent, reporting back to his superiors about conditions in Garmisch, noted sarcastically at the end of his report: "All black-market investigations were being made by units of the CIC. I have nothing to add to this statement." All these motley factors had their effect on the success (or otherwise) of the investigations into the Reichsbank affair and have a bearing on the final outcome of this long and complex story.

Such, then, were the outfits that were unleashed by the Americans on the Reichsbank case and the Garmisch affair between 1945 and 1949. Excessively compartmentalized, with no clear overview, no overall direction, no central coordination, no master file, no watching brief, blundering about in the half-light and the dark, not knowing what they were looking for, getting in one another's way and on one another's nerves—no wonder one of the first and best of the investigators, Walt Snyder, described the Reichsbank case succinctly: "It was a fucked-up mess!"

Walter Snyder appears to have been the first agent to be put on the Reichsbank case after General Patton's intervention. It seems that the Provost Marshal for Third Army (in whose office some of the Reichsbank gold and money had been stored at Bad Tölz) had referred the matter to the CID Chief for Third Army, who in turn had passed it up the line to his superior, the CID Chief for European Command, Lieutenant-Colonel Eugene Smith, who had handed the matter down to the CID unit nearest to the scene of operations—the 13th CID Detachment at Munich. Walter Snyder, one of the 13th CID's best agents, able, honest, and a good German speaker, was sent to Garmisch to conduct a preliminary investigation. He was joined in the autumn of 1945 by a team of German detectives borrowed by the 13th CID from the Munich Police Department. Acting as Police Liaison Officer in Munich, coordinating all activities between the Germans in the Munich Police Department and the Americans in the Criminal Investigation Division (CID), Counter-Intelligence Corps (CIC), Military Police and Military Intelligence was Sergeant William C. Wilson. It was through Wilson that the case was referred as it progressed and through him that the Munich detectives forwarded their report to the CID at the end of their investigation. It was to Wilson that Snyder confided his private impressions of the case.

There could have been no more crucial investigation into the Reichsbank affair than this one, for the corpse was still warm, so to speak, and the evidence still scattered around. The names and whereabouts of the people principally involved with the treasure in one capacity or another were already known. None of these people had yet vanished or died; all could be easily located for interrogation. Motives, evidence, suspects—all were still fresh. Vital preliminary spadework had been done by Brigadier Waring and the local CIC and—theoretically at least—their findings were available to the American and German CID now probing the case.

In Bill Wilson's opinion no one ever knew more about the Reichsbank business than Walt Snyder and his CID chief, Gene Smith, who were first-class men. And yet—next to nothing came of it all. The mountain labored and brought forth a mouse. Snyder blamed it on "too many fingers in the pie," with CIC, CID, Military Government Public Safety Branch, and Special Branch all claiming an interest. Sadly, neither Snyder nor Smith can tell us more now. Snyder was shot and killed in May 1948 while working on a different case, and Smith died in an air crash a year or two later.

One can only surmise what else went wrong with the Garmisch investigation. The greatest handicap was not knowing how much gold and currency was supposed to have disappeared. The Foreign Exchange Depository (FED) was still a year and a half away from discovering that its Reichsbank currency account was short to the tune of some $2,000,000 in foreign exchange. The investigators do not seem to have followed General Patton's instructions to hand over "those civilian bastards" in order for the CID to "find out what happened to the rest of this hoard." Instead they concentrated on only the one part of the Reichsbank treasure for which they could find a finite figure and a tangible exhibit—the $404,000 or so dug from the von Blüchers' garden and taken away by General Patton's own personal interpreter, Fred S. Neumann. Since they could find no trace of any deposit corresponding to 404,000 American dollars, the investigators came to the conclusion that it was this which comprised the missing portion. This was perfectly understandable, given the circumstances, but it was the wrong track and would lead nowhere.

The investigators seem to have ignored the facts already on file in Third Army headquarters at Bad Tôlz concerning the strange circumstances in which certain enemy subjects—Rauch, Warth, Schreiber, and Groeger— were known to have handled large quantities of foreign currency shortly before the American military police made their recovery. Though Rauch and Warth were arrested and interned by the CIC during the course of the investigation—they were both picked up at the same time and place at the end of November 1945—they were confined only because they fell into the Supreme Headquarters Allied Expeditionary Forces (SHAEF) Automatic Arrest category as known or suspected Nazis and SS men, not because of the Reichsbank investigation, and they do not appear to have been interrogated about missing U.S. dollars while in internment. If the investigators turned up any details of a deal over American dollars between Rauch and certain Americans in Third Army—and there must have been one—they left no record of them.

The conclusion finally arrived at by the CID in 1945 was that Captain Neumann and a Master Sergeant from the Finance Office had made away with the missing dollars. "They had considerable testimony to back up their conclusion," one U.S. Army CID agent recalled. At a subsequent inquiry a senior officer from the Inspector General Division declared that he was "unable to obtain any proof of delivery to the Finance Department or to the Central Depository of German Funds" of Nazi assets for which Neumann had signed a receipt. When Neumann himself was subsequently confronted with the CID conclusion, he does not seem to have provided a satisfactory explanation—why not must remain a mystery—and though he was not formally charged by the American authorities, he fell under a towering storm cloud of suspicion, which lingered for years.

While the German Police CID in Munich had been looking into the currency aspect of the case, Walt Snyder had been trying to check on the gold. Aware, perhaps, of discrepancies in the subsidiary gold cache discovered in the hills above Walchensee—of boxes of gold coin being dug up where German records indicated that gold bullion had been buried—Snyder came to the conclusion that there had probably been two gold shipments down to Mittenwald, one of bullion and one of coins. But that was about as far as he could go. The FED could provide no leads. It is doubtful whether anyone had thought to tell him of the 10th Armored Division's order authorizing Sergeant Singleton's bullion recovery from the gold bunker near Mittenwald, or of the two alleged Office of Strategic Services (OSS) agents who drove off with the contents loaded on two 2½-ton trucks, never to be seen again. All he could do was pursue rumors and false clues laid by overly optimistic informants. One informant sold the CID a map of the area where the missing gold was supposed to be buried —near Füssen—but all they ever dug up was a golden dinner service belonging to a private family. Another informant announced that the missing gold was buried near Goering's palace at Valhalla, but when the cache was exhumed it amounted to no more than a small collection of coins and a rather large cellar of vintage French cognac. As for the rumors, they grew wilder and more fantastic by the day:

A group of U.S. officers bribed Swiss guards and took the gold to Switzerland.

A group of U.S. officers who were sympathetic to the Zionist movement turned it over to members of the Zionist underground.

A group of U.S. officers smuggled it to Italy, where exiled Mafia types used it to set up a narcotics smuggling racket.

The Nazi underground got it and it wound up in South America.

By Christmas 1945, Walt Snyder had been pulled off the Reichsbank case. Almost six months were now to pass before the CID again turned their minds to the matter of the Reichsbank currency and gold. Meanwhile a set of papers on the Snyder investigation was deposited more or less unread in a safe in the CID headquarters of Third Army, which had now moved from Bad Tölz to Heidelberg. It was there that the new CID Chief for Third Army, Captain Charles I. Bradley, found them when he took over the job on May 1946. Bradley recalled later:

I had all this stuff in the safe. I had money and everything else when I took over. There was a whole bunch of stuff about some Germans, you know, that said they came up to the Americans and that they knew where there was a lot of money buried and if they gave them some of it, and American passports, they'd tell them where it was. The money was gotten together and then about 130 million—120— disappeared. And nobody paid any attention to this, so I went to G-2 [Third

Army military intelligence] and talked with them and let them read it, and I said: "Who do you want to carry the ball on this? Do you want Intelligence to carry the ball or do you want the Criminal Investigation Division?" They said: "You carry the ball. If there is anything of an intelligence nature—cut us in." So I went ahead and got the 481st CID to get on it. The case concerned the Reichsbank gold—the stuff they moved out of Berlin. I thought it was fantastic. I don't know what happened to the rest of that money either. It's kind of peculiar, you know.

By the autumn of 1946 the CID investigation had spread its tentacles from Garmisch and Heidelberg to Frankfurt and London. The chief of the 481st CID Detachment, Jack Grindell, had assigned one of his ablest and most industrious investigators—Jack Ketcham, a law graduate and qualified attorney in civilian life—to spearhead the investigation. In October, Ketcham accompanied Bradley on a six-day fact-finding mission to London, where they consulted with three British officers who had worked on the Reichsbank case soon after the end of the war, including Brigadier Waring (then at the War Office), an inspector at Scotland Yard and "the vice-president of the British Electric Company." In November, Ketcham and another agent from the 481st CID, Ward Atherton, a former forest ranger and an honest and competent agent, spent two days poring over the Reichsbank records at the FED in Frankfurt. "Ketcham and I were there trying to track down what had been turned in and what was unaccounted for," Atherton recalled. "I remember that quite distinctly because that was the day I saw the Hungarian Crown of St. Stephen, which the United States recently returned to the Hungarian Government." Atherton could no longer remember the sums involved, but Ketcham had a rough idea: "It was an awful lot," he confirmed on the phone from his home in Concrete, Washington, in March 1978. "Wagon-loads full."

Jack Ketcham left the case after three months to join the FBI as a special agent. His place in Garmisch was taken over by Ward Atherton. It soon became apparent to him that he was working in a forlorn cause. "These things had taken place in June or July of '45," he recounted, "so our entire agency was more than an entire year after the facts. And with the dispersal of several million American forces personnel back to the U.S. and out of military service, and no records on where they went and so forth—why, it was extremely difficult for us in the CID. Most of the names that we encountered—people we wanted to talk with and so forth—were long gone. That's what was so frustrating about the whole matter."

The U.S. Army Criminal Investigation Division was strictly concerned with criminal activities by American personnel in the American Army. Though their investigation proved "frustrating," this did not mean that

NAZI GOLD

during 1946 no progress had been made by American investigations as a whole. Since the end of the war the American Counter-Intelligence Corps had maintained a permanent station in Garmisch-Partenkirchen engaged in monitoring border crossings by outgoing Nazis and incoming Soviet agents. Inevitably the Garmisch CIC became involved in the Reichsbank case, sometimes parallel to the CID, sometimes in tandem, but generally always from an opposite and complementary point of view—the CIC was more interested in the illegal activities of Germans and other foreign nationals than in Americans.

It was the CIC that initiated the most direct and aggressive surveillance operation of all the investigations to date. The spearhead of this operation was a Czech-born American member of the CIC Special Squad with a knowledge of languages and a talent for eavesdropping by the name of Lieutenant Leo de Gar Kulka. Kulka had joined the CIC early in 1946 on the strength of his linguistic ability and his inside knowledge of Soviet Russia and its postwar satellites. Seconded to the Special Squad in April, he was soon engaged in a Top Secret counter-intelligence project, codenamed Tobacco, monitoring Soviet and Czech espionage in the U.S. Zone and Soviet-motivated subversion in Bavaria. During this time Kulka became something of an expert in clandestine sound-recording techniques, which was probably one reason why he was temporarily taken off the anti-Soviet project and sent down to Garmisch on a bugging operation involving the Reichsbank gold and dollars.

Kulka recalled later: "I was asked whether I would mind going to a place in Garmisch and bugging a house that was empty but would be occupied two nights hence and recording the conversation."

I went to Garmisch, [Kulka recalled] arrived there late in the evening and was taken past the house in question. I examined it rather carefully, then got myself entry into the building by jimmying the lock, found out what the layout was, and then returned. I secured all the equipment I needed for the job and placed a couple of microphones in the living room, one in the den, and one in the bedroom, and then buried wires to a house about half a block away which was secured. I was to monitor any conversation that was going on.

Well, it seems that everybody got together in the house and there was a lot of conversation. My main purpose was to see that we got the conversation recorded as best as possible on the cumbersome disc and 35-mm film equipment which we were using at that time for sound-recording purposes. I do remember the conversation centered around money, dollars, pounds sterling, and a number of times Goering's gold was mentioned. The specific gist of the conversation was the problem of transporting certain funds. No decision was arrived at, but a few suggestions were duly noted and handed to the CID and CIC.

So far, so—in a manner of speaking—good. Just what was meant by Goering's gold is not clear, and though it would be tempting to guess this might be a misnomer for Ribbentrop's gold on the part of the men doing the talking or the man doing the listening, the matter must remain uncertain. But at this point in Kulka's recollections the plot thickens. And he continues:

I remember specifically that I was surprised that the names of certain agents were mentioned who were part of the Garmisch CIC. However, without knowing any of the background it didn't make much sense to me. I delivered the recordings to the CIC headquarters in Munich and I remember one of the agents was a little perturbed that I had got involved in this and kept asking, "How much did I find out, how much did I find out?" and I told him really I found out very little but maybe somebody else could make sense of the discs. The recordings were good and clean and easy to understand.

A year later Lieutenant Kulka was to be involved in a much tougher and rougher investigation into the same matter, where the target this time was none other than Ivar Buxell and the technique of investigation a good deal more intrusive. This incident will be related at a more appropriate stage of the narrative. For the moment it should be said that if Lieutenant Kulka had gotten any idea that some members of the Garmisch CIC were less than objectively involved in this case, he was probably not far wrong.

For the aficionados of this case, that small but undiminishing coterie of students of the world's greatest robbery—"The Friends of the Reichsbank," so to speak—the stakes were greatly raised when W. Stanley Moss's book, *Gold Is Where You Hide It* (see Introduction), was published in 1956. For Moss made an allegation which was to color the case forevermore. Moss's allegation was a very wild one. According to him, the 728 bars of gold bullion from the Berlin Reichsbank were not recovered by the proper authorities in the summer of 1945 but spirited across the border into Switzerland with American help. We have already proved conclusively that the 728 bars were not stolen but ended up where they were intended—in the FED vaults in Frankfurt—and Moss's case therefore falls to the ground.

Hubert's comment in 1982 was brief and to the point. "Utter piffle. Pure nonsense!" he exclaimed. "You have got to get this into your head. Gold, physically, was never seen by anyone in the entire group. Neither touched nor seen." The views of one postwar Military Governor of Garmisch, Major Melvin Nitz, was based on more practical aspects of the matter. "I have to laugh, you know," he commented. "Because you know what gold weighs, and you know what a problem it is carrying gold, and you're talking about moving literally tons of gold. Just how is a person going to be doing something like this, going through border checks and these other things? When I was there the rumor was that the gold had gone. There was no gold. The gold had gone. I wish to Christ I *had* gotten some—if there had been some."

It is a curious fact that neither Major Nitz, nor any other Military Governor of Garmisch-Partenkirchen, nor in all probability any other single officer in American-occupied Germany was ever in any position to know all the facts or at least have an overall view concerning the fate of the Reichsbank treasure and other assets that had been brought into the area during the last days of the Third Reich. Only now, with official documentation made available from the U.S. archives along with first-hand accounts and other information from other sources, is it possible for a single investigator even to begin to piece together the whole picture. After so many years the picture is necessarily still incomplete. Even so, the final reckoning is astonishing.

13

The Reckoning

The fate of the money dug up in the garden of Haus Hohe Halde and carted off in three batches by Captain Neumann can be traced, at least in part, in official Military Government documents that have survived from that time. These clear up the controversy surrounding Captain Neumann, but only serve to deepen the mystery overall.

As we have seen, the first recovery, totaling $251,374, was safely transferred from the Military Government in Garmisch to the Military Government in Munich.

The second recovery, described in the Annual Report of the Garmisch-Partenkirchen Military Government Detachment as worth "about $50,000," was initially processed by the Garmisch Military Government Property Control and Fiscal Officer, Captain Charles W. Snedeker, who had a curious story to tell about this particular recovery. In a letter from Chicago dated 4 October 1977 he wrote:

I believe that it was one of Oscar Koch's officers that came to my Command Post about 2 A.M. (at my request) to count the money that I had uncovered. The comment he made to me after being asked who knew that I had found the money was: "Let's split it." I requested a receipt acknowledging the amount and then turned it into Frankfurt with other valuables.

In fact, the money was duly passed up the line to Munich in the proper way, and Captain Snedeker received an official receipt for it. The precise value of this second recovery amounted to $50,905 and included the $1,634 worth of English pounds recovered from the von Blüchers' garden a few days previously.

The third and final recovery from the von Blücher house—the $104,956 taken by Captain Neumann on 24 August—was in fact handed over to

Captain Snedeker at the Military Government office in Garmisch. The second and third recoveries seem to be referred to in a Third Army Weekly Intelligence Report at this time: *"Money Cache.* A total of $152,000 in U.S. currency, part of the Reichsbank reserves, was uncovered in Garmisch-Partenkirchen, 25 August. Money has been turned over to Military Government Garmisch-Partenkirchen."

After a recount which brought the grand total of foreign currency recovered from 38 Gsteigstrasse to $1,634 worth of English pounds and $407,235 — not the $404,840 stated in the receipt given to the von Blüchers — the third recovery was transferred like the first and the second to the Military Government in Munich. Written in longhand on the receipt given to Snedeker on 1 September was the name "von Blücher."

So far everything had been done by the rule book. The recovered funds had been sent through normal channels to the proper authority, all correctly accounted and signed for. The next step, too, was perfectly in order. The $104,956, like the two previous deposits (Nos. 7 and 14), was transferred by the Military Government to the Land Central Bank in Munich, and there deposited as Deposit No. 18 by the Currency Section, Financial Branch. And there it stayed and from there, in the course of time, it vanished — like virtually every other component of the Reichsbank treasure that had been deposited in that particular cranny.

The correct procedure for the handling and shipment of recovered funds was well-known to the finance officers of American military government in Bavaria. All gold and silver bullion and coin, precious metals, gemstones, jewels, foreign exchange, and other valuables recovered by tactical units were bound by Occupation regulations to be turned over to the fiscal and property control section of the nearest Military Government Detachment, and from there shipped up the line via the Regional Military Government Detachment for Upper Bavaria to the Chief of the Finance Division in Munich. There the recovered funds could be held for safekeeping in the vaults of the authorized Military government bank, the Land Central Bank (which served the banking needs of American Occupation authorities) until such time as arrangements could be made to ship the funds in question to their next destination — the Foreign Exchange Depository (FED) in Frankfurt.

Even the FED — from which deposits had about as much chance of escaping as light from a black hole in space — was not home base. The gold held in store there was earmarked for the Tripartite Commission for the Restitution of Monetary Gold, in Brussels, while the U.S. currency was destined for the Federal Reserve Bank in New York, to which all U.S. dollar currency recovered in Germany and stored in the FED was finally shipped in January 1949.

The various American authorities in the chain stretching from the Military Government office in Garmisch to the FED in Frankfurt were perfectly conversant with the correct procedure for the transmission of funds. This is proved by the history of two shipments — a wooden box containing $141,225 worth of English pound notes and 15 bags of silver coins that had belonged to dead British airmen. These items were passed on from the Garmisch Military Government to the FED in July 1945 via the Regional Military Government in Munich in a copybook transaction which turned out to be virtually unique.

But no shipment of recovered Reichsbank assets sent from Garmisch through normal channels was ever to get through to its proper destination in Frankfurt. Indeed, only *one* of the recoveries of Reichsbank treasure made in the following month in the Garmisch area ever reached the FED. This was $4,000 found by Lieutenant Roger Ernst, U.S. Army, while hunting for hidden documents in the vicinity of the Klausenkopf currency caches in the second week of August. This little hoard (probably part of the $5,000 which disappearead from the $120,000 Mielke delivered back to the Munich Reichsbank in April) only got through to the FED because Lieutenant Ernst inadvertently bypassed the normal Garmisch-Munich channels. He had placed the dollars in a box containing recovered German documents and they later turned up in the Berlin Document Center, and were passed on from there to the Frankfurt FED. It follows that if funds recovered at one end of the transmission line did not eventually wind up at the other — at the FED, or, failing that, the Federal Reserve Bank — the inescapable conclusion must be that the funds had disappeared at one or other of the intermediate staging posts. In the case of the Reichsbank dollar currency recovered in the Garmisch area in August 1945 that staging post was not the first, or even the second. Captain Neumann did *not* make off with over $400,000 as has been believed for the best part of the last forty years — though this does not prove he did not make off with anything. Still less did Colonel Pfeiffer, or the von Blücher brothers, or their associates Mathias Stinnes and Klaus Bremme. Where the dollar hoards recovered by Captain Neumann — and not just those, but the gold bullion recovered by Sergeant Singleton, and in all probability the millions of dollar bills recovered by Major Rawley, and other assets — were finally blocked and eventually vanished was at the next-to-last stage of their ordained progress "through channels" — in Munich.

The detailed gold and currency inventories of the FED and the Federal

Reserve Bank between the beginning and the end of United States rule in Germany reveal that none of these valuables from the Reichsbank reserves and related sources were ever deposited in their respective vaults in Frankfurt or New York. The gold and currency shipped up the line to Munich in the summer of 1945 was left stranded high and dry at the mercy of the officers who had virtually absolute control over them—the Chief of the Finance Division of OMGB and his immediate subordinate, the Chief of the Enforcement and Investigation Branch, Property Control.

It was not only recovered funds from Garmisch that were swallowed when they reached Finance Division in Munich. It will be remembered that some of the Reichsbank treasure from Berlin, including two gold bars and a sizeable quantity of foreign exchange, was diverted from Mittenwald to Berchtesgaden at the end of April, and that some of it disappeared soon afterwards in the hands of *Landrat* Jacob. What was left—the two gold bars (part of the original shipment of 730 bars from Berlin) and a bag containing $19,840—was stored in the Berchtesgaden Savings Bank (*Sparkasse*) under the control of the local Military Government Detachment.

On 12 August 1945, following the usual procedure, this consignment was passed on to the Munich Land Central Bank, where the gold bars and U.S. dollars appeared as Deposit No. 10 on a list of valuables held for the FED by the Bavarian Military Government authorities in Munich. But this consignment never reached the FED; the two bars of gold were not passed over to the Tripartite Commission for the Restitution of Monetary Gold, nor did the $19,840 form part of the U.S. currency shipment sent back to the United States in 1949. Two weeks later, on 28 August, the $40,350 worth of English pounds still left in Berchtesgaden were handed over for forward transmission to Munich. Like the rest of the assets emanating from Berchtesgaden, the $40,350 worth of English pounds, which were entered as Deposit No. 15 in the Land Central Bank in Munich, do not appear to have reached their proper destination.

Even more extraordinary was the fact that, just three weeks after the two bars from Berchtesgaden had been delivered to Munich, the Finance division at Headquarters U.S. Group Control Council issued a 31-page report classified Secret entitled *Report on Recovery of Reichsbank Precious Metals* which indicated, *inter alia*, that the two gold bars in question were actually missing. The report was very detailed and very thorough. It showed that subsequent to the Merkers recovery, $41 million worth of non-Reichsbank gold and just over $14 million worth of Reichsbank gold had been recovered by the U.S. military and the Gold Rush team. This left $3,500,000 worth of Reichsbank gold unaccounted for, made up as follows:

50 bars never heard of after evacuation from the Weimar branch of the
   Reichsbank in April 1945
40 bars left in the Berlin Reichsbank at the time of the shipment to Merkers
147 bags of coin originally in the Magdeburg Reichsbank
2 bars "lost somewhere in the chain of evacuation from Erfurt to Wallgau" (meaning while in German hands in April)

The report clearly established that the two bars were originally part of the
shipment of 730 bars from Berlin; it gave their precise weight (54.538
pounds), and it even quoted their bar numbers (41919/41920). Yet for all
their thoroughness and for all their grasp of detail, the Finance Division
people of the U.S. Group Control Council — a devoted team of specialists
with all the resources of the U.S. Army behind them — were unable to locate two gold bars held in official U.S. custody since 12 August 1945 in a
bank vault run by the finance division of their own Military Government
almost on their own doorstep in Munich. By October 1948 the FED
seemed to have accepted that the two gold bars had gone for good, and in
a handwritten reply to a FED request for information regarding Reichsbank gold which had not been recovered, Albert Thoms, former head of
the Reichsbank's Precious Metals Department, listed these two bars along
with the bullion and gold coins lost when the Russians overran the Reichsbank vaults in Berlin.

The two bars stored in Munich should have been shipped to the Tripartite Commission for the Restitution of Monetary Gold. For reasons unknown the Belgians seem to have been deprived of at least 54½ pounds of
monetary gold, and morally if not legally were entitled to compensation
for their loss from the U.S. government, for they formed part of the 11,405
bars of the Belgian gold reserves plundered by the Nazis five years previously. Though the amount in dispute here is relatively small — two bars
worth $30,000 in 1945 and $435,000 today — the principle could well be
extended to the infinitely greater quantities of gold which disappeared at
the same time and under similar circumstances.

The discrepancies in the gold count were discovered much sooner at the
FED than the very considerable shortfall in foreign exchange. A whole
year was to pass before FED officials began the laborious task of balancing
the account of the Currency Section. Between the late autumn of 1945 and
the summer of 1946 the FED seems to have lain almost completely dormant, continuing to act as a repository for the valuables in its possession
but doing little else (primarily because of lack of manpower). At the end
of July 1946, however, the FED began to stir into life. At last it began to

count the paper money in its possession. On 24 July it brought out a "Register of Valuables." A week or so later two officials of the Currency Section, Frank Roberts and his assistant, Rona Geib, began to look into certain odd and puzzling features to do with the currency recoveries of the previous summer.

On 7 August 1946, Rona Geib paid a visit to the office of the intelligence section of OMGUS in the I. G. Farben building in Frankfurt. The purpose of the visit, according to Rona Geib, was to determine the source of certain valuables in the FED "about which we had incomplete details." Miss Geib was passed on to the CIC Records Section. Three million names were held on file in records, Miss Geib was told. Which names was she interested in? The next day she came back with a list of 16 names. Most of these names were connected with quantities of SS loot which had been recovered and subsequently deposited in the FED. But two of the names were also connected with the fate of some of the original contents of the Berlin Reichsbank vaults. These were General Gottlob Berger and General Josef Spacil, who had between them deprived the Reichsbank of nearly $10,000,000 worth of assets at the end of the war. Their appearance on the preliminary list of suspects gave a clear indication that the FED was now settling down to its task.

The CIC Records Section produced files on eight of the 16 individuals, including Berger and Spacil, and informed Miss Geib that any of the individuals could be interrogated by making the appropriate arrangements with the Interrogation Center in the I. G. Farben building. "Rather unexpectedly," Miss Geib reported, "I ran into the background of Shipment 31 in the folder of Josef Spacil." Shipment 31 consisted of such assets as had been recovered from the $9,000,000 worth of valuables stolen by General Spacil from the Berlin Reichsbank in April 1945. The facts on Shipment 31 alone should have suggested that further inquiries and subsequent interrogation might be desirable. But while Miss Geib was considering the case, the final inventory of Shipment 52A—which included the Reichsbank currency recovered from the Klausenkopf caches in June 1945—was at last completed. This revealed that everything in Shipment 52A was not quite as it should have been either and that something very odd had been happening to the Reichsbank reserves.

Things now began to move, albeit slowly. On 12 September the Deputy Director of the Finance Division of OMGUS telephoned the Chief of the FED (Colonel William G. Brey) asking for details of the serial numbers of U.S. dollar bills held at the Depository. Colonel Brey, a much respected career soldier, knew little about financial matters. This side of the FED was run by his able Deputy Chief (and eventual successor), Frank C. Gabell, the man in charge of the secret distribution of new German currency to West German banks prior to the historic currency reform of June 1948. "Brey was the 'picture' at the FED," wrote Gabell, "and I was the 'works.'"

On 1 November two agents from the Army CID visited the FED to examine the files "in connection with an investigation of persons and organizations involved in the finding and delivery of valuables." On 12 February 1947 Rona Geib was again at the CIC Records Section in the I. G. Farben building. This time she was looking for anything they might have on the financial set-up and dealings of the Reich Security Head Office (RSHA). By 7 March matters were drawing to a head. Rona Geib made yet another call at CIC Records "for the purpose of gathering information from G-2 files on certain German individuals connected with various shipments of valuables received in the FED." These individuals were:

Josef Spacil (Head of Amt II of the RSHA)
Rosenberg-Lipinski (Reichsbank Director)
Friedrich Rauch (Lt.-Col. in Schutzpolizei, Berlin)
Walther Funk (Reichsbank President)
Hans Neuhauser (*Wehrmacht* Captain)

Someone at last was putting two and two together. The four new names, in addition to that of Spacil, were all individuals who had been closely involved in the fate of the Reichsbank reserves. By 17 March the FED was right in the middle of the investigation. The Chief of the FED wrote to the Fiscal Officer of OMGB in Munich:

On 13 April 1945 a large amount of currency held at the Reichsbank Berlin was sent from Berlin to Munich. Much of this currency was subsequently recovered in Munich, Mittenwald, and St. Johann and brought to the FED where it is still retained. Since there are many discrepancies between the list furnished recently by the Berlin *Staatskontor* (successor to the Berlin Reichsbank) and the count which was made in the FED, it would be appreciated if you would make inquiries and if possible procure such lists and other records as may have been kept in the Munich Reichsbank regarding the movement of this currency.

Shortly afterwards — nearly two years to the day after the currency was driven off from the Berlin Reichsbank under a hail of bombs and Soviet artillery fire — the FED produced a final five-page report, signed Rona L. Geib and entitled "Currency Sent from the Reichsbank Berlin to Southern Germany in April 1945," which reconstructed "at least in part" what had happened to the SS and Reichsbank currency shipped out of Berlin just before the end of the war. For the first time the very considerable discrepancies were listed.

According to the FED's findings, about a quarter of a million dollars worth of foreign currency dispatched form Berlin to Munich on behalf of the SS (including funds thought to have been Himmler's personal property) had disappeared. The total value of the missing SS currency by today's values would amount to $1,375,000. The report continued: "Regarding the regular Reichsbank currency balance the discrepancies consist almost exclusively of deficits, the most noticeable of which are U.S. dollars, French francs, Swiss francs, Turkish pounds, and English pounds." The complete list of discrepancies, with their 1945 dollar equivalent, was as follows:

Currency	Amount	1945 U.S. $ equivalent
U.S. dollars	1,164,990	1,164,990
English pounds	92,004	368,016
French francs	1,000,000	20,149
Swiss francs	499,960	116,813
Turkish pounds	221,650	180,203
Norwegian kroner	119,900	18,166
Portuguese escudos	69,000	2,760
Palestinian pounds	1,700	6,800
Egyptian pounds	197	814
		Total U.S. $ 1,878,711

So at long last it was officially confirmed that nearly two million dollars worth of foreign currency had disappeared from the Reichsbank currency caches on the Klausenkopf above the Walchensee—the contents of the 17 bags found to be missing when the caches were discovered by the Americans in June 1945. Together with the missing SS currency, therefore, the grand total of currency missing from the original shipment from Berlin amounts to over $2,000,000. Immediately after the war many of these currencies, particularly the dollars, would have fetched many times their face value on the black market. By 1983 the equivalent value of the U.S. dollars alone would be $6,407,445 and of the English pounds $2,024,088. The remaining currencies, revalued in dollars on the same basis, would be worth a total of $1,901,377. By 1983 values, therefore, the total haul from the Reichsbank currency reserves (including the SS currency in the Reichsbank's custody) would be worth $11,707,910—an immense sum even by the standards of present-day robberies.

The final page of the FED report was entitled "Recommendations." Though very belated, they were very well founded, and they pointed future investigators—if there were any—in pretty much the right direction. The recommendations were:

1. That Rosenberg-Lipinski be interviewed to find out what he did with the bag of SS currency he retained.

2. That Mielke (who still works at the Munich Reichsbank) be interviewed. Why and when did he bring some currency back from Mittenwald to Munich? Also what happened to what was left behind?

3. That Fritz Rauch (formerly a Lt.-Col. in the Schutzpolizei in Berlin) be questioned. Who was the *Wehrmacht* colonel who with Rauch selected the hiding place for the treasure in Mittenwald? How much currency does he believe was removed from the cache after his first trip to get the currency (27 June 1945)?

4. That Funk be interviewed. What relation is there between valuables evacuated to Munich and those sent to Salzburg by order of Kaltenbrunner?

5. That Groeger and Schreiber who helped recover the valuables of 52A (currency recovered from the Klausenkopf) be questined to see if more details can be developed.

6. That Reckow of Berlin *Staatskontor* be contacted again to check whether list submitted is completely accurate (i.e., whether there is a possibility that some of the currency may have been returned to Berlin). Also whether currency in this list constituted practically all of currency left in Reichsbank or whether sizeable sums remained.

The last sentence is a particularly significant one, for it seems to indicate that for the first time American financial officialdom was fumbling towards the unpalatable concept that more currency may have been hidden in 1945 than was contained on the Reichsbank's inventory.

Strictly Reichsbank currency was the only currency which had any degree of accountability, because its origins were of an official nature, unlike the semiofficial funds of such organizations as the German Intelligence Service, which were provided without accountability and not listed on any inventory. Not all foreign exchange in the Reichsbank's custody was on the Reichsbank's books, and this was obviously where the trouble started in assessing just what else had disappeared. The $2,000,000 worth of foreign currency posted as missing by the FED was only known to be so as the result of a process of accountancy—comparing a list of what went out from Berlin in April 1945 with a list of what came into Frankfurt a few months later. The accuracy of the estimated debit balance therefore depended entirely on the completeness of the two sets of figures to be balanced. If, as has been suggested, the list of currency that went out from the Reichsbank in Berlin was incomplete, it follows that the $2,000,000 worth of currency that was missing and believed to have been stolen was merely the tip of the iceberg. In the final Secret report to the Office of Financial Affairs, Civil Affairs Division, OMGUS, entitled "U.S. Dollars Found in Germany" and dated 28 March 1949, Frank J. Roberts, now Acting Chief of the FED, concluded: "It is appreciated that the data and exhibits as submitted, though voluminous, by no means present a clear picture of the disposition of the foreign exchange after it left the Reichsbank, Berlin. Obviously a considerable portion has never been found."

Nor was it ever found. The missing dollars were not part of the shipment of dollar currency that had been sent from the FED to the Federal Reserve Bank in New York in the previous January. Nor were they part of any of the additional deposits accepted by the FED right up to 29 November 1950, or of further shipments to the United States in 1951. Nor were any of the dollars that had ended up in the Land Central Bank in Munich in 1945 — or any other valuables known to have been there still in May 1947 — ever actually *seen* again after that date.

The role of the Land Central Bank in Munich in the story of the Reichsbank reserves and associated funds is an odd one. At least $427,075 (worth $2,348,125 in 1983) recovered from the Reichsbank foreign currency reserves are known to have been deposited in this bank — $19,840 from Berchtesgaden and $407,235 from Garmisch. A total of 10,405 English pounds worth $183,128 in 1983 is also known to have been deposited there, along with two bars of bullion worth $30,000 ($435,000 today). In addition, a further $400,000 (worth $2,200,000 today), found at Oberau, together with a large but unquantifiable quantity of gold bullion recovered from the Mittenwald area by the local Provost Marshal, Sergeant Singleton, was reported to have reached the American fiscal authorities in Munich, and it is possible that an extremely large consignment of U.S. dollars recovered on the Garmisch-Oberau road by Major Rawley of the 10th Armored Division was channeled to the same destination. In other words, nearly a million dollars' worth of Reichsbank treasure (now worth a formidable $5,166,253) and possibly a great deal more, was delivered to the Land Central Bank during the course of the summer of 1945 and from there, at a later date, removed by a person or persons with the ability or authority to dispose of such funds.

At the time of the American occupation there was only one person who had the requisite knowledge and power in Munich and that was Colonel Russell R. Lord, Chief of the Finance Division of OMGB, the superior — and the intimate — of one of his most important departmental heads, Major John R. McCarthy, in charge of the Investigation and Enforcement Branch. Between them, these two soldiers of fortune were to carve up the financial fiefdom of Military Government in Bavaria as their own domain and in due course endure the closest scrutiny and incur the deepest suspicion of a whole series of secret investigators from the Army's Criminal In-

vestigation Department, the Inspector-General's Department, and the
Counter-Intelligence Corps in their attempt to unravel the true facts about
the great Reichsbank robbery and the financial and criminal irregularities
that ensued in Munich and Garmisch-Partenkirchen.

Given the circumstances, it was a supreme irony that both Lord and
McCarthy should have become regular visitors at the house next door to
the von Blüchers, in whose garden a sizeable portion of the missing
Reichsbank reserves was buried shortly after the end of the war. For when
Mathias Stinnes was led away to internment in October 1945, a Captain
Pope, one of Lord's officers from Property Control in Munich, who was a
good friend of Mathias' wife, Tucki, became a frequent visitor to the
Stinnes house at 40 Gsteigstrasse in Garmisch, and both Lord and
McCarthy were often at the house as visitors, commuting from there to
work in Munich. Colonel Lord always professed ignorance of anything to
do with missing currency or bullion. "I heard about it," he told the authors
in Owosso, Michigan, in January 1978, "but I didn't know anything about
it. You could probably get 10,000 rumors. I read about it in the *Stars and
Stripes* even. Well, they never knew. To tell the truth, there were a lot of red
herrings suggested by the Nazis during the denazification program to keep
everybody off balance, so I never knew how much was true and how much
wasn't." As for McCarthy, Colonel Lord had this to say: "He worked in investigating for financial intelligence. He wasn't a Treasury man, but *he
worked in investigating funds that were taken from one bank to another* —that sort of
thing" (Authors' italics).

Neither Colonel Lord nor Major McCarthy was in any doubt as to
what his proper duties were. In October 1946 they were briefed in these by
no less a person than General Eisenhower himself, then Army Chief of
Staff in Washington, who visited Munich in the course of an inspection
tour of U.S. Army installations and headquarters in the American zones
of Germany and Austria. Eisenhower was particularly explicit about the
function of Major McCarthy in the Finance Division. "The mission of the
Investigation and Enforcement Branch of Finance Division," ran Eisenhower's briefing notes, "is to develop facts and evidence from information
obtained and to see that proper action is taken against those persons found
guilty of violating Military Government laws dealing with Properties and
Finance." In the light of McCarthy's nefarious activities later in this story,
Eisenhower's notes for this meeting are the height of irony—an irony
doubly compounded by Eisenhower's cable to President Truman a day or
two later: "You will be pleased to know our troops are upholding the finest
traditions of the American Army."

By early 1947 the status of the deposits held at the Land Central Bank in Munich was becoming a cause of some concern to the Finance Division. On 5 March a representative of OMGUS Finance Division, David Schwarz, went over Colonel Lord's head and convened a meeting with officials of the Land Central Bank in Munich without inviting him. This was like letting the internal auditors loose on a firm without bringing in the executive officer. Lord was offended and suspicious and his response was swift. In a memo to the Director of the Finance Division of OMGUS he protested testily: "As Mr. Schwarz did not contact this office while in Munich we are in no position to advise or supervise on the work laid out as we have no first-hand knowledge of the discussions and requirements laid down to the Land Central Bank officials..."

Four months later the FED took steps to have a closer look at the contents of the Land Central Bank's vaults. In July 1947 the heads of the Currency Section and the Depository Section of the FED began checking the sources of various assets held for Military Government in German banks in order to see whether they properly belonged in the FED. An inspection of the Land Central Bank in Munich revealed a number of deposits in sealed bags and other containers. These were not opened, but though there was very little information on the source and historical record of these items, it was felt that many of them were clear candidates for the FED — as, for example, two gold bars weighing 55 pounds and a deposit containing various gold items weighing about 317 pounds. The inspectors pointed out to Colonel Lord that fuller information should be forthcoming on other items to determine whether they should be in the FED.

By November 1948 the Head of the Currency Section, Joseph A. Angotti, was able to report to the FED that the Land Central Bank in Munich was holding, in addition to a quantity of foreign exchange recorded on the accountant's books (mostly rather useless currencies like Russian rubles, Hungarian pengos and Polish zlotys), a quantity of foreign exchange in considerably more desirable currencies which mysteriously were *not* recorded on the accountant's books, including sums of $251,165, $19,840, $50,905, $104,956, and $40,035 and $1,634 worth of English pound notes — familiar totals which had, of course, emanated from Garmisch and Berchtesgaden in August 1945. Angotti explained that these probably represented captured or confiscated funds. He pointed out that captured funds were the property of the U.S. Army and that often so-called confiscated funds were really captured funds too. Angotti believed that this was the case with the items in the Land Central Bank in Munich, and he recommended that the funds listed there be collected by the FED. This does not seem to have been done.

Two months later U.S. currency recovered in Germany was loaded under guard in 14 sealed containers in the hold of the U.S.S. *General Harry Taylor* homeward bound for New York from Bremerhaven. The Munich dollars whose checkered career we have tried to follow from their vault in the ruins of the Berlin Reichsbank, via the bowling alley in the Mittenwald *Kaserne*, the bunker on the mountainside overlooking Lake Walchen, the inside of Colonel Pfeiffer's backpack, the tomato bed of the von Blüchers' garden in Garmisch, the back of Captain Neumann's jeep, to their next-to-last resting place—Colonel Lord's inner sanctum in the Land Central Bank in Munich—were not on board that ship.

Shortly after the arrival of the dollar currency in America, the United States Department of Justice (the body now responsible for the dollars recovered from Germany) raised some question about the currency believed to have been held in the Land Central Bank in Munich. On 3 February 1949 Murray Van Wagoner, the Land Director of Bavaria, was obliged to write to the Deputy Military Governor of the U.S. Zone, Major-General George P. Hays, pursuing this elusive matter. "The United States Department of Justice has requested certain information from the Land Central Bank in connection with deposits made under Military Government Law No. 53.... The Land Central Bank was unable to furnish the information desired to the United States Department of Justice." And at this mysterious point official documentation dries up.

When the U.S. authorities, as a result of growing native German interest in the matter, were asked for information and assistance in a letter from the Land Commissioner of Bavaria in 1948, they replied: "U.S. policy has reached the stage that we no longer have an interest in the possible recovery of the property involved."

So far as the fate of the Reichsbank assets deposited in the Land Central Bank was concerned, there remained one last possibility—that some had never been removed from the bank at all, either officially or unofficially, but were still on deposit there when Allied Military Government came to an end and West Germany became a sovereign state in May 1949. The assets in questions would then have been at the disposal of the Land Central Bank or the Ministry of Finance of the Federal Government of Germany.

In July 1979 the Land Central Bank in Munich was approached with a request for their help in determining the final disposition of Deposits Nos. 7, 10, 14, 15, and 18—items of recovered Reichsbank treasure held in the account of the American Military Government for Bavaria until at least November 1948. The inquiry met with a positive and favorable response until the matter was passed on to the German Federal Bank (Deutsche Bundesbank) in Frankfurt. A lengthy silence then ensued until a reminder elicited the following curious reply dated 9 January 1980:

Thorough and inevitably time-consuming investigations at the Land Central Bank and this office have revealed that some records appertaining to the matter in question still exist. Since these records refer to specific details and persons we feel unable, to our regret, to make them available to you, as the official secrecy regulations to which we are subject require us not to disclose such details to third parties. This secrecy requirement takes precedence over historical or literary interests.

Broadly speaking, however, one can say that the deposited assets which were not claimed by the military government were returned to the persons originally entitled to them (while these could be traced) after their general release in 1955. Worthless assets were destroyed some time ago. Undeliverable assets were sold at public auctions in accordance with the general provisions governing undeliverable objects held by public authorities and the proceeds were transferred to the Minister of Finance. [On 21 February 1955 the Allied High Commission for Germany formally released all assets deposited at the Land Central Banks under the provisions of SHAEF and Military Government Law No. 53.]

If the U.S. authorities had known just how much property had been involved they might have been less indifferent. But they never did know. There were, as we shall see at a future stage of the story, a number of official investigations conducted into the affair of the Reichsbank treasure and its aftermath; but because of the unwieldy nature of the military system, the lack of coordination between the different elements in the American occupation bureaucracy in Germany, and the extraordinary difficulties put in the way of the investigators, the full extent of the Reichsbank robbery was never discovered.

No central file was ever kept on the Reichsbank affair which integrated the progress and the results (if any) of the separate and uncoordinated investigating bodies. In a sense, this present book now serves the place of that nonexistent central file. For the first time ever it is possible to integrate in a single list the long succession of hits and heists, gunpoint snatches and petty purloinings, disappearances and discrepancies that nibbled and gnawed and gobbled away at the helpless carcass of the Reichsbank reserves before and after the collapse of the Third Reich. The perpetrators were German, Russian, and American soldiers. Their motives were a mixture of political stratagem (General Spacil), *vis victis* (rights of conquest — the Red Army), and private opportunism and greed (most of the

The backgarden of Haus Hohe Halde, the von Blüchers' villa in Garmisch where more than $400,000 of Reichsbank currency was buried in the vegetable beds.

Another $400,000 in US currency, found under a hayshed on Klaus Bremme's farm at Oberau, is counted at 10th Armored headquarters in Garmisch. Neither sum (each worth more than $2,000,000 today) ever reached the proper authorities.

Hubert von Blücher at the age of 19, photographed between air raids in Berlin in the spring of 1944, a year before he returned to the family home in Garmisch.

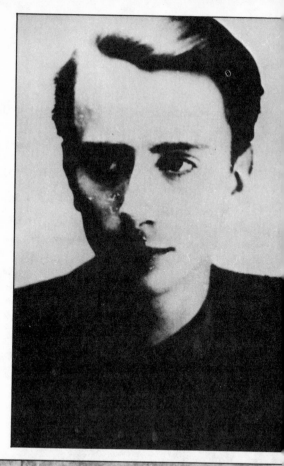

Captain Neumann's famous receipt for the dollars buried in the garden at Haus Hohe Halde, with the signatures of Pfeiffer, Rauch and Bremme as witnesses. When the money subsequently disappeared it was thought Neumann had made off with it.

28 August 145

TO WHOM IT MAY CONCERN:

Lüder von BLUECHER AND Hubert von BLUECHER have turned over to the US Army the following sums of money entrusted into them by Colonel Franz PFEIFFER, former Commandant of the Gebirgsjager-schule Mittenwald Germany. This constitutes the entire amount originally entrusted into them.

$ 404.849:88
465:88 English pounds

The undersigned acknoledge the reсipt of the above stated amount.

Fred S. Neumann
FRED S. NEUMANN
Capt FA. CIB
THIRD UNITED STATES ARMY

Signatures of witnesses present during the transaction appear below.

Signatures of witnesses:

Franz Pfeiffer
FRANZ PFEIFFER

FRITZ RAUCH   *Fritz Rauch*

CLAUS BREMME

Some of the money men of American Military Government in Bavaria. *Top left*: Major Kenneth A. McIntyre, Town Major of Garmisch in June 1945, who 'processed' a lorry-load of US dollar notes from the Reichsbank reserves worth up to $8,000,000. *Top right*: Captain Charles W. Snedeker, who passed the money dug out of the von Blüchers' garden from Garmisch to Munich. *Bottom left*: Colonel Russell R. Lord (in civilian suit and spectacles), Chief of the Finance Division in Munich and the ultimate custodian of recovered Reichsbank funds in Bavaria. On his left is Brigadier General Walter J. Muller, Military Governor of Bavaria. *Bottom right*: Major John R. McCarthy (on right), Chief of the Investigation and Enforcement Branch under Colonel Lord in Munich, and one of the American occupation's most ambitious operators. On his left is Colonel Charles M. O'Donnell, Chief of Public Safety in Bavarian Military Government.

Allied officers in early pursuit of the missing Reichsbank millions included a British Army Staff Officer, Brigadier Michael Waring (*top*), pictured here at the Indian Army Staff College at Quetta during the war (centre of top row), and an American Military Police Battalion commander, Colonel Robert M. Allgeier (*bottom*, second from left), who was responsible for the recovery of one of the caches of Reichsbank gold and dollars (pictured here at US Third Army Advance HQ in Nancy in 1944).

rest). Little of what was stolen was recovered and none of those responsible was ever indicted or brought to trial.

Here, then, is our summary of the principal robberies of the Reichsbank reserves described in this book, with the 1945 values of what was taken converted into dollars where necessary, followed by the 1983 dollar equivalent.

1.   90 bars of gold and 4,580,878 gold coins taken from the Reichsbank in Berlin by the Red Army in May 1945.
     Total 1945 value: $3,434,620   1983 equivalent: $49,801,990

2.   Gold Currency Bonds (Westphalia, Weimar, Industrial) taken from the Berlin Reichsbank by Major Feodor Novikov of Red Army Intelligence on 15 May 1945.
     Total 1945 value: $400,000,000   1983 equivalent: $2,200,000,000

3.   Jewels, diamonds, securities, and foreign currencies worth $9,131,000 taken at gunpoint from the Berlin Reichsbank by General Joseph Spacil on 22 April 1945 and handed over to Colonel Skorzeny for safekeeping.
     Total 1945 value (after deducting known recoveries amounting to $492,401):
     $8,580,143   1983 equivalent: $47,190,786

4.   1 bag of SS foreign currency taken from the Munich Reichsbank by Reichsbank official Rosenberg-Lipinski on 24 April 1945 and 12 sacks of SS foreign currency totaling over $2,000,000 taken from the same place on the same day by SS General Gottlob Berger, $1,816,805 of which was recovered from St. Johann in May 1945.
     Total 1945 value: $218,727   1983 equivalent: $1,202,298

5.   85,000 Swiss francs taken by a Dr. Österreich and a Reich Security Head Office official from the Munich Reichsbank on 25 April 1945.
     Total 1945 value: $19,859   1983 equivalent: $109,324

6. $5,000 taken by Reichsbank official Mielke from the *Kaserne* at Mittenwald on 25 April 1945, of which $4,000 was probably found hidden on the Klausenkopf by Lieutenant Roger Ernst, U.S. Army, in August 1945.
     Total missing, 1945 value: $1,000   1983 equivalent: $5,500

7. $67,120 U.S. dollars taken from the Savings Bank (*Sparkasse*) at Berchtesgaden by Karl Theodor Jacob on about 1 May 1945.
     Total 1945 value: $67,120   1983 equivalent: $369,160

8.   2 gold bars worth $30,000 ($435,000 in 1983) together with 19,840 American dollars ($109,120 in 1983) and 10,000 English pounds worth $176,000 in 1983 taken from Berchtesgaden Savings Bank and deposited in the Land Central Bank, Munich, from which they subsequently disappeared.
     Total 1945 value: $89,840   1983 equivalent: $720,120

9.   One truck-load of foreign currency, estimated maximum value of $8,000,000 recovered by Major Roger Rawley on the Oberau road in June 1945 and handed over to Major Kenneth Asa McIntyre, Town Major

10.   of Garmisch-Partenkirchen. A portion of this recovery was last seen in
        Major McIntyre's office.
        Total 1945 value: $8,000,000   1983 equivalent: $44,000,000

10.   11 boxes weighing 330 pounds each, and believed to contain gold, deliv-
        ered to Einsiedl from Berchtesgaden on 25 April 1945.
        Total 1945 value: $1,856,705   1983 equivalent: $26,922,229

11.   25 boxes containing 100 gold bars from Konstanz to Einsiedl for burial.
        No official record of recovery. If this was the gold recovered by Sergeant
        Singleton in the Mittenwald area in June 1945 it never reached official
        custody and must be listed as missing, believed stolen.
        Total 1945 value: $1,406,595   1983 equivalent: $20,395,627

12.   6.5 tons of Ribbentrop gold last seen at Schloss Fuschl, near Salzburg,
        Austria in May 1945.
        Total 1945 value: $7,431,693   1983 equivalent: $107,759,500

13.   17 bags of foreign currency from the Berlin Reichsbank taken from the
        currency caches on the Klausenkopf and environs in May and June 1945.
        After initial inquiries at the FED, suspicion fell on Colonel Fritz Rauch,
        Helmut Schreiber and Helmut Groeger. The $400,000 found at Oberau
        and the $407,235 and $1,635 worth of English pounds found at Garmisch
        and recovered by the U.S. Army in August 1945 may have formed part
        of the 17 missing bags (leaving over $1,000,000 still unrecorded and unex-
        plained). If so, they subsequently disappeared—the latter sum from the
        Land Central Bank, Munich, where it had been deposited.
        Total 1945 value of missing bags: $1,878,711   1983 equivalent: $10,332,910

The overall total of funds missing or stolen from the Reichsbank's custody
thus amounts to $432,985,013. In 1983 this sum would be worth
$2,508,809,444.

Nearly forty years after the event, the robbery of the Reichsbank reserves
can still claim to be the greatest robbery in modern history. But because
the facts of the case were largely unknown to the public at large for many
years—were, indeed, deliberately suppressed by the powers that be—a
number of other robberies laid claim to be considered the greatest ever in
the years that followed.

    The first of these was the Brinks robbery. In Boston, Massachusetts on
17 January 1950, a gang of eleven men raided the headquarters of the
Brinks Transport Company (a firm specializing in the top security transportation of bank cash, payrolls, and other valuables) and within the space
of just fifteen minutes made off with a haul of $2,500,00 in cash.

$2,500,000 in cash. For six years the robbers kept a low profile and avoided arrest. But in the week before the expiration of the Statute of Limitations, one of the men made a confession to the police, as a result of which eight of the gang were convicted and sent to prison for life. To the world at large the Brinks robbery appeared to be far and away the biggest robbery known to civilized man. But between 1945 and 1950 there had been 30 percent inflation in America, which would put the true value of the Brinks robbery at only $1,750,000 by 1945 values — or somewhat less than the total amount of official Reichsbank currency looted from the currency caches on the Klausenkopf alone.

The Brinks robbery was patently *not* the world's greatest, and in any case was eclipsed by a more sensational one in England thirteen years later — the notorious Great Train Robbery. In 1963 the Glasgow-to-London night mail train was held up by a large gang of professional criminals and relieved of $10,000,000 in used five-pound notes on their way back to the Bank of England for pulping. In the popular imagination this robbery continues to be regarded as the greatest in history — in Britain, at least. In fact, it is far surpassed by the robbery of the Reichsbank reserves, taken as a whole; and if due allowance is made for inflation, even the relatively modest losses of the Reichsbank funds in the region of Mittenwald alone total at least as much as the haul of five-pound notes taken from the ill-fated English mail train 18 years later.

Since the early 1970s soaring inflation has relentlessly eroded the real value of more recent large robberies — the estimated $6,000,000 known to have been taken from the safe deposit boxes in Nice, France in July 1976; the $6,000,000 of platinum stolen in South Africa in January 1982; the theft of $15,000,000 of securities (later found to be out of date) stolen in London on 3 December 1982; the $8,000,000 stolen in New York less than two weeks later; and the $9,500,000 in cash, jewels, and other valuables stolen from the bank in Marbella, Spain, on Christmas Day of the same year. Such raids are of course breathtaking in their magnitude. But they are still dwarfed by the Reichsbank robbery of 1945 — and their inflation-adjusted totals still do not exceed the losses sustained by the Reichsbank reserves buried in Mittenwald all those summers before.

In order to map the full extent of the Reichsbank robberies and trace the slow dawning of awareness on the part of the American authorities which in 1947 led the FED to name Rosenberg-Lipinski, Mielke, Rauch, Schreiber, and Groeger, it has been necessary to run ahead for many months and even years beyond that fateful morning in late August 1945 when Captain Neumann of Third Army drove through the shattered gate of 38 Gsteigstrasse with the last of the pecuniary offerings from the von Blüchers' back garden loaded in the back of his jeep. It is now time to go back to those earlier and more volatile and chaotic days in Bavaria soon after the end of the year and follow the movements of those leading players who are now about to bow themselves off the stage and into the wings.

In 1946 Klaus Bremme, who had an Argentinian wife, was allowed to emigrate to Argentina, almost the only country which at that time welcomed German immigrants. He was followed after a little while by Mathias Stinnes.

As for Colonel Rauch, he was allowed to leave Garmisch after the final recovery in Gsteigstrasse, in spite of his SS affiliations. Such indemnity from arrest as he may have obtained, one way or another, as a result of his cooperation with the Americans over the Reichsbank money soon ran out, however, and in November 1945 Rauch's Nazi past caught up with him. On 27 November he was arrested by Counter-Intelligence Corps (CIC) Special Agents and detained at the Tegernsee city jail before being transferred to the Civilian Internment Enclosure at Stephanskirchen. The reason given for his arrest was that he fell into the SHAEF Automatic Arrest category as a past member of the Nazi Party and Allgemeine and Waffen SS — there was no question of an investigation into the missing Reichsbank millions. Rauch admitted his membership in the proscribed organizations and in February 1946 the camp screening officer appended this comment to Rauch's evaluation report: "Automatic Arrest — Waffen SS service as Captain and a SECURITY THREAT. Continued internment pending directives from Higher HQ."

Exactly how long Rauch languished in American internment is not known. He was probably released later in 1946 or perhaps 1947 — unlike his friend, Karl Warth, who managed to escape from the American internment camp at Dachau in April 1946 and disappear. Subsequent investigations revealed that Rauch had no income of any kind between the end of the war and 1948, and lived on his own resources. He was, however, sufficiently in funds to be in a position to emigrate with his wife to Argentina in 1948 — the third signatory of the Neumann receipt to do so. Rauch got out down the so-called Römische Weg or Roman Way, the Nazi escape route via the Vatican. According to the records of the Argentinian Police Headquarters in Buenos Aires, "Jose Federico Rauch" entered Argentina on 16 February 1948 and soon afterwards became a partner in a metallurgical firm by the name of Exact SCL, a company formed by Germans and based at Santa Rosa 3350, Florida, Province of Buenos Aires. The initials SCL stand for "Collective Society," which has a special status in Argentine law. A Collective Society does not have the obligation to publish details of its formation, share capital, and board of directors in the official bulletin, and for this reason the share capital, directors, and balance sheets have never been placed on public record. Exact SCL, it seems, had a business relationship with a firm called "Efeve" which manufactured bath taps sold under the trademark FV and renowned for their high quality. Rauch, whose profession in the police records was given as "Industrialist," was the production manager for the Efeve taps. The Argentinian police report concluded with a statement to the effect that Rauch had contributed a sum of between 100,000 and 150,000 U.S. dollars to the capital of the company.

After the final currency recovery from Gsteigstrasse, Colonel Franz Pfeiffer, holder of the Knight's Cross, was allowed to leave Garmisch and return to Austria, where he resumed his duties with the French Army and continued the task of demobilizing fugitive German soldiers in the mountains of Tyrol and Vorarlberg until the operation was successfully completed in the autumn of 1945. Pfeiffer was then reemployed by the French Army as an instructor in mountain infantry techniques and tactics at Seefeld in the Tyrol and then acted as advisor to the French Mountain Riflemen—the Blue Devils—in Chamonix, in the French Alps, for three months. Colonel Pfeiffer continued to live in Austria until December 1948, after which time, according to the Innsbruck police, he emigrated to Argentina.

According to Pfeiffer, he was able to afford the trip because he had inherited a legacy from an uncle in Munich. But in his application for a visa Pfeiffer advised the Innsbruck police that he had been born in Vienna, Austria, on 14 May 1907, whereas according to the Registry of Births in Munich he was registered as being born in Munich, Germany, on 23 October 1907. Colonel Pfeiffer eventually received his official passport from the Argentinian Consul in Berne, Switzerland, and allegedly sailed with his wife from Cannes on the S.S. *Conte Grande* bound for Buenos Aires. He did not give the impression of being an inordinately rich man when he left Europe, and after he reached Buenos Aires he called himself Francisco Guillermo Pfeiffer.

A report in the possession of Police Headquarters in Buenos Aires alleges that Pfeiffer left Austria in December 1948, arrived in Argentina in March 1949 (a year after Rauch), settled in Florida district, and joined the board of Exact of which Rauch was also a member. The Buenos Aires police believed that Pfeiffer had, like Rauch, made a sizeable contribution to the capital of the company—in his case to the tune of some $100,000 U.S. dollars. There was one anomaly in the report. Pfeiffer's place and date of birth were given as Munich, 18 June 1912, which was different from both of the Austrian police records and the Registry of Births in Munich. It is not known why three different records in three different countries register three different birth dates for Colonel Pfeiffer.

If this information is correct, by today's values $100,000 would be worth $550,000 and $150,000 would be worth $825,000. If sums of money of this order were indeed contributed to the share capital of Exact by Rauch and Pfeiffer, it is unlikely that they represented the total sum that was or had been in their possession, since a portion would be required for travel and contingencies. But in any case, it would be quite extraordinary to find this kind of money in the hands of former German Army and police officers at that period of time — especially in the form of U.S. dollar currency, possession of which by German subjects was still illegal in occupied Germany and Austria as late as 1948

In an interview with the authors in 1983 Pfeiffer fiercely denied ever having put any dollars into a firm called Exact.

"That is a lot of lies!" Pfeiffer declared. "What absolute rubbish! One hundred thousand dollars invested by me in the firm! You know, now I've really had enough! Who is saying that? And what is this about police records? I never had anything to do with the police in Buenos Aires.

"I refuse to answer any further questions. Saying I invested 100,000 dollars — it's a cock-and-bull story! Me and 100,000 dollars, it makes me laugh! I'm sorry, but the police in Buenos Aires are talking a lot of poppycock. I never paid in 100,000 dollars. I never had that sum.

"I have always regretted talking to you at all. I should have kept my mouth shut. All this toing and froing, and *they* said this and somebody *else* said that, and so on and so on. Send my warmest greetings to the police in Buenos Aires and tell them to sell their lies and nonsense to somebody else. I certainly never paid 100,000 dollars into the firm."

Moreover, Pfeiffer swore he had never been a director of Exact, had never even heard of Efeve, and had never been to Switzerland. However, he *had* owned a small toy company in Buenos Aires called Inoco and he *had* worked on occasion for a company — a West German copper firm — represented in Argentina by Exact. At some stage, it seems, he had paid a small sum into Exact, but it was a "pure formality."

"It was purely *pro forma*. I don't recall exactly — it was a few Argentine pesos, a certain share in the firm, and I never saw the money again. In any case it was a ridiculously small sum. As far as I am concerned the whole matter is finished. It's a long time ago and I now have other worries. I have to pinch and save to make both ends meet. I am going to end this conversation. I am sorry, I do not want to be rude. I have done nothing to reproach myself with but I'm not going to have anything further to do with it."

Given the staunchness of Pfeiffer's denial, the Argentine police report is something of a puzzle.

Unfortunately Fritz Rauch has chosen not to shed any further light on the matter. "I am completely unqualified to say anything," he told the authors in his one brief interview on the telephone. "I can give absolutely no information on this subject whatsoever. Tell me, who betrayed my telephone number to you? Normally only my friends have my telephone number, if you see what I mean. So it must have been someone from among my circle of friends. I am making no statement and I wish not to be consulted further about these matters. Firstly I know far too little, and secondly I do not know who is really hiding behind all this. Listen, I am now seventy-seven and I have only one wish and that is to be left in peace. I think I have deserved that."

Hubert von Blücher also went to Argentina, arriving there in October 1948 on a Swedish passport. According to the Argentinian police records in Cordoba he registered his profession as photographer and his name as Huberto von Bluecher Corell. Even in South America the aura of legend continued to surround this unusual young man, and before long it was bandied about that he had, on his arrival in Argentina, presented a priceless Gobelin tapestry as a gift to Eva Peron, the President's charismatic and glamorous wife, and she had graciously agreed to accept it. "All a lot of nonsense," Hubert told us years later. "Like Bormann in the Hotel Plaza in the Argentine. And me being seen with him. And me bringing him the money he had handed over to me in the German Reichsbank in Berlin—80,000,000 dollars or so—and with the money he founded the National Socialist Party of Argentina."

Those who knew him in those days recall that he was often seen in smart society in the Argentinian capital. In 1950, after working for two years as a photographer in Buenos Aires, he left for Cordoba province, where he set up residence in La Cumbre and spent considerable time in the nearby province of Mendoza. In 1951 it seems he made his way to the United States, where he worked for the Color Corporation of America in California for a while and wrote occasional film scripts for Hollywood, including the commentary for a Walt Disney film set in the Amazon. In 1960 von Blücher returned to Buenos Aires, but later he left South America for West Germany where he wrote several intelligent and futuristic novels and founded a company in Düsseldorf specializing in research and development for antichemical warfare products, backed by government contracts.

So by a curious coincidence, perhaps, five of the German names on the famous receipt for the $404,000 dug up in the von Blücher garden ended up in Argentina: Klaus Bremme, Fritz Rauch, Franz Pfeiffer, Mathias Stinnes, and Hubert von Blücher. Only Lüder stayed at home, though eventually, many years later, he too went abroad—in his case to South Africa, where he bought a large farm near Pretoria.

As for Helmut Schreiber, he was employed for a while as an entertainer by the British Army in the British Zone of Germany, and later established a worldwide reputation as a conjuror of the highest order—Kalanag the Magician, the "Eighth Wonder of the World." Of all the Germans involved with the Reichsbank money only Helmut Groeger was ever investigated for illegal possession of foreign exchange suspected to have been stolen (although a 1948 CIC report, under the heading "Illegal Possession of Foreign Currency," cross-references Rauch, Warth, and Schreiber with Groeger). Towards the end of 1945 Groeger left the employ of Third Army and set up on his own as a professional black marketeer—funded, in all probability, by a portion of the Reichsbank currency which disappeared on the Klausenkopf. Groeger came under suspicion when it was discovered that in 1946 a former member of the 503rd Military Police Battalion attached to Third Army had illegally shipped to the United States $25,000 in greenbacks inserted in the folds of heavy wrapping paper used to wrap five large packages containing small, inexpensive souvenirs. The $25,000 in question—worth $137,500 by present values—were traced to Helmut Groeger. Subsequently the Munich CIC conducted an investigation into his affairs in order to determine his connection with the military police and his possible complicity in illegal American currency dealing. Groeger, the CIC reported, was one of the first persons to discover a huge cache of foreign currency "hidden by the Nazis shortly after World War Two."

"Helmut Groeger lives exceedingly well," the report continued, "and his income is derived from both black market transactions and from the money he appropriated from the German cache he found. Subject recently had in his possession 2,050 U.S. greenbacks in $1 denominations."

In his defense Groeger explained that the money was part of a packet of $5,000 which had been delivered to his home at Rottach in the summer of 1946 by an unknown messenger for an unexplained reason. At first, he said, he hesitated to spend such a substantial quantity of dollars since Germans were not allowed to possess foreign currency in 1946. As time went by, however, he began to spend small amounts of it on food and other necessities and later bought himself a house with part of it—an indicator, perhaps, of the considerable purchasing power of such relatively small sums of dollar exchange in those immediate postwar days.

It was about that time, according to Groeger, that he began spending more freely and made a deal with the MP of the 503rd MP Battalion. He claimed that he gave the MP $2,000 on the basis that the MP would keep $1,000 for himself and use the remaining $1,000 to send CARE and other packages to Groeger from the United States. It was an unlikely story—for a start the MP was caught shipping home $25,000, not $2,000—and the American authorities evidently thought so too, for they set in motion the preparations for Groeger's trial. In a secret memo dated 25 May 1948, CIC Special Agent Max L. Marshall said this about Helmut Groeger:

This investigation was inaugurated when a Request for Investigation from Special Agent Coopman came to this agent accompanied by a memo alleging that Groeger had helped in recovering foreign currency originally owned by the *Wehrmacht* that somehow he had retained large quantitites of American dollars for himself and that he had been involved with an American soldier in illegal currency dealings. Current investigations have revealed that these allegations are true in substance.

And at the end of a later report Marshall added a final comment: "Notify FBI to work on case in States."

That was as far as the matter seems to have got. At this point, for reasons which will become more readily apparent at a later stage in this story, further proceedings were blocked by some powerful hand from on high. Three investigative agencies had maintained eight files on Helmut Groeger, the associate of Colonel Rauch and plumber of the Reichsbank currency holes at Walchensee. All eight files were now destroyed. If Groeger ever did go to trial, the results of his hearing are no longer a matter of public record. What is strange is that a man under the gravest suspicion of having played a significant part in the greatest robbery in history should have proved such an embarrassment to certain elements among the U.S. Army occupation authorities that his case was suppressed and his trial hushed up—if indeed it even took place at all. Helmut Groeger, we must conclude, was a pawn in a greater game. Who the other players were, and what form the great game took, is a matter for a later chapter in this book.

A former Gebirgsjäger officer who knew Garmisch in the uncertain days before and after the end of the war remarked recently:

You will never, never find out now exactly what happened to the gold and the money. Someone—one of the main participants—would have to be on the point of death and decide to confess and tell the truth before it is too late. Too many people are involved. It will never come out into the open. Even then I doubt if anyone would confess under oath on his deathbed, as too many relatives would be harmed. One does not have to be a super-detective, a Sherlock Holmes, to see what was going on. To my way of thinking—and this was what I could not stomach at the time—it's all been covered up. There have been investigations here in Germany and in the United States. I've been asked over and over again. But nothing comes out. It's all been covered up.

II. CORRUPTION
AND COVER-UP

14

The Collapse of a Great Army

At the end of the war more than 150 small Military Government detachments had fanned out into the towns and villages of Bavaria to carry through the unprecedented experiment of American occupation. It had always been thought that after the German surrender all that Military Government would have to do would be to take over intact an existing system of German government and control it from the top. It had not been envisaged that the Germans would fight to the last, that in the process the entire system of government would be destroyed and that the occupying powers would have to run the whole of the country themselves from the bottom to the top. The occupation developed into one of the most extraordinary regimes in modern history. "The world had never known before a situation in which four peoples lived and tried to cooperate in a country inhabited by a fifth," wrote one historian of this bizarre episode. "Although backward peoples have often come under foreign rule, there are few precedents for civilized industrial nations actually taking over the governments of another (instead of giving orders to a puppet regime)."

The problems confronting Military Government amid the ruins of Germany and among a morally and economically shattered population were enormous. Its success in solving them depended (in part) on the abilities of the individuals who composed the Military Government teams. In the American Zone these were often looked down on by the men in the tactical echelons of the Army and were often impeded in their duties by the prejudice and incomprehension of their commanders-in-chief. Often this was because Military Government consisted of personnel who were unfit for combat service, because they were either overage, or wounded, or surplus to their units' requirements. The average age of officers in the early days of American Military Government was 46, but many were well over that

age, and some of the most able and energetic were 55 or more. Many of
these officers were highly qualified, successful, and wealthy men in civilian
life, and included lawyers earning $100,000 a year (in 1945), editors of
large newspapers, and presidents of major universities. These men had
volunteered for Military Government while the war was still being fought
in the expectation that their special skills as engineers, agronomists, teach-
ers, bankers, public health workers, and so forth could be put to good use
in the task of postwar reconstruction in Europe. Such men approached
their difficult tasks with almost missionary fervor and in Germany often
achieved miracles in getting things working again, restoring some kind of
rough order out of chaos and establishing a firm foundation for the new
Germany of the future.

There were also misfits reassigned from their regular Army units. Often
these men were harmless self-indulgers, like the young captain who "liberated" an immensely powerful prewar Porsche racing car and could be
heard, in the small hours of each night after curfew, roaring up and down
the Munich-Augsburg autobahn at stupendous speeds like some demon
nightrider. Or like the billeting officer they called "King James," who held
sway over his requisitioned properties like a petty medieval monarch and
with two pearl-handled Colt 45s at each hip reigned over his subjects from
a Bavarian castle on whose high flanking walls he had had painted a giant
yellow Texas rose. Or like the Military Governor of the small Bavarian
town of Eichstätt, a baronial young American captain of rich Bostonian
Catholic descent, who ruled his domain dressed in the papal court costume
of the Vatican (of which he was a genuine member), complete with sword,
chain, and robe.

American Military Government attracted rascals and rogues. These
were the men who were destined to take advantage of their privileges and
power in Germany to perpetrate the most outrageous rackets and biggest
robberies in history.

There had been early-warning signals in the American Army well before the end of the war. During the fighting in the Ardennes in December
1944, when the last great German counterattack had threatened to throw
back the Allied advance, the Americans had been hampered by the activities of an estimated 19,000 U.S. Army deserters engaged in large-scale robbery, gangsterism, and black marketeering in occupied territories. Indeed
the whole American effort was put in jeopardy by the criminal, not to say
treasonable, conduct of certain members of the U.S. Army Corps of
Transport, who devised a profitable scheme which involved rerouting
whole train loads of gasoline tankers away from the Ardennes front, where

the gasoline was urgently needed for American tanks, southward into liberated France, where it was siphoned and sold for a fortune on the French black market. In Italy, too, a small section of the American Army, mostly soldiers of recent Italian origin with probable American Mafia affiliation, gravitated into organized crime with remarkable alacrity, linking up with their local Italian Mafia cousins and indulging in gang warfare and Chicago-style shoot-outs in the cafés of Rome. With the end of the war and the collapse of morale and discipline that the end of the fighting inevitably entailed, serious crime among members of the military soared.

It was not only the Americans who turned to crime after the German surrender. In Berlin armed gangs of deserters and DPs — Russians, Poles, Frenchmen, Spaniards (from the former Spanish volunteer battalions of the Waffen-SS), and some Americans — terrorized the city. In May 1945 one such gang, a hundered strong, attacked a train at the Anhalter Bahnhof railway station. Other gangs moved out into the Zones. Convoys of British Army trucks approaching Berlin were held up at gunpoint by armed men, and on one occasion British troops were engaged in a running gunfight with American train bandits who had earlier shot their way out of an ambush. Even the soldiers of the Red Army deserted in untold numbers and roamed the countryside in predatory packs.

Booty and women had been the perquisites of conquering armies from time immemorial. This was so in 1945 almost as soon as the first foreign soldier crossed the German frontier, and it went on being so long after hostilities had ceased. Not even the highest-ranking service chiefs were exempt from the general rule of *vis victis* (rights of conquest). At the last great conference of the Allied war leaders at Potsdam in July 1945, several of the supreme British military chiefs — including the Chief of the Imperial General Staff, Field Marshall Sir Alan Brooke, Marshal of the Royal Air Force Lord Portal and Admiral of the Fleet Viscount Cunningham — were seen to loot rare antiquarian books from the Royal Library in the Cecilienhof Palace; and President Truman's special aide, Brigadier General Harry Vaughan, quickly discovered the Berlin black market, and while his colleagues were otherwise engaged in sorting out the world, proceeded to dispose of his spare clothes for a brisk profit amounting (he was to boast later) to "a couple of thousand bucks." There was no accounting for tastes. In Bavaria one official of the Office of Military Government, Bavaria (OMGB) made off with the Reichspost stamp collection, another purloined a death mask of Napoleon, and a third stole the large collection of lead soldiers from the War Museum.

What distinguished the American Zone from the other three Occupation Zones was the persistence and magnitude of the criminal acts that were committed there. There seems to be no comparable record for such widespread wrongdoing in the British, French, or even Russian Zones. Though two million American soldiers had been demobilized and sent home from Germany by the first Christmas after the war, this still left a million or more combat veterans marooned among the ruins—homesick, bored, unmotivated, and malcontent. Some of these men entertained a very different attitude to their role as occupation troops from that of their European counterparts in the other zones. The French, Russian, and British soldiers came from homelands which had been bombed, invaded, or blockaded by Hitler's forces, and instinctively perhaps they experienced a greater sense of involvement and responsibility in the occupation of the former Nazi state and had a more acute perception of their role. The American troops, by contrast, hailed from a continent on the other side of the world; they had helped win the Europeans' war for them and many of them felt that they had done enough and that it was time to go home.

There were other contributory causes. The Americans came from a country where the frontier spirit of the Old West, with its pioneer individualists on the one hand and its renegade outlaws on the other, was still strong; in the frontierlike chaos of posthostilities Germany this spirit found fresh strength. Coming from a country where, in the dictum of President Calvin Coolidge, "the business of America is business," they found themselves in a country where the spirit of private enterprise enshrined in this "proverb" could be pursued *ad absurdum*—and outside the usual rules. Many of the Americans in Military Government were of recent German or German Jewish origin, and once back in Germany their loyalties were torn in a variety of directions, not all of them legal. But perhaps the single greatest cause of immorality and crime on the part of the American occupation was the corrupting ambience of the Germany in which they had to live and function—an ambience which provided daily opportunities for enrichment.

The occupation forces lived well in Germany. Those at the top lived and ruled like kings. Generals in the U.S. Zone had their own private trains, fully staffed and under steam 24 hours a day to whirl them from one end to the other of their kingdoms. Junior officers lived like millionaires, and even GIs had German servants to look after them. In their luxurious off-limits ghettoes the victors lived the good life while all around them thousands starved in the rubble.

"We became an 'India Service,'" wrote a former U.S. Chief Information Officer in Frankfurt—"poobah Sahibs—masters of a conquered people, rulers of an occupied colonial state. Little people from the States haughtily ordered German mayors and governors to appear before them, delivered speeches on democracy, and received homage and presents. Like India Service personnel, in the midst of ruins and near starvation, we lived well. We requisitioned the best houses. We wined and dined as we had never done at home. Like conquerors, we affected fancy uniforms and fancy leather boots. The most beautiful women in Germany we had at our price. There were servants to minister to our every need. For a few packs of cigarettes, we even had music with our meals. And on the streets, before the opera, groups of Germans gathered to fight each other for our cigarette butts."

George Kennan, a highly-placed advisor in the State Department, formed an even more derogatory opinion of the occupation elite in the U.S. Zone, and wrote in his memoirs:

Each time I had come away with a sense of sheer horror at the spectacle of this horde of my compatriots and their dependants camping in luxury amid the ruins of a shattered national community, ignorant of the past, oblivious to the abundant evidences of present tragedy all around them, inhabiting the same sequestered villas that the Gestapo and SS had just abandoned, and enjoying the same privileges, flaunting their silly supermarket luxuries in the face of a veritable ocean of deprivation, hunger, and wretchedness, setting an example of empty materialism and cultural poverty before a people desperately in need of spiritual and intellectual guidance, taking for granted—as though it were their natural due—a disparity of privilege and comfort between themselves and their German neighbors no smaller than those that had once divided lord and peasant in that feudal Germany which it had been our declared purpose in two world wars to destroy.

Some Military Government officers resigned in disgust. "In one of the more idealistic decisions of my life," one of the explained later, "I decided to get out before I was completely demoralized by the rich life, the castles, the women, the drink, and black market."

The first two years after the war witnessed in Germany a sociological phenomenon without precedent in the history of modern Europe—that of universal concubinage. This practice was widely observed from the lowest to the highest ranks of the Allied armies. Among the lower ranks in the U.S. Zone it was so widespread that German girls were kept quite brazenly in the barrack rooms of the big Army bases, and regular bed checks were necessary to root out female guests who were off-limits. Among the top brass the spate of high-class German mistresses—many of them of dubious Nazi background—threatened to spill over into public scandal. As a consequence of total promiscuity, the incidence of VD reached epidemic proportions. Now the Army posters on the autobahn read: "Beware of *Veronika Dankeschön.*" But few did. "When we came up against our first 19-year-old Rhineland blonde," one GI was heard to explain, "with blue eyes, pink cheeks, braids, and very desirable, we were just clean bowled over."

For the women of Germany—lonely, hungry, out of work, and greatly outnumbering their own men, millions of whom lay dead on the battle-fields of Europe or rotting in prison camps abroad—the Allied soldier was the best short cut to survival that could be found. In December 1945 a German police report declared: "It is impossible to distinguish between good girls and bad girls in Germany. Even nice girls of good families, good education, and fine background have discovered their bodies afford the only real living. Moral standards have crashed to a new low." The German Fräulein became an item of mass consumption like any other and could be acquired by barter like a commodity on the black market. No Allied soldier need be without female company if he carried a few packs of cigarettes or a can of bully beef or a pair of silk stockings from the PX in his knapsack.

The principal instrument of corruption was the black-market cigarette. In the German cigarette economy the PX cigarette was the prime source of every American's wealth over and above his pay. One Camel or Lucky Strike in 1945 was worth more than double a German's pay for a hard day's work clearing the rubble in the streets. One packet of cigarettes would finance fifty double scotches. A few cartons would enable a GI to deal in antiques, Persian rugs, Meissen porcelain, Leicas, binoculars, paintings, sculptures, silver, and jewelry. With several million cigarettes issued by the PX in the American Zone each week, it is not surprising that a U.S. Army lieutenant could earn as much as $12,000 a year on the cigarette economy and go home with a nest-egg of $25,000 on top of his pay. In October 1945 the American occupation forces in Berlin sent home nearly $5.5 million more than they had been paid. Officers were the biggest operators, often leaving their desks for more lucrative earnings from black-market deals in the streets. "Those conditions," wrote one American official on assignment from Washington, "created an atmosphere so unreal, so nightmarish, so demoralizing that official work was almost impossible." Since the practice was so prevalent and so many high-ranking officers were involved, it proved virtually impossible to eradicate.

Even the Military Governor himself, General Clay—or more exactly, his wife—was allegedly involved. According to one U.S. Army Criminal Investigation Division (CID) agent, "it was common gossip that Mrs. Clay was engaged in extensive black-market trading and that her acquisitions were being sent back to the States by the General's personal plane." At first, it seems, General Clay was unaware of the situation, but shortly after it was reported to him by an agent of the CID the black-market situation was declared to be a "security threat" and every effort was made to cover the matter up — a task made more difficult when the U.S. Customs, Florida District, sent a letter of complaint with a long list of landings of Clay's personal plane in the Miami area. In each case the pilot reported "classified mission" and thus avoided Customs inspections. However, investigation disclosed that none of these overseas flights had been logged in with the Air Force. The Air Force investigation disclosed that all of the Berlin departures had simply been logged as "training flights." Charges were laid against the pilot. "I can't remember if he was actually tried or if he resigned," our CID informant reported, "but it was pretty obvious that he was taking the fall, as the saying goes."

Many profited from the occupation; a very few hit the jackpot. Those that did seem mostly — for no greater reason, perhaps, than sheer opportunity — to have hailed from Office of Military Government of Bavaria (OMGB), whose headquarters town was the still-ruined Bavarian capital of Munich and whose sin city was Garmisch-Partenkirchen.

In October 1945 command of OMGB fell to Brigadier-General (later Major-General) Walter Muller, formerly Third Army's supply officer. Muller was destined to remain Military Governor of Bavaria throughout the greater part of the period covered by this book and the immediate chief of a number of the senior American officers who take part in our story. He was seen by the Germans with whom he dealt as a rough professional soldier who was both good-hearted and helpful. But he was also touchy at the beginning, when Military Government underwent a transition from a system based on the organization of the occupying army to a system based on the organization of German local government, and the Germans never knew whom he would arrest next. Muller's reign presented a paradox: on one hand the MPs and the CIC, with their unrestrained powers of arrest, terrorized the populace with arbitrary arrests and mass confiscations of homes; on the other hand widespread crime and corruption flourished as never before or since. No fewer than three of the main divisions of Military Government in Bavaria were seen to be rather less than perfect. One was the Legal Division, which suffered from a shortage of officers adequately qualified in the practice of law and the dispensing of justice. "With a military government code of justice and no legal precedents to speak of," recalled one CID agent, "the law was what in effect the legal section said it was. What a collection of carpetbaggers!" Another was the Financial Division, whose Chief, Colonel Lord, and his aide from Property Control, Major McCarthy, we have already met in connection with the disposition in Munich of gold and dollar currency recovered (and subsequently mislaid) from the Reichsbank treasure. Yet another was the Transportation Branch, which over a period of several years involved itself in one of the OMGB's major scandals.

By late 1946 it had become evident that a staggering number of German civilian automobiles requisitioned by OMGB for the use of the U.S. Army had been stolen or embezzled. Out of over 5,000 vehicles originally requisitioned, only 1,500 could be accounted for. 3,500 had been illegally disposed of on the black market — enough to equip several army divisions — generally under the subterfuge of having been declared unfit for military use or "cannibalized" for parts. Many of these had then reappeared in the vicinity of Munich with licence plates indicating they had been sold into private ownership, whereas they were or should have been under U.S. military control.

Alarmingly, it was found that the Transportation Branch of OMGB was staffed, almost to a man, by personnel who were, in the words of the official report, "inefficient or dishonest, or both." This situation, the report continued, "has favored thefts of automobilies and fraudulent transactions in automobiles, which transactions, there is reason to believe, have been, and are still, conducted on a large scale. And this highly unsatisfactory condition will continue as long as crookedness is, as at present, at a premium." For all that, most of the extremely serious cases of larceny, embezzlement, forgery, and fraud perpetrated by American personnel in Bavaria were not prosecuted by the American High Command — for reasons that will become apparent in due course — and the proper exercise of law and justice was interfered with to an alarming degree in the few cases that did reach the courts. This extraordinary state of affairs should be borne in mind as a background to the curious affair of Garmisch-Partenkirchen, to which town this story now turns.

It so happened that the Military Government of Garmisch had one of the poorest records for honesty and efficiency in the U.S. Zone. Shortly after its capture the town had been made a U.S. Army Recreation Center for American personnel on local leave. Every kind of facility was lavished on it, from hotels and shopping centers to a ski school and a Hollywood-style nightclub, and for a while the whole town became virtually one huge American hotel. After the rigors of the war years and the dreary monotony of the ruined cities, Garmisch proved a seductive place for the American officers who ran it, and some of them were all too easily seduced. They were seduced not only by the easiness of the life there but by certain members of the local population who, for their own advantage, put opportunities in their American masters' way that were both unique and (frequently) irresistible. If some of the Military Government officers who reported for duty in Garmisch were not corrupt before their arrival, they were soon corrupted after it. For these men, the temptations for personal enrichment simply proved too great.

Surviving records for the period immediately after the German surrender are too fragmentary and confusing to give any clear picture of the web of intrigue and corruption that enmeshed the Military Government in Garmisch during that first fall and winter. As early as the beginning of 1946 the unacceptable face of American rule in Garmisch had come to the attention of the military authorities, but bemused investigators were forced to confess that they found the whole situation "very confusing." Enough emerged, however, to indicate that "most people in the employ of Garmisch Military Government were making an effort to, and in some cases succeeding in, bettering their positions and obtaining property and probably money illegally" and that "collusion and liaison was employed by German civilian employees and U.S. Army officials for the purpose of self-satisfaction and personal gain." A subsequent Inspection Report by a colonel from OMGB bluntly concluded: "This was the most poorly administered detachment I have seen."

In a town as politically and criminally exposed as Garmisch, it might have been expected that the American High Command would have taken quick, firm, and decisive action to keep the situation there under control. This, for some reason, they failed to do until the summer of 1947. For a full two years after the end of the war, every imaginable crime was committed in Garmisch, until in time the town bore a closer resemblance to a wild cowboy town in America's Old West than to a fashionable winter resort in southern Germany. The records speak for themselves. During a period of just over one-and-a-half years no less than *seven* officers served as Military Governor in Garmisch. Of these, several — though not all — had to be reassigned for sheer lack of ability or for feathering their own nests. No other Military Government detachment in the U.S. Zone — and there were nearly 150 — had such a high turnover of commanding officers. "They changed like a revolving door," one CIC agent in Garmisch recalled; "they were always being investigated for one thing or another." Of a total of 24 American personnel ordered out of Bavaria for prejudicial acts over the period of a year up to the autumn of 1947, four were from Garmisch Military Government, including two Military Governors, one Legal Officer, and one Public Safety officer.

This, then — the worst-run town in American Germany — forms the unpredictable background for the remainder of our story of the Reichsbank robbery and its aftermath, a lamentable tale of corruption and cover-up.

15

The White Horse Inn

Garmisch-Partenkirchen was one of the nicest small towns in Germany. Thanks to Major Pössinger and his fellow Gebirgsjäger officers it had not been laid waste in battle like many other small towns, and it gave off the same discreet air of unostentatious wealth and well-to-do Bavarian Alpine charm after the war that it had enjoyed before.

Lying in an open mountain basin beneath the snowy ramparts of the Wetterstein range and the highest peak in Germany, the 9,720-foot Zugspitze, Garmisch-Partenkirchen was the principal town of the so-called Werdenfelser Land, a seductively beautiful region of lakes, forests, gorges, waterfalls, snowfields, peaks, and Alpine pastures. Originally two separate villages of picturesque narrow streets and pretty Bavarian-style frescoed houses on either bank of a tributary of the River Loisach, Garmisch and Partenkirchen had long grown together as the metropolis of the Bavarian Alps and the leading winter sports resort of Germany. The 1936 Winter Olympics had taken place there, and the high-jump platforms of the Olympic Ski Stadium and the great rinks of the Olympic Ice Stadium were still in existence when the war came to an end. Into the latter the Americans threw every German in uniform they could find, and when that was full they herded the remainder into the green expanse of the Kurpark in the center of the town, while suspected Nazis were locked up in Gebirgsjäger barracks until such time as they could be processed.

There were a great many Germans in captivity in Garmisch in the first

---

Editor's note: Due to strict libel laws, the following two chapters have been edited to mask the identities of persons who are still living and who had substantial involvement in the disappearance of millions of dollars in American currency and German gold.

weeks and months after the end of the war. The town had been an important staging-post on the route into Austria and the heart of Hitler's national redoubt; many *Wehrmacht*, SS, and Hungarian units had straggled here in their southward retreat from the Americans, while many thousands of Nazi functionaries and notable personages (including the Kaiser's daughter-in-law, the Crown Princess of Prussia, and members of the French Vichy Government) had holed up here in the hope of avoiding retribution in suitably comfortable and elegant surroundings. The population of Garmisch swelled enormously during the last days of the war and eventually there were five times the number of people living in the town as there had been in the year before the German collapse. Among the newcomers were many Germans of real wealth—much of it already salted away in Swiss bank accounts until better times returned. Inevitably, after the surrender Garmisch became a gathering place of adventurers and dealers of all kinds.

At the end of the war, then, Garmisch-Partenkirchen was an unscathed and inherently well-to-do town in a relatively remote and exceedingly beautiful corner of southern Germany within striking distance of both the Swiss and the Austrian borders—and, of course, the burial caches of the Reichsbank reserves. If it had been a cosmopolitan place before the war, it was doubly so after it. For crowded together within the small confines of the town and the mountain-bound district surrounding it were men and women from every corner of Europe—German and Eastern European refugees, evacuees, enemy prisoners of war, Allied prisoners of war, hospitalized wounded, and Jewish survivors of the concentration camps—along with the occupation soldiers from far-off America. As well as German, a whole babel of tongues could be heard in the streets—English, French, Russian, Yiddish, Czech, Polish, Lithuanian, and all the languages of the Balkans. In the political and economic chaos that prevailed, people from many nations and from all walks of life—from ex-officers, diplomats, and ladies of society to opportunists, rogues, and professional crooks—did what was necessary to survive the rigors of peace. In the diversity and audacity of the racketeering that ensued, there were probably few towns in Germany that could compare with Garmisch in the first four years after the war. As the former head of the Garmisch CIC recalled "Garmisch was like the Klondike. We had every creep you can imagine."

In Garmisch, as in the rest of Germany, sheer survival was every German's topmost priority. For Germany in 1945 was a land of hunger and desperate need, where the simplest, smallest object was unobtainable and the very means of existence had ceased to exist, where everyone lived from hand to mouth, where the daily fat ration weighed less than an empty matchbox and it was calculated that the average German could expect a new dinner plate once in five years, a new pair of shoes once in twelve years, and a new suit once in fifty years.

The black market existed over most of war-ravaged Europe, but nowhere was it blacker than in Germany. There the basic cause—extreme shortage of consumer goods leading to astronomical prices—was exacerbated by a virtually worthless German currency and a rigid monetarist policy of rationing and price controls imposed by the Allies with the object of preventing the soaring inflation of the kind experienced in Germany after the First World War. This policy had two effects. The first was to paralyze the economy. The second was to abolish one of civilization's main foundations—money. In place of money came barter. A Bokhara rug could be bought for 100 pounds of potatoes, a piano for a suckling pig, a dinner plate for a set of false teeth—or anything and anyone, from diamonds to love, for American (or English) cigarettes.

For three years after the end of the war Germany became a cigarette civilization. Tobacco plants flowered in Rhineland vineyards and town window boxes, and two new folk figures of the time appeared—the tobacco baron at one end of the spectrum, and the *Kippensammler,* the collector of butt ends, at the other. Ten butt ends made one cigarette, and for one cigarette a man could get a whole bottle of schnapps, and for one bottle of schnapps he could get two pounds of butter from a country farmer. Germany, it was said, had become a nation of bowed heads.

For many millions of Germans the black market was the only means of existence. In time it developed into a well-organized illicit underground economy, based on an eternal triangle of market forces in which the immutable law of supply and demand was determined between three main groups—the people of the towns, the people of the countryside, and the soldiers of the occupation armies. The starving townspeople traded their valuables (jewelry, watches, furs, Leicas, Zeiss binoculars, objects d'art) for the soldiers' PX luxuries (coffee, sugar, chocolate, white bread, silk stockings, cigarettes), and the country people traded their surplus food (potatoes, bacon, poultry, flour, and eggs) for the townspeople's valuables or the luxuries they had obtained from the soldiers. After the first postwar harvest the whole of Germany went on the move as the people from the towns flocked into the countryside to exchange their barter goods for the farmers' produce. Many traveled hundreds of miles on the crowded trains, often riding on the bumpers or the carriage roofs. Each train had its black market nickname. The Potato Train ran from the industrial Ruhr to agricultural Lower Saxony. The Calorie Express went from hungry Hamburg to the farmlands of Bavaria. The Vitamin Train took Dortmünders out to the cherry harvest around Freiburg, the Nicotine Line ran to the tobacco fields of Pfalz, the Fish Express from the North Sea to Berlin.

The black market was personally and socially corrupting and economically damaging, for no modern industrial society could possibly be organized as a barter system. But for some it provided exceptional opportunities.

Two categories of people stood to make money on the black market in Germany. The first were the soldiers, whose access to an almost unlimited supply of cigarettes and other luxuries was a potential source of great profit. The second were the big-time operators, the *Scheiber* or pushers, who ran large, illegal, Mafia-style organizations dealing in the wholesale supply of basic black-market consumer goods or in high-risk, high-yield commodities like narcotics, industrial chemicals, old masters, precious stones, and — perhaps the hottest prime commodity of all — penicillin or "white gold." These were the men who controlled the black market, who fixed the prices, moved goods around from one zone to the other by the wagonload, kept control of their gangs with the help of ex-professional boxers and other heavies, and waged a fierce power struggle with their rivals. Some of these organizations were highly sophisticated. The Duisburg Railway Station Gang, for example, had its own headed notepaper with an embossed coat of arms on it and kept typed lists of commodities, with dates and prices, like a legitimate business. Another gang stole complete trains, locomotive and all, which they used to transport to enormous consignments of potatoes and other black-market perishables in bulk.

One of the most successful black marketeers was a former concentration camp inmate. He had acquired a million sewing-machine needles that had disappeared from the inventory of the Singer Sewing Machine Co. in Darmstadt while it was under a custodian of American Military Government. He smuggled the needles to Italy, where he sold them to the Necchi Company. Though he only received a nominal sum for the needles, he also received as part of the deal the U.S. sales rights for the Necchi sewing machine. He then emigrated to New York and with a small amount of capital set up a commission order office. Within two years he had made over a million dollars.

In Garmisch-Partenkirchen there was no "Mr. Big" but rather a loose confederacy of rascals, many of whom were habitués of the same haunt — a notorious establishment called the *Weisses Rössl*, or White Horse Inn. This was a rectangular, two-storied building which stood at right angles to the long main street known as Bahnhofstrasse, almost opposite the grandest and most expensive hotel in town, the Partenkirchner Hof, and barely a hundred yards from the American Military Government headquarters in the *Rathaus* on the other side of the street. Along one side of this modest edifice a whitewashed facade bore a typical Bavarian fresco depicting the principal *dramatis personae* of the popular operatta which had lent its name to this establishment, pride of place being given to a galloping charger, the white horse itself. The other side of the building overlooked the rushing, soapy-looking waters of the River Partnach, which separated Garmisch from Partenkirchen, and, tumbling headlong down a narrow, boulder-strewn gorge beneath a tangled overhang of beech and sycamore trees, would eventually find its way into the distant Danube and Black Sea.

In 1945 the place was not really an inn. Its function was rather that of a *Nachtlokal*, a bar-restaurant which stayed open late at night. The building still stands today, albeit under a new name and new management. The original fresco is covered as far as the eaves in a luxuriant growth of Virginia creeper which in autumn enlivens an otherwise undistinguished edifice with a spectacular display of crimson foilage. Nowadays the place is part of a popular chain of restaurants serving decent meals at modest prices. In 1945 it was one of the most notorious sinks of iniquity in the whole of Upper Bavaria.

The White Horse was leased in those days to a remarkable and short-lived woman by the name of Zenta Hausner, who was destined to play no small part in the making of the Garmisch legend. In due course the American press in Germany would come to call her Garmisch Nell or the Queen of Hearts, and among the Germans of Garmisch she was known by the no less evocative nickname of *die Königin der Nacht* (the Queen of the Night). At the end of the war Zenta was 35 years of age, an attractive woman by all accounts, with a full figure and a shock of bright red hair, a long track record in the business, and an overriding ambition to achieve riches and luxury in a world singularly lacking in either.

Frau Hausner's past was not greatly more wholesome than her future. She was born in October 1910 in Mühldorf, a small Bavarian town on the River Inn, the daughter of a well-to-do brewer. She was a pretty girl, and a pushy and ambitious one. By the age of 18 she had already become the owner of her first establishment — a beer tavern in the city of Munich. Two years later she came to the notice of the police when she tried to shoot herself in Munich's most fashionable hotel, the Vier Jahreszeiten, following the break-up of her love affair with a well-known violinist. Fortunately she was interrupted, with a pistol at her breast and a scratchy record playing a weepy violin solo — *"Das Lied der Sehnsucht"* ("Song of Yearning") — on the phonograph. Zenta survived her heartbreak and was thus granted a stay of execution for 17 more years.

With the profits from her tavern the youthful Zenta bought a restaurant in a respectable spa town in Lower Saxony, and married a racing car driver by whom she had one child, a daughter. After her divorce in 1938 she moved back to Munich, where she ran a nightclub and brought and managed the Hotel Post near Munich railway station. During one of the mass air raids on the Bavarian capital in 1944, Zenta's hotel was bombed and destroyed and in compensation she received from the Nazi government 30,000 Reichsmarks. With this money she removed herself to unscathed Garmisch-Partenkirchen just before Christmas 1944 and rented the hotel-restaurant Zur Schranne. This hotel was situated next to the office of the *Kreisleiter*, the head of the Nazi local government, and inevitably became a popular location for local Nazi dignitaries, who used the restaurant as a meeting place and held elaborate parties there during the evening. The entire community, it was said, regarded Zenta's restaurant as a disgrace to decency. Zenta Hausner herself was considered to be an ardent Nazi sympathizer and was known to have been the mistress of Gauleiter Giesler, the Nazi governor of Bavaria. According to the postwar *Landrat* of Garmisch, only because of her connections with the local governor was Zenta granted the lease of the Zur Schranne at all.

All of this should have been rather a handicap to Zenta Hausner when the war to eliminate Nazism ended in an Allied victory and the occupation of Germany. But it was not. Like hundreds of thousands of other Nazis or Nazi sympathizers in Germany, this lady of fortune escaped retribution by taking advantage of the moral ambivalence of the occupation regime. Though the punishment of Nazis and the total eradication of Nazism was one of the main postwar goals of the Allied occupation governments in Germany, in practice the process was snarled by almost insuperable administrative difficulties and bogged down in human reality — the social, sexual, and financial rapport that developed between victors and vanquished, and the mutual satisfaction of private need and greed between the Allied soldiers and the German civilians.

In order to continue her career as a restaurateur in Garmisch, Zenta Hausner had her eyes on the White Horse. But when she applied for a licence she was refused on the grounds of her previous affiliation and connection with Nazi organizations and officials. There was only one way out, it seemed, and that was via an American officer's heart. Frau Hausner was a comely woman and only a week or two after the end of the war she had

already caught the eye of a certain U.S. Army captain called Korner—
"one of the most unglorious representatives of the occupation powers on
German soil," according to one who knew him in those days. Later that
summer Captain Korner was appointed Commandant of a local Civilian
Internment Camp for suspected Nazis and became an influential member
of the American military establishment in the town. Their liaison seemed
almost preordained. Frau Hausner wanted the White Horse Inn and Captain Korner wanted Frau Hausner. *Ergo,* Captain Korner would get her
the White Horse Inn and he would have Frau Hausner.

As Commandant of the Internment Camp, Korner had become experienced in reaching accommodations of this sort. Like many members of
American Military Government in Germany he was more German than
American and seems to have had difficulty in determining where his patriotic loyalties lay. Born and brought up in Germany, he had emigrated to
the United States in the Thirties. Allegedly Korner brought a large sum of
money to the States which he misappropriated from a *Wehrmacht* unit with
which he had been serving before his defection. Korner's military records
are missing from the appropriate U.S. Army archives in the United States,
so nothing of his career is known until he surfaced in Garmisch at the end
of the war as a German expert in the U.S. Army Counter-Intelligence
Corps (CIC) and thus fatefully crossed the path of "Garmisch Nell."

What *is* known is that Captain Korner abused his position at the internment camp to make a personal profit out of the inmates, most of whom
were known or suspected Nazis. Korner's business was selling *Persilscheine,*
or Persil certificates, to the highest bidders. A Persil certificate was a whitewash document, generally bogus, which officially cleared the bearer of
complicity in Nazism during the Hitler era. It was one of the most highly
prized items on the German black market—and one of the most expensive. What Korner peddled were not, as it happened, bogus papers but
genuine official discharge papers, properly signed but wrongfully issued.
Some of the Germans who were released in this way were such notorious
Nazis that they were later rearrested, and the process would begin all over
again. Whenever Korner found he had run out of bidders he merely recruited more by the simple expediency of having a man arrested "on suspicion." Through professional go-betweens Korner would then get in touch
with the prisoner's relatives and fix a price that would secure his release.
The payment was almost obligatory in those circumstances, for there was
no habeas corpus and a man could be held "on suspicion" for an indefinite
period, regardless of his guilt or innocence. Such was the man who aspired
to Zenta Hausner's bed, who became in quick succession her lover, her

confidant, and her business partner, and who played such a decisive role in the beginning—and the end—of her peacetime career in Garmisch-Partenkirchen.

With a man like Korner on her side, Zenta's difficulties with local German officialdom were quickly solved.

Captain Korner bulldozed his way through the opposition. German advisors to the Garmisch Military Government were fully aware of Frau Hausner's activities during the war and knew that her *Fragebogen* contained false statements about her Nazi connections. One of them even threatened to see to it that Hausner left Garmisch with only a suitcase in her hand. Against such opponents Captain Korner was both bullying and dismissive. In his capacity as a Civilian Internment Camp officer he had personally screened Frau Hausner, he emphasized. He could confirm that she was "OK," so how dare they bandy false information? How dare they cause the lady offense? "Why don't we keep quiet about the past?" he suggested to them conspiratorially. "Between us we could rule Garmisch." So the lease was granted. The White Horse Inn was now in Zenta Hausner's hands to make of it what she would.

What Zenta made of the place probably confirmed everybody's worst fears. The underlying function of the White Horse—the source of its future notoriety—was not what any official had had in mind. But there was no doubt that Frau Hausner knew her job and was an excellent businesswoman. Both professionally and privately she was everyone's idea of "the hostess with the mostest." She was charming and personable. She was easy on the eye and easy to get on with. She was a cheerful, jolly soul—*lustig* in the Bavarian manner—and she laughed a lot and helped others to laugh in a gloomy and uncertain world. And she was as generous as she was shrewd. Diners in her restaurant did not have to produce their ration cards to get a meal; in the White Horse, it was said, *gibt es alles "ohne,"* everything is "without." If one of the *Herren* did not have enough money with him to pay the bill, no matter—she gave him credit "on the slate," and entered his name and his debt in her little black notebook.

The White Horse offered warmth, hospitality, conviviality, and escape. In the simple, cryptlike Bavarian room, the schnapps flowed, music played, the conversation swelled and the blanket of black-market Virginia tobacco smoke thickened. All kinds of people came to Zenta's *Nachtlokal* for a night out and a respite from the realities of postwar Germany—civilians and soldiers, Germans and foreigners, nice girls and tarts, the good, the bad, and the ugly. And among them, seated in a huddle in the darker corners, their earnest discussions submerged under the noise and the smoke,

were the men who bestowed on Zenta Hausner's night haunt its quintes-
sential reputation—the wheeler-dealers. Failed businessmen, banned by
occupation law from the pursuit of legitimate commerce and trade, they
used the White Horse like an industrial club or a commodities exchange,
covertly manipulating the underworld forces of supply and demand in
Garmisch and Upper Bavaria, and busily operating the black market by
means of a primitive but complex system of barter in contraband and
under-the-counter goods of every description: furs, diamonds, gasoline,
automobiles, salt, cognac, optical equipment, insulin, precision instru-
ments, and anything that could be turned for a quick profit. A Garmisch
journalist who was Zenta's close friend later recalled: "Over the tables,
wagonloads of coal, alcohol, and petrol were brought and sold. A great
deal of money was also made by buying and selling diamonds and opium.
Gradually all those people who could be considered respectable stopped
going to the White Horse." One of the most active racketeers was Zenta's
manager of the White Horse, a man known to everyone as Charlie. In the
past, Charlie had achieved the unusual distinction of being thrown out of
the Hitler Youth and obtaining a fraudulent discharge from the *Wehrmacht*
in wartime. In postwar Garmisch he emerged as a big-time black marketeer, morphine addict, and local thug—"a bad and very dangerous guy," in
the words of one who knew him.

For the big-time operators, Zenta Hausner—who was a big-time operator herself—made available the inner sanctum of her own private quarters. Above the nightclub she had a small apartment looking down on the
river: a modest sitting room with four chairs and a round occasional table,
a bedroom with a double bed and a kitchen and bath. Here, after the club
had shut for the night, she would invite a few close friends or business part-
ners for a nocturnal poker party or other entertainment. Here, too, she
would confirm her latest deal and embrace her latest lover, others besides
Captain Korner, though he was her most constant.

Something else helped to make the White Horse the most notorious dive
in Garmisch—and in Garmisch itself had, in the words of American
Counter-Intelligence, "the worst concentration of international gangsters
in postwar Europe." Here was the easy access to foreign borders—Switzerland, Austria, Italy. Here too, in extraordinary amount and variety, were
valuables of all kinds that had been dumped and cached in the area as the
tide of war receded. For in addition to the Reichsbank reserves, the *Abwehr*
funds, and the war chest of the Brandenburg Division, large stocks of military and strategic materials of all kinds had been abandoned throughout
the Werdenfelser land—platinum, uranium, heavy water, morphine,

cocaine, precious metals, jewels, and much else besides. These abandoned dumps were soon discovered and ransacked by local racketeers and formed the basic stock-in-trade of the big-time black marketeers and international smugglers operating from Munich and Garmisch as a base.

The fate of some of these valuables we have attempted to describe already. Portions of the remainder came to the attenton of the authorities from time to time. Ten cases of platinum, for example, which were said to belong to the Italians, arrived in Mittenwald too late to be properly hidden and had to be buried under a manure heap in the backyard of Joseph Veit, the local hunter who had been asked to find a hiding place for Funk and other Nazi VIPs in April 1945. AFter the Americans had occupied Mittenwald, Veit handed over the cases of platinum to a couple of officers who were carrying out a house-to-house search, obtaining a receipt from them in return. On a number of occasions during the next few months several American Counter-Intelligence Corps officers called on Veit and demanded to know what he had done with the platinum that had been placed in his charge. On each occasion Veit showed them his receipt and the CIC investigators went away puzzled. It seemed to Veit that either there was a total lock of coordination between the different department of the U.S. Occupation or the ten cases of platinum (like a portion of the Reichsbank treasure) had not reached the right hands once they had been recovered by the Americans.

Much of the uranium disappeared, also. The uranium, in the form of small cubes, had been stockpiled by the Germans during the war at their atomic bomb research station in the foothills of the Kreuzeck, one of the heights above Garmisch-Partenkirchen. With the approach of the American Army the entire stock of uranium cubes was loaded onto trucks, driven down to the River Loisach, and tipped into the water. One day later in the summer — not long after the first atomic bomb had been dropped on Hiroshima on 6 August 1945 — a group of children paddling in a shallow stretch of the river chanced on some of these metal cubes lying among the rocks in the riverbed. To their delight, they found that when they struck the radioactive cubes against a stone they emitted a flash about a foot long, like a magic lighter. Naturally the children took a few of these strange cubes home with them and showed them to their parents, and it was not long before the astonished adults surmised what it was the children had found.

This was the beginning of Garmisch's great uranium rush. It had not escaped some of the more astute citizens of the town that the basic fissionable material of the atomic bomb must have some kind of value on the local black market and they were soon scouring the riverbed in search of this precious new commodity One man even went to the extent of making fake uranium cubes out of lead studded with splinters of flint. (There was a similar case of mineral counterfeiting in Garmisch a few years later, when an American sergeant and a German accomplice attempted to pass off gold-painted iron bars as bullion from the Reichsbank gold reserves.) Many of the uranium cubes ended up in Berlin and East Germany, but a number of them — because of the great difficulty of fixing a price for this kind of commodity— remained for a while in the possession of the people who had found them, often with embarrassing results. A local Lothario, who took great pride in his success with the ladies, hid his cube under the seat of his car, and was temporarily rendered impotent (so the story goes) by the radioactive properties of the metal he sat on each day. Another Garmisch man, a dentist who had hidden a cube in a cupboard of his surgery, found that his x-ray equipment refused to function properly— until the day he sold his uranium cube.

When the Americans eventually got wind of the business they treated it with the utmost urgency. "We put a big hush-hush on it," recalled one of the American investigators. "The goddamn State Department sent over a couple of spooks and they went up to the river with a guide. I guess they got it all up and put Top Secret on it and headed back to the States with it." Several wooden slatted boxes of uranium oxide were recovered, together with two carboys of "heavy water" (deuterium oxide, employed as a moderator in nuclear reation), and at least 35 loose cubes which were being peddled on the black market in Garmisch. Twenty more cubes were apparently traced to Switzerland but an untold number of uranium cubes — one estimate puts the figure at nearly 700 — were never accounted for, at least not publicly.

Platinum, uranium, and radium were sensationally precious windfalls for the black marketeers of Garmisch and the Werdenfelser Land. But they were short-lived phenomena; for regular day-to-day profits the professional racketeers relied on another windfall commodity in rather more continuous supply— narcotics. Narcotics were the ultimate in black-market contraband, then as now. They were the most profitable, in terms of the ratio between volume and profit, and the most perilous, in terms of the ratio between profit and penalty. In the course of time the narcotics problem in Bavaria was to escalate from a breath of rumor to a clamor of scandal. The resulting brouhaha was to become so insistent and so inextinguishable that higher command in the U.S. Zone was eventually compelled to set Army investigators on Garmisch in an attempt to sort out this and other large-scale infringements of public order and military discipline. The outcome of these investigations is the subject of a later chapter. Regardless of the result, the narcotics traffic had a solid basis in fact.

The original stock of drugs for the postwar narcotics trade derived from the large quantities of morphine, opium, cocaine, etc., held in German hospitals and the warehouses of the German pharmaceutical industry at the end of the war. These drug stocks were purloined by German civilians and American military alike, but since these thieves did not have the necessary contacts of their own they could only distribute their supplies of narcotics through the dealer of the German black market, though later the Americans began to sell the drugs to the United States directly.

One of the biggest stocks of German narcotics consisted of a huge deposit of cocaine left in the Garmisch area by the German Army Medical Corps shortly before the end of the war. This depot was apparently not discovered by the Americans after the occupation and very few people knew of its existence. Those that did know seem to have included a group of Polish ex-POWs from Murnau, near Garmisch. In 1946 the people who had taken possession of the cocaine began to move it into Italy via Mittenwald and into France via Konstanz at a highly profitable price of $1 per gram. When the reserves of narcotics from German wartime medical sources dried up, other sources had to be found. Some stocks were filched from factories legitimately manufacturing new supplies of narcotic drugs in Darmstadt, Mannheim, and Berlin. Large shipments of drugs were also imported from London into north German ports, transported to Munich, and thence smuggled across the borders to Italy and France. Small dope rings in Bavaria also resorted to a degree of agricultural or chemical expertise to obtain the base product of their trade; some grew the Asiatic poppy for its opium, others used chemical processes to extract narcotic ingredients from various medications legally purchased in bulk.

The narcotics trade was widespread throughout Upper Bavaria and spilled across the borders into Austria, Italy, Switzerland, and France. Though the principal source and concentration point of the traffic was Munich and not Garmisch, as the American investigators had been led to believe, Garmisch nevertheless remained a highly important staging post on the smuggler's route south, and additionally possessed a sizeable drug-trafficking population of its own.

In some respects, Munich and Garmisch represented not so much separate hubs of activity as different ends of the same axis. Regarding the Munich-Garmisch "axis," one American investigator — Philip Benzell — in December 1947 reported that American personnel involved in illegal activ-

ities in Upper Bavaria included the Chief of the Investigation and Enforcement Branch, Finance Division, Office of Military Government of Bavaria (OMGB) John McCarthy, and an officer of the Public Safety Branch,
OMGB:

American personnel possibly involved in illegal activities in Upper Bavaria are a
former Major McCarthy, now civilianized, and Major O'Donnold, Public Safety
Officer, OMGB. While no concrete evidence [sic] exists linking them to narcotics
trafficking, it is noteworthy that their names have repeatedly and persistently appeared in other than official capacity, in this and varied other types of investigations conducted in Upper Bavaria by both the theater and local CID in the past
year or more. Allegations have been made that the above named persons are in
league with Dr. _____, a suspected narcotics operator, residing in Beidwag-
strasse in Garmisch and a "wanted" personality by the Austrian authorities. The
associations and social intercourses of McCarthy and O'Donnell with notorious
and suspected German personages certainly does not inspire the placing of confidence in them by this law enforcement agency. Further information was being
sought concerning Dr. _____ through an informant, Frau Hausner of Garmisch,
who was acquainted with the doctor. Frau Hausner, a suspected narcotics dealer
and addict, was the proprietress of the notorious Garmisch café "Wiesses Rossel"
[sic] a well-known rendezvous of black marketeers and criminal types. Information from this source, presumably supplied for self-interest, has proved invalu-
able.

With our return to the Weisses Rössl, and Zenta Hausner's surprising
metamorphosis into a member of the United States Intelligence community in OMGB, we have come almost full circle. The wheel takes a final
turn when we discover that Hubert von Blücher and one Mucki Clausing
were also involved with the Americans, one as a CIC investigator, the
other as a Special Investigator for Military Government in Garmisch,
both charged with, among other things, the task of helping to unravel and
expose the narcotics rackets in the area.

The role of Mucki Clausing and the younger von Blücher brother in the
narcotics affair in Garmisch-Partenkirchen is confusing and contradictory.
In the documents that have survived from the time — the secret reports of
CIC agents and so on — the activities of these two remarkably resourceful
and versatile young Germans are mystifying in the extreme, and today
neither of the men are (after a gap of so many years) able to throw much
light on the obscurer episodes. Though the main course of events can be
charted in outline, their significance is not always readily apparent.

Mention has already been made of the huge stock of German army
cocaine found in the Garmisch area at the end of the war. It seems that it
took black marketeers a number of months to organize a means of infiltrat-

ing this cocaine onto the narcotics market. As late as the end of January 1946, Military Government reports stated: "There are no known large operations in narcotics at this time in Bavaria." As far as Garmisch-Partenkirchen was concerned, the medical supply officer of OMGB was able to report to the chief of the Public Health Branch that on the basis of his inspection between 25 May and 27 May 1946 there were no apparent irregularities in the narcotics situations in that town. However, it soon became clear that by now this optimistic report was more a reflection of official ignorance than a statement of the real state of affairs. For a few weeks later the situation was to undergo a dramatic change.

In July 1946, in the words of one Garmisch resident close to the center of the action, "all hell broke loose in Garmisch." A top secret list of persons suspected of illicit cocaine dealing had fallen into the hands of Zenta Hausner. A number of the people on this list were known to her personally, and since they were all in danger of imminent arrest she was forced to act swiftly to save them. Some she was able to warn in time, others she struck from the list and substituted the names of people she wanted to get rid of. Among the innocent names now added to the list were those of some people who lived in Grainau. Naturally they did not know they had been put on any list, nor did one of their visitors, Lüder himself. Also arrested were Roman Roussell, Baroness von Hirschberg, Herr DuBois and Mathias Stinnes' former wife, Tucki, who was detained in Düsseldorf and brought back to Garmisch for questioning.

The arrest of Lüder was clearly not at all what had been intended. For six weeks the elder brother languished in jail on suspicion of dealing in narcotics. Hubert wasted no time in trying to arrange for his brother's release from prison. He went straight to the new military governor of Garmisch-Partenkirchen. The new official, a recent appointee by the name of Major Melvin Nitz, was a cool, stocky, 27-year-old American of German descent, with impeccably correct manners and a fierce Alsatian dog which he took with him everywhere he went. His legal officer in Garmisch, Captain Edward E. Bird, still remembers the major clearly as he was at this time: "He was rather an athletic, stocky type. I mean a real heavy, broad-shouldered type — a football-player type. I would say about five-foot-ten or five-foot-eleven. He had close-cropped, light colored hair, and I think he had light eyes." Major Nitz had been in the job for only a short time when Hubert sought him out, but he had several years of wartime combat and military government experience behind him. Originally an airborne infantry officer in Italy, he had served as a military government officer in Belgium, Luxembourg, and the Rhineland before being posted to Bavaria as deputy military governor at Berchtesgaden.

He could have been no stranger to Garmisch, for after Berchtesgaden he was posted to Starnberg, which was only 43 miles away on the Munich road. Major Nitz was, however, relatively a new boy when it came to dealing with the corruption of the area in his charge. It was Nitz's misfortune to have inherited one of the worst-run military government districts in Germany. Garmisch was probably already out of control when he took up his post and was to get worse during the period of his governorship.

"General Muller was military governor of Bavaria," he recalled at his office in Fresno, California, where he was public defender, in January 1982. "[He] told me to go down to Garmisch and straighten out the mess. There was a lot of trouble with the German government — American troops having a lot of trouble with the Germans and so forth. One of the problems was the American troops, you know — like a particular colonel I remember well. I remember him vividly because he was such an obnoxious person. He was the one I really ran into; he had one of the chalets and he put in a telephone and had telephone lines to all over Europe...had his shack [girlfriend] dropped up there and then he had this girl and, Christ! American families were coming in and it was necessary for us to find them somewhere to live; and, hell, I was damned if I was going to throw some German family out when this tootsie was up there on the hill with this big place. So I booted her out and put an American family in there and that's when I ran into the colonel. We would have found some place for him and his shack if he had been reasonable."

As for rather more criminal matters, like narcotics, Nitz admitted: "It was only when I got down there that I got word that there was supposed to be narcotics coming through the area." But he seems to have done the best he could in the situation in which he found himself, and though his methods were occasionally unorthodox, he gives the impression of having been open to any suggestion in his endeavor to investigate the profitable operations mounted by the criminal fraternity in Garmisch.

His first step in this direction was to release Lüder von Blücher from prison and appoint Hubert as his special investigator. That at any rate is how Mathias Stinnes described Hubert's new role. The description was confirmed by Special Agent H.A. Deck, the CIC chief in Garmisch, who in a top-secret report to the Special Squad dated 26 September 1946, described Hubert as "presently working in military government, probably as an investigator of one type or another." In another CIC report filed a month later, Agent Karl Sussmann stated that: "Clausing was asked by Captain Bird, at present legal officer of Garmisch-Partenkirchen, whether he could help them to clean up and to investigate the dope ring in Bavaria. Clausing was told by Major Nitz, MGO [Military Governor] Garmisch-Partenkirchen, that he had to work with Hubert von Blücher, who had volunteered to work on the case."

Whatever Hubert's exact status in this affair, it seems to have been an informal *ad hoc* arrangement with the military governor and his aides rather than an official appointment by OMGB, for his name never appeared on the Garmisch Military Government Detachment's Civilian Roster during the period of Nitz's command. Despite the obvious differences between the two men—nationality, age, role, background, and rank—they apparently got on well together and shared interests.

Close relationships between the alien rulers and their native subjects were not entirely uncommon in the Rajlike atmosphere of occupied Germany barely a year after the end of the war. As military governor, however, Major Nitz was like a proconsul of old; he could do more or less what he liked and keep what company he chose. And young Hubert was not such bad company. The son of an ambassador, leading member of one of Garmisch's most distinguished families, which had entertained some of America's most honored generals (Patton, Bradley, Truscott) around the fireplace of the family home in Gsteigstrasse—on the face of it the younger von Blücher, despite his slightly gamy reputation about town, was not such a bad German for the local representative of American rule to know. He was engaging, intelligent, humorous, and inventive; there was never a dull moment in his company and one never knew where the conversation might lead. Hubert von Blücher in his turn had the highest regard for the American major. "I met him about twenty or thirty times," he recalled later. "He was living in the officers' building and very often invited me over for a snack. He was a very fair, extremely decent man, there is no other way of putting it, a very sportsmanlike nature."

Nitz's recollection, by contrast, was of a somewhat more distant relationship. Asked in 1982 about his friendship with Hubert von Blücher back in 1946, Nitz replied: "I met Hubert in Garmisch for about four or five times at maximum because I had no reason to meet him there or see him." Moreover, Melvin Nitz could not recall ever having employed Garmisch citizens as special agents. "I never hired local people to be special agents or anything because that wasn't our capacity. All our capacity ever was was to contact people. I had other contacts, people that I would go and talk to and ask to accumulate information. Then I used to submit—I think it was a weekly report—that used to go to Berlin to General Clay's office—and it went direct, it didn't go through any type of channel." As far as narcotics smuggling was concerned, Nitz said: "The only source of information I ever had was a lady, Zenta Hausner. She had a restaurant in Garmisch, and we got the word there was a lot of questionable activity going on at the place. Whether she was feeding us a line of crap I don't know, but whatever information I got from her — that there was going to be some narcotics coming through on a certain day or something — I always used to send to headquarters in Bavaria, because there was no question of the fact that *somebody* was trafficking in narcotics — they were coming up from Italy, through Innsbruck, Garmisch, up into Munich, and then apparently on from there."

Surviving documents, however, indicate that when Melvin Nitz was military governor of Garmisch-Partenkirchen he played a much more vigorous part in pursuit of the drug trade in his area and that from time to time Hubert von Blücher assisted him in this difficult but worthwhile endeavor. Much of the information to this effect comes from Mucki Clausing, who in documents dating from 1946 was reported to be a Counter-Intelligence Corps investigator and in his interview admitted as much. It seems that neither von Blücher nor Nitz were aware of Clausing's intelligence role in 1946. Hubert was genuinely surprised to learn about this in 1982, while Nitz could conjure up no recollection of anyone by the name of Clausing whatsoever. "I really don't place Clausing at all at this time in any capacity," he said. "I just don't know where he would fit in. We didn't have too big a staff there at the time, and the chauffeur I had was an elderly gentleman and God, I'm sure he must have died by '55 or so because he was pretty old when I had him."

Melvin Nitz himself now views the whole business with weary resignation. "I've been trying to work out why the hell does this thing keep cropping up all the time?" he pondered in 1982. "It comes back to life, then it disappears, then it comes back to life. I've been trying to figure why the hell does it keep cropping up?" Casting back through his mind 36 years after the event, however, the former military governor of Garmisch-Partenkirchen did come up with one unequivocal recollection, one salvaged piece of jetsam that perhaps validated those narcotic-hunting days before the hunters become the hunted.

"As far as I was concerned," Nitz remembered, "whatever we got I always sent it up to headquarters. I had been sending this stuff up for a couple of months, and then I discovered that the very American whose name came up all the time was the person who was given to investigate the thing. For some reason the name of McCarthy came up. As far as I know he was a major or lieutenant-colonel. He had been given all these reports, because his name was on those reports I was sending out. I was sending out the same reports to Berlin and I went up and talked to the general [Muller] about it and he said, 'Well, you don't have to worry, I know all about it. Just keep giving me information.' And I said, 'Well, if his name keeps coming up, I'm going to keep putting it it.' And he said 'Fine, just go ahead and do it.'"

As we have seen, it was not just in Major Nitz's reports that McCarthy's name kept cropping up.

16

"Garmisch Residents of Dubious Character—"

The next episode in the story revolved around a character with whom we have already made a fleeting acquaintance. This was the Polish DP and one-time member of the former circle of Hubert von Blücher — Ivar Buxell. An unusual person by any standard.

Ivar Buxell was a man of many parts, some overt, many mysterious; but by far his greatest part was that of professional survivor. Only a tiny minority in postwar Germany rose above the morass of suffering humanity to profit from the chaos in which they found themselves. These were the true survivors, the masters of the survival game. They came not just from Germany but from all over Central and Eastern Europe, wherever war and conquest had destroyed the normal fabric of society. Such people were the Artful Dodgers of the postwar world, men and women whose special attributes — be they social, professional, financial, sexual, or linguistic — enabled them to exploit the opportunities and lucky breaks that arose out of the extraordinary disarray of the time. One such survivor was Ivar Buxell.

Buxell was in many ways a typical product — and victim — of his age and geography. The vicissitudes of parentage, political frontiers, and war deprived him of a single abiding homeland, so that though he was to become a citizen of several states, he was a true native of none, equally fluent in German, Russian, Polish, and Spanish, and speaking English, French, Czech, and Ukrainian besides. Born a German Baltic in Lithuania, brought up in Russia, educated in Switzerland, Buxell had worked as a shipping expert in the Polish Ministry of Commerce in Gdynia and Warsaw until the outbreak of war. But the German invasion of Poland was to reshape Ivar Buxell's life as irrevocably as it reshaped every Pole's.

The Nazis provided Buxell with his first big test of survival. The Gestapo decreed that he was not a Pole but a *Volkdeutscher* of German Baltic stock. He became the partner in a paint factory in Warsaw, manufacturing camouflage paint for the German Air Force on the eastern front. At the same time he became a member of the German Military Intelligence (*Abwehr*) in Warsaw. His loyalty to the German cause seems to have been a matter of convenience rather than conviction, however. While he sported a portrait of Adolf Hitler on his office wall in Warsaw for the benefit of his German business clients, his Polish partner in the office next door sported a portrait of the Free Polish leader, General Sikorski. "I did not care for Hitler," Buxell said later. "I was not anti-Nazi. I just had an antipathy for Hitler. Most of the *Abwehr* in Warsaw were anti-Hitler." After the war it was rumored that Buxell had in fact been a double agent, working for both the *Abwehr* and the Polish Home Army. But he has consistently denied this. "I was a member of the *Abwehr*," he affirmed later, "but never a double agent. On the contrary, we had an order from our director to help the Polish and the Jewish people."

A few hours before the Polish uprising in September 1944, Buxell left Warsaw and headed for Berlin. In February 1945 he made his way to Prague, ostensibly to help activate the anti-Soviet armies of Russian and Ukrainian rebels under General Vlassov and General Shandruk, but in reality to obtain new papers and passes, without which his safety, even his life, remained in jeopardy.

For Ivar Buxell was in a precarious position. He had lost all contact with his headquarters. His old *Abwehr* documents were out of date. For the sake of his own personal security he turned to the Ukrainian General Shandruk for help. "General Shandruk supplied me with all necessary documents as a member of his staff," Buxell later recalled, "as well as with an order to organize for him in Garmisch a new intelligence office. The general and I knew perfectly well long before that all was lost." It was, of course, purely a stratagem for survival. There was about as much point in opening an intelligence office for a virtually nonexistent army in a war with only days to run as there was in opening a zoo or a bank. But Ukrainian papers were better than no papers at all — and Garmisch was a better place than most in which to hole up in the coming chaos.

So, in the early spring of 1945, some weeks ahead of the American 10th Armored Division, Ivar Buxell arrived in Garmisch-Partenkirchen, where he was later joined by his brother Erhard. His arrival was viewed with suspicion by the local Gestapo chief. Buxell recalled him asking: "What are you doing here? Are you a spy or something?" No, Buxell told him, *Abwehr*. "But what are you *doing*?" the Gestapo chief persisted. "Are you a deserter?" "No," Buxell replied. "I am with the Ukrainian Division, SS Ausland. Why don't you ring my Belinda office, telephone number Adele 208, Berlin. My cover is such and such, my code name is so and so." All day, Buxell recalled later, the local Nazis in Garmisch tried ringing the number in Berlin. "They didn't know what I knew," Buxell recounted. "The office had been abandoned."

So Ivar Buxell was allowed to stay in Garmisch-Partenkirchen. He found accommodation with his family in a large and unusual guesthouse belonging to a Frau Hirth who catered exclusively for famous writers, musicians, and aristocrats such as Ernst Jünger, Helen Keller, Richard Strauss, and Prince Ludwig of Hesse. The house was under the protection of the Gestapo, and in addition to Ivar Buxell and his wife and three-year-old son a number of other specially privileged foreign families were housed there, including several fugitive members of the French Vichy Government and the family of Mussolini's commander-in-chief in North Africa, Marshal Graziani. Unlike most of the other guests, Buxell stayed on at Haus Hirth after the American Counter-Intelligence Corps (CIC) requisitioned the place as their headquarters and thus became familiar with several of the CIC special agents operating in the Garmisch area.

Buxell had come a long way. The years as a maritime expert in the Polish government, a Russian specialist in German Intelligence and (briefly) a German advisor in the Ukrainian Army were now behind him. In his 40th year, at a crossroads in the history of the world, he found himself forced to play yet another role in yet another unforeseen scenario in a land ruled by people from an entirely different continent: the Americans. From his Polish ID card and passport and his Russian and German birth certificates, the Americans did not know what to make of Ivar Buxell. "The CIC lieutenant was very confused," he recalled. "Eventually he decided, 'You are Stateless.' So I became a Stateless Displaced Person (DP)." Now he was required to play the greatest trick of survival in his life.

Ivar Buxell was formidably equipped for this difficult virtuoso role. He was well accustomed to adjusting to changing foreign regimes, languages, and lifestyles. Small, wiry, and pixie-faced, with gray hair, blue eyes, and a dark complexion, he abounded in a quick, nervous energy, radiated charm and intelligence, and was quick to extablish a widespread network of well-placed and like-minded friends. "You can only survive in times after war or revolution," Ivar commented years later, "if you are smarter than the other people. People started to think how to make money and how to live again. We were all criminals."

Ivar joined the local Polish Committee, drawn from the ranks of some 6,000 Polish officers who had been kept in a prisoner-of-war camp at Murnau, near Garmisch-Partenkirchen, and before long he was making regular automobile trips to the Swiss border to pick up Red Cross parcels provided for the Committee. The freedom to travel — if only as far as a foreign border — was a highly prized dispensation in Germany after the war and was to prove a valuable privilege for Buxell and his friends in the months to come.

At some point not long after the American occupation of Garmisch, Buxell's widening radius of local acquaintances finally took in certain individuals with whom his name was to be intimately associated for as long as they continued to live in Garmisch: Hubert and Lüder von Blücher, Mathias Stinnes, and the three newcomers to the story, Mucki Clausing and the brothers Ardo and Roman Rousselle. In due course these men were to fall under the gravest suspicion of the American investigative authorities — Ivar Buxell, perhaps, above all. And yet, though Buxell was to be subject to the most extreme forms of investigation then practiced in the American Zone of Germany, it was not his name that was to be perpetuated in the folk memory of those wild postwar Garmisch days; in due course his involvement in the events that gave Garmisch its notoriety after the war was to vanish without a trace. This is surprising. For out of all the people engaged in dubious derring-do at that time, only Ivar Buxell has an investigative file which has survived to the present day.

For reasons which will be revealed later, much of the documentation deriving from the various official investigations mounted in Garmisch-Partenkirchen between one and two years after the end of the war disappeared under mysterious circumstances. What was left resembled archaeological fragments, potsherds and papyri that by chance had survived the ravages of time, circumstance or intention, to prove the existence, if not the totality, of some vanished historical event. These bits and pieces, culled from various sources and cross-referenced without explanation under Buxell's name in the archives of the U.S. Army's Intelligence Agency in Fort Meade, Maryland, give a direct glimpse into the cross-currents of suspicion, denunciation, accusation, and counteraccusation that eddied and swirled around Garmisch-Partenkirchen in the murky times following the end of the war.

By the time Major Melvin Nitz had arrived in Garmisch to take up his post as Military Governor in 1946 it had begun to dawn on the local CIC that all was not right in the area. We have already seen how various rumors and allegations about the fate of some of the Reichsbank dollars began to spread around the town and how these became linked with other rumors and allegations about illegal border-crossings, narcotic trafficking, and other serious black-market activites. Some kind of crisis seems to have occurred in the first half of June, a fortnight or so after Major Nitz's arrival when (in Mathias Stinnes' words) "the cocaine bomb went off." Lüder von Blücher, inadvertently arrested with certain friends, under the pressure of events began to turn on his old comrades. By July, Mucki Clausing was closely involved with the Garmisch CIC and he had also begun leaking stories about the activities of his friends. So by the beginning of September the CIC had become apprised of the considerable ramifications of the case and the pivotal role of Ivar Buxell. On September 6, Special Agent Gene Gutowski filed the first background report on Buxell:

Subject on April 1945 came to Garmisch. Since then, he was involved in a number of large-scale black-market operations (American currency, dope, etc.). Subject's girlfriend is one Mrs. Rouselle, recently divorced from Ardo Rouselle, brother of Roman. Connected also with Mathias Stinnes and von Blücher family. It is still unknown how far is subject involved in Hubert von Blücher's operations. However, it is for sure that he knows much more about them than he says. Subject has a very large circle of friends, some of them in high positions. Has some connections with Munich CID.

Little more than two weeks after Gutowski's report, Mathias Stinnes denounced Buxell (and just about everybody else) to the U.S. Constabulary. In a memo dated 26 September 1946 and headed "Alleged handling of TS [Top Secret] information by Germans," Special Agent Deck of the Garmisch CIC reported to the Special Squad at CIC headquarters in Frankfurt:

Information comes to this office from reliable sources, through a Constabulary colonel, name not given, that one Mathias Stinnes, now living in Garmisch, approached this Constabulary colonel in social converasation with information denouncing one von Blücher, presently working in MG [Military Government], probably as an investigator of one type or another. Von Blücher, according to Stinnes, is closely connected with black-market operations. Von Blücher, according to information, is also closely working with 2 Polish brothers named Buxell.

Stinnes alleges that Buxell contacted him, offering him a car and papers if he would go to Switzerland and deliver a package, at the same time picking up a package and returning to Garmisch. According to Stinnes, he was told by Buxell that this mission was of top-secret nature, in the interest of the U.S. Army, and connected with anti-Russian operations. Stinnes, however, thought that the package contained narcotics.

A further item in Ivar Buxell's file is a photocopy of the famous receipt for $404,000 given to the von Blücher brothers by Captain Neumann in August 1945. There is nothing in the file to indicate *why* the receipt was included and some explanation is necessary for its presence. It had always been assumed by the U.S. military authorities on the spot at that time that the $404,000 recovered from the von Blüchers' garden had been stolen, and for a long time the finger of suspicion had pointed at the American officer who had made the recover—Captain Neumann. We have already shown this suspicion was unfounded. The money was handed over by Captain Neumann in a perfectly proper manner to the correct military government authorities and was then passed by them through normal channels as far as Munich, where its progress stopped and whence it later disappeared, either physically or on paper. The U.S. occupation authorities were therefore right to show concern about the ultimate fate of the money, since they could find no record of its having ended up at its required destination, the FED, and appeared to have no means of monitoring its deposition in Munich. It followed that since to all intents and purposes the von Blücher money *had* disappeared—even though not in the way that was generally believed—some mark had to be made against the von Blüchers' involvement in the affair. It further followed that anyone known to be a close associate of the von Blücher brothers, like Ivar Buxell, would also have some record of the dollar affair entered in his own dossier. Hence the copy of the receipt in Buxell's file. But at this point the matter takes a new twist.

The twist is this. Ever since the Reichsbank currency had been retrieved from the von Blüchers' garden in Gsteigstrasse, the rumor had spread around Garmisch that not all the currency had been dug up and handed over and that a considerable quantity remained in the hands of Hubert and Lüder von Blücher. According to a statement by the von Blücher's erstwhile next-door neighbor, Mathias Stinnes, a "goodly number" of dollars were still hidden behind the books in the library at 38 Gsteigstrasse *after* the handover to Captain Neumann. "It was from there," Stinnes confessed, "that I pinched a genuine fifty-dollar bill as a keepsake. And to this day I do not know to whom I owe that money." The inference drawn by Stinnes is enlarged upon in another official document contained in the Buxell file in the U.S. Army's Intelligence Agency in Fort Meade. This document consists of an undated report written by CIC Special Agent Karl Sussmann and typed on official U.S. Army paper bearing the letterhead: Headquarters, Counter Intelligence Corps, United States Forces

European Theater, Region IV, Garmisch Sub-Region. Under a subheading, "The Dollar Affair," Sussmann had this to say: "At the end of the war the Blücher brothers had $400,000 or $500,000, which belonged to the Foreign Ministry, in American currency. They have a receipt signed by a Captain Neumann of the American Army, that they turned in all the money they had. However, Messrs. Rousselle, Roman, and Ardo, two brothers, and one more witness only known to the Rousselle brothers, have seen $100,000 which the Blücher brothers kept."

According to Ivar Buxell, Ardo Rousselle was Lüder and Hubert von Blücher's closest friend. "Ardo is extremely reliable," Buxell recalled in a letter from Caracas, Venezuela, dated 16 May 1977. "He told us—my brother and me—that he was present when Hubert was counting the dollars in Gsteigstrasse No. 38 in Garmisch. It was an enormous quantity and Hubert offered Ardo some of them, but Ardo refused." Since it is known that neither of the Rousselle brothers were present at No. 38 in August 1945 at the time the dollars were being exhumed and counted at the behest of Captain Neumann, Buxell is presumably referring to the dollars allegedly left over after the Neumann collection. Ardo Rousselle himself, perhaps, has made two further comments on the matter.

In the sixth of a curious series of fourteen unsigned articles which appeared in the local Garmisch newspaper *Garmisch-Partenkirchener Tagblatt* between January and March 1956 entitled "*Dunkle Rätsel aus dunklen Tagen*" ("Murky Riddles from Murky Days—Little Known Incidents from the Early Post-War Days in our Landkreas"), the following allegation was made about a prominent Garmisch resident named Graf Heinrichstein: "[He had] Money worth millions of marks, consisting mainly of dollars, part of the Reichsbank treasure of Lake Walchen. Careful estimates of our informant state that at the time [the count possessed] about four million dollars."

According to Ivar Buxell, the kind of inside information revealed in the *Tagblat* article strongly indicated that "our informant" was none other than Ardo Rousselle, Hubert's closest associate. *The article further alleged that a prominent citizen of Garmisch named Heinrichstein succeeded in befriending officials of the American military government in Garmisch-Partenkirchen, agreeing to share the loot with them fifty-fifty.*

From these officials Heinrichstein was supposed to have received travel documents and the loan of a car—a powerful Mercedes bearing the American numberplate "M 1"—with which he was able to drive a number of times into Switzerland without any hindrance—this at a time when it was strictly forbidden for Germans to travel abroad. "Inside the car—which was never checked—were large bundles of dollar notes," the *Tagblatt* continued. "At that time the control of the borders was so superficial that any colorfully printed paper was sufficient to get past the American and French guards and across the border. Heinrichstein's route always took him via Lake Konstanz and through the French zone of occupation. Careful estimates state that during the two years following the end of the war he had brought about 2,800,000 dollars into Switzerland."

If this story is true, and if the figures are accurate, the dollars "still around" after the Neumann recovery would be worth the prodigious total of $22,000,000 by today's values, and the amount allegedly smuggled into Switzerland would now be worth $15,400,000.

Enlarging on this account, Ivar Buxell has stated in the course of correspondence from Caracas that Heinrichstein was accompanied on some of these trips to Switzerland by his own girlfriend of the time, a well-known cinema actress by the name of Frau von Meyendorff, and at other times by the American military government officials. "Ardo confirmed," Buxell wrote after a meeting with Rousselle in Bavaria in the spring of 1977, "that one part of the money and maybe other valuables were transported by the son of the late owner of the Post Hotel in Garmisch, and his girlfriend, Yvonne von Hoesch (now dead). They got a lot of money for the transportation. The "Bad Boy" and prime mover [of the gang] was Graf Heinrichstein, the smartest of them. Mucki's closest American friend and intimate companion was a military government captain from whom Mucki and Yvonne repeatedly obtained travel permissions to Austria and Switzerland.

Ardo's allegations in the *Tagblatt* — if they *were* Ardo's — were made at a time when Heinrichstein was safely out of the country and had, to all intents and purposes, vanished somewhere in South America. But twenty-three years later, long after Heinrichstein had returned to West Germany and established himself as a wealthy and distinguished industrialist with international connections and a considerable degree of financial and legal muscle, Ardo had still not changed his tune and resolutely stuck to the story he had first broached to the Garmisch CIC in 1946 and apparently elaborated in the Garmisch local paper in 1956. In an interview with Ardo Rousselle in Munich in May 1978, shortly after his precipitate flight from Angola following the Portuguese colonial pull-out (bringing with him, he said, only the clothes on his back), he confirmed that after large currency handovers to the Americans, citizens in Garmisch were still in possession of "several million dollars in U.S. dollars rather than hundreds, thousands, or hundreds of thousands." More than this Ardo could not, or would not, say. He was extremely nervous and reticent and made it clear that he risked his life by giving the interview at all. He had agreed to it, he said, only at the wish of his old friend, Ivar Buxell.

"I frequently changed U.S. dollar bills on the black market in Munich for them," he stated in a letter dated 20 July 1976. "I presume that a considerable amount of the paper money landed in their hands." In addition to the greenbacks, a quantity of these dollar bills turned out to be large Gold Dollar bills, a form of currency which had become obsolete in the United States before the war and which—as we have already seen in statements by Colonel Eckles (of the Currency Division of the FED)—had constituted a large portion of the Reichsbank currency hoard recovered from the Walchensee. "The bills were very old and very used," Buxell commented in July 1979. "When I changed them for them on the black market, they told me that they were savings of the family."

Only a relatively small proportion of the money could be disposed of in this way, however. It became evident that the rest would somehow have to be transferred to Switzerland and properly banked. This, too, was an extremely difficult thing to arrange. Germans were not normally allowed to travel abroad at this time. Even if they could find suitable transportation to the border, the American, French, and Swiss border guards would stop them if they did not have official papers. It was essential to obtain passes and travel documents from the American military government. And it would help to have an American military government car as well, and even an American military officer to drive it. This is, as we have detailed, is precisely what Heinrichstein managed to arrange.

As a cover for their dollar shuttles into Switzerland, the confederates told people that they were investigating narcotics smuggling in the region on behalf of the military government. Sometimes the three Germans drove into Switzerland on their own with dollars concealed in the car, sometimes they drove across with the American officers in an offical military government car. The comings and goings of these make-believe sleuths eventually came to the attention of the U.S. Army CID, who noted in a secret report to the Commander-in-Chief European Command:

...Numerous opinions have been expressed...that several American officers have been involved in the trafficking of narcotics. Such opinions have not been supported by concrete evidence and have generally been based upon rumors originating from unreliable sources. In an effort to determine whether military personnel have been or are involved in narcotics traffic, this Agency examined all available reports of the local police agencies and the Counter Intelligence Corps. This Agency also interviewed German civilians who allegedly had information relating to activities of former U.S. Army officers in the Garmisch-Partenkirchen area.

Upon the basis of all information gathered, it is the opinion of this Agency that a former colonel was involved in a minor capacity with organized narcotics smuggling in the Garmisch-Partenkirchen area. A captain and former Legal Officer of Garmisch Partenkirchen Military Government has also been suspected. While there is no conclusive evidence to implicate the captain in the trafficking of narcotics, yet, in his military government position, and in view of the fact that he enjoyed a close personal relationships with,* suspected dealers in narcotics, he must certainly have had knowledge of such trafficking. Further investigation is being made into his motives. He is at present located at Landkreis (W)olfrathausen [sic] as a Military Government officer and will be interrogated by this Agency at such time as more conclusive evidence which might implicate him in illegal activities is uncovered. Information received from informants would implicate the colonel in the illegal traffic of narcotics with a Frau Diefenthal and her daughter Unita, as well as several other German civilians who are discussed in the next paragraph. Efforts are being made by this Agency to locate the Diefenthals, as their present whereabouts is unknown. The extent of the alleged traffic by this group is unknown to the informants who supplied the information.

Rumors current in Garmisch during the period when Nitz was Military Governor were that Garmisch residents of questionable character were involved with the colonel in the trafficking of narcotics in the Garmisch area and in other illegal dealings between Garmisch and Switzerland. It has been alleged that they made several trips into Switzerland with the authorization of the colonel. It cannot be established whether such trips were for the express purpose of transporting narcotics; however, from available evidence, the trips ostensibly were not made for any legitimate purpose. Photographic copies of letters authorizing travel throughout the American and French Occupied Zones of Austria, signed by an American captain, are in possession of this Agency. The letters authorize the three (3) German civilians *to carry large sums of money* [emphasis added] in the currency of various countries and American cigarettes and liquor. Such letters state that these persons were employed on a special mission for the Military Government of Garmisch-Partenkirchen.

Information obtained by Lt.-Col. Smith during his investigation, revealed that the colonel had directed the captain to issue the above-mentioned letters of authorization. The letters supposedly were issued to the three (3) German civilians who were working for the Military Government as informants and investigators of the narcotics situation in Upper Bavaria. It is believed that the true purpose of such letters was a guise to cover up illegal transactions.

The following named persons are German civilians residing in Garmisch who are suspected to be involved in the trafficking of narcotics in this area: [Individuals are then named in the report]....

During the course of these events an estimated $2,800,000 in dollar bills were smuggled into Switzerland and safely deposited in Swiss bank ac-

---

*Individuals are then named in the report.

counts. By then the colonel was on the point of being demobilized from the Army and Graf Henrichstein was in jail in Garmisch after having been caught crossing the frontier one last time—on this occasion without proper papers. He did not stay in jail long. Sentenced by the captain to three weeks of imprisonment for illegal border crossing, Heinrichstein was released immediately on the grounds that he had already spent more than three weeks in prison. For some reason Heinrichstein was now in a great hurry. He did not collect his things from his cell, nor does he seem to have returned to his home. Instead he made straight for the Swiss border in his BMW. In 1947 it was still against the law for a German to travel out of Germany and it was only possible to do so with forged documents or genuine travel warrants issued to Germans by the Allied authorities for special reasons. Therefore the German did not drive into Switzerland by car at all—or so he claims.

I swam across the Rhine [he recounted to us] and was picked up on the other side. I had been told that I could come to Switzerland to start studying. No problem. We had many friends on account of my father's profession. You probably know this from your own family. However, I simply could not get an exit visa. It was simply too difficult. It had to go via Berlin and the Allied Control Council, goodness knows what else. So I decided to do without one. I watched the sentries and frontier guards for three hours and then swam over. One had learned that sort of thing since the age of nine—we had been brought up as soldiers.

So there I was, over on the other side, looking quite obviously like a German wearing a sopping wet suit of clothes, and I marched into a café where—and I regard this as the most spectacular personal coup of my life—I managed to borrow the money for a telephone call to Oerlikon. And then a great big beautiful motor car arrived with a driver and every luxury, as if it was [sic] the Pope that was being picked up, and into this car crept a wet, shivering little chap, clutching a receipt for 2 francs 50 for the telephone call, which the chauffeur had settled on my behalf. Apart from that he refused to exchange a single word with me.

Then I entered a house, a veritable palace, the home of my father's friend. It was like coming home on vacation, as a pedestrian, from hell. Unimaginable.

I began by exercising horses every morning, as I had no work permit in Switzerland, and no passport, and in any case it was difficult at that time as a German. The final incident of this whole affair came during my Swiss period. An Englishman and an American came to see me. They had obtained official permission from the Swiss to interrogate me. At that time I was at the *Eidgenössische Hochschule*—the Swiss Federal High School. They came in, accompanied by Swiss police, and demanded, "Where is Captain Neumann?" I answered their questions. If one leaves Germany without an exit visa, as I had done, it is best to be somewhat careful. And that was the last I heard about the whole business.

Only once in the next ten years—for a brief period of two weeks—did he visit Germany again. This was four or five months after he had gone to Switzerland, he recalled, when he heard that his mother was seriously ill and it was feared that she might die. His return to Germany was necessarily illegal, the German explained. "I could not get an entry permit into Germany from Switzerland because I never had an exit permit from Germany in the first place. I did receive a Swiss "Letter of Safe Conduct," but I could not travel to Germany with this because there was no official body in Switzerland which would stamp a visa on it for me. So, being then a physically active person, I said (speaking in English): "Same way out as in—input equals output." And so I swam over again, into the French Zone, got a few lifts, walked a few yards—and was home again."

By a curious coincidence it seems that the same day Heinrichstein was discharged from prison, his friend the colonel was honorably discharged from the U.S. Army. That day, or the next, he too arrived at the Swiss border, bringing with him the attractive German girl who was soon to become his wife. Some said that these two crossed over the border together. There is no evidence for this but it is known that for a while both of them shared the same house at 50 Aarbergerstrasse in Berne, a very desirable residence in the center of town, where by a curious coincidence they were joined at one stage by the Swiss Secret Service man—an advocate and doctor of jurisprudence called Armin Läderach—with whom they had had dealings when they both lived in Garmisch. Later Heinrichstein was best man at the colonel's wedding in Berne in June 1947. At the end of September both men left Berne, the German for foreign parts, the American (with his wife) for a small lakeside town near Lucerne, where he studied law for a few months before finally returning to the States in March 1948. An important stage in the story was at an end.

17

The Inspector General Calls

Ivar Buxell, during most of the winter, spring, and summer of 1947, remained in confinement in the *Rathaus*. A week after his arrest the Garmisch Counter-Intelligence Corps (CIC) filed a secret memorandum on his case to the CIC headquarters in Frankfurt. They clearly believed they had got hold of a big fish. The memo concluded with the agent's comments:

It is recommended that the proper authorities in France be checked to determine the authenticity of the papers found in Buxell's possession. Although subject alleges to have obtained them legally, he is known to have mentioned to informant X–6–IV–G that he "was able to obtain the visa for Venezuela for only 375 dollars, although the normal black-market price is quoted as slightly more than 600 dollars." Buxell is known to have worked as a double agent for the German Intelligence Service against the Polish Underground, and is strongly believed to have undercover connections to the Polish Warsaw Government. His activities and contacts in this area have been under observation for some time. Interrogation of all arrestees is being continued.

Three days later, on 12 March 1947, the Munich CIC sent an urgent telegram to other CIC stations. One of Buxell's associates, Kasimierski, had jumped train while being transferred under guard to Frankfurt. "Subject is to be arrested on sight," the telegram requested. "If apprehended subject is to be transferred to the I.G. (Inspector General's) section, USFET, attention Lt.-Col. Smith, Room 216, I.G. Farben."

The Lieutenant-Colonel Leonard H. Smith introduced here by the legerdemain of a U.S. Forces telegram was destined, as an Inspector General of the U.S. Forces, European Theater (USFET), to prove one of the most significant players in the next act of this unfolding drama. At this point he was at the very begining of what was probably the most crucial of all the investigations into the many misdemeanors in Garmisch, and Kasimier-ski, and more particularly his associate, Ivar Buxell, were of more than passing interest to him. For by strangest coincidence, he had met Buxell before, not in Germany but in France. Now he was destined to meet him again, not in France but in Germany. "The same man turned up in both places," Colonel Smith recalled, "which is very strange." Especially as in both places he was in prison, and in both instances confined on suspicion of illegal border crossing.

The IG investigation under Colonel Smith began in Garmisch in the early spring of 1947. It took over more or less where the Criminal Investi-gation Division (CID) investigation had left off and largely as a result of what the CID had stirred up. By now the buzz of rumors circulating in and about the Military Post and U.S. Army Recreation Center of Gar-misch-Partenkirchen had become loud enough to have reached even the ears of the Governor of the American Zone, General Lucius D. Clay, in distant Berlin. The rumors reached Clay at a particularly critical time. It had escaped no one's attention, least of all Clay's, that the American occu-pation of Germany was in a shambles. The occupation army, over which he still had no direct control, had got out of hand. Officers and men alike lived for the black market. Bored troops turned to drinking and fighting. Malcontented units rioted through the streets. The *New York Times* des-cribed the occupation army as "an aggregation of homesick Americans shirking their jobs to figure out ways to make money, courting German women, counting up points." The occupation elite—the officers and their dependants—lived a life of ostentatious luxury such as few had enjoyed be-fore or would ever enjoy again. The lower ranks, who could not live like feudal lords, behaved like robber barons. Street violence and the molesta-tion of women were widespread. Looting was wholesale. "The ragged Ger-man," the troops were told in a 1946 orientation pamphlet, "has a lot in common with a trapped rat."

Not until the end of 1946 did this hate policy change. Not until March 1947 did 49-year-old, four-star General Clay finally gain control over the occupation army as well as the military government. The former engineer officer and Supreme Headquarters Allied Expeditionary Forces (SHAEF) problem-solver, who was once described to President Roosevelt as "the most competent man in the executive departments...give him six months and he could run General Motors or U.S. Steel," now wore two hats, one as Commander-in-Chief, U.S. Army and Air Forces in Europe, the other as Military Governor of the U.S. Zone of Germany—thereby becoming very nearly an independent sovereign in the part of Europe under his command. He assumed his new role only just in time to stop the rot from becoming a total collapse. Shortly afterwards the Chief of the Foreign Exchange Depository (FED) announced the discovery of the disappearance of some $2,000,000 from the foreign exchange reserves of the former German Reichsbank—a loss even greater and potentially more embarrassing to the American occupation authorities than the $1,500,000 robbery of the Hesse crown jewels at Kronberg in the U.S. Zone in 1945, at that time the greatest robbery on record.

Clay was aware of the problem, if not yet of the extent of it. He was to write in his memoirs: "During this period of unavoidable confusion, charges of almost every kind appeared to be part of the daily fare. Unfortunately many of them had some basis in fact. A victorious army of combat veterans had defeated the enemy in hard fighting. Released from the discipline of combat, it was not ready to accept the more rigorous discipline of garrison and peacetime training." Clay was concerned because he knew that back in the Pentagon, an army commander was judged by the absence of trouble in his command. That was one cogent reason why, shortly after he had assumed supreme command of the American Zone of Germany, he began to take a more than passing interest in the affairs of Garmisch, the worst-run town in Germany.

At the end of April 1947 General Clay issued a verbal directive to his Inspector General at European Command headquarters, Major General E. P. Parker. "On 26 April 1947 General Clay told me personally that he desired an investigation of certain conditions in Garmisch," General Parker reported in a memorandum two days afterwards. "He had been informed that there were large black-market dealings in jewels and narcotics between Germany and Austria in which U.S. personnel in the Recreation Center in Garmisch were involved. He was told that the local CID had ignored this. Also he desired an audit made of construction costs of the skating rink [nightclub] at Garmisch as he had been informed that much work material had been purchased (some from Italy) but not used on the job."

Colonel Smith was the Inspector General selected to head the investigation in the field. The colonel saw his brief as a rather general, exploratory one. "I was just trying to find out what was going on," he was to recall afterwards. "There were so many rumors reaching the Commanding General. I was working on leads that said gold, on leads that said counterfeit currency, leads that said drugs, and leads that said diversion of U.S. government funds and property. You name it. Across the board. And the leads led me all over the place."

The investigation was initiated on 13 May 1947. In the early days one particular rumor dominated all others. This was the matter of the Casa Carioca. This was not in fact a mere skating rink, as General Clay had thought, but a large and very lavish nightclub for the entertainment of American forces personnel in Garmisch. This sophisticated establishment boasted a sliding roof so that on fine nights one could dine, drink, and dance to a live band under the stars, and an ice stage where one could watch spectacular ice shows over champagne and strudels—and it was built entirely through the efforts of one man, Frank Gammache (pronounced Gamma-shay), formerly the Garmisch Post Engineer. Gammache, 41, a civil engineer and mine inspector by training, had served in the war as a sanitary engineer in the Engineering Corps in the Ruhr and Bavaria. In October 1945 he was transferred to Garmisch to assist in setting up what was to become the Garmisch Recreational Center and continued in this job as a civilian after leaving the Army in September 1946. The construction of the Casa Carioca (now, alas, burned down) was a truly remarkable achievement on Gammache's part. In building it Gammache was, in Colonel Smith's view, "imbued with a spirit of creating a *magnum opus* which would redound to his professional career." The Casa Carioca was put together out of bits and pieces—materials in short supply in both military and German stocks, including steel from the Ruhr—foraged and scrounged for throughout the German hinterland. "It didn't cost the U.S. Government a penny," Gammache remarked later. But Colonel Smith commented subsequently: "Where did the money come from?" Where indeed? Rumors abounded. A former Executive Officer of the European Command CID recalled: "I was told that the nightclub was built and paid for with a diverted train of coal." A CID agent who later went down to Garmisch remembered:

The Army to this day has never been able to ascertain whose property this thing was built on or where the money came from to build it. The Army was supposed to be putting up the funds to build the place but the amount of money they put in was about enough to do the bathroom. It cost hundreds of thousands of dollars to put the floor in and the ceiling, even in those days. But a lot of the money for it came from deals. They would send trucks around and they would pick up, oh, maybe a whole flip-side truck of bags of potatoes. Now we're talking about five or six tons of potatoes, and they would take these potatoes and they'd drive like mad over to Czechoslovakia and bring back Bohemian crystal and glass. All this was really illegal—and that's the way the whole damn place was built. Several people got rich from these deals, and quite a few of them got caught.

When the Inspector General's team began to probe the matter, it was not potatoes and cut glass they turned up but British urinals. U.S. Army trucks, it seemed, were in the habit of driving into the British Zone of Germany to pick up urinals and other fittings for the Casa Carioca and then staying in the British Zone and undertaking other work for the personal benefit of the U.S. Army personnel in Garmisch. But when 14 serious misdemeanors were brought to the attention of the Post Commander, Colonel Dodd, his reaction was to say: "Forget it, too many people are involved." It was soon evident to Colonel Smith that he should investigate the activities of certain members of the Garmisch Military Post in general and the activities of Frank Gammache in particular.

Frank Gammache, not unnaturally, took exception to being singled out for such intensive scrutiny and cast around for the handiest means of airing his grievance. As it happened, the handiest means took the form of two bored journalists who were passing through Garmisch looking for a story shortly after Colonel Smith had moved into town. The two journalists were Ed Hartrich of the *New York Herald Tribune* and Tom Agoston, an Englishman with the International News Service. According to Agoston, he and Hartrich had been assigned to cover the story of the denazification of the man who was to play the part of Christ in the first Passion Play at Oberammergau since the war. Things were very quiet at the time so they decided to try and scrounge a trip down to Garmisch on one of the liaison planes belonging to the U.S. Constabulary. One of the generals they were friendly with agreed, and in late May they made a somewhat dangerous flight down to Garmisch, the nearest airstrip to Oberammergau, in two planes. Once in Garmisch they checked in at Clausing's Post Hotel. Agoston's story continues:

We were sitting at the bar and somebody, an American chap, said: "Are you Mr. Agoston?"

"Yes," I said

"Would you mind stepping outside for a minute?"

"What do you want to see me about?" I said. "Why don't you come and have a drink?"

"Oh no," he said. "I don't want to go in there. You see, everybody knows me. I don't want to go in there."

We didn't know what it was all about, so he said: "Look, you're there with a colleague of yours. I don't know who he is. Can you please come up to my room?"

So we went up to his room and to cut a long story short, he said: "Look, the Army is trying to throw the book at me. I am only a tiny cogwheel in this great big crookery. Everybody else is a crook, but not me."

We didn't know what the hell he was talking about. He was so scared that something was going to happen to him that he was a bit incoherent. He was afraid of the Judge Advocate General and he told this story about the gold and the drug running and everything else. He was scared to death. And this is how we got the story, you see.

It was a remarkable story—though Gammache subsequently denied ever giving it. But for reasons that will be presently explained, it was eight months before Tom Agoston was able to file it. When it finally did appear in *Stars and Stripes* it did so under a banner headline:

HUGE DOPE RING PROBED IN BAVARIA

The magnitude of the case which has shaken the U.S. community of Bavaria and threatens to have grave repercussions was revealed by American and German sources first some eight months ago in Garmisch. They said the affair involved a whole series of separate cases, including the high-powered narcotics ring and black market headed by a former German SS officer.

A German ringleader and other members of the gang were able to operate due to "close connections" with a former U.S. Army officer now civilianized and reported to be a member of Bavarian Military Government, evidence indicates.

This official, acting as "protector" of the gang, first contacted the ring in the capacity of a narcotics investigator, according to information.

Investigators have also checked the activities of another former officer now believed living in Switzerland with his German girlfriend on proceeds of the black market. Informants said this former major may be able to solve the mystery of cached gold bullion estimated at $750,000 [equivalent to 50 bars weighing over half a ton], as well as an additional $2,500,000 worth of U.S. dollar notes.

A third former officer, who is reported in possession of information relating to the gold and bullion caches, is said to have returned to the U.S. where he is now living.

These hoards are reported to have been discovered shortly after the war's end by the U.S. Army.

Ed Hartrich had filed a similar story with the same dateline in the *New York Herald Tribune*. At the request of the Army both had been withheld for eight months for fear of prejudicing the investigation. But it was as a result of the original leads that General Clay first became personally acquainted with the more alarming aspects of the Garmisch affair. On 28 May 1947, less than two weeks after Colonel Smith had opened the Inspector General's (IG) investigation, a message from European Command Headquarters in Frankfurt confirmed that "all possible influence" had been put on Hartrich and Agoston to prevent their publishing the story. On 2 June Clay discussed the situation in Garmisch with his Chief of Staff and acknowledged that "the original tip on the conditions reported to be existing in Garmisch was given him by a newspaper man." On 3 June Colonel Smith traveled to Stuttgart to talk with General Clay personally about certain aspects of the Garmisch case and to clarify his initial directive. Clay reiterated that he wanted the investigation into conditions in Garmisch to be conducted in such a way that *"no person guilty of major improper action... shall escape identification, location, apprehension, and prosecution"* (authors' italics). It was now clear to Colonel Smith that the case was a matter of the utmost seriousness, and that he had the Commander-in-Chief's complete support in his efforts to clear it up.

Colonel Smith was operating at theater level, which meant that no boundaries or local echelons of rank would interfere with his investigations. This not only implied the existence of what were described as "serious and extensive irregularities" in the area within his scope of investigation, but also the possibility of U.S. military involvement, since the Inspector General's Division was primarily an internal examining body of the U.S. Army — the equivalent of the present Army's Internal Affairs Division or Scotland Yard's A10 (the police who watch the policemen).

The IGD investigation conducted in Garmisch-Partenkirchen by Colonel Smith lasted from May to July 1947. Smith was directly assisted by Lieutenant Kulka, from ICI's Special Squad, who on this, his second assignment in Garmisch, was to act as Smith's interpreter (in several languages). After a bugging assignment in Garmisch the previous summer, Kulka had returned to his counterintelligence duties on Operation Tobacco — the investigation of the Soviet Repatriation Commission and the fate of the Russians who were forcefully repatriated by it. After a fracas at a Russian refugee camp, during which Kulka had placed the Soviet officers of the Commission under arrest for usurping their authority in American territory, Kulka had been taken off Operation Tobacco and assigned to Colonel Smith's IG investigation in Garmisch instead. Walt Snyder from the CID in Frankfurt, who had already worked on aspects of the case a year and a half previously, also joined the team, and further assistance came from the CIC Special Agents and CCD wiretap censors in Garmisch.

It soon became apparent to Colonel Smith that there was something particularly untoward, even sinister, about this particular investigation. "I could not help but sense from the very beginning," he told a subsequent inquiry, "difficulties which did not belong in the ordinary routine investigation, and which caused me to suspect that some interference was being imposed." In his report to General Clay, Smith spoke of "widespread perversion of the truth" and "conflicting testimony" which was caused by "a state of fear on the part of many of the witnesses." The Colonel laid the blame for this on a particular American whose reputation in Garmisch, Smith wrote to Clay, "has been such that only the bold were willing to openly risk incurring his enmity." Even in his own interrogation this individual displayed a belligerent manner towards the Inspector General, and always tried to shout him down. Smith had never experienced anything like it in his life. His senior rank and the status and aura of the position of Inspector General were normally sufficient to command military respect and compliance. Not so in Garmisch-Partenkirchen. It seemed that he was opposed by shadowy forces intent on eavesdropping on his investigation and sabotaging it by every means at their disposal. These means were not inconsiderable. Money was one. Fear was another. Duplicity another. Smith's suspicions pointed in the most unlikely directions and in the end he grew frightened for his own security.

His suspicions were aroused almost as soon as he arrived in Garmisch on 13 May 1947. Initially the plan had been for the team to live in a hotel — Clausing's Post Hotel — and do their work at the Post headquarters. This proved impossible. "The first time we left our hotel room," he wrote later, "my interpreter and I each unobstrusively placed a match stem between one entry door and the jamb, breaking the stem of it flush with the jam so that it would be inconspicuous. If it were not in place on our return we would know our rooms had been surreptitiously entered. When we got back the match stems were gone." Not only was the hotel insecure, but it was also blindingly clear that the identity of any witnesses arriving for interrogation at the army headquarters would instantly become a matter of public knowledge. Colonel Smith asked for a separate building, away from the headquarters, where some semblance of confidentiality and security might be maintained. He was allocated an attractive Bavarian chalet hidden by a screen of conifers at 40 Kleinfeldstrasse on the outskirts of the town. Two secretaries (one a WAC, the other a civilian girl from the States) and a German cook and driver completed the complement. In addition, Lieutenant Kulka arranged some special services via contacts of his own. Through a Polish contact (who was wanted for murder and robbery in the French Zone) he arranged for a detail of former Polish prisoners-of-war, organized into security troops, to provide an armed guard and to patrol the outside perimeter of the house. And he arranged for his own personal informant, a former SS man who had a police record of convictions for forgery, fraud, and embezzlement, to work as a technician on the case and handle the document photography in the cellar laboratory under the house. By ordinary standards the IG team in Garmisch was a very large and elaborate one.

"Once physically installed," Colonel Smith recalled, "I set about opening a rudimentary office. The most important item, clearly, was a safe for hiding the documentary evidence I collected. An Army field safe was supplied and a chain by which it was padlocked to a cast-iron radiator. Removal of the safe would have meant tearing out part of the heating system. The weak link was the fact that the safe opened not by a combination but a key."

Obviously if any of the nosier inhabitants of Garmisch felt impelled to look at confidential documents inside the safe they would have to get hold of the key. Since the key was always in the possession of Colonel Smith, this was no easy matter. But it seems there were people in Garmisch with nerve enough to give it a try. The Colonel's bedroom was on the first floor of the house in Kleinfeldstrasse, at the front. Very early one morning shortly after he had moved in, he was awakened by a squeaking sound in his room. It was a very quiet sound, barely more than a rustle, but it persisted and it was probably the persistence of the sound which disturbed his slumber. The Colonel rolled over and, as he did so, he heard in his half-comatose state a soft Bavarian female voice whisper, "'Scuse me, please," and then she was gone.

Colonel Smith sat up in bed and switched on the light. He looked around the room. Nothing had gone. He cocked his ear for some telltale sound, but nothing disturbed the deep tranquillity of the Alpine night. He noticed that the drawer of the bedside table was half open. Had he left it like that? Then he realized. "Accustomed to the German habit of placing the contents of one's trousers in the night-table drawer," he wrote afterwards, "she had obviously gone there looking for the keys to the safe. And all that time they were in the pocket of my trousers, lying on a chair at the other side of the bed! Need I say I am happy she did not know! And profoundly thankful her visit did not have a more sinister motive and disastrous ending—for me!"

A check next morning showed that the Colonel's nocturnal visitor had somehow evaded the Polish guards and got in and out of the house through a basement coal hole. "My conclusion," Smith told an offiical inquiry later, "was that this was not an ordinary housebreaker, as food and valuable photographic equipment in the house was passed up and not touched." A sentry had actually seen the woman leave the house but he jumped to the conclusion that she had been paying the German chauffeur in the house a nocturnal visit and made no effort to arrest her. Later Smith suspected that the intruder was none other than Zenta Hausner, the notorious racketeer from the White Horse. To be on the safe side the original guard detail were dismissed and a new Polish guard posted in their place. Two days later the new guards were forced to open fire on a gang of three men trying to break into the house for a second time. No one was hit but it seemed advisable to stiffen the defenses still further and the guards' pistols were replaced with U.S. Army-issue submachine guns. And so, under siege inside the make-shift stockade of a requisitioned private house in Garmisch-Partenkirchen, the American colonel and his Czech-born lieutenant, fed by a German and guarded by Poles, sat down to unravel the misdeeds of certain American officers and their Bavarian friends in this small but iniquitous town in southern Germany.

Colonel Smith carried through his assignment in Garmisch like a man under siege. He was not the sort to be easily intimidated but in Garmisch he continued to feel a genuine concern for his personal safety. What he remembered most about that time, he admitted in later years, was "being cooped up in one house, not being able to go anywhere, working night and day, trying to get the reports out, trying to keep the people at top headquarters satisfied that things were progressing and not making the progress I ought to be making and wondering when things were coming to a head. I didn't know a thing about the town. I didn't get around it. I wouldn't know one street from another."

For Lieutenant Kulka the memory of those days was even more traumatic than it was for Colonel Smith. "Several attempts were made on my life," Kulka explained when first contacted in the course of research for this book. The investigation and its aftermath led to all kinds of accusations being leveled against him and was allegedly to result in his forcible severance from the Service. For years afterwards he struggled to bury the past, to suppress the bitterness, paranoia, and fear he experienced as a consequence of the part he played in the Garmisch investigation. "I decided that the way to sanity for me would be to completely forget and to dissolve into my subconscious all the happenings that had transpired in the previous years," Leo Kulka told us in the spring of 1979. "I buried myself in a new career and became a workaholic, if you will. The first time that this entire matter cropped up again was when you called. I must confess that I was more than just shocked. I was absolutely flabbergasted. You caught me so completely unaware."

In Kulka's memory the centerpiece of the IGD investigation, though not its original cause, was Ivar Buxell. Buxell, it will be remembered, had been consigned to the *Rathaus* jail on 24 February 1947. He was still in jail when the snow stopped falling and the spring flowers came into bloom on the *alpages* and the skiers finally abandoned the ski slopes. He was still in the jail when a high summer sun beat down on the copper roofs of Garmisch and the hikers roamed, bare-kneed and feather-hatted, through the green-leafed woods, and the *Queen Elizabeth* set sail for the Americas with-

Top left: Garmisch blackmarketeer and lessee of the notorious White Horse Inn, Zenta Hausner, shortly before her sensational murder in 1947. *Top right*: The apartment at the back of the White Horse in Bahnhofstrasse, Garmisch, where Zenta Hausner was found dead (in the kitchen, third window from right on first floor) at Christmas 1947. *Bottom left*: An ice show at the lavish (but controversial) Casa Carioca night-club. Built out of surplus material and scrap, this was one of the most famous recreation centres of the American occupation, and triggered the first investigation into Army corruption in Garmisch. *Bottom right*: Polish DP Ivar Buxell, professional survivor and early victim of the truth drug Pentothal (from the photo in the French passport issued during his ill-fated flight to Paris in February 1947).

Top: The boys from the CID – at a wedding party in the 32nd CID HQ at Esslingen in 1947. 'Operation Garpeck' agents attending include Frank Purcell (seated on floor), Thomas Gardiner (holding the bride) and Victor Peccarelli (in dark suit to left of bride). Also in the picture is Charles Bradley (seated next to Peccarelli). *Bottom left*: CID Chief Agent Philip Benzell, agent in charge of 'Operation Garpeck', 1948. *Bottom centre*: Agent William C. Wilson of the US Army CID in Garmisch in March 1947. *Bottom right*: CID Agent Walter Snyder, one of the US Army's first investigators at Garmisch, photographed a week before his murder in May 1948.

Faces of the American Raj in Germany. *Top*: The American Military Governor of Bavaria, Brigadier-General Walter J. Muller (standing) presides over a meeting of his detachment commanders in Munich in 1946. *Bottom left*: The Governor of the US Zone of Germany, General Lucius D. Clay, after successfully covering up the Reichsbank robbery and Garmisch affair with the help of US Secretary of the Army, Kenneth C. Royall (centre), chats about other things to comedian Bob Hope (in Germany to entertain American troops). *Bottom right*: One of the Military Governors of Garmisch-Partenkirchen, Major Melvin W. Nitz (on left), pictured on the balcony of his house at 88 Hauptstrasse in Garmisch with Lt.-Colonel Jackson, Legal Officer from Munich, in the summer of 1946.

The Reinhardt Memorandum eventually blew the lid off American Military Government in Bavaria. In addition to former FBI and CIC agent Guenther Reinhardt himself (*top left*), other Americans were involved in one capacity or another. Leo de Gar Kulka (*top right*), the CIC's anti-Soviet and bugging expert, was twice sent to Garmisch to help investigate gold, narcotics and other irregularities. Lt-Colonel Leonard H. Smith (*bottom left*), US Army Inspector General, headed a major investigation into corruption in Garmisch in the summer of 1947. Gordon Gray (*bottom right*), seen here with President Eisenhower in the 1950s, was the Assistant Secretary of the Army who processed Reinhardt's exposé of American military rule in Germany.

out him on board. The vision and the dream—of a new start under the palms in some tropic Shangri-La on the opposite side of the world—sank from sight and finally vanished from Ivar's inner eye. As the days went by he grew uncharacteristically pessimistic and distressed. What did the Americans want with him? When would they bring him before a court and get this thing over?

By the standards of the U.S. Zone in 1947 Ivar Buxell and his brother were kept in imprisonment without trial for an inordinately long period. In Summary Military Government Courts in the larger cities, such as Munich, a case was normally tried within five days of arrest, and in smaller towns, such as Garmisch, within three days of arrest, unless the person in question was released on bail. In more serious cases tried at the Higher Military Government Courts, the person was usually tried within 15 days of arrest and almost always within 30 days. But Buxell was held for five months, an exceptional period of detention indicating the exceptional circumstances of the case. The Americans were to turn their attention on Buxell soon enough. As the IGD investigation proceeded and leads opened in various directions Buxell's name began to crop up with sufficient frequency to indicate that the incarcerated Pole merited closer scrutiny. But Buxell presented a special problem. "I knew through Counter-Intelligence Corps (CIC) channels," Smith confirmed afterwards, "that this man was able to send communications in and out of the Garmisch city jail at will. I concluded it was unwise to interrogate him *and* let him remain in the Garmisch jail."

Smith then took a most unusual step. He went over his immediate superiors' heads and sought an interview with the Commander-in-Chief and Governor of the American Zone, General Clay. The two met in Stuttgart on 3 June 1R947, the day after Clay had first become apprised of the true state of affairs in Garmisch. According to Smith the meeting was arranged "because of a peculiar position which required a decision from someone who commanded both military and military government." The outcome of the meeting was that General Clay gave his permission for Buxell to be transferred from the jail in the Garmisch *Rathaus*, which was under Military Government control, to the Military Prison in Garmisch, which was under U.S. control and therefore within Colonel Smith's aegis.

The day after his meeting with General Clay, Colonel Smith requested from CIC Headquarters in Frankfurt a status report on the Buxell brothers. When the CIC in Garmisch were chased on this they pointed out that the papers they had "on that gold and dope deal" had been handed over to the CID during Ward Atherton's investigation earlier in the year. They were assured that the Buxell report need only contain what had transpired since May, when Colonel Smith had opened the IG investigation.

Smith and Kulka now began to work on Buxell. "All of a sudden," Kulka recalled, "Colonel Smith came down extremely hard on him. He badgered him, he interrogated him, he did everything he possible could to make a nervous wreck of the man." Kulka himself kept out of the interrogation at this stage, but one day Colonel Smith let it be known to Buxell that he was going away for a few days and a colleague of his would take over the questioning — Lieutenant Kulka. "I returned back to the cell of the Polish individual," Kulka recalled subsequently, "and had a very friendly conversation with him, making him trust me because of my Slavic background — being Czechoslovakian by birth and able to speak both Czech and Polish. I agreed with him what a terrible SOB the Colonel was, and when he complained that he was a complete nervous wreck — which had been totally planned — I mentioned I had a friend in the local hospital and would arrange for him to be taken there for a couple of days while Colonel Smith was away to allow him to regain his strength and get a sedative for him."

One night, it seems, Ivar was picked up from the *Rathaus* cells and transferred to a special cell of the Military Police. A bright light burned day and night in this cell, and a guard kept constant watch through a peep hole. Buxell was not interrogated, but after a few days an Army Medical Officer with the rank of captain came to ask him how he felt. Buxell admitted to being nervous, so the doctor gave the guard some tablets which he had to issue three times a day to the Pole "for his nerves." Buxell, who was a chemist, became suspicious and did not take the tablets. He put them under his tongue and when the guard was not looking he threw the tablets in the slop bucket. Some days later Lieutenant Kulka called for him in the middle of the night. "I arranged for him to be released into my custody," Kulka related, "and took him in my care to the local Military Government Hospital and got him into a room. They allowed him a beautiful hot bath and a chance to clean up, and I stayed with him all the time, of course, to make sure he was safe. Then he climbed into bed and I told him that my friend, the doctor, would give him a shot which would allow him to sleep a little bit. That was a little ploy of mine. He said, 'Fine,' and he really looked on me as a friend."

The shot which Ivar Buxell was given in the American hospital — and which Smith today stoutly maintains he never authorized or had any knowledge of — was sodium pentothal, popularly known as the "truth drug" and then a relatively new tool in the U.S. police repertoire of investigative and interrogative techniques. Pentothal is a barbiturate anaesthetic commonly injected intravenously to induce anaesthesia at the commencement of surgery. Its induction is rapid and pleasant, leading to sedation and calming in smaller doses and to sleep in full doses. Pentothal is cleared from the bloodstream so rapidly that moment-to-moment control of the anaesthesia is possible and a subject can be kept in a twilight state of diminished inhibition for a relatively prolonged period. In subsequent years its widespread use in surgery became a matter of concern for the CIA because of the tendency by the CIA operatives to reveal secrets while under its influence during surgery. The CIA got around this by swearing-in the operating theater personnel under the U.S. Secrecy Agreement. The use of sodium pentothal for nonmedical purposes in the United States in 1947, however, was a little unusual, but this did not prevent the subtance being pushed into the veins of the unfortunate Buxell's upper arm in the U.S. Zone of Germany.

In Buxell's memory he did not get into a bed but was put on an operating table to which he was fastened. A few seconds after being injected — it seems he was put on some kind of intravenous drip — he found himself in a semiconscious state. He was then slapped around the face and regained consciousness, though only to the extent of attaining a trancelike state. He saw a number of people standing around the table. At the foot were two colonels, two secretaries, the doctor, and a captain. One of the officers — probably Kulka — started to ask him a number of questions very rapidly. The questions did not seem to make much sense and were apparently not related. "When and where were you born?" "Where were you on 20 May 1938?" "What is your opinion of the philosopher Hegel?" "Are you a member of the Communist Party?" They asked over a hundred questions, and unanswered questions were repeated.

Then Kulka went off at a tangent. "I brought up the subject of a certain Garmisch resident," he recalled. "To my biggest surprise, the minute I started to mention the name of this man it rang a bell, and he got extremely uncomfortable."

Buxell, it seems, then went on to talk about the burial of portions of the Reichsbank treasure in the von Blüchers' back garden, its recovery by the Americans, and its subsequent fate. As it stands Buxell's story now is somewhat garbled — the effect of the sodium pentothal doubtless compounded by the lapse of time since the event — but the main drift is clear enough. A few days after the Americans had made their recovery from the garden they returned to the house and demanded the receipt back on the pretext that it contained some mistake. According to Buxell's unconscious rambling it seemed that once they had retrieved the receipt the Americans — a colonel, a major, and two GIs — would have a free hand to do what they wanted with the treasure because there would no longer be any material evidence to show that they had taken it or that it had even existed. The receipt was duly handed over to the American colonel, who then tore it up. But then one of the Germans "reached into his pocket and produced a photocopy of the original receipt and in a rather sarcastic tone turned to the Colonel and said: 'Would the Colonel care to have another copy to tear up, because there's lots more where this came from.'" At this point Buxell's mind wandered down another track and came to the subject of gold. Kulka later recalled what the Pole had told him.

"The gold bullion," Kulka continued, "which was in mahogany boxes, was taken to a bowling alley in an inn in the first little town north of Garmisch-Partenkirchen on the way to Munich [possibly Farchant]. There it was put at the back of the bowling alley, at the end of the *Kegelbahn*, and a false wall built in front of it."

Though this was not the last we are to hear about the gold bullion at the back of the bowling alley in Franchant, it is the last we are to hear from Ivar Buxell under the influence of the truth serum. Kulka made Buxell as quiet and comfortable as he could and got him back to his cell.

On the removal of the injection [Kulka recounted] the Polish individual was directed to wake up. I reassured him and gave him the posthypnotic suggestions that he was perfectly all right, that he had rested and I would let him aleep for about ten minutes more. Then he would have to get dressed and get back to his cell before anybody knew that he was missing. A few minutes later I helped him to get dressed, got him in the car, and took him back to the cell. Of course, any recollection of the interrogation was completely erased. I made him comfortable and asked him to rest and he fell asleep for the whole afternoon and the whole night. When I came back the next day he was extremely grateful that I had made it possible for him to rest and regain his composure. This was the first sleep he had had in God knows how long.

Unfortunately the incident had some rather unpleasant consequences for this Polish DP. The next day he was interrogated by five or six American officers, including two already known to him — Captain Livingstone of the CIC and Captain Skelton, the Garmisch Public Safety Officer. By confronting him with fact after fact which he had admitted to in the hospital, he finally broke down and made a full confession and related the story verbatim while conscious. This was immediately typed up by the secretary, who was a WAC, and the "Polish individual" signed it.

Then [Kulka continued] the colonel released the Polish individual, much against his wishes and pleadings. The Polish man kept begging and begging the colonel to provide security for him. I pleaded with the colonel to provide security for him but he said: "We have no authority or way of holding him, therefore we have to let him go."

He was released and completely disappeared. I have no idea what happened to him. It wouldn't surprise me if he was one of the many unidentified corpses that were found around Garmisch at that time. But I heard a rumor he was turned over to the Russian Repatriation Commission for return to Poland, and of course, at that time internees were being executed as they crossed the border.

In fact, Buxell did not perish but lived to tell the tale and became the prosperous vice-president of a large engineering company in Venezuela. He still remembered it all very clearly, even 30 years after the event.

I disappeared for 18 days [he related]. Even my wife couldn't find out where I was. The fact was that I was in the hands of the Army and not the Military Administration. The German police did not know what was happening to me. I was forced to keep secret and not tell anything to anybody about where I was during those 18 days. Later on, I do not remember when it was, we were taken to the Military Court in Munich. The U.S. Prosecutor told us not to worry and after the trial we went free. A few months later the American judge paid me a visit, together with his wife, and we spent a couple of hours together in my house. He acted in a very mysterious manner and told me that many things had happened that were unknown to me. He assured me not to be worried, as the whole gold affair was over and all problems had come to a good end.

One explanation why "the whole gold affair was over" has been provided by Leo Kulka, though it cannot be substantiated from any other source. Some weeks after Buxell had been injected with the truth serum and talked about gold bullion hidden in a bowling alley, Kulka recalled, a quantity of gold came to light under rather curious circumstances. "The noncommissioned officers of the Military Police detachment in Garmisch held a party of some sort in the bowling alley," Kulka related. "One sergeant got into a rather hefty argument with another. They started breaking and pushing things, the bar was broken up and the sergeant, who by that time was quite drunk, decided to do some bowling with some funny bowling balls that they had over there, which completely lacked holes to put your thumb into." This kind of bowl had to be pitched rather than rolled, but being a little worse for drink the Military Police sergeant wildly overpitched the bowl, which went hurling down the alley, bounced, and smashed into the wall at the back and disappeared. The Americans tried to retrieve the bowl but found it too difficult to do so without dismantling the wooden boards with which the wall was constructed. When they eventually climbed through they found, to their complete surprise, not only the wooden bowl but a stack of wooden boxes and six cardboard boxes, like shoe boxes, as well, To their even greater surprise they found that the wooden boxes contained gold bullion and the cardboard boxes contained concentration camp tooth gold compressed into square bricks which still contained human teeth.

The gold was loaded onto a truck and deposited with the Military Police. The sergeant was charged with starting a brawl and causing damage to property. The circumstances surrounding the discovery of the gold were largely suppressed. When Lieutenant Kulka demanded to see the gold and where it was stored he received, he says, "the royal run-around":

The Military Police claimed it had been given to the Military Government because the Military Government was responsible for all judicial matters. Therefore the Military Police didn't really have the gold. I saw one box of bullion in the Military Police office. After I started looking for the rest in order to get a count I had to go to the Military Government and that's where the path started to go in all sorts of different directions. The curious thing was that there was no record anywhere of who had what or how much. The only one, strangely enough, who had a proper count was the innkeeper from whose place the bullion had been removed. He informed me how many boxes he thought he had counted and swore that he had absolutely no knowledge as to how they could possibly have gotten there. He had sworn his innocence to the Military Government and they believed him — or a deal was made — and that was all there was to it.

So about two weeks passed and I went back to the innkeeper and the inn was closed. There was nobody there any more. Rumors had it that he had been picked up by the Americans. Military Police had no record of him having been picked up and Military Government refused to have anything to do with it. They claimed that they had turned the matter over to the German Criminal Police and that the gold had been transported to Munich to be put in the hands of the then Director of the Police Department for Bavaria, a certain Herr Pitzer. Working for Herr Pitzer and Head of the Criminal Police was a Herr Grassmüller, who was a very good friend of mine. Herr Grassmüller, however, didn't know what had happened to it either. He had heard about it but he insisted it was a matter that the American Military Government had taken over. Having known Herr Grassmüller for many years I believed him to be a very honorable man of the old school and that he really did not know anything about it.

No more was ever heard of this particular stash of gold. There is no record of it in the gold inventory of the Foreign Exchange Depository (FED) or in the surviving files of Office of Military Government of Bavaria (OMGB). Curiously, as in the case of several other gold recoveries discovered in this book, it is to Munich that the trail leads and in Munich that the trail grows cold.

Lieutenant Kulka's problems with the gold were as nothing compared with Colonel Smith's difficulties with the case as a whole. After the investigation was finished all sorts of allegations were made to U.S. Army higher command about the "almost incredible power wielded by the American conspirators and their German associates." Some witnesses approached by Colonel Smith, including Germans, openly defied and obstructed the colonel. Others were just spirited away. Two of the three Civil Censorship Division (CCD) monitors were alleged to have been reached by the gang and from then on failed to produce satisfactory excerpts of suspects' telephone conversations. Later, important sections of the files relating to this large-scale wire-tapping operation (code name "Operation Comic Strip") disappeared. "I didn't feel that I had cooperation in the Post at all," Colonel Smith admitted subsequently. "I didn't feel comfortable there at any time." The Garmisch Post Inspector was up to no good. He was in the remarkable position of having two identification cards, one in his real name, the other in a false name. "He made it a point," Colonel Smith testified in 1948, "to become extremely familiar with one of my two secretaries, posted my telephone numbers in the Bachelor Quarters in Garmisch as that of his office, and conducted himself in such a manner that I was called three times by the Post Headquarters to ask whether he was my assistant. He apparently tried in every way to create the impression that he was associated with me in conducting the investigation. Although I had no ground except suspicion, I felt it was quite likely he was implicated in some of the improper actions of the Post. I have been told he is presently in Bologna, Italy, together with my former secretary, and that he is no longer on active duty with the American Army."

Then exceptional pressure was put on both Colonel Smith and Lieutenant Kulka from above. During the course of the investigaton two German girls, who shared house with the Garmisch Military Post Commander, Colonel Francis Dodd, and two of his subordinate officers, were arrested on the technicality of illegal border crossing. They had been caught taking a considerable quantity of jewelry of questionable origin out of Germany on behalf of their boyfriends, the two American colonels, and it was hoped that by prosecuting them to the limit on the border-crossing charge they would break down and turn state's evidence, thus assisting in the preparation of well-founded cases against members of the Garmisch "gang." But suddenly Smith was told to lay off the two girls. As he subsequently reported to General Clay, he was directed by Brigadier-General Muller, the Military Governor of Bavaria, not to try them on any charge "until the receipt of further instructions from him." Later, at a further inquiry into the Garmisch affair, he enlarged on this intercession by Muller in the case of the two German girls. "While they were still under arrest," Colonel Smith testified a few months later, "I received a personal telephone call from General Muller, Director of Military Government, Bavaria, in which I was asked why these women should be tried. I knew this information could not get to General Muller except through the means of some officer of high rank who was in a position to call General Muller. I have been told Colonel Dodd was a classmate of General Muller. Obviously, Colonel Dodd had interceded with General Muller to obtain special treatment for these two women." (In fact, West Point records show that Dodd and Muller were *not* classmates, but that Muller and Clay *were*.)

Then Colonel Smith discovered that the regional headquarters of the Counter-Intelligence Corps (CIC) in Munich were trying to pull his assistant, CIC Special Agent Lieutenant Leo Kulka, off the case before he had completed the job. "Most of the time," Kulka recalled, "I felt like a mushroom—kept in the dark and covered in manure." When Smith went over the regional CIC's head and appealed to the CIC Command Headquarters in Frankfurt for permission for Kulka to be retained on the IGD investigation in Garmisch, the Munich CIC—fearful of what the Garmisch investigation might reveal about some of their own activities—resorted to dirty tricks to harass Kulka. One morning Kulka telephoned Smith in Garmisch. "I am in Munich," Kulka told him. "I am supposed to be back Monday morning but I cannot get back until Tuesday. I have been asked whether I will accept punishment under the 124th Article of War because I have been seen without the proper insignia on my uniform." Colonel Smith had never see Kulka without his proper insignia. It was outrageous that his assistant should be threatened with a court-martial on such a contrived charge, deliberately designed to interfere with the Inspector General's investigation, which had begun to implicate members of the Munich CIC itself.

In spite of the obstructions the investigation progressed and the dossier grew. "The amount of information we received was overwhelming," Leo Kulka remembered. "A multitude of Germans would flock to my office or ask me into their confidence and meet at secret places and divulge a host of information about the wrongdoing of people within the Military Government, the CIC, CID, police, and what have you. It seemed that the Germans felt the Inspector General's Department gave us a stature above everybody else's. We were considered to be the elite of the American Gestapo, as it were—a chance for everyone to get even. So I was writing and dictating reports of sergeant so-and-so living with so-and-so and stealing silver and diamonds from some poor family and selling it on the black market or shipping it home..."

Kulka was prepared to go to considerable lengths to obtain his information. In order to pursue his inquiries inside the prisoner-of-war camp for German officers near Garmisch, he was briefed for two weeks by a Gebirgsjäger general and then infiltrated into the camp dressed as a high-ranking German ex-officer. On another occasion Kulka was sent to an American Bachelor Officers' Quarters in a converted civilian house in Garmisch to investigate a report that a U.S. Army Lieutenant was sharing his quarters with a German baroness, which was strictly against military orders. Unusually, Lieutenant Kulka wore his insignia of rank — and as a consequence was mistaken for somebody else by the German *Hausdame*, "a nice little old lady," at the Officers' Quarters.

She looked at me [Kulka recalled], and she said, "Oh, you must be the young man who came to pick up the briefcase with the papers for Switzerland." I said, "I guess so." She said, "Oh yes, the lieutenant told me that you were coming to pick it up and that you are a young pilot." So I said, "Yes." The *Dame* came down and handed me a briefcase and a larger attaché case which was sealed with a diplomatic seal. So I took them and hastily left. I took them to my room in the house and opened up the diplomatic case and to my intense surprise found it filled with British pounds in rather large denominations and also some jewelry. The briefcase I found to be filled with about ten folders which contained very neatly written columns of names of people with dates and their rank, their location, and sums of money — all the instructions and records of how the money had been transported across the border. I immediately contacted Colonel Smith and he was extremely interested. We went through the paperwork and found a great number of important names, including a number of colonels from headquarters. The one thing they all had in common was that they all belonged to units that had one time or another controlled the border crossing to Switzerland — Military Police, Military Government agencies, and CIC.

By June it was apparent to Colonel Smith that the Garmisch case was a very big one indeed and made up of many parts which were often interlinked. "My investigation led to the pointing of suspicion at a considerable number of people," Colonel Smith reported after the end of the investigation. Suspects included a high-ranking American officer in Garmisch, who was "uncooperative" and "does business with a certain clique of Germans." Smith added: "...As to narcotics, I was forced to the conclusion that there was good reason to suspect some of the military personnel." Whether they had been infiltrated or not, the Civil Censorship Division (CCD) telephone tappers continued to produce transcripts of conversations dealing in black-market furs, diamonds, cocaine, tapestries, cameras, valuable Japanese vases, cars, and border passes.

According to the unofficial report of an officer with an ear close to the heart of the investigation: "The preliminary evidence alone was sufficient to implicate a dozen or so officers ranking from captains to brigadier-generals who at some time or another between 1945 and 1947 have been connected with the administration of Garmisch or military organizations there or Military Government units both in Garmisch and on the Bavarian State level. Also in the preliminary evidence there seemed to be sufficient grounds to believe that at least two dozen German nationals ranging from German mistresses of various officers to German building contractors and former Nazi politicians would go to jail for as long as life terms."

By the middle of July 1947 Colonel Smith had finished his preliminary report and dispatched it to the Governor and Commander-in-Chief, General Clay. The report indicated that there was sufficient evidence to warrant a full-scale investigation and recommended that a strong force of highly qualified and specially selected CID, CIC, and CCD personnel be assigned to prepare a series of criminal prosecutions. On 18 July General Clay expressed an order to the effect that he desired the Garmisch Military Post to be given a thorough shake-up and all the old-timers removed, along with any individuals specifically mentioned as questionable in the report. On 24 July 1947 the Inspector General's Department (IGD) investigation under Colonel Leonard H. Smith, Jr. was officially concluded. "I had reasonable concern for my own life," Colonel Smith recalled afterwards, "and when this operation was finished I just decided to terminate. I knew that any protection I had was gone, so I promptly made a request to get transferred. I got transferred back to Berlin, and so I was totally out of the way and totally unaware of what developed afterwards."

What developed afterwards was indeed curious. Some of the immediate consequences of the investigation were not entirely unexpected. Four colonels were banished from Garmisch-Partenkirchen. The Military Governor and the Post Commander were shipped back to the States. One of the Post Commander's executive officers was transferred to Vienna, and the Post Inspector went to Italy, dragging Colonel Smith's civilian secretary, an attractive American girl, with him. A week or so after the end of the investigation, Frank Gammache was arrested and placed in confinement to await court-martial on charges of misappropriation of U.S. military property and disorderly and discreditable conduct. A special CID unit was sent down to Garmisch by the Theater Provost Marshal to clean up the town and arraign other miscreants. All this was as it should be. But there were other consequences of the IGD investigation which were quite unexpected — and some of them were distinctly sinister.

The first untoward incident came to the attention of Lieutenant Kulka. According to Kulka, the IGD investigation was *not* terminated by Colonel Smith but suddenly called off on the orders of higher authority. "The entire story got awfully hot," Kulka has stated, "because it started involving more and more people. I was asked to keep my mouth shut because there were too many people involved in the CIC and Military Government. Some very high-ranking people were involved in this and their palms had been greased somewhere along the line. If one of these people had ever been caught or grilled, then half of the U.S. Command would have been in very serious trouble." In a letter from San Francisco, dated 18 April 1978, Leo Kulka enlarged on this. "General Lucius Clay was in command at the time of the investigation and it was his command which had ordered the sudden stop of the investigation. I specifically remember a remark made by Colonel Smith of the IG at the time that we must have gotten too close to home... This might explain why the entire investigation came to a sudden standstill and why the files were burned in the house which served as our headquarters."

According to Kulka, the destruction of the investigative records occurred in this manner: "When Colonel Smith and I were ordered back to our stations, overnight, there was an officer that came from the United States Air Force (USAF) or United States Forces European Theater (USFET) headquarters and demanded all the files, which was about two filing cabinets full, and he told Colonel Smith that they were going to be forwarded to Frankfurt. However, when I returned unexpectedly I found him sitting there putting them all in the fireplace." For the authors of this book the image of an American Army colonel feeding an open fire with the precious documentation on the Garmisch affair is one of the most melancholy of the entire story. Through three preliminary reports by Colonel Smith were eventually located in the U.S. Archives, these bore no mention of such contentious aspects of his investigation as gold and currency, and no reports on these aspects have yet been traced.

For 26-year-old Lieutenant Kulka, worse was to follow him. He alleges that he was sent back to Munich by the CIC, held incommunicado under house arrest for about three or four weeks and told never to write any further reports about the case. Then a variety of bizarre allegations were thrown at him. He was accused of gun-running after it was found that he had sent three target pistols back to the States. He was accused of harboring an alien in his quarters — to wit, his 87-year-old grandmother, whom he had smuggled out of Czechoslovakia just before the Communist coup — and of wrongly collecting subsistence allowance from U.S. Army funds on her behalf while she was awaiting emigration to the United States. Kulka's security clearance was revoked, which effectively terminated his employment as a special agent. His German informant, one Anton Ditt, was arrested and later tried and sentenced to two years imprisonment for false representation as a CIC agent. When Kulka asked for a court-martial so that he could learn the real nature of the charges against him he was simply shipped off to the Zone of the Interior (i.e., the United States) as "unsuited for CIC duty." The girl he was proposing to marry (and who is now his wife) was forbidden to accompany him. Though Kulka claimed she was a Jewish DP, it was ruled that she was a Sudeten German expellee from Czechoslovakia and therefore ineligible for marriage to a U.S. citizen. When Kulka reported the affair to his Senator, so much pressure was put on his fiancée and grandmother that he decided it was prudent to keep his mouth shut. "Even while I was separated from the Service," Kulka commented bitterly recently, "my fiancée and her relatives were harassed by the American Military Government and the officers in my Corps. I was told in no uncertain terms that if I ever wanted to see my fiancée again I had better keep my mouth shut about the entire story. It wasn't until about a year later that purely by accident my fiancée was able to get her exit permit and get to the United States.

Some years after Kulka's bride-to-be left Germany for the United States, Colonel Leonard H. Smith was posted from Berlin to distant Ecuador, in Latin America. The principal agents of the Inspector General's investigation into the Garmisch affair were thus as far from Germany and from each other as it was possible for them to be.

The Garmisch affair was to continue to haunt Leo de Gar Kulka for years afterward — even after he was recalled from the Reserves to serve in the Korean War. When friends and colleagues began to be killed or commit suicide he grew paranoid about the whole business. "Just recently," he wrote from San Francisco on 14 April 1978, "a friend of mine, who was my CO in Japan and Korea and was with the Provost Marshal's office in Garmisch, was mysteriously killed in Los Angeles. He was described as having suffered a heart attack following an attempted robbery, during which the contents of his filing cabinet were stolen — nothing else. He was writing something about the bullion incident. Coincidence? I consider myself lucky to be alive and able to talk about it since the Statute of Limitations has run out for everybody."

Kulka wrote again recently: "Though my first gut reaction was to let sleeping dogs lie, my present feeling is that this scandal has been hushed up far too long. Apparently Watergate is not the only matter to be hushed up." But then he had second thoughts. "I wonder if at my age helping you write a book is worth the risk of my personal safety and the undisturbed emotional tranquillity I have enjoyed. If you have found me, so could those who have enriched themselves. Do you want to know how much I know? Why? What then? Why should I trust you?"

In the light of what was to follow in the Garmisch affair, Leo Kulka's suspicions were not difficult to comprehend.

18

The Reinhardt Memorandum

The Inspector General's team, after fighting off the Garmisch "gang" for the best part of three months, finally staged a tactical retreat from that unholy town in the last week of July 1947. Their departure, unbloodied but bowed, did not mark the end of the hostilities. For shortly afterwards the Army returned to the attack with a two-pronged assault designed to regularize the irregularities which had been highlighted by the Inspector General's investigation. First they moved in a Criminal Investigation Division (CID) Special Project Team inaugurated by General Clay, and then they sent poor Frank Gammache — small fry, fall guy, and ingenious creator of the luxurious Casa Carioca nightclub — for trial by court-martial. Neither of these events, however, was to prove an outstanding triumph for the Army's forces of law and order in Garmisch-Partenkirchen.

The strange business of the Casa Carioca had been one of the Inspector General's main preoccupations in Garmisch. It was known that it had cost a fortune to build, but it was not known where the fortune had come from, and the resulting investigation had led down many dark alleys and into many murky corners. There were those, like the newspapermen Ed Hartrich and Tom Agoston, who had some inkling of what was really going on in Garmisch and expected great things from Frank Gammache's court-martial. They were to be greatly disappointed. When the charges were finally read out in court at Bad Tölz on 9 September 1947 they proved to be somewhat less than earth-shattering. Gammache was charged on a total of eight counts under the 94th Article of War (knowingly and willfully misappropriating military property) and the 96th Article of War (disorderly and discreditable conduct). In sum, the builder of the most fabulous and costly fun palace in the whole of Bavaria was charged with misappropriating 11-7/10 tons of coke, 17 ½ cubic feet of gravel, and some wood for building dog kennels valued at $5.26. He was further charged with wrongful use of labor intended for the military service (mending a German's car) and wrongful occupation of a hotel without proper authority (living with a German girlfriend). He was found guilty on account of the coke but not the gravel or the dog kennels, and guilty on account of the German car but not the German girlfriend. He was then fined $1,500, taken under escort to the nearest port of embarkation, and shipped home to the United States.

The charges against Frank Gammache were so trivial that Ed Hartrich, to whom Gammache had spoken at length in May about all the various goings-on in Garmisch, believed that something peculiar had happened. The U.S. Army judiciary's Pre-Trial Report contained statements about the "scope of this investigation" and "the aid of CID investigators, [a] CCD team, and so forth" and stated: "The extensive investigations which preceded this pre-trial investigation have given it many unusual aspects." It hardly seems credible that these remarks could apply to a case where, in terms of monetary value, the loss to the U.S. military authorities was less than a hundred dollars or so. Obviously there was more to it than that, but nowhere in the Record of Trial was there any further information on the deeper implications at stake. The matter had to be much more serious to involve the Inspector General's Department (IGD), Criminal Investigation Division (CID), Civil Censorship Division (CCD) *and* a court-martial. But if it *was* much more serious, why did it not come out at the trial — unless there was a concentrated plot in existence to prevent the whole truth from becoming known? And if that were the case, what was it that had caused the matter to be suppressed at the very highest level?

According to a recent review of the case by the officer who acted as Frank Gammache's defense counsel at the court-martial — Colonel Clifton H. Young — Gammache should not really have been on trial at all, even though what he had done was, strictly speaking, illegal. "I think it was General Eisenhower [who] told Lucius Truscott to outdo the Nazis in fixing up a recreation center at Garmisch for the occupation troops," Young related in 1978." He wanted it better than anything the Nazis had built. So this gave Gammache, who was the nuts-and-bolts man, the authority to do exactly what he did do. What he did was illegal in one sense, but he had the privilege of doing it because he was ordered by his superiors. He wasn't the one to be tried — they really should have tried General Eisenhower."

It was against this background of uncertainty in the field and double standards at higher headquarters that the CID Special Project Team swung into action. Headed by Victor H. Peccarelli, who until then had been Chief Agent of the 32nd CID in Esslingen (a suburb of Stuttgart), the team had been set up on General Clay's instructions as a criminal investigation to follow up the Inspector General's preliminary investigation that had recently ended. Operating at the very highest level. Peccarelli was answerable only to the European Command Provost Marshal and reported directly to a selected high eschelon of the European Command, cutting out all intermediaries in the chain of command. This not only made the CID Special Investigation a very high-powered operation, but a very hush-hush one as well. Its leading members—Victor Peccarelli and his assistant, Philip von Pfluge Benzell—were the *crème de la crème* of the American Army's internal police force in Germany. According to one who knew them both, Peccarelli was "a typical BTO [big time operator]," an ex-detective who was attended by much noise and commotion wherever he went. His great friend, Benzell, was a "first-rate investigator," a former District Attorney investigator in civilian life, who was now divorced and had "no steady girlfriend but played the field." A fellow CID Agent, Bob Shaw, remembered him as a "very, very bombastic type. He could be a typical Colonel Blimp and he made enough noise that he kinda got his way in a lot of things because people didn't want to outshout him." He must also have had (or needed) a sense of humor. A spoof "Wanted" notice, complete with mug shots, was produced by his CID colleagues at about the time of the Garmisch investigation. Headed WANTED! $2.50 REWARD, the spoof read:

Apprehend and detain the following named man:
PHILIP vP BENZELL
Alias "Benny the Bum," alias "Baldy-locks,"
alias "That S.O.B., Benzell,"
DESCRIPTION:
Height: 5′ 10′
Age: 34
Weight: 190 lbs
Eyes: Two
Hair: Two
Sex: About twice a week
Has a very even disposition (mad all the time), sometimes seen in the company of a tall, dark man known as "That big Guinea Bastard."
WANTED FOR:
Murder, arson, rape, sodomy, larceny, fornication, highway mopery with intent to creep, and impersonating a CID agent.

Several other enlisted men made up the CID team, which was known familiarly as Peck's Bad Boys and officially worked under the code name "Operation Garpeck," a compound of the words Garmisch and Peccarelli.

Since they were working undercover on this particular operation, all wore plainclothes.

During August 1947 the team moved into a large and secluded Bavarian-style house called Haus Duisburg (formerly the property of the Bayer Company and known as the Bayer Hof), which was situated three miles out of Garmisch on the old Garmisch-Mittenwald road. The team's mission was wide-ranging. Surviving documentation is incomplete and neither Peccarelli nor Benzell is now alive to tell the tale, but Peccarelli's wife, Alice, who was working in the CCD in Germany at the same time as her husband was working in the CID, remembered the case clearly and was in no doubt that her husband had been assigned to investigate the disappearance of a large quantity of gold bullion which had been carried up into the hills in the Garmisch area on the backs of "donkeys." Though it is known that Operation Garpeck was also investigating narcotics trafficking in the area, Alice Peccarelli had no recollection of her husband talking about that. "It was gold from the German National Treasury," she affirmed from Stockton, New Jersey, in 1980, "which they claimed had been melted down into bullion."

Frank Purcell, who was a key member of the Garpeck team, confirmed and enlarged on Mrs. Peccarelli's recollection in a telephone conversation from his home in California in 1982. "We were not investigating narcotics," Purcell stated; "we were investigating gold bullion and military records." With another CID colleague by the name of Thomas Gardiner, a fully qualified attorney, Purcell was specifically involved in the investigation of one man, a former Military Governor of Garmisch, whose rank he gave as colonel. "The investigation was directly against him. No one else was involved. He had absconded with a lot of military records, a lot of gold bullion out of Garmisch. I know that there was a lot of gold bullion involved — no one could even imagine how much. They talked about astronomical figures. But I know the colonel had access to a lot of wealth in the Garmisch area. I say I know — I suspect and I know. It was quite an important case. There was a lot of time expended on it. What I do know is it had to be a court case because Victor Peccarelli assigned Thomas Gardiner and myself to the case and I automatically assumed, 'Well, I'm working with an Operations Agent who was extremely important to the organization and it's got to be a very important case.'"

Philip Benzell confirmed at a subsequent inquiry into the case that there was a "mass of information" on the officer in question and that he was alleged to have "embezzled or converted to his own use, monies belonging to the German Government" which had been deposited in Switzerland for safekeeping. "At the present time," Benzell stated, "Messrs. Gardiner and Purcell of the 32nd CID are investigating in Switzerland." He made that statement on 3 February 1948 — some weeks *after* Garpeck had been called off. The matter was obviously taken *very* seriously.

The search for the bullion and the former Military Governor took Purcell and Gardiner all over Europe. "We went up into Sweden, we went on into Denmark, France, and on into Switzerland. I think the colonel was located in Switzerland and we tried to extradite him and we were unsuccessful because of the extradition law in Switzerland. We did a lot of work with the Swiss Police — the Canton Police in Switzerland. We relayed the information back to the CID in Frankfurt but what action the CID took I don't know."

There was not much action the CID *could* take. Public Safety Officer Elmer Pralle recalled later: "It was in Switzerland that we lost control of that. We could not get any information out of Switzerland because of the accounts and the secrecy. I wrote letters down there and we called down there but they would not reveal anything at all on that." A check on the "colonel's" background and bank account in his home town in the United States by investigators sent in by the Provost Marshal General at Peccarelli's request also drew a blank.

Even Colonel Franz Pfeiffer, the Gebirgsjäger commander who had originally been responsible for the burial of the Reichsbank gold near Mittenwald in the last days of the war, was recalled from obscurity in Austria, where he was instructing French troops in German Alpine warfare techniques, to answer fresh questions about the gold from Philip Benzell. It was Captain Sauteau, the French Intelligence agent, who had arranged the rendezvous. But Pfeiffer declared — as he has continued to declare ever since — that he was sick to death of the whole business and could add nothing new, and Benzell was obliged to leave empty-handed.

The ripples eddying out from Garmisch washed even farther afield than Austria, Switzerland, and Scandinavia and eventually reached as far as California, on the West Coast of the United States, half a world away. Dollars as well as gold came under the scrutiny of the investigators, and the mysterious business of the $404,000 taken from the von Blüchers' garden and the receipt for it signed by Captain Fred Neumann was looked at afresh. Early investigators had never been satisfied with Neumann's explanations as to what happend to the money and after he had returned to the States and left the Army, suspicion still lingered in his direction. Now, in September 1947, Operation Garpeck reopened the inquiry. It was decided to send a U.S.-based agent to California where Neumann was working as the western representative of a coin-operated cigarette vending machine company in San Francisco, and the Internal Revenue Service was requested to keep a check on Neumann and his former Master Sergeant for signs of conspicuous spending.

In the second half of September CID Agent Howard Hyatt arrived in California and contacted the San Francisco Office of the FBI. On 19 September 1946 the San Francisco FBI wrote to the Director of the FBI in Washington, D.C.:

Subject: Frederick Siegfried Neumann
        Theft of Government Property

A Special Project of CID has been established in Garmish-Partenkirchen, Bavaria, to determine among other matters the ultimate disposition of some $404,840 and £405, allegedly receipted for on 24 August 1945 by one Captain Neumann, CIB, Third Army.

In this connection, investigation has been undertaken by CID to determine if Neumann may have misappropriated funds turned over to the Army by captured prisoners of war. Agent Hyatt of CID was in possession of a photostatic copy of the purported receipt obtained from Captain Neumann. As of 27 August 1945 [sic], however, Finance records of Headquarters, European Command, failed to disclose such an amount of money had been received by the U.S. Army from Captain Neumann.

Upon completion of this investigation Neumann is to be interviewed by CID to determine the validity of the receipt and if valid what disposition was made to the funds involved, following which a report is to be forwarded to the Office of the Provost Marshall General, War Department, Washington, D.C.

Agent Hyatt advised that his investigation is proceeding and at the appropriate time the FBI would be notified in the event it became necessary for this Bureau to undertake investigation. It appears that should Neumann exhibit a receipt regarding the disposition he made of this large sum of money he will be temporarily in the clear and further efforts made by CID to trace these funds.

In view of the huge sum of money involved, and because the Bureau may be called on to undertake investigation, the above is being furnished to the Bureau at this time for its information.

All, it seemed, in vain. Whatever the outcome of the inquiry in California, Neumann remained at large, the FBI was never called in, and the mystery of the $404,000 was never solved. In all probability Neumann was not the man, but whatever explanations he might have been able to give, he took them to the grave. For in June 1970 Fred Neumann, one of the prime suspects in the Great Reichsbank Robbery, died of tuberculosis in the National Jewish Hospital in Denver, Colorado.

But there were other key suspects. As Operation Garpeck progressed the name of John McCarthy, the 31-year-old, $7,000-per-year Chief of the

Investigation and Enforcement Branch of the Finance Division, recurred time and time again in the course of inquiries into narcotics, finance, and numerous other matters conducted by both the local and theater CID. But McCarthy was a difficult and apparently dangerous man to get to. Files and other information which had a vital bearing upon certain of his activities mysteriously disappeared from the Finance Division on a number of occasions when the investigators came to examine them. A witness who, in Philip Benzell's words, "could give us the absolute rock-bottom factual information on McCarthy," refused to do so while he was still in Germany. "This reluctance," Benzell stated at a later inquiry, "was attributed to fear of bodily injury or harm in this theater." According to one witness, some of the CCD wire tappers were in with the Munich "bunch," and when Benzell requested that a tap be put on McCarthy's civilian phone, McCarthy soon got wind of it. "McCarthy suddenly moved out of such quarters as he was occupying in Munich," Benzell testified, "and was living in a residence along the banks of the Isar, and the CCD was having a difficult time in determining precisely where he lived in order to tap his phone." But McCarthy was nothing if not resilient. Even while he was being hounded by the CID, quietly living along the Isar, he bounced back into the limelight with a sensational announcement to the press which could no nothing but help refurbish his tarnished image. The subject of the announcement — McCarthy's continuing hunt for missing treasure — was the height of irony under the circumstances. "MG PRESSING WIDE SEARCH FOR HIDDEN NAZI TREASURE," the Army newspaper *Stars and Stripes* reported from Munich in December:

Military Government officials here revealed that an extensive search is being pressed throughout Bavaria in an effort to find the hidden treasures of Hermann Goering and other prominent Nazis whose loot was buried or stored away before the capitulation of Germany.

J.R. McCarthy, chief of the investigation and enforcement branch of the finance division of Bavaria MG, said millions of dollars in gold, silver, diamonds, and paintings already have been recovered. He asserted there still remain hidden somewhere in Bavaria treasures estimated to be worth millions.

Faced with so many difficulties, Operation Garpeck investigations into gold, dollars, narcotics, embezzlement, and other chicanery, began to bog down. It should have had everything going for it — even a new Military Governor who was on their side. Colonel Kenneth E. Van Buskirk, whose avowed mission was "to clean up Garmisch," was a thick-set, square-headed, balding man from Special Services, who had been General Patton's "housekeeper" and (it was said) his "favorite court jester." He was, *mir-*

abile dictu, straight as a die and honest as a saint, and that should have helped. But somehow the investigation just did not go as it should. Victor Peccarelli reported: "The progress of this investigation has often been materially impeded by the reluctance of informants to supply information. Informants have met with threats on their lives. Furthermore, there has been a definite reluctance to identify or supply information about American or Allied personnel in connection with the illegal activities in this area for fear of reprisal...."

Victor Peccarelli and Philip Benzell, hitherto the closest of friends, even fell out over the conduct of the operation, and when Peccarelli was reassigned in early December, Benzell took his place as Chief of Garpeck. Why, people began to ask, after the concentration of so much talent and ingenuity and the expenditure of so much time and effort, were there still no charges made, no arrests, no seizure of tangible evidence? Even the narcotics side of the case, which had produced plenty of leads, fouled up at critical moments. When they tried to buy morphine and cocaine from the narcotics rings as criminal evidence, something usually went wrong. Five hundred grams of cocaine which they bought from the Garmisch ring for a dollar a gram through a Chinese pusher named Leo turned out to be fake, and they had to forego the purchase of a kilo of cocaine from a Polish ring when the money to clinch the deal failed to turn up in time from the CID cashier. Benzell did succeed in buying 250 grams of morphine, of a type only used by the former *Wehrmacht*, for 12 cartons of cigarettes, but for some reason the pusher, a well-known figure in Garmisch, was not detained and nothing came of the transaction. And when they tried to obtain the services of Zenta Hausner at the notorious White Horse Inn, they eventually arrived too late.

Ed Hartrich and Tom Agoston — whose newspaper stores on Garmisch, filed in May, were still being kept on ice by the Army High Command — grew so impatient with the progress of the Garpeck investigation that they decided to carry out their own private investigations using their own informants. It was at about this time that their paths fatally crossed with that of another ex-newsman, then a member of the same CIC Special Squad to which Lieutenant Kulka belonged, and a member of the Munich Press Club to which the newsmen belonged, by the name of Guenther Reinhardt. Both Hartrich and Agoston on the one hand and Kulka on the other had a lot to say about the Garmisch affair— and Reinhardt, flabbergasted, listened avidly. The consequences — the so-called Reinhardt memorandum — were to blow the lid off Garmisch and the Office of Military Government, Bavaria (OMGB), once and for all.

Like many of the Americans who have featured in this story, Guenther Reinhardt was a native of Germany. Born into a well-known German Jewish banking family in Mannheim in 1904, he had studied economics at Heidelberg University, been a member of the German ski team for the ill-fated 1924 Olympics (which never took place), and at the age of 21 emigrated to the United States, where he continued his postgraduate studies at Columbia University. His first job had been in a New York bank, but in 1933 he became a freelance journalist and wrote a syndicated foreign affairs column for McClure Newspapers. Because of his preoccupation with the rise of Nazism in both Germany and the United States Reinhardt was commissioned by his banking associates and a couple of large civic groups to carry out a private investigation into the question of Germany's likely furture international relations. The information he uncovered concerning Nazi activities in the United States was subsequently turned over to the House Committee on Immigration and Naturalization, the forerunner of the McCormack Committee, a Congressional body investigating the spread of foreign subversive activities within the United States, and itself a predecessor of the House Committee on Un-American Activities.

This led to Reinhardt's early involvement with the American intelligence world. In 1934 he was appointed to act as a liaison link between the McCormack Committee and the FBI. In 1936, after time abroad as foreign correspondent for a Swiss newspaper, Reinhardt returned to New York and claimed to have been appointed a "Special Employee of the FBI." In any event, he used his freelance journalistic work and his continuing undercover operations against Nazism, Fascism, Communism, and other subversive movements in America as a cover for his FBI activities, which involved a confidential mission to Mexico and continued after America's entry into the war. While working for the Foreign Press Association Reinhardt was allegedly credited with a scoop predicting the Japanese attack on Pearl Harbor 13 days before it actually occurred. The item was published on 24 November 1941, but its warning went unheeded by the State Department.

During 1942 and 1943 Reinhardt masqueraded as a Communist in order to infiltrate American Communist organizations and then passed on the results of his investigations to the authorities. In a routine Loyalty and Character Report at this time he was described as a "respected citizen with a good family background, and of good character." But though personal references rated his character and integrity as "excellent," his emotional stability was generally reckoned to be no more than "average." Between 1944 and 1946 Reinhardt served as Adjutant to the Manhattan Squadron of the Civil Air Patrol (Auxiliary Army Air Forces). For a few months in 1946 he worked as Foreign Correspondent on the European Staff of the International News Service (INS), for a few more months as a reports officer in the Public Safety Branch of Military Government in Frankfurt. It was during this period that Reinhardt was involved in hunting down six Hungarian SS guards responsible for murdering downed American airmen and securing the evidence for their conviction at the Nuremburg War Crimes Trials. Then he reentered the American intelligence world, to which he believed it was his destiny to belong, and joined the CIC in Germany.

Reinhardt, it must be stressed, was not a mere lightweight in this particular world. He was a highly intelligent, educated, and talented man, a substantial figure who ranked quite high in the OMGUS hierarchy, first as assistant to General Clay's Chief Public Safety Officer, and later as press representative for General Clay's Intelligence Chief of Staff in the European Theater. A confidential report on Reinhardt compiled by the Inspector General's Division of the U.S. Army in Germany in April 1948 as a consequence of events which form the main subject of this chapter, sums up his checkered career with the American occupation authorities in Germany as follows:

The records reflect the fact that Mr. Reinhardt was employed in the command on 7 September 1946, primarily to serve as press representative for the Deputy G-2 USFET. He appeared at that time to be unusually intelligent and energetic, at first displaying a great capacity for work, a prodigious memory, and a marked ability to gather information. It was necessary to relieve him of this assignment on 4 May 1947, however, because of a displayed lack of tact and common sense, plus a peculiar persistence in breaches of security involving discussions of classified military matters with unauthorized persons, and by unauthorized contacts with officials of State Department and Military Government, to whom he misrepresented his position and the scope of his authority. On 5 May 1947, Mr. Reinhardt was employed by CIC, because of his linguistic ability, education, FBI experience, and knowledge of Germany, he having been born and educated there.

In fact, Reinhardt was never an actual member of the CIC. Though he was made available to the CIC in an agent capacity, he was really a civilian employee of the Office of the Director of Intelligence at European Command Headquarters. Initially based at CIC headquarters in Frankfurt, Reinhardt was assigned in June 1947 to the CIC regional office at Munich, first as an agent on the Special Squad — importantly, the outfit to which Lieutenant Kulka, then working on the IG investigation in Garmisch, belonged — then later as Case Officer (Communist Desk). In this latter capacity Guenther Reinhardt was acknowledged to be the top Communist investigator in the CIC. In his memoirs of his CIC career, published in New York in 1952 in a book called *Crime Without Punishment*, Reinhardt regarded his role in Germany as a kind of personal crusade against the forces of wickedness, in whatever form they appeared.

"For two years after the end of the war," he wrote, "I was able to follow the trail of the Soviet secret terror against America in Europe as a Control Investigator of the U.S. Counter Intelligence Corps. Part of that time was spent as a case officer directing intelligence agents in the field. In many respects it was fruitful work. During that period I was able to participate in the 'breaking' of the cases of Ingeborg Petersen, the German girl spy who posed as a WAC, and of Siegfried Kabus, the young Nazi fanatic who had taken to planting time bombs in the dead of night."

Guenther Reinhardt pursued subversion of American interests in Germany, whether from within or without, with the demonic energy and fanatical single-mindedness of a man possessed—the Don Quixote of the U.S. Zone. He never let up. Even his holidays were used to further the cause. "During my work in Germany," he was to write afterwards, "I had discovered an appalling penetration of American security agencies in Germany by Soviet agents. In all cases the agents engaged in the penetration were receiving their orders and relaying their information to Prague. I was, however, supposedly restricted at the time to investigations in Bavaria, and an intensely complicating atmosphere of interservice jealousies made intrusion into the Prague area unpopular." Undaunted, Reinhardt decided to pursue his case and indulge his obsession by taking a vacation in Prague. But the tentacles of the forces of darkness had reached everywhere in Guenther Reinhardt's life, or so it seemed. In Prague he discovered that the Czech Secret Police already had a copy of his personal file in their possession and that it was a girl working for the Civil Censorship Division of the U.S. Occupation Forces in Germany who had transmitted it to them.

Reinhardt was to bring the same obsession and paranoia to bear when he turned his attention to corruption in the American occupation of Germany. His enthusiasm was not always appreciated by his fellow Americans, for it sometimes transgressed not only the bounds of geography but the demarcations of his brief and protocol as well. Once he bearded Clay's Chief-of-Staff, Brigadier-General Charles K. Gailey, about the record of a certain political suspect by the name of Markovitch. The next day his commanding officer carpeted him for it. "General Gailey told me you'd stuck your nose into something that didn't concern you," his commanding officer told him. "If you want to keep your job with me, forget about the whole thing and be glad General Gailey isn't going after your scalp."

There were plenty who would have liked to have gone for Reinhardt's scalp. He was not a very popular man with his colleagues. He was, for a start, a sneak. Most recalled him as a boastful, rather unbalanced character, who suffered from persecution mania and was prone to exaggeration. CID Agent Bill Wilson described him as "full of crap." A former CIC operative in Munich, Werner Michel, remembered that Reinhardt suffered from persecution mania to such an extent that on one occasion when Michel was present he rushed out of his hotel, drew his service revolver, and opened fire, exclaiming that "they" were after him. Tom Agoston, who worked for INS as Reinhardt had once done, and knew Reinhardt well, recalled:

He was unbalanced up to a point. In Frankfurt he used to call me at 2 o'clock in the morning and say, "I just want to say goodbye."

And I'd say: "Well, what's happening? Are you going home?"

And he'd say: "No, I'm going to commit suicide."

And I'd say: "For God's sake, where are you? Don't be a bloody fool!"

And I went round there to his flat and found he was wearing a white tropical uniform. He was in the Coast Guard, he told me. He had three pistols on his desk and he said: "Well, all right. Well, I'm going to blow my brains out."

I had to stop him. But he was a fantastic chap. He looked just like Erich von Stroheim.

Agoston recalled a second incident concerning Reinhardt which illustrated another facet of his personality:

There was a crazy German girl who was a mascot, a camp follower, and she picked up GI English. Her American English was so fantastic she was able to pass as a CIC officer and she borrowed a stolen jeep and forged papers, and checked into various hotels and billets and ran up bills. Now the first person to interrogate her was Reinhardt; and he put out a release about this *"most dangerous Mata Hari"* — and she was just a good-time girl!

By June 1947 — halfway through Colonel Smith's and Lieutenant Kulka's IG investigation in Garmisch-Partenkirchen — Guenther Reinhardt's personal behavior began to be a matter of serious concern to his superior officers. He would react strangely to minor situations, or burst into tears, or throw violent fits of temper during which he would hurl himself to the ground and roll back and forth. At other times, to the embarrassment of his superior officers, he would go about posing as the Chief of the CIC, and on vacation in Czechoslovakia it was said he had described himself everywhere as the "Chief of the American Intelligence in Germany." These signs of incipient breakdown coincided with a growing awareness on Reinhardt's part of the true extent of the corruption endemic in the American Zone. Indeed it is possible that — for a man with such a taut and rigid sense of morality, and such an extreme and manic black-and-white perception of good and evil — the former was partly a consequence of the latter. It is probable that a significant part of Reinhardt's information came from his disaffected colleague in the CIC Special Squad in Munich, Leo Kulka, who at the end of July returned from the Garmisch investigation fully aware that the place was a hotbed of crime and corruption.

By the late summer of 1947 both Reinhardt and Kulka were beginning to perceive that their careers in the CIC were, for possibly different reasons, in jeopardy. Both men had fallen out of favor with the organization that employed them and both were harassed mercilessly over trivial formalities, presumably as a means of hindering their work and breaking their morale. We have already seen how Kulka complained of being confined to his quarters and charged for not wearing his proper insignia during the IG investigation in Garmisch. Not very long afterwards it was Reinhardt's turn to bear the brunt of this kind of calculated and petty officiousness from his superiors. In a letter to Tom Agoston sent by Reinhardt from New York some months after the event, he described at length the humiliations to which he was subjected:

Being on the operations level I saw for the first time — and was aghast at — the incredible extent of brazenness of irregularities. You know that I can't keep my mouth shut when I see something wrong or crooked. The result was that the Regional Commander [of the CIC] hounded me in the rottenest way you can imagine. As I had a superior work record there was nothing they could do about that. So there was a thousandfold chicanery in different ways. They gave me difficult assignments and then took my vehicle away from me under some pretext and made me hitchhike 100 miles a day; they took the furniture out of my room on the pretext of an adjustment of inventory; they gave me assignments calculated to keep me from headquarters (30 miles in the country) during meal hours and when I returned they would call my attention [to the fact] that military regulations forbade feeding men outside the announced mess hall hours; they made me spend hours night after night rewriting agents' reports in addition to my other duties "because I was the only professional writer in the office"; they gave me "Charge of Quarters Duty Agent" duty over weekends at headquarters "because I needed this special training"; despite a written request from the Army hospital in Munich they refused me permission for hospitalization "because there was too much work to do" and threatened that if I had to go to hospital for a rest I would be sent back to the States as useless to CIC; they refused me permission to go to headquarters in Frankfurt to complain; they tore up formal communications through channels asking for reassignment; etc., etc. But I stuck it out.

In the meantime I was powerless to do anything about the irregularities of the agents under me. Even formal charges were disregarded. Then I personally made two arrests of Germans on whom I had the goods 100% but who had terrific MG connections. One case was that of the chief German in the Garmisch black-market ring about which you have written several times (anything you published was completely accurate but only 10% of what is really there!). The other [case] was former SS man who was trafficking in genuine forged papers (if you know what I mean) and smuggling former Luftwaffe personnel wholesale out of Germany. In both cases the guys were out of jail in less than twelve hours and the evidence which I had turned over to the appropriate authorities was handed back to these men! In both cases I was reprimanded for "unauthorized" arrests—simply because I had not observed the formality (disregarded in 99 and 8/10ths of all cases!) of securing written permission from the Regional Commander for the arrest. Both cases were reported to Frankfurt that I had brought three American correspondents to a Halloween party at the CIC Cloak and Dagger Club in Munich without permission, that they had seen all the German girls there, the CIC boys drunk, the CIC boys talking about classified stuff, the German girls in their cups spouting Nazi propaganda, etc., etc.

Well, I got orders transferring me to Berlin and to stop over in Frankfurt for two days duty at CIC headquarters.

And then Reinhardt learned that his superiors had arranged "secretly but very efficiently" to send him home. "G-1 and Civilian Personnel had been told that it was a Top Secret security case," he complained bitterly in his letter to Agoston, "and that's how they even arranged for a berth on the next ship."

There was no appeal against this peremptory expulsion. Reinhardt was forbidden to go to the Inspector General under threat of immediate arrest. He was warned that if he made any move to get another job in Germany, or spoke to the press about what had happened, he would be arrested and charged with violation of security regulations. If he stepped so much as an inch out of line his German girlfriend, whom he hoped one day to marry, would be publicly dragged through the mud "because I had whored around with her. You know, of course," Reinhardt confided to Agoston, "that that tied my hands."

It is not difficult to imagine Reinhardt's state of mind on hearing this news. Shock followed by outrage, followed by a blind desire for revenge. That he should be bounced from the country by the very authorities whose corruption he had sought to expose was too much to bear. He would reveal all. So before he sailed from Germany he dictated a formal 48-page report at CIC headquarters in Frankfurt "about all the irregularities and the faking of intelligence reports in the Munich Region." This was the first of two reports Guenther Reinhardt was to present to the American authorities in connection with this affair. The report amounted to a blistering attack on the people who had just fired him. It accused the CIC of widespread corruption, incompetence, and idleness, all owing to the rivalry and lack of coordination of five overlapping Army Intelligence Agencies, and predicted that the United States faced "another Pearl Harbor in Germany" because of the conditions prevailing in the CIC. Though it was actually written in Frankfurt in November as an embittered and angry valedictory to the U.S. Occupation, it had its genesis in Munich in the preceding September, when it was first conceived in marginally less emotive circumstances at the suggestion of CID Agent Philip Benzell, then a member of the extensive CID investigation in Garmisch-Partenkirchen. Benzell subsequently provided a formal Army inquiry with this account of the strange meeting at which the first Reinhardt memorandum was discussed:

I met Mr. Reinhardt at the billets of the 13th CID in Grünwald, which is a suburb of Munich. Present were—myself, Mr. David Gallant (the Chief Agent of the 13th CID), and Reinhardt. At the outset of our conversation he handed me a typewritten sheet which outlined his personal history and accomplishments in the field of reporting and writing. He also stated that he had been a special employee of the Federal Bureau of Investigation and added that as proof his income tax returns be examined. After I had read this typewritten page he stated as follows (or words to that effect): "Benzell, I have asked that you meet me to discuss the investigation that you are conducting in Garmisch. I have heard that you are an 'honest cop' and feel that you will take action on the matters which I have given you." Thereupon he told me a long story concerning the alleged misdeeds, misdoings, and misconduct of a Major McCarthy...and a number of other indigenous persons. He alleged that all of these persons formed a combine, or ring, dealing in narcotics, currency, gold, jewelry, stolen cars, and other assorted types of felonies.

The entire story was disjointed and not in sequence and at the conclusion of the interview, which lasted perhaps one-half to three-quarters of an hour, I requested that he reduce his story to some form of writing—coaching him, however, not to identify himself with the written story. I suggested that he neither date it not write it in his own handwriting and that preferably it should appear as merely a typewritten piece of paper, on the theory that Reinhardt should enjoy the status of an informer and his identity be protected. He agreed to that and stated that he would be in touch at a little later date. It was also agreed that when I called him, the code word to be used was that I wanted to see him "at the movies." (This reference was in connection with the Bavarian film colony, which is also located in Grünwald.) After a passage of several weeks I called him on at least three occasions but was never able to contact him.

It took the painful trauma of his summary dismissal (which happened on 12 November) to force from Reinhardt his long-promised denunciation of the American Occupation in Germany and of the organization to which he himself had been attached, the CIC. Its contents were explosive. According to Reinhardt, "there were terrific personnel shake-ups—the operations chief for Bavaria was dismissed instantaneously, the executive officer was transferred, the commanding officer about to sail for home was held over for weeks to explain things, etc., etc., but there was also a terrific cover-up and mutual protection operation going on from Garmisch to Augsburg and from Munich to Nuremburg."

Having fired his first shot, Guenther Reinhardt set sail from Bremerhaven on 15 November 1947 on board the U.S. transport *General Black* and arrived in New York on 26 November. His German girl, Nora, sailed a few days later and arrived in New York on 4 December. Her arrival only served to complicate the private side of a life that was already publicly complicated enough. For at his apartment on Christopher Street, New York, Reinhardt also kept a wife. For years she had been a hopeless invalid, totally paralyzed and mentally incompetent, but under New York law Reinhardt was permitted no divorce, and Nora was destined to remain no more than the Fräulein "from over there."

Reinhardt's 48-page report had evidently not gotten things off his chest and the sea air and the ocean crossing had done nothing to blow away his gloom. On the contrary, the 12-day voyage had provided him with nothing but time to brood, and it did not help that the ship itself seemed like a floating appendage of the U.S. Occupation Zone he had just left, peopled by disgraced black marketeers from the American PX, peddling diamonds and Leicas at $230 apiece. By the time Reinhardt sailed past the Statue of Liberty he was half out of his mind.

When I got back to the States [Reinhardt wrote in his letter to Agoston], I was so damn mad I wanted to blow my top. Unfortunately at the Press Club in Washington, just before I was going up to Capitol Hill to lay the rotten mess of graft, stealing, smuggling, incompetence—and the danger to our entire Intelligence system—before some of my contacts in Congress, a couple of "newspapermen" (who I did not know until much later were fixers for [Secretary of the Army] Royall) got hold of me and told me that it was my patriotic duty not to let any of this scandal out. Did I want to give gratis ammunition to the Russians? Didn't I want to have things righted? Well, the best way—the only way—was to go directly to the Secretary of the Army and lay all my evidence before him. Mr. [Kenneth C.] Royall would surely act—he was interested in discovering what really went on in Germany. He would act drastically—I would get all the reforms that I wanted.

So on December 8th and 9th I saw all the top boys at the Pentagon. On December 16th I was appointed and sworn in as Special Consultant to the Secretary of the Army at $35 a day plus per diem expenses and given an office and a secretary next to the Assistant Secretary of the Army, Gordon Gray.* They even moved out his Executive Officer, a full colonel, temporarily. I was told to dictate my report and the Secretary would take action as each section was handed to him.

Like a fool, I dictated everything.

This, Reinhardt's second and principal memorandum, was longer and more substantial that the first, consisting of 55 pages of typescript, each page stamped TOP SECRET and (in the copy which has survived to the present) annotated by an unknown hand. The document bore no title or date and no signature of authorship, though the name of the author was soon to become a household word throughout the Department of the Army and the American Zone of Germany. The Reinhardt memorandum was divided into nine main sections, each section dealing with a particular abuse or set of abuses commonly practiced (in Reinhardt's opinion) by American personnel in Germany, and each further divided into subsections, citing particular examples and concluding with Reinhardt's recommendations for future action. According to subsequent Army analysis, the two Reinhardt memorandums together contained 134 specific charges against the U.S. Occupation, 47 of them against the organization which had just fired him, the Counter-Intelligence Corps.

The opening section of the 55-page memorandum was entitled LOOT AND SMUGGLING SITUATION. It described how American military and civilian personnel were continuing to smuggle into the United States vast quantities of loot — rugs, art objects, furniture, porcelain, cameras, diamonds, and jewelry amounting to more than three-quarters of a ton in individual cases — acquired illegally on the German black market. The higher the rank, according to Reinhardt, the worse the offense, and he cited the case of a general whose baggage to the States amounted to 166 crates, boxes, and cases full of silverware, drapes, paintings, and very valuable china which had formerly belonged to the castles and landed estates around Hesse. A second section of the memorandum, entitled BLACK MARKETING BY AMERICAN DEPENDANTS, alleged that "greedy American wives are exploiting German misery and are acquiring valuable heirlooms in return for a few scraps of food." Another section, headed, PUBLIC DISPLAY BY ARMY OFFICERS OF EXCESSIVE LAISHNESS, singled

---

* Gray was later Secretary of the Army under President Truman and Director of the Office of Defense Mobilizaiton under President Eisenhower. In 1955, as Chairman of the 5421 Committee, he became one of the most powerfully placed men in the United States. This Committee (also known as the Special Group) consisted of Gray, the Secretary of State, the Secretary of Defense, and the Director of the CIA, and was the most secret committee of the United States government, dealing with issues too sensitive even to be discussed by the National Security Council. Its main function was to protect the President and no covert action could be taken without its approval.

out "the lavish private railroad trains of certain general officers which are kept fully staffed and under steam 24 hours a day and which are used perhaps once every six weeks," and the accommodation of a young army captain and his wife (typical, in Reinhardt's view, of hundreds of similar cases) who "occupy a 12-room mansion and estate which can be compared with an American millionaire's country residence. Their four servants cost them a total of $10 a month." Another section, SCANDALS IN CONNECTION WITH GERMAN MISTRESSES OF AMERICAN PERSONNEL, cited the amorous career of "an exceptionally beautiful and clever German woman" who was "among the last batch of mistresses of Nazi Propaganda Minister Goebbels," and who worked her way up the officer ranks of the CIC in Bavaria until the last in the line shipped her off for a 30-day pleasure trip in New York, where she was accommodated in some style at the Waldorf and the Ritz. At CIC regional headquarters in Munich, Reinhardt continued, "there were available on 1 October 1947 more than two dozen cases of irregularities of CIC agents in connection with their German Fräuleins which should have required drastic disciplinary action but which were covered up. (One of the "two dozen cases," it must be said, would have been Reinhardt's own.) Other sections dealt with black-market scams by the American civilian staff of the PX in Germany, failures in Army screening of visa applicants, suppression of important information to Washington, and the deficiencies of the CIC. But the major accusation of the memorandum, and the one of greatest significance to this story, was the fourth, which bore the heading ORGANIZED CRIMINAL BLACK-MARKET ACTIVITIES OF AMERICAN PERSONNEL. This section dealt with Garmisch and opened with a broadside:

Organized large-scale black-market activities which in themselves are criminal and which have additional criminal amplifications have reached a point where a major scandal seems imminent due to the fact that American correspondents in the Theater have initiated investigations of their own recently, after becoming impatient with what they call the "do-nothing attitude of the Army."

The Garmisch case is probably the most important because of the huge amounts involved, the extent of the criminal activities and criminal conspiracy, the danger of its "breaking" soon and the possible ensuing criticism of the Army, the nature of the crimes committed, allegations of inefficiency in the investigation and tardiness or failure in bringing the culprits to justice. The Garmisch Army Recreation Area, with its luxurious facilities and high living, has been the focus of much talk and allegations of grave irregularities allegedly indulged in by Army and government personnel ever since May 1945. A number of investigations were conducted but somehow were always killed or failed to produce prosecutions because of alleged lack of evidence.

On 22 May [sic] 1947, Lt.-Colonel Harold [sic] Smith, General Clay's personal Inspector General, arrived in the Garmisch area of a Top Secret mission to investigate what by then had become almost a certainty of widespread irregularities such as embezzlement of several hundred thousand dollars in cash and in jewelry of German Government, Nazi Party, and German Army funds and property; misappropriation of U.S. government funds; bribes given and accepted by Army personnel; large-scale organized black-market ventures of U.S. Army and War Department personnel; large-scale trafficking in narcotics; large-scale trading with the enemy; etc., etc.

Selected personnel from CID and Regional CIC worked with Colonel Smith under conditions of extreme secrecy and this writer conferred several times with Colonel Smith at the latter's secret headquarters in Garmisch. By the middle of July, Colonel Smith had prepared his preliminary report to General Clay which showed sufficient preliminary evideance to warrant a full-scale investigation, and he consequently recommended to General Clay that a strong force of highly qualified and specially selected CID, CIC, and CCD personnel be assigned to prepare a series of criminal prosecutions.

Reinhardt recounted in his memorandum to assistant Secretary of the Army, Gordon Gray, his version of how Colonel Smith's investigation was hampered and interfered with by the Garmisch "gang," then went on to describe how the follow-up CID investigation under Peccarelli and Benzell was meted much the same treatment.

The CID investigation by a special team recommended by Col. Smith got under way early in August 1947, but it was soon apparent to this writer that it did not proceed as well as it should. The team was headed by CID Agent Peccarelli and on 26 August 1947 it was learned that Peccarelli had been "bought off." Through the machinations of the gang he had been offered the position as head of the Belgium Branch of the "5th Avenue Shop," a big New York export firm with a guaranteed annual salary of $25,000 a year. When verifying this information on the same day, it was established that a Chief of the Munich CID was no more than lukewarm towards the investigation and privately expressed the opinion that it was "not worth pressing this thing too much because the gang was too powerful and had too much influence in Military Government." He also stated in this confidential conversation that "it did not pay to fight this thing as a number of people who became too nosy had suddenly found themselves back in the United States." Peccarelli's chief assistant in the Garmisch investigation, CID Agent Benzell, also gave the impression of either having been discouraged by the obstructions placed in the way of the investigation or of losing interest.

Guenther Reinhardt then came to the centerpiece of his allegation. A "gang" of American conspirators and their German associates were involved in a wide range of criminal activities and wielded incredible power in Garmisch. The head of the American group was the Chief of the Investigation and Enforcement Branch of the Finance division, OMGB, John McCarthy (now a civilian after leaving the Army with the rank of Lieutenant-Colonel), and the chief German confederate of this group was a certain notorious doctor. Reinhardt's memorandum continued:

It was established that one of the headquarters from which criminal activities had been conducted in the past and at present was a house at Garmisch occupied jointly by Mr. McCarthy and his German girlfriend. The same group also occupied a house in Munich which was and still is being used for black-market activities. The chief German confederate of the American group is "the doctor," who frequently lives at the two addresses given above and also maintains a residence in the city of Munich. "The doctor" owns and runs five different automobiles which are also regularly used by McCarthy and other Americans associated with him. Some of these automobiles have been traced as having been used in narcotics shipments. The investigation has also established that the association between McCarthy and "the doctor" dated back to April 1945, when McCarthy moved into Innsbruck with the 103rd Division and found "the doctor" there. The latter had been a notorious racketeer and active Nazi storm trooper. On the strength of Nazi atrocities committed by him in Innsbruck "the doctor" is still on the Austrian wanted list as a Nazi criminal. Subsequently, McCarthy had "the doctor" denazified before a German Denazification Tribunal at Garmisch on the strength of a letter in which he stated that "the doctor," by a certain action, the nature and details of which could not be divulged for military reasons, had saved the lives of thousands of Amrican soldiers during the combat phase.

Preliminary investigation, Reinhardt continued, also pointed to highly irregular deals between McCarthy and his gang and a Public Safety Officer working in Munich and several other adjacent counties.

Also implicated were three colonels...and a former American officer who at present resides as an American citizen in Switzerland and who apparently lives on his share of the proceeds of black-market deals and embezzlements and who, according to substantial leads, has repeatedly acted as middle man in transmitting and depositing individual sums of as much as $10,000 each.

"The effect of activities as described above in the United States," Reinhardt warned at the conclusion to the Garmisch section of his memorandum, "when, as, and if they break, does not need any further elaboration." And he recommended that, in view of the failure of Theater agencies properly to investigate cases like this, "special personnel be dispatched from Washington to handle such cases."

Such was the main tenor of the Reinhardt memorandum, extruded in a white-hot fury of indignation and self-righteousness in a high-level office of the United States' central military complex at the Pentagon, Washington, in the week before Christmas 1947. "I dictated everything," Reinhardt explained in his letter to Tom Agoston, "with all the evidence, names of witnesses, black-market purveyors to high-ranking personnel in Germany, dates and details of transactions, etc., etc. I went into the fullest details on your Garmisch deal: gave everything on the fake and phony investigations of 1946 and 1947, who had made which witnesses disappear, etc., etc. Among the remaining witnessess whom I urged be guarded and protected was the girl who (*after* my written report!) was murdered."

The "girl" was Zenta Hausner. Suspecting cause and effect, Reinhardt added: "What I did not know at that time was that each section of my report was sent to Clay personally in special code after I handed it in."

So the Reinhardt memorandum, like a bomb primed and set, was delivered to its target. The American Army in Germany reacted violently to its receipt, first diving for cover, then shooting back with all the weapons it could muster. There were bound to be casualties, though not the ones intended. Zenta Hausner, in all probability, was one. Guenther Reinhardt would, in due course, be another.

19

Death of a Red Princess

Zenta Hausner's complicity in black-marketeering, international smuggling, and narcotics trafficking was an open secret in Garmisch-Partenkirchen. Her cafe-nightclub, the Weisses Rössl or White Horse, was notorious as a meeting place for the local underworld, and her name was on every informant's lips and perpetuated in report after report by the Counter-Intelligence Corps (CIC) and Criminal Investigation Division (CID) during the first two years after the war. And yet Frau Hausner continued to survive and prosper.

In 1946 she survived investigations by the local CIC, the Military Governor, and the Special Branch. When it was reported that she was taking dope from Munich to Garmisch (for further shipment over the border into Switzerland) for 20,000 marks each trip, nothing happened. When she was on the point of being arrested by a German investigator working for the Garmisch Military Government, the investigator was prematurely thrown off the case and held incommunicado for two days on the orders of her American-German lover, Captain Korner. Nothing happened when it was discovered that she was allowing the White Horse to be used for clandestine meetings of the local Communist Party. Nothing happened when Charlie, the notorious racketeer, became Zenta's manager at the White Horse. And nothing happened when the Inspector General, Colonel Smith, began yet another American probe into the Garmisch way of life in the summer of 1947. Nothing untoward ever happened to "Garmisch Nell." For one thing she enjoyed the protection of her well-placed boyfriend, U.S. Army Captain Korner. For another, as a double agent reporting directly to the Military Governor, she was more useful to the Americans out of prison than in it. So Zenta Hausner did as she pleased and graduated by easy stages from paltry deals to big business in the free-wheeling world of the Garmisch black market.

By late 1947, however, it was clear that life was not working out entirely as she had hoped. Her plans to sell and emigrate to sunnier climes and a freer, more secure life in Argentina—a country kind to Germans and persecuted Nazis and favorable to the acquisition of emeralds, ranchers, colonels, and furs—had fallen through and she was nervous and despondent. It was December now. Alpine winter, German austerity, foreign occupation, another Christmas looming as joyless as the last...Argentina, oh, Argentina! Her American lover did nothing to lighten the gloom. Captain Korner had been to America to spend his leave with his wife. He came back a changed man. Changed for the worse, if that were possible. His love had cooled, it seemed. One evening, she taxed him about it.

"Was geschieht mit unserer Liebe?" she asked him. "What is happening to our love?"

"Das warnur ein Abenteuer," Korner is supposed to have replied. "That was just an adventure."

For the Christmas of 1947, Zenta had planned to visit her family at Moosburg. She was not to know that in the week before Christmas Guenther Reinhadt had named her as a Military Government double agent in his coded report cabled from the Pentagon direct to General Clay in Berlin. Nor was she to know that this information had been passed down in clear from Berlin "through channels" to Garmisch and that as a consequence it was possible her life was in peril. On the evening of 22 December 1947, in her role as an American agent, she had paid a call on the Garmisch Military Governor, Colonel Van Buskirk. Van Buskirk had recently been sent (in his own words) "to clean up Garmisch, which was the worst concentration of international gangsters in postwar Europe." One of his sources in Garmisch was Zenta Hausner, whose White Horse Inn, according to Van Buskirk, was "the headquarters of international illegal activities." Hausner, Van Buskirk recorded, reported to him on the arrivals and departures of international hoodlums. On the evening in question he had strongly urged her not to come to see him. "She was just about to pull off a big schnapps deal," the colonel related years later. "She'd visited me that night and told me all about it—how she reckoned she was going to corner the whole market. I reckon I must have been one of the last people to see her alive."

In fact it was established that five other people had spent at least a part of the evening of 22 December in Zenta's apartment over the White Horse. This was not particularly unusual. Zenta was well known for entertaining men friends in her flat long after the nightclub had closed. After the last of the visitors had left at about 3:30 A.M., Zenta got ready for bed. She put on her nightdress, switched on her bedside lamp, and went to bed. At this point, it seems nothing untoward had happened. Her dog, Ali, was asleep in the sitting room, the doors were securely locked, and Zenta had settled down to read a magazine in bed. It was past 3:30 A.M. and she was due to catch the 7 A.M. train from Garmisch to Munich later in the morning. The night was still, the footsteps of the passersby in the street were muffled by the soft cover of fresh snow outside Zenta's windows, the river burbled loudly as it rushed over the boulders under Bahnhofstrasse Bridge and plunged between ice-bound banks towards the Isar and the Danube. Later several people would testify that they had seen a man standing for a long time by the gateway of the White Horse. But nobody stopped to watch or ask. And so the eventful night passed.

It was still dark when the first visitors arrived at 6:45 next morning. Karl Roesen, 53 years old, was Zenta Hausner's lawyer. He was also a CIC informant and a large-scale black-marketeer in his own right. During the previous spring he had been under the surveillance of the Civil Censorship Division (CCD) telephone tappers for suspected illegal currency dealing. In the coming summer he would end up in Garmisch jail for falsification of documents. But early on the morning of 23 December 1947 Roesen was at the White Horse simply in the role of Frau Hausner's friend and advisor. It had been planned that they would travel together on the 7 o'clock train to Munich, where they had legal matters to attend to. After that Frau Hausner would continue by car to Moosburg to join her family for Christmas. That, at any rate, was the plan. But when Karl Roesen and a friend of his tried to rouse Zenta there was no response. They banged on the door, they called up to her bedroom window, they tossed up snowballs against the panes. But still there was no response, and still the front door remained firmly closed and the curtains pulled. The men stood in the snow staring up at the silent apartment, their faces flushed pink with the wintry cold, breath rising in clouds. Behind them the river tirelessly chattered down under the bridge and over the boulders. The men had no way of knowing why Zenta refused to answer their call. Had they known they might not have given up so easily. But deciding that Zenta had changed her mind about going to Munich, or was sleeping it off after another late night, they eventually reversed their steps and left without her.

The White Horse housekeeper, Anni, had been awakened by the shouts of the two men outside. Fearing her mistress was late for her appointment, she got up hurriedly, put on her dressing gown, pattered along to the door, and banged on it in the hope of waking Zenta. She, too, found there was no reply, and when she tried to open the door she realized it was locked, which she found surprising. Anni had counted on having the day off and was vexed that her mistress had apparently overslept and missed the trip to Munich. She went back to bed, lay there for another hour or two, then got up at about 8:30 to prepare breakfast. She unlocked the door and went up the stairs to the kitchen, which was shared between Frau Hausner, the lessee of the White Horse, and the actual owner, Karl Wagner, who kept a *pied-à-terre* above the restaurant. For the sake of privacy a door separated the kitchen from the hallway leading to the bedroom and sitting room of Zenta's private accommodation. The curtains in the kitchen were drawn when Anni entered and only a dim half-light percolated through. For a few moments the girl busied herself with cups and spoons, then out of the corner of her eye she saw on the floor near the window, the sprawled figure of her employer, clad in a striped dressing gown.

Zenta's back was towards her and at first Anni thought she must be unconscious. She knelt down at her side and bent to turn her over. Then, in the dim gloom, she saw her mistress' face and let out a piercing scream. The right-hand side of Zenta Hausner's forehead had been smashed in and her face had been savagely and grotesquely mutilated by cuts and slashes with a carving knife so that she was virtually unrecognizable. The handle of the carving knife was sticking out of her neck and its blade pinned her head to the kitchen floor. Blood encrusted her shoulder-length red hair and was spattered on the wall by the stove and had spread all over the linoleum. It had already darkened but was still tacky underfoot. The corpse of the woman they called "The Red Princess" and "Garmisch Nell—the Queen of Hearts" was cold but not yet completely stiff. Anni let go of it and rose, still screaming, and fled the room, down the stairs and out through the door into the street, where she stood in her bedroom slippers in the last night's snow and the morning's icy rain, and screamed again.

Neighbors were quickly on the scene. They jostled up the narrow stairs and stood fighting in the kitchen doorway for a peep of the grisly scene inside. There was nothing useful they could do. Someone called the German police, who arrived at about 9 A.M. By the time they got there the place was overrun by Americans. As police investigations go, this one was a shambles. Nobody had arranged to have the apartment cordoned off and a lot of people were wandering around the rooms without any kind of restriction. This meant that within an hour a lot of crucial evidence had been destroyed and positive fingerprinting of the apartment's contents was no longer possible. The police did notice that the telephone in the hallway was off the hook and that a cake and several half-full cups of coffee stood on a table in the sitting room. But in the crush nobody bothered to check how many pieces of cake had been eaten or exactly how many coffee cups had been drunk out of, if any at all. There facts were not established during the initial inquiries and later attempts to reconstruct the crime showed that many investigative opportunities of a similar nature had been carelessly thrown away.

The death certificate indicated that Zenta had been killed by wounds administered by a blunt tool (probably an ax) and a kitchen knife. The time of death was given as approximately 4 o'clock in the morning. The door from the small hallway at the top of the stairs to the corridor leading to Zenta's bedroom and living room was found to be locked when Zenta's body was discovered. It seemed that Zenta must have got up and gone to the shared kitchen to prepare coffee and cake for herself or her visitor and that the door to her private quarters had been locked behind her while she was in the kitchen, thereby cutting off her one line of retreat. The murderer must have taken the keys with him, since they were discovered later in a neighboring garden.

The police were left with the problem of motive and suspects. Was robbery the motive for the murder? There is plenty of evidence to suggest that it might have been. For a start, Zenta's famous platinum bracelet was found to be missing. So were two strings of pearls, a gold signet ring, a large gold brooch studded with diamonds and rubies, and a golden cross with amethysts. A reward notice was posted on every advertisement board: MURDER WITH ROBBERY IN GARMISCH-PARTENKIRCHEN. 10,000 RM REWARD. But there were stong doubts that robbery *was* the motive. There were, it seems, more pressing reasons for doing away with Zenta Hausner, and if the murderer's purpose was robbery, why did he leave behind a large stack of banknotes (thought to have been U.S. dollars) which were lying on a sideboard in the kitchen at the time of the murder? The apartment had not been ransacked and two large 5-carat diamond rings which she habitually wore were still on one finger. *Crime passionel* was another possible motive, but it was widely felt that the most likely explanation was that Zenta Hausner had been killed to keep her mouth shut — possibly at the behest of an American.

The possibility of American complicity in the death of Frau Hausner was strongly discussed at the time and is firmly believed today by many who had known her well in Garmisch. This could be one reason why the U.S. military insisted on conducting their own investigation into the murder, even though, under normal circumstances, crime involving German citizens was a matter for the German police. There were other reasons. For one thing, Zenta had been an American agent. She was generally believed to have worked for the local CIC detachment, and documentary evidence indicates that she had also worked for the CID and the Theater Provost Marshal. Most importantly, at the time of her death Zenta Hausner was working specifically for the American Military Governor of Garmisch, Lieutenant-Colonel Kenneth Van Buskirk. As a known narcotics trafficker, Zenta may have posed a threat to a certain person or persons because of her connections with both the drug business and the American investigators who were inquiring into it, and it is possible that she was silenced at a crucial point in the investigation. The dope rings were well informed, and since one of their members was reputed to be a high-ranking official in the Office of Military Government of Bavaria (OMGB), it is certainly possible that he arranged for Zenta to be eliminated as quickly as possible before the investigators, with her assistance, got too close for comfort. The urgency would have been all the greater when, in the week before Zenta Hausner's murder, Guenther Reinhardt in Washington began sending reports and naming names in coded cables to General Clay in Berlin. Zenta's death blew the lid off OMGB. But the damage would have been even greater if she had been left to continue as an informant.

For these and other reasons the U.S. military kept the German police out of the murder investigation for a full 17 days. It is debatable whether or not they did this on purpose. It may have been indifference or thoughtlessness. Or it may have been a concern to ensure that there would be nothing left lying around to indicate the identity of the killer. At any rate, by the time the German police, led by an Inspector Johann Venus from Bavarian Country Police Headquarters in Munich, formally took over the case on 8 January 1948 they were no longer in a position to undertake an investigation which stood much chance of success. Much of the evidence had disappeared and the German police's own position was invidious, for in the immediate postwar period they could command no respect or authority from either the civilian populace or the occupation troops. American officials constantly interfered with the German investigation, interrupted interrogations, and released witnesses of their own accord. It was said that when one German official refused to give an American woman journalist a photograph of Zenta Hausner, she simply struck him across the face with her riding crop.

Nevertheless, in spite of every handicap the German police perservered with their inquiries. They made a crime plan of the White Horse flat and sketched in Zenta's body in the kitchen and the position of her dog, her bloodstains, her handbag, and her suitcase, presumably packed for the trip to Munich and Christmas in Moosburg. They interrogated witnesses and arrested at least ten suspects, some of whom were detained for as long as four weeks and interrogated as often as twenty times. They made an inventory of what had been taken from the flat and combed the area looking for it. They found the keys to Zenta's quarters in a neighboring garden. They also found the little black notebook in which she had kept a record of the White Horse customers—but with a page torn out. They did not find Zenta Hausner's diary, which supposedly contained a day-by-day account of her black-market business activities and, according to the U.S. Army CID, "allegedly implicated the Garmisch Chief of Police, Ellinghaus, and Chief of Criminal Police, Hoffmann, together with American personnel." Nor did they find the other murder weapon—the ax—or the missing jewelry. The police ascertained that five people had visited Zenta's flat on the night of her murder and that the murderer must have called after the last of them had left. They also ascertained that the murderer must have been a friend of Zenta's, for her dog did not bark and there was no sign of a forced entry. Zenta herself, it seems, had let the man in willingly and gone to the trouble of producing coffee and cake for him at the unholy hour of 4 A.M. Who was he? Did he have an accomplice? What about the five people who had visited Zenta on that final night? How good were their alibis?

Three of the people were checked out by the police and immediately deleted from the list of possible suspects. The other two, who had gone to the White Horse flat in the hope of a late-night poker game, soon became prime suspects. This would have surprised nobody. For one was our old friend, the dope smuggler and business partner of Zenta Hausner, "Charlie," and the other was another White Horse black-marketeer by the name of Michael Hugo Knoebel, alias Baron Michael von Knoebel, alias Herr Major, a well-known local weirdo—and until recently Zenta Hausner's lover. The redhead took all types into her organization and into her bed, but 29-year-old Michael Knoebel—a tall, well-built, good-looking man with impeccable manners but considerable problems in adjusting to civilian life—was one of the most peculiar. During the war he had served as air crew in the Luftwaffe on the Russian Front and claimed he had been shot down no less than six times. He first came to Garmisch in May 1945 as a hospital case. He was known to suffer headaches as a result of a serious head wound sustained in air combat with the Red Air Force in 1943 and it was probably this which explained his erratic behavior in Garmisch after the war. A CIC report on Knoebel, prepared shortly after the Hausner murder, confirmed that the poor man seemed to be teetering on the edge of certifiable insanity. "Subject is suffering from a serious mental psychosis (schizophrenia)," ran the report, "which he became affected with during the Second World War. Subject lives in another world most of the time and believes that he has been placed on earth to revolutionize world politics and that he plays the part of a Soviet agent, U.S. intelligence man, Soviet International Brigade recruiting officer, and a good friend of Tito of Czechoslovakia [sic]."

In the White Horse one evening Knoebel had been heard to remark in his cups that he ought to become a Soviet agent because the Americans were destroying what was left of Germany. He actually did try to join the local Garmisch branch of the KPD (German Communist Party) but his application was rejected because he was "not in control of his mental faculties and talks too much." Twice he tried (unsuccessfully) to join the Yugoslav Air Force and once he claimed he had been invited to join the Greek Air Force (a Royalist organization) by a high-ranking Greek officer named General Markos (the Commander-in-Chief of the Greek Communist Army). It was when he tried to recruit an innocent Garmisch resident for the Soviet Internatinal Brigade that the CIC moved in on Michael Knoebel. They reported that since Zenta Hausner's death he no longer wanted to live because his "very best friend was killed," and concluded he was not capable of normal mental functions and was "therefore to be regarded only as a threat to German society and not as a security threat to the U.S. Armed Forces."

Both "Charlie" and Knoebel were duly picked up by the German Criminal Police and detained in custody as suspects in the Hausner murder. Knoebel, it seemed, had an ironclad alibi and was soon released. Charlie claimed to have been "en route to Munich" at the time of Zenta's death, but turned himself in to the German police the following day. He was questioned and then released for Christmas, at which time he went to visit a girlfriend in Frankfurt. When he returned to Garmisch in February, he was arrested but again released for lack of evidence after spending six weeks in custody. Inspector Venus, in charge of the German police investigation, found himself in the curious position of having any number of suspects but virtually no evidence to lay against any of them. Working on the sensible theory that the killer must have been someone very close to Frau Hausner, Inspector Venus turned his attention to her current lovers, of whom there were two — the long-established Captain Korner, and a recent acquisiton, a 41-year-old local trucker and member of an important narcotics ring operating between Garmisch, Munich, Hamburg, Innsbruck, Konstanz, and Bolzano, by the name of Ernst Virnich. Of these,

Captain Korner was an American and had an alibi — he was en route to Nuremburg for a court-martial on the night in question — while Virnich was a German and didn't. Virnich was taken into custody and remained in police hands for six months as a prime suspect before he, too, was released for lack of sufficient evidence to bring him to trial.

Captain Korner was not the only American to be questioned. Captain Bird, the former Military Government Legal Officer in Garmisch, was also required to account for his movements on the night of the murder. "I was hearing Christmas Eve Mass in a little church," he recalled in 1977. "My wife and two children were with me, so I don't think I would have been able to nip down to Garmisch and murder that woman. I had a very good alibi!"

There, for several years, the matter rested. In 1950 it seemed a breakthrough had been made in the case when Zenta Hausner's daughter found a gold chain and other pieces of jewelry down the side of an old armchair which had once stood in her mother's flat above the White Horse. But the jewelry did not include the platinum bracelet or any of the other especially precious missing pieces and the discovery in the end led nowhere. Then in the summer of 1952 came a fresh development. Charlie, who was by now 18 months into a 6-year prison sentence for his part in a robbery at a jeweler's store in Augsburg, notified Inspector Venus that he wanted to make a statement. He knew the identity, he said, of Zenta Hausner's murderer. He knew because Knoebel had confessed to him a week after the murder on New Year's Eve 1947. Knoebel killed Zenta because she had left him for another man. His alibi was phony. It was true that he had visited a girlfriend in Garmisch on the night of the murder. But he had slipped a sleeping pill into her wine, and when she fell asleep he hurried back to the White Horse with an ax under his jacket. Though he still had the keys to Zenta's apartment, he chose to wait until the last of her guests had left and then knock on the door. Zenta let her ex-lover in and he asked her if she would get him something to eat. They both went into the kitchen, where an argument developed. In his rage and fury, Knoebel knocked Zenta down with the ax and then stuck the kitchen knife into her throat. He then relocked the flat, threw the ax into the river and the keys into a neighboring garden, returned to the room where his girlfriend still slept soundly in a deep, drugged sleep, and got back into bed.

As a result of Charlie's statement his former friend, Michael Knoebel, was rearrested and imprisoned in Munich jail for three weeks on remand. He denied having confessed to Charlie, and the girlfriend in question could throw no further light on his movements on the fatal night more than four years ago. Since there was insufficient evidence to sustain a conviction, Knoebel was again released, and vanished into obscurity. No more arrests were ever made in the Zenta Hausner case and her murder continues to be shrouded in seemingly impenetrable darkness.

People who knew Frau Hausner or were involved in the case have sharply divided views about the identity of her killer. Generally, the Germans believe she was murdered at the instigation of an American — perhaps by a hired hit-man, if not by the American himself. The Americans, on the other hand, believe she was murdered by Germans. This was certainly the view of the American Military Governor at the time, Colonel Van Buskirk, the man who was sent down to clean up Garmisch. "It was like this," he revealed a few years after the murder. "Five hundred people cleared out of Garmisch the day I arrived down there. But a lot stayed on. Zenta started working for me. I had several other German informers on my payroll too, but she was the best. They'd been threatening her for a long time. They killed all my informers one night — every one on a single night. They shoved one guy off a cliff and they tied a rock around another's neck and then chucked him in the lake. And you know what they did to Zenta Hausner, the bastards." About "them" Colonel Van Buskirk had no doubts: "A black-market gang. Gangsters. Germans, I reckon. For my money I reckon it was an all-German outfit." And he added: "She was really a damned nice kid. I liked her a lot."

The death of the "Red Princess" had a galvanizing effect on the American occupation in Bavaria. Until now the occupation authorities had managed to keep the extraordinary state of affairs in their territory from public view. When two journalists, Ed Hartrich and Tom Agoston, inadvertently stumbled on the story of the Reichsbank treasure and the crime and corruption in Garmisch during the previous summer, the newspaper copy they filed was suppressed on instructions from General Clay — an unusual curtailment of freedom of the press in a time of peace. So long as the Americans were working on the case, even the murder of Zenta Hausner was kept from the press. But the moment they handed the investigation over the the German police, the story broke. On 8 January 1948, the very day the Germans took over, the first of what was to become an avalanche of press indictments of Army irregularities appeared in the American press. Under the banner headline, NELL, THE GIRL WHO SAW IT ALL AND TOLD IT TO THE U.S. SLAIN, the story was carried by the *Chicago Herald Tribune*, having been filed by Hal Foust from Garmisch the day before.

"Nell, known as the Queen of Hearts in the American military government rest center here, is dead in an unsolved murder mystery involving

black marketeers, smugglers, international financiers, international gangsters, and spies of several nations," wrote Foust. "She had been found in
the nude," the American reporter continued, "killed by a single slash across
the face, and her death was a heavy loss to the Military Governor. 'She was
valuable to us,' said Colonel Van Buskirk, who was General Patton's
housekeeper and 3rd Army special service officer during the war. 'She was
counterintelligence personified. She knew the barons and baronesses, and
the riffraff of international idlers and mischief-makers.'"

The next day, Foust filed a second story, this time implicating an un-
named American officer in the killing, under a headline which read: U.S.
CAPTAIN TO FACE VICE SLAYING QUIZ. "German police," wrote Foust,
"were promised today that they would have permission of the occupation
authorities to question a United States Army captain in the murder of
Nell, Queen of Hearts, purveyor of vice, illicit booze, and underworld information. The officer is not suspected of using the knife which silenced
the pretty informer, but police hope he may be able to name her more
threatening enemies." Foust was almost certainly referring to Captain
Korner here, an obvious witness with a more than passing interest in the
fate of the deceased lady. Significantly, at the end of his piece Foust broad-
ened his view somewhat, and for the first time made public the possibility
of a "general investigation of American occupation corruption, draining
towards Garmisch like the successful underworld is attracted to Miami in
the winter."

On 12 January, Tom Agoston and Ed Hartrich swarmed through the
breach in U.S. Army censorship blasted by Hal Foust's earlier articles and
finally filed the Garmisch stories that the Army had suppressed in the summer. Both men used the Hausner murder as the news item around which
to wrap their indictment of the American occupation in Bavaria in general
and in Garmisch in particular. "Postwar Germany's biggest black-market
scandal, involving a gang of international narcotics pedlars, threatened to
blow up in the lap of U.S. Military Government today," wrote Agoston in
Stars and Stripes. "The case came to a head with the murder two weeks ago
of Garmisch Nell.... Serious charges, said to involve U.S. MG [United
States Military Government] officers in Bavaria, as well as the daughter of
an internationally known German industrialist, a princess, prostitutes,
and others, have been lodged with Army Secretary Kenneth Royall." For
the first time Agoston hinted at the possibility of a top-level U.S. Government investigation into conditions in the American Zone of Germany—
the inevitable reaction to the Reinhardt memorandum and the growing
clamor in the press.

Ed Hartrich filed a similar story in the *New York Herald Tribune*, head-lined ARMY REVEALS HUGE BAVARIAN DRUG TRAFFIC. But Hartrich was more specific in his allegations:

Persistent reports say a wealthy Bavarian was director of the narcotics ring. He is said to have been discharged by a Garmisch denazification court through the intervention of an AMG official [Major McCarthy], though the French government lists him as a "wanted SS (Elite Guard) officer." His key agent is said to have been a daughter of a German industrialist long "friendly" with certain AMG officers. A Bavarian princess is said to have been the actual "fence."

Two former American Army officers are believed to be implicated, according to the CID. The German industrialist's daughter is said to have been the friend of an American captain while he was assigned to duty with the Military Government for Bavaria. He has since returned to the United States.

The other officer, a former major, is reported to be hiding in Switzerland, where he fled when Army investigators began to look for $750,000 in gold bullion and $2,000,000 in American currency which the Army found in Bavaria toward the end of the war but which afterward disappeared.

The Provost Marshal's office said some of the clues in the "Garmisch case" extend as far as America.

The press exposure of the Garmisch affair, already unwelcome to the U.S. occupation authorities, began to assume deepening political significance when the story was picked up by the East European Communist press and recycled as propaganda against the U.S. Forces of Occupation. A Soviet-run East German newspaper wrote scurrilously of "an international underworld worthy of the best that Chicago could produce" and spoke of the murdered and mutilated "Titian-red Queen of the Underworld" as the link

between the German and American gangsters who had jointly engaged in narcotics smuggling and white slavery financed by gold bullion and currency stolen from the financial reserves of the Third Reich. Involved in this gangster-dance for warm flesh and cold gold — amounting to millions — are the highest heads of the SS and Nazi *Wehrmacht*, Fascist displaced persons (who in their turn took away the Nazi gold), industrialists and their daughters, and a number of American officers who are not fit to belong to an army created by Roosevelt. "We have closed the mouth of the Titan-redhead for good — it's a pity about her nice legs," say the gangsters — and they are still at large.

On 20 January 1948, only a week after Hartrich and Agoston had first filed, the official Czech Communist Party organ, *Rude Pravo*, published its own inflammatory version:

AMERICAN GANGSTERS' AND GERMAN NAZIS' ACTIVITIES IN GIRL AND COCAINE TRADE

Neither the American nor the German police seem to have a clue for the mysterious murder of a young German girl, whose body was found in the renowned Bavarian winter sport center, Garmisch-Partenkirchen.

As ascertained by an autopsy, the victim was drugged before being murdered. Several symptoms prove the girl was a cocaine addict. Apparently, the girl was either a member or victim of a big gang of white flesh dealers engaging in large-scale recruiting of German girls for brothels in South America, smuggling simultaneously various drugs, mostly morphine, cocaine, and opium, from American and French sources.

One part of the gang is comprised of Germans, particularly of members of the Nazi underground.

Another branch of the gang, being on particularly good terms with the U.S. forces of Occupation, deals in confiscated property of Nazis, such as gold, jewels, and furniture. Their racketeering activities total for the past quarter of a year over 3 million dollars.

The American Embassy in Prague immediately protested to the Czech Foreign Office. The article — which they described as "one of the opening shots in the Czechoslovak election campaign" — was "abusive" and "vicious" and contrary to the Czech Prime Minister's undertaking to discontinue "abusive articles" (as distinct from "legitimate criticism of the United States") in the Czechoslovak press. But the damage had been done. The affairs of Garmisch now not only served deeply to embarrass the honor and authority of the American role in Germany in American eyes at home, but provided ammunition for the nations' critics and enemies abroad. Garmisch was no longer a parochial issue, but a domestic and international one as well. Something would have to be done about it.

20

The Cover-Up

To say that the American army in Germany did not like the Reinhardt memorandum would be to understate the case. They abhorred it. But they did not abhor it half as much as they abhorred its author, who in the season of good cheer and good will to all men continued to sit in his Pentagon office next to Assistant Secretary of the Army, Gordon Gray, content that he had done the decent thing for American civilization in Germany and as yet blissfully unaware of the approaching shock waves that would blast him from official favor and ruin his life.

The memorandum had been transmitted to General Clay by encoded cablegram page by page as it was written — with possibly fatal consequences for Zenta Hausner and several other German informants in distant Garmisch-Partenkirchen. The 55-page typewritten manuscript of the main memorandum landed with a faint puff of brimstone on the Commander-in-Chief's desk in Berlin immediately after the Christmas season, on about New Year's Day, 1948, and the original 48-page memorandum, dictated in Frankfurt in November, found its tortuous way through Army channels to Berlin some weeks afterwards — not too late to play its part in the ensuing storm. The 55-page memorandum was immediately turned over to the Inspector General of the European Command for investigation. Initially there was still a chance that the whole thing could be handled quietly within the confines of the U.S. Army in Germany. The murder of Zenta Hausner and the resulting newspaper publicity, with its revelations of crime and scandal in Garmisch and the Office of Military Government of Bavaria (OMGB) as a whole, soon squashed that possibility. One way or another, the newspaper revelations and the Reinhardt allegations would have to be answered in public and in the glare of national and even international publicity. The department of the Army and the United States

Forces in the European Theater were thus faced with two broad options: they could clean up or cover up.

In exercising this option their hands were to a large extent already tied by the scandal arising from an earlier case of major crime by Army personnel — the sensational Kronberg jewel robbery. Kronberg Castle was the seat of the former royal family of Hesse and after the war it had been turned into a U.S. Army officers' recreation club. In April 1946, shortly before the wedding of Princess Sophie of Hesse, youngest of the Duke of Edinburgh's four sisters, it was discovered that a large portion of the Hesse crown jewels, valued by the Army at $1,500,000 and by the Hesse family at more than twice that amount, were found to be missing. A team of Criminal Investigation Division (CID) investigators, including Agent Philip Benzell, were put on to the case, and it was eventually proved that the valuables — rubies, pearls, and jade torn from their settings, along with two quart jars of diamonds, a solid gold dinner service, and nine volumes of letters from Queen Victoria — had been stolen by a former welfare officer at the castle, Captain Kathleen Durant, and her husband, Colonel James Durant, with the complicity of Colonel Durant's former aide-de-camp, Captain David Watson. Since this was believed at the time to have been the greatest robbery in history, the ensuring court-martial attracted immense publicity — and inevitably an extremely unfavorable international view of the conduct of the U.S. Occupation Forces in Germany. Though the culprits were duly found guilty and sentenced (Colonel Durant to 15 years hard labor, his wife to five years, and Watson to three), it was inevitable that the Commander-in-Chief and Military Governor of the U.S. Zone would look unfavorably on further criminal revelations of a similar magnitude in his territory. The Reinhardt allegations, however, indicated scandals even more scurrilous and demeaning than the Kronberg case. The Kronberg robbery had been the biggest in the world. Now Clay was threatened with the revelation of another robbery — the Reichsbank robbery — which was even bigger. The world's greatest robbery and the world's second greatest robbery, both committed in the American Zone of Germany within a few months of each other — it was too much to contemplate! Clay's choice between a clean-up or cover-up was really made for him, given his well-known dislike of unsavory incidents in his command.

The Kronberg case had not been the only scandal to come to light in the U.S. Zone since the end of the war. In March 1947 a 37-year-old Swiss-born American intelligence officer, Captain Victor J. Haig, was tried in Garmisch-Partenkirchen at a court-martial which disclosed misdemeanors of the most sensational kind. Posted to Garmisch in June 1945, Haig had shared a house with a fellow intelligence officer and two girlfriends. His fellow officer's girlfriend was a well-known Czech movie actress and one-time mistress of the Nazi Propaganda Minister Dr. Joseph Goebbels. Haig's girlfriend was a self-styled baroness who had been on "intimate terms" with the Gestapo chief, Ernst Kaltenbrunner.

Late in 1945 Captain Haig began a political investigation for the Frankfurt Counter-Intelligence Corps (CIC) into the conduct of a leading German industrialist by the name of Arnold Rechberg, the so-called German Potash King, who had been interned by the Nazis during the war. Rechberg had political ambitions to restore the old Bavarian monarchy and to form a separate Bavarian state backed by high Catholic officials and the Bavarian nobility. In due course Rechberg enmeshed both the baroness and Captain Haig in his illegal and subversive schemes, and before long they were both living in his various castles in the countryside north of Garmisch. Rechberg also involved Zenta Hausner's lover, Captain Korner, in his activities. During the time that Korner was Commandant of the Civil Internment Camp for suspected Nazis in Garmisch, and later when Haig took over Korner's job there, Rechberg joined in Korner's fake release racket, securing the release of Nazi prisoners on phony health grounds for the sum of 125,000 RM ($12,000) per prisoner. This money Rechberg then used to bribe people to publish his political propaganda articles in Germany and the United States.

Naturally none of this endeared him or his associates to the American authorities when they finally got wind of it. In January 1947 the Americans raided Reichberg's castle at Eschenlohe. The baroness was arrested. A four-inch-thick bundle of classified American documents and a quantity of weapons were found in Captain Haig's quarters in the castle. More weapons were found in his official quarters in Garmisch, bringing the total haul to 28 rifles and pistols, which it was believed Haig was supplying to an underground faction. The baroness was thrown into prison in Garmisch. Arnold Rechberg was detained, but soon died of a heart attack under American interrogation.

Haig was accused of passing Top Secret documents to the baroness, and evidence indicated a "sponsoring connection" between Rechberg, the baroness, Haig, prominent German industrialists, and profiteering Nazis. Haig's court-martial revealed an unbelievably tortuous tale of skullduggery and double-dealing from which it emerged that Haig's mistress, the baroness, was among other things a Communist agent who had been passing American secrets via her CIC lover, the nefarious Haig, to Communist Party contacts in Germany. To cut a long and extraordinarily complex story short, Captain Haig was found guilty on seven out of nine charges, sentenced to be reduced in rank to the foot of the list of officers in his grade, to be reprimanded, and to pay a fine of $1,500. He was then sent back to the United States.

On 13 January 1948, less than a fortnight after the Reinhardt memorandum had landed on Clay's desk, the Director of Intelligence in Washington sent a Secret message to the European Command that Victor Haig was back in Europe, even though he was "an undesirable who should have been denied entrance." The Haig case, Washington pointed out, indicated "possible gun-running, furnishing of information to German Communists from Secret reports, and extensive black market in Garmisch area with contacts in Switzerland." The Haig case, following the Kronberg case, inevitably helped to reinforce the Army's hostility to the Reinhardt memorandum and in all probability played a role in the final outcome.

Nevertheless, Guenther Reinhardt's allegations concerning personnel, policies, and conditions in the European Theater were treated with the utmost seriousness by the Inspector General's Division. For the purposes of investigation they were carefully analyzed and broken down into 134 separate incidents grouped into nine main categories. These were then "thoroughly" investigated — so the Inspector General was to claim — utilizing the combined efforts of seven experienced senior officers working over a period of two months.

The first report covered the allegation that THERE EXISTS A HIGH LEVEL POLICY OF SUPPRESSION AND DISTORTION IN THE PRESENTATION OF INTELLIGENCE AND RELATED TOPICS TO THE DEPARTMENT OF THE ARMY. According to Reinhardt, reports to Washington on intelligence, political conditions, occupation frictions, and criminal incidents were variously suppressed or toned down on the direction of the Theater Commander, General Clay, in order to avoid criticism or restraint from Departments in Washington. In view of what was to happen to the Reinhardt memorandum, this first report was a highly relevant one. The investigation on which it was based was initiated on the verbal orders of General Clay and undertaken by Major General Louis A. Craig of the Inspector General's Department (IGD) between 2 and 29 January 1948. It was not an impartial investigation. Given the set-up, there was no way that it could have been. General Craig limited his investigation to asking the people allegedly involved whether or not they had done what Reinhardt claimed they had done. Not surprisingly they all seem to have said no. It is difficult to see how an independent investigation into allegations made principally against General Clay could be undertaken by a senior member of his own IGD who had not only launched the inquiry in pursuance of General Clay's verbal order but also filed his report with him on completion of his investigation. All the personnel questioned were key members of Clay's staff and unlikely to risk demotion or worse by criticizing the actions or policies of their chief. Thorny issues such as the withholding of information from the press were avoided. Thus there was no mention of the Army "exerting all possible influence" and "prevailing upon" newspapermen like Ed Hartrich and Hal Foust to withhold or radically alter their news stories on the Garmisch affair. "There is no factual basis for the allegations," concluded Craig. "Testimony is unequivocally negative and completely in contradiction to the allegations made."

The other investigative reports by Clay's IGD — on loot, black-marketeering in the PX, CIC inefficiency, and so on — were written in much the same vein and drew much the same negative conclusions. The report containing Reinhardt's allegations about the Garmisch affair, based on an investigation by Major R. B. Hensley, Assistant Inspector General, was no exception. But in the light of our accumulated knowledge on this subject, drawn from contemporary American documents and other sources, it is possible to evaluate the accuracy or otherwise of Reinhardt's statements and the impartiality or otherwise of the Inspector General's assessment of those statements. The result is interesting.

Major Hensley's investigation, the fifth of the nine investigations by the Inspector General's Division into the allegations contained in the Reinhardt memorandum, lasted from 6 January to 25 February 1948 and necessitated inquiries in Berlin, Frankfurt, Bad Homburg, Bremen, Munich, Weilheim, Stuttgart, Starnberg, Bremerhaven, and Garmisch-Partenkirchen. Evidence specifically relating to the Garmisch affair, including the IG investigation of the previous summer and the Garpeck investigation which followed it, was given by Lieutenant-Colonel Smith (of the IGD), Lieutenant David Gallant (Chief Agent of the Munich CID), and Chief Agent Philip Benzell (Provost Marshal's office).

At the end of his detailed examination of Reinhardt's allegations about the Garmisch affair, Major Hensley added two summary sections entitled "General Discussion" and "General Conclusion." Both were shrill in tone and characterized by the very qualities which they accused Reinhardt himself of displaying. Reinhardt's allegations, wrote Hensley, were "broad" and "malicious. It is evident," he contended, "that the writer completely distorted the facts intentionally, or took parts of incidents in which there was a thread of truth, grossly exaggerated it in proportion to its true worth, and proceeded to reap a field of conclusions that would make sensational and outstanding reading against the Department of the Army."

Everything, wrote Hensley, must be seen and understood — and, by implication, forgiven — against the ruinous state of postwar Germany. "Germany, as well as the entire European Continent, still is in the backwash of World War II...It is an economic fact, based upon the law of supply and demand, that following all great wars, both victors and vanquished are in most cases war-ravaged people forced of necessity to barter their luxury possessions for a mere existence." The conditions in Germany, observed Hensley, were "grossly abnormal," but the Americans were "making every effort to do their part in a situation that is monotonous at best." Hensley continued: "It is realized that some individuals take literally and practice assiduously the precept of 'To the victor belong the spoils'...Nevertheless, it is dangerous to generalize from such examples, since they do not represent the true overall picture." The detective forces were doing their best, Hensley maintained, but black-market operations and illegal barter could never be stamped out entirely until Germany was restored to a normal healthy economy again.

Major Hensley then turned to the question of Guenther Reinhardt himself. Reinhardt made his allegations, Hensley suggested, simply in order to secure for himself a high-powered job in Germany as a Washington-based trouble shooter. Furthermore, he was himself guilty of being a "big-time operator" on the German black market. Major Hensley concluded his "General Discussion" with a punishing *envoi*:

By such generally unfounded and fanatical allegations as those contained in this document the prestige of the European Command has been damaged considerably. Open resentment on the part of witnesses was encountered throughout the course of this investigation. Such resentment was based upon their lack of faith in Mr. Reinhardt's sincerity of purpose, his unsavory reputation in the Theater, and his obvious disregard for the truth.

Major Hensley followed this with his "General Conclusion" which stated:

That the allegations sent to the Secretary of the Army by Mr. Reinhardt as contained in this report, with minor exceptions, consist of gross misstatement of facts, misleading excerpts of reports, and exaggerations of incidents. From these, erroneous and sometimes vicious conclusions have been drawn by the writer for the evident purposes of selfish and sensational publicity, in an effort to discredit the European Command as reprisal for his discharge from his position in the CIC and to create further employment for himself.

The Major then concluded — somewhat piously, given the circumstances:

That the matters contained in the allegations have been and are under constant surveillance and study by those in authority in the European Command and progressive steps and sincere efforts are being made constantly to bring about elimination of undesirable conditions.

Hensley's report is unsatisfactory on a number of counts and certain things have to be said about it. For one thing, it avoids the main issue. For another, it is both platitudinous and evasive. It discusses relatively trivial aspects of the allegations (and dismisses most of them out of hand) but almost totally ignores infinitely more serious charges which we know to have had a solid basis in fact. The bulk of the "General Discussion" is devoted to petty black-marketeering, which is excused on the grounds of the "grossly abnormal" conditions in Germany, but glosses over the very grave allegations involving American military personnel ranking from captain to general in large-scale robbery and embezzlement, misappropriation of U.S. Government funds and property, international narcotics trafficking, murder, and flagrant interference in the processes of law and justice. Reinhardt's allegations, according to the "General Conclusion," consisted of gross misstatements of fact, misleading excerpts of reports and exaggerations of incidents — "with minor exceptions."

One is bound to ask: Was the theft of more than $404,000 — described by the FBI as "this huge sum" and actually acknowledged as missing from U.S. custody in Hensley's report — a "minor exception"? Was proof of narcotics trafficking in Garmisch "minor," or Colonel Smith's testimony that his investigation had been interfered with, or the fact of Zenta Hausner's murder, or the evidence of misappropriation of U.S. Government property, or the acknowledged suspicion that the Garmisch Post Inspector was a member of a criminal gang, or the established conclusion that Major McCarthy had, quite apart from anything else, presented false testimony before a denazification court and destroyed evidence in the Finance Division? In reality, far from making "gross misstatements of fact," Reinhardt was meticulously precise about verifiable names, dates, and incidents, and it is remarkable that very few factual data were corrected by Hensley.

Instead of answering Reinhardt's most important allegations, or even taking into consideration the fact that some of them were actually upheld in the evidence presented within the text of Hensley's own report, a violent attack was launched on Reinhardt's character and motives. He was described variously as a liar, a fanatic, an opportunist, a position-seeker, and a black marketeer, and his motives were ascribed to selfish ambition and a desire for revenge. In fact, the motives behind the allegations are strictly irrelevant, for the allegations stand or fall on their own account. On the other hand, the motives behind the Army's response to the allegations, as embodied in the Inspector General's report, are highly relevant. At stake, Major Hensley averred, was the prestige of the European Command, and everything possible would have to be done to preserve that prestige intact. This certainly did not include the "constant surveillance" and "progressive steps and sincere efforts" that Hensley contended were being made "to bring about elimination of undesirable conditions." Quite the contrary, as we shall see. To the Army's everlasting shame, no further action was ever taken to deal with the issues which remained outstanding in the Reinhardt memorandum. Instead, Major Hensley appended his "Recommendations" to his IG report. It baldly proposed: "That no further action be taken and this case considered closed."

And it was.

Major Hensley's report on the Garmisch allegations (and related matters) reached General Clay's desk on about 1 March 1948. Other reports by other officers of the IGD were still being compiled and it was not until April that the findings of the Inspector General's investigation were complete and had been finally digested. On 22 April Colonel F. J. Pearson, the Inspector General, submitted to the Commander-in-Chief nine Reports of Investigation and one CIC dossier on Guenther Reinhardt, together with a letter summarizing the Inspector General's final views on the matter.

Of the 134 definite allegations identified by the IGD, only 11 were sustained. Most of these were held to be the products of administrative error rather than misdemeanors requiring disciplinary action. The one recommendation for disciplinary action (against a lieutenant-colonel not involved in the Garmisch case) was disapproved by the reviewing authority. The letter reinforced the views already advanced by Major Hensley and added some new ones of its own:

The vast majority of Mr. Reinhardt's allegations have not been sustained [Colonel Pearson reported to General Clay]. It was the combined opinion of the investigative officers in this case that for a command of this nature, scattered over a wide area in relative small subdivisions and in a foreign country where the indigenous population has suffered an almost complete breakdown of economy and morals, there have been remarkably few cases where the conduct of American personnel has reflected adversely upon the integrity of the Occupation Forces and, likewise, upon the integrity of the U.S. Government. It appears particularly well established that, when such instances have come to the attention of those in command, prompt and efficient corrective action has been taken.

The author of the Reinhardt memorandum, the Inspector General maintained, was guilty of untactful handling of arrests (including, it should be

remembered, the notorious ringleader of the German element of the Garmisch "gang"). He was guilty of using CIC credentials to impress authority
to which he was not entitled. He appeared to be temperamentally unsuited
to work with the Army. His disregard for orders suggested psychopathic
tendencies. His judgment was unsound. He was a big-mouth, a scandal-
monger, and a purveyor of rumors and hearsay. He could not be trusted
with a secret.

The Inspector General was not finished with Guenther Reinhardt.
"While serving in Munich until sometime early in November," wrote Pearson, "Mr. Reinhardt repeatedly displayed an utter lack of sound judgment, as well as a marked emotional instability. He was unable to bring
the simplest case of investigation to a successful ending, weaving into the
matter involved fantastic plot, wild conjectures, unwarranted insinua-
tions, and unsupported conclusions.

"Early in June 1947," Pearson revealed, "Reinhardt's superior officers became convinced that he was mentally ill and in need of psychiatric treatment...Mr. Reinhardt was persuaded to seek psychiatric advice and made
visits to an experienced psychiatrist at the 98th General Hospital during
the first two weeks in June 1947. This psychiatrist expressed the professional opinion, following these visits, that Mr. Reinhardt's mental disturbance
was such that he would soon be unable to carry on satisfactorily, unless improvement were experienced."

It seemed that Reinhardt was not only wrong, in the Inspector General's
view, but he was mad; and not only was he mad, he was bad as well. For
example, he had a girlfriend in Germany at the same time as he had a wife
in the United States, and — horrors of horrors — he traded cigarettes on the
black market! There were, Pearson suggested, "ample reasons" for termin-
ating Reinhardt's CIC career—"to wit: immorality, inefficiency, black
market operations, and breaches of security."

Guenther Reinhardt always maintained that he had only done his job
and that as a Control Investigator of the CIC it was his sworn duty to ob-
serve and investigate irregularities and recommend action. As far as the
U.S. Army was concerned, however, Guenther Reinhardt was a dead
man. He had, in a manner of speaking, been executed long before he had
been sentenced. He was never called before the Inspector General to defend or explain his allegations and he was given no opportunity to defend
his name or his integrity which (unknown to him at the time) was becoming increasingly impugned. He was beheaded without a trial. Long before
the first IG report on Reinhardt's allegations had been completed, the European Command and the Department of the Army had begun to exact

their revenge on him. In a letter to his old newspaper friend, Tom Agoston, written from his New York apartment, this embittered target of the military establishment outlined what befell him while the IG inquiry was still in progress in Germany:

Things began to happen. On 21 January 1948 I was notified that my job in Berlin had been cancelled by the Theater Commander. On 27 January I was called to Washington and informed that I had been discredited. The boys in the theater had manufactured the damndest file on me you ever saw — after I left and *after* the investigations got going. I also learned that during a one- or two-day stay in Washington around 26 January, Clay had raised hell at the Pentagon about his command being investigated. Well, what they had concocted about me had no resemblance whatsoever to my personnel file that I had seen in Frankfurt the day I left. My commendations seemed to have disappeared. Nothing was said about my good efficiency ratings. Derogatory statements about me by the dozen had been added. The *one* speeding ticket I got in my life — for doing 40 miles [per hour] in a jeep on the autobahn — had been blown up into a *major disciplinary action*. The day in April 1947 when I wore the wrong shade uniform (civilian U.S.) jacket at the Casino and was apprehended by one of Huebner's lieutenants was made into a formal arrest for insubordination against a commissioned officer and grave misconduct, and *dozens* of statements added — (mostly from persons against whom I had filed charges!) from "associates and co-workers" describing my "unreliability,' "inefficiency," "emotional unstableness," "immorality," "irresponsibility," "immaturity," "lack of judgment," "violations of security," "sex mania," etc., etc.

During the ensuing weeks I got letters and word from CIC people on the methods used to get these statements — the *official* orders given, threats, persuasion, etc.

I wrote the Secretary a formal letter apprising him of my knowledge of the derogatory dossier, the phony way it had been manufactured, and called his attention that both under the law and Constitution, I had a right to see it and to answer every statement. I pointed out to him that in one of his letters to me he had rejected my argument for protection of the identity of informants and witnesses in the *preliminary* phase of our investigation with the counterargument that under our American system anybody accused of anything derogatory *must* be permitted to see the exact charges and be informed of the identity of the person who makes them. I further volunteered to submit myself to the jurisdiction of the U.S. Civil Service Commission, the Department of the Army, and even to a court-martial in Germany. But I wanted this file to be brought out in the open, even if it meant preferring charges against me. Failing that, I demanded that a formal investigation of me be launched by the Inspector General and that I be examined under oath. I also said that I did not seek reinstatement in my job although my contract, which had had still nine months to run, had been cancelled in violation of and disregard of six different specific provisions of law and regulations — but all I wanted was to have my name cleared.

The Assistant Secretary wrote me back that in view of the fact that I was not under investigation and that no charges had been filed against me there was no reason for any action!

The Inspector General's investigation was not the only reaction to Reinhardt's bombshell. A day or two after the 55-page memorandum had landed on General Clay's desk, the special CID investigation in Garmisch, code-named "Operation Garpeck," was abruptly terminated, ostensibly on the orders of the Theater Provost General, General George Weems, and allegedly because "it wasn't getting anywhere." At a time when Garpeck's services might have been even more in demand by the High Command than ever, Chief Agent Philip Benzell and his team were called off, much to Benzell's disgust. "I always felt that Peccarelli and his team were wasting their time in Garmisch, living off the fat of the land, chasing women, etc., etc." Lieutenant-Colonel Lester J. Zucker, Executive Officer of the European Command CID, wrote to the authors in 1979. "Apparently General Weems thought so too and cut it all short…Whatever they were investigating, and it may well have been the gold and currency, nothing ever came of it. No recovery was ever made, no one was ever charged." All there was to show for months of toil and frustration were two reports on narcotics trafficking in Upper Bavaria — one dated 2 December 1947 signed by Victor Peccarelli, and the other, dated 10 January 1948, written by Phillip Benzell. Of the results of the probes into the gold and currency cases there was no trace — they were simply missing. Much of the most relevant material from the narcotics reports, relating to the more nefarious activities of some of the more nefarious American and German inhabitants of Garmisch-Partenkirchen, has already been cited in earlier chapters. The two reports in their entirety were submitted as exhibits in the IG investigation into the Reinhardt memorandum. The concluding paragraph of the concluding report barely concealed the concern of its author at the information he must have been reluctant to convey: "In view of the withdrawal of this Agency from the investigation of illegal trafficking in narcotics, all informant nets in that field have been withdrawn and the operation, orginally established for such type of investigation, has been discontinued."

Having got Operation Garpeck — and the possibility of further embarrassing revelations — out of the way, the Army proceeded to get rid of another potential embarrassment to its threatened image. While Reinhardt had been producing his report in the Pentagon, the Secretary for the Army, Kenneth C. Royall — an important member of the American Government with personal access to the President of the United States — instructed his personal representative, Judge Earl Rives from North Carolina, who was in Germany at the time, to look into Reinhardt's charges.

"Rives came back on 18 January 1947," Reinhardt told Agoston —

...and there was a hell of a blow-up which reached the papers only in part. Rives told them that he found things even worse than I had charged. As he is a reserve officer and aspires to be a general, and as he is a close political associate of Royall in North Carolina state politics — where Royall wants to become governor and Rives the state political boss — he felt he could not handle the investigation without lousing himself up forever with the big Army boys and embarrassing his friend and associate Royall. On the other hand Rives would not lend himself to a whitewash. So he resigned "because of urgent personal matters in his personal affairs at home.' That put he boys on the spot...

In the meantime they got an old guy, Orville Taylor— one of those typical "prominent citizens," a lawyer from Chicago — to take up Rives' job as special emissary of the Secretary to investigate the German situation. He sailed from New York on 4 February 1948. They had not allowed me to see him. They did not give him the assistants from Washington whom I had named as honest and not subject to the EUCOM influence. On 14 April he returned and on 4 May they released his report. It was the most godawful whitewash I had ever seen.

It was indeed. The Taylor Report available to the public took the form of a Department of the Army press release issued by the Press Section of the Public Information Division — an organ of public relations intended to promote a favorable image of the U.S. Army in the U.S. media. Under the heading "FOR RELEASE IN A.M. PAPERS, THURSDAY, MAY 6, 1948 — ARMY RELEASES TAYLOR REPORT," the release began:

The Department of the Army today made public a report by Orville J. Taylor, Special Assistant to the Secretary of the Army, based on findings of his recently completed survey of personnel, policies, and general conditions in the European Theater.

The complete report submitted by Mr. Taylor to Secretary Royall follows.

What "follows" was in fact the second of two reports by Orville Taylor, the first concerning itself with Reinhardt's 48-page criticism of the CIC, the second with his 55-page memorandum on the general state of the U.S. Zone.

The first Taylor Report had been submitted to Secretary of the Army Royall at the end of March 1948. It was concerned solely with Taylor's investigation into the allegations made against the CIC. Though Taylor conceded that the CIC "did not enjoy an unblemished reputation" and that "approximately 20% of the men were unqualified for counterintelligence duty," he was of the opinion that Guenther Reinhardt's allegations of widespread moral corruption, professional incompetence, indifference and laziness were no more than glittering generalizations emanating from the fantastic imagination of which the reporter must be possessed." After attending conferences with General Clay (and other top brass) and CIC briefings with the CIC Chief and his regional commanders all over the U.S. Zone and in Berlin, Orville Taylor— not surprisingly— became satisfied that "these excellent and efficient officers" were doing a "magnificent job" and that there had been a "week-to-week, and almost day-to-day improvement and correction, where necessary, of the organization." The first Taylor Report was in effect another, last-minute IG report, and read like it. The so-called Taylor Report submitted to the press by the Department of the Army was something else again.

It is regrettable [read the press handout] that critics are apparently unwilling to accord consideration to the magnificent performance and full achievement of our Army of Occupation...I am satisfied that the Army of Occupation is doing a fine job, making due allowance for the abnormal conditions which prevail in Europe today. The incidence of blackmarketing, as well as of crime, drunkenness, and immorality among American personnel stationed in Europe, is extraordinarily low.

The handout concluded on a cozy note: "America has every reason to be proud of the Army of Occupation and the men and women who compose it. They are serving their country well and merit our full confidence."

There was not a single reference to the very serious charges which Reinhardt had made concerning the state of affairs in Garmisch-Partenkirchen. These had evidently been dealt with by the simple but effective expediency of ignoring them completely.

The American press, for whom the doctored version of the Taylor Report was intended, were not greatly impressed by this. Many papers did not carry the Report. Others thought it was spurious. The *Chicago Tribune* of 6 May wrote:

Taylor's report was described as a "whitewash" in some [Washington] quarters. His findings, it was asserted, bore out earlier charges of considerable corruption and misconduct among military government officials.

In his letter to Tom Agoston, Reinhardt confirmed the general press reaction:

Ninety percent of the newspapers refused to print it. Going over the report I could see in 16 different places that the report had been written — by Clay's boys! Furthermore, I learned subsequently how the investigation was rigged, how some of the very people whom Taylor was supposed to investigate had actually done the investigating for him, had taken him in hand, etc., etc.!!! I simply cannot understand how an intelligent man could have been so *completely* bamboozled and turned in a report that only a nitwit could not recognize as a blatant piece of hogwash.
  And that was that.

But I still have enough friends in the theater and in certain spots in the Pentagon to learn that there was also an Inspector General's report on a detailed investigation they made separately. And that report was a lulu! My friends told me about the many, many recommendations for prosecution that that report contained. They were all turned down by the topside boys because a big scandal might break and because too many careers would be ruined.

If there was anything General Clay liked least it was scandal among his own forces in his own zone of Germany, especially after the Kronberg jewel case and the Haig case. Nor could the U.S. Government at a time of mounting international crisis and threat of all-out war with the Soviets (culminating in June with the Soviet blockade of Berlin and the Allied airlift to counter it), afford any besmirching of the reputation and honor of the American forces in Europe. Germany was the new front line. It was paramount that the American Army in Germany, which was supposed to be a bastion of freedom and the democratic way of life, should be seen to be good and true. The Taylor Report helped to ensure that it would.

From the day of its release the questions of corruption in the U.S. Zone, of crime in Garmisch, and of the theft of gold and of currency from the former German Reichsbank were dead and buried issues. They ceased to be a matter of formal investigation in the European Theater. They were not raised in the American press again. There were no embarrassing prosecutions either in Europe or in the United States. By means of a systematic cover-up and whitewash initiated at the highest levels of the Department of the Army and the European Command, the whole scandalous mess was brushed away and hidden from public sight. Investigative dossiers known to have existed on key suspects were destroyed, and the same fate seems to have befallen many of the investigative files and reports kept by the principal investigative agencies involved in the activities described in this book. Many documents still existed, but the archives of these agencies in the U.S. either maintained a stony silence or could not or would not accede to requests for information. Amazingly, the CID — which had 1,500 pages of documents on the Kronberg jewel robbery— claimed to have no papers whatsoever relating to the investigations they had conducted into the gold, dollar, narcotics, and murder cases in Garmisch-Partenkirchen between 1945 and 1948. The CIC had very little. The FBI stated that as they had not investigated the matter they could be of no assistance. The CIA could find no records relating to the matter, nor could the United States Secret Service, or the U.S. Treasury or Department of State. The Offices of the

Provost Marshal General, the Adjutant General and the Attorney General gave similar negative responses. So did the archives of the Chief of Staff of EUCOM and the Civil Affairs Division. Even the most senior officers of the time professed remarkable ignorance of the matter. The then Commander-in-Chief, General Lucius Clay, replied (through his secretary) from New York in 1978 that "if $3 million in gold or in U.S. dollars was taken from our area it does not seem possible for this to have happened if it was money belonging to the U.S." The then Assistant Secretary of the Army, Gordon Gray, stated in 1977, "I don't have any recollection of any specific allegations of anything." Then then Military Governor of Bavaria, Murray van Waggoner, could not remember anything about gold and narcotics either. "That's all news to me," he told us over the phone from Michigan in 1977. "General Clay gave me only one instruction and that was to see to it that cigarettes didn't get in the black market. Narcotics? Who was bothered with that?"

For years official American silence was total. When the *Guinness Book of Records* first included a version of the Reichsbank robbery in its 1957 edition under the heading, "Robbery: Biggest Unsolved," it was unable to elicit any further elucidation of the facts from the official bodies in the United States. As late as 1975 requests for corroboration were met with the same stone wall from the Department of the Army in Washington:

Based upon repeated research of the official records of that period occasioned by previous inquires over a 10-year span [a spokesman replied] United States Army archives regard the Guiness [*sic*] entry as an unverified allegation... By the way, how are things with the Loch Ness monster these days?

There was no way that that Army spokesman could have found and collated the myriad pieces of documentary evidence and eyewitness testimony that eluded even the official investigators in Garmisch in the immediate postwar years. There was no way he could have known of the Flying Fortress that blew the Reichsbank to pieces in the great raid of February 1945; of the flight of the gold and dollar reserves to the illusory safety of the national redoubt; of its transportation into the Mittenwald hills on the backs of mules; and its burial by Colonel Pfeiffer's men. There was no way he could have known of the piecemeal disappearance of hugely valuable portions of the Reichsbank treasure; or the parts played by Rosenberg-Lipinski, Gottlob Berger, Karl Jacob, and Karl Warth, Helmut Schreiber, and Helmut Groeger; or the $407,235 taken by Captain Fred Neumann from Hubert von Blücher's garden; or the two truckloads of gold bullion found by Albert Singleton, or the $2,000,000 of Reichsbank banknotes that were never accounted for in the Federal Exchange Depository (FED); or the dollars and the gold spirited over national frontiers in those first frenzied days of peace. There was no way that that Washington spokesman, now so remote in time and place from the events on which he chose to comment, could have added his sums and shown that a mammoth $432,683,469 worth of funds had been stolen from the German Reichsbank; or picked the brains of former German officials and demonstrated that more than six tons of Nazi gold had gone astray; or pieced together all the scattered fragments of evidence that showed the parts played by officers of the SS, the *Wehrmacht*, and the U.S. Army in all these huge, historic heists — crimes of opportunity which were the product of a time and morality shattered by war.

And since the Department of the Army had officially cleared the name of General Clay's Army of Occupation in Germany once and for all, how could that Washington spokesman have uncovered the cover-up and reconstituted the incinerated and shredded files that illuminated the dark gangland days of Garmisch-Partenkirchen and the OMGB? How could he have known about the international narcotics ring financed with stolen Reichsbank money, of the fleets of cars and trucks enough to equip whole armies looted from the U.S. Army in Bavaria, of all the scandalous deals and extortions and swindles and embezzlements, the smuggling and big-time black-marketeering, the financial manipulations and top-level illegal expropriations practiced by Americans and Germans, separately and in collusion, who found themselves in uniquely privileged positions in a chaotic world — and bowed to temptation.

When the Reinhardt investigation came to an end with the command decision "That no further action be taken and that this case be considered closed," the United States Army finally evaded the task of fixing responsibility for these crimes or indicting the guilty men. Most of the names that could have been indicted were listed in the Reinhardt memorandum, although even today, because of English and American libel laws, we still cannot reveal them all. But in the ultimate analysis, perhaps, these names are incidental to our major finding, which is that in countenancing a blatant cover-up of misconduct on the part of some of its senior personnel, the Army made it possible for the perpetrators of the greatest robbery in history and the instigators of some of the Army's biggest rackets to escape scot free.

21

The End of the Affair

This sorry story is not quite done. The American cover-up had left most of the actors still on stage, so to speak. Many of them had yet to say their last lines and make their final bows. Some had their most dramatic exits still to come. Others had new parts to play, and would go out with their names in lights. Only one could be said to have been howled off the stage by the summer of 1948. This was the unfortunate Guenther Reinhardt. The rest of his melancholy tale is told at the end of his long letter to his English reporter friend, Tom Agoston — an agonized *apologia pro vita sua* which almost makes a tragic hero out of this strange and misunderstood man.

In December 1948 I was offered a very exciting job with the U.S. Displaced Persons Commission. Because of some very flattering recommendations I had been chosen unanimously among many applicants for a top job. Germany. The salary was *very* nice. I was appointed, sworn in, got my credentials, my diplomatic passport, my military entry permit, and my plane ticket. In addition the largest labor organization in the country had entrusted me with a mission that had the State Department's blessing as well as the DP Commission's.

As I was sitting with the commissioner to say good-bye, the Army phoned. A Lt.-Col. Clark in Security Group of Intelligence Division in the Pentagon said that they would not under any circumstances allow me in Germany. That the moment I had landed in Frankfurt they would cancel my military entry permit and send me out of Germany on the next plane. He stated in so many words that this was not a security matter and said specifically that the matter did not involve my loyalty. That I was a trouble-maker — had made charges that caused an investigation which in turn showed my charges wildly exaggerated, etc., etc.

The commission told me to go over to the Pentagon and straighten the matter out. I got the famous runaround and this Clark character even denied knowing anything about the matter! But some of the colonels who had been in Frankfurt with me told me quite openly that the Army had it in for me because I had ruined so many careers.

Well, the Army boys invited the chairman of the commission to have a look at their secret dossier on me and told him if after seeing that he still wanted to employ a − − − character like me it was all right with them and they would withdraw their objections.

The meeting took place and the commission got scared—told me that they depended so much on the goodwill of the Army—that the Army was doing everything it could to sabotage the DP program in Germany—that if I insisted on keeping my job it would anger the Army and result in adverse effects on the Jewish DPs—so would I please, please resign.

I went to New York to confer with my friends at the top of the Jewish organizations and they said flatly that there was no alternative but to resign—that I had to do it for the sake of the Jewish DPs.

What could I do? Of course I resigned.

Of course in anticipation of going to Germany I had given up all my other work—a nice teaching job, lucrative magazine articles, good lecture work, etc. Naturally I also had completed certain arrangements as to my household, etc. The sudden development left me without a job. For the past six weeks I've tried to get back into the swim of things but it has been difficult.

Nora has had a pretty tough time too. However, I finally got her the job she always wanted and she is very happy working for one of the finest fashion places in New York. She also goes to college at night and is doing remarkably well in her studies. We still can't get married because of my domestic situation. As you know my wife has been a hopeless invalid for ten years. For the past year and a half she has also become mentally incompetent and more than 80 cents out of every dollar I earn goes for her care and up keep. New York law does not permit any divorce in such situations as she is not insane in the legal sense of the word: inasmuch as she is completely paralyzed she does not conform to the legal requirement of insanity that she "could be a menace to others or herself."

Some day things must right themselves after all this long streak of adversity. Then we'll have a couple of drinks together and a good laugh at the days of "*Sturm und Drang*," as the Germans would say.

It is doubtful whether Guenther Reinhardt ever managed to enjoy the "good laugh" he had promised himself and his friend. There was destined to be no decisive upturn in his long streak of adversity. For ten years he worked as a private eye for a San Francisco lawyer called Crum. For another four years he worked as an insurance investigator in New York. Then in 1969, at the age of 63, he suffered a heart attack in St. Vincent's Hospital, New York, and died. So passed the one man who had tried to right American rule in Germany and in the process turned it upside down —and destroyed himself.

Meanwhile, what of other Americans in this drama? In spite of the blatant attempt of the U.S. Army to cover up the misdemeanors of some of their personnel in Germany, heads did begin to roll—particularly in the so-called Transportation case, to which reference has been made earlier in this book. Here there was carnage in Military Government, as a letter dated 3 April 1948 from Colonel Thomas H. Young, of the Inspection Section, to the Director of Military Government in Bavaria indicates:

This section had conducted investigations which culminated in the removal of approximately forty key individuals from Military Government. It was found that not only were these persons all guilty of conduct calculated to bring discredit upon the service, but many of them were found to have committed serious crimes while in our service. Attention is particularly drawn to an investigation just completed by this section. This investigation revealed the most serious inefficiency, neglect, and wrongdoing in the administration of the transport program in Bavaria. This wrongdoing resulted in the failure, for all practical purposes, of this program. This investigation was a means for eliminating from Military Government the unworthy officials responsible for this sad state of affairs. This one investigation alone resulted in formal charges being preferred against fifteen individuals.

This is strong stuff, and the removal of 40 officials represents the loss of the total American staff of Military Government in Bavaria. At first sight it even gives the impression of a significant deviation from the general policy of covering up the misdemeanors of the American forces in Germany. But as events proved, there was no deviation. Only one American was brought to trial, along with two Germans and two DPs. The cases of five other Americans were duly processed, found in every respect to be strong cases, and actually referred to a General Court Martial, only to have the trial blocked in each case by higher authority. One of the five, who faced serious charges of embezzlement and defrauding the U.S. Government, was allowed to resign without prejudice and according to Colonel Young was "now roaming over Europe, including the American Zone of Occupation in Germany, with a freedom of movement denied to more than a hundred million other *honest* Americans." Three of the five went absent without leave, fled to the United States by air, and were allowed to resign—"allowing these three individuals to go completely unpunished for offences similar to those for which more deserving Americans in the Theater are now serving several years in prison." Only one of the five, a U.S. Army sergeant, ever appeared before a court-martial but, in a scandalous interference with the course of justice, his trial was interrupted on orders from higher military authority. "The defense is willing to call several high-ranking officers in the United States Army to testify in this case," the Defense Counsel told the court, "to indicate that higher authority—EUCOM—has requested that this case and other cases...be taken out of the court."

This was the sort of thing that gave rise, in Colonel Young's view, to "the confusion and dismay to be found in the minds of the majority of right-thinking, conscientious American personnel in Bavaria...Our failure to prosecute known American criminals has raised justifiable doubt in the minds of many Germans as to the impartiality of our justice...the alarm ing leniency of courts, in so far as American personnel are concerned, can be attributed to the miscarriage of justice in the many cases covered by this investigation." Colonel Young came to a solemn conclusion in his report, which could be given a far wider application than the transportation case alone. He wrote:

"There has been a failure on the part of higher headquarters to fully support and encourage law enforcement agencies in Land Bavaria. This failure to apply the law...has resulted in a lowering of respect for all law in the community and the loss of prestige by the occupying forces in the eyes of the German population and our Allies."

That old trooper, John McCarthy, the man every Criminal Investigation Divison (CID) agent in Germany loved to name, was among those who continued to arouse "confusion and dismay" among right-thinking Americans. McCarthy, the notorious head of the Investigation and Enforcement Branch of Property Control, was to survive to fight yet another scandal and yet another assault against the integrity and honor of his good name. That scandal was the Property Control Case. This was to bring about his downfall and that of his superior, Colonel Lord, and the removal of the last of the bad men from American Bavaria, and from this book — not, many thought, soon enough.

There will always remain a mystery around McCarthy. As head of Investigation and Enforcement Branch of Property Control — the department of American Military Government in Bavaria responsible for the confiscation and redisposal of former Nazi property — he had long been in the best of all possible positions to manipulate the department's affairs to the personal financial advantage of himself and certain of his closest colleagues, who were also intimately involved in the affairs of Property Control, not only in Munich, but in Augsburg and, of course, Garmisch. That much became clear to his superiors in the U.S. Occupation in due course. But it seems McCarthy was up to more than falsifying the books. We have already seen how CID Agent Philip Benzell and other investigators of the Garmisch affair reiterated in their reports the fact that McCarthy's name cropped up time and time again in connection with various aspects of their investigations — including narcotics trafficking. We have also seen how McCarthy, though the object of deepest suspicion on the part of the investigative authorities, always remained one jump ahead of them — largely as a result of tip-offs from members of the investigative networks who also happened to be members of his own criminal confederacy. So when the Civil Censorship Division (CCD) tapped his private phone in Munich he was able to receive due warning of the fact and move to a secret abode "along the banks of the Isar" where, incredibly, his colleagues in the close-knit fraternity of the American administration were unable to locate him. And when they came to look at the books in Finance Division, McCarthy was forewarned and destroyed them — or destroyed at any rate those accounts and records which he knew to be incriminatory. In this way the investigators were denied the concrete evidence that could bring McCarthy to trial — and so, it goes without saying, were the authors of this book. And yet there was, as one of the investigators, CID Agent William C. Wilson, told us, "not much doubt as to his dishonesty and lack of integrity." Even the Inspector General charged with examining that part of the Reinhardt memorandum relating to this particular matter was forced to concur that McCarthy had provided false testimony to facilitate the denazification of his chief German confederate, whom we have been obliged to refer to as "the Doctor." (He was not a medical man, but had a doctorate in another field of learning.)

The circumstances leading to the denazification of "the Doctor" lie at the heart of the mystery surrounding John McCarthy. McCarthy, then a Major, was the G-2 (Intelligence) officer of the 103rd Infantry Division when it took the surrender of Innsbruck, the capital town of the Austrian Tyrol, during the first week of May 1945. Almost immediately after the entry of the division into the town, McCarthy made the acquaintance of "the Doctor," a young German-born Nazi civilian who two months previously had sought refuge in the Tyrol from the rigors of the war front near the Rhine. There was nothing untoward about the fact that these two, the American Intelligence Officer and the Nazi civilian, should have made each other's acquaintance. It would have been part of McCarthy's job to follow any lead or contact he thought fit in the pursuit of military intelligence. Since "the Doctor" claimed to have been a member of the Resistance in Austria, and to have saved the lives of thousands of American soldiers by disarming (through means still unknown) the enemy forces attempting to stop the 103rd Infantry Division from entering Innsbruck, it would have been eminently reasonable, even necessary, for McCarthy to have made contact with "the Doctor" at the earliest possible juncture. What is extraordinary is that McCarthy should have gone to the length of rigging "the Doctor's" denazification. "It is highly desirable," he wrote in a testimonial certificate to be presented before the denazification court in Garmisch, "that [the

Doctor] be cleared of any blemish which may appear on his record. Further information will be furnished to U.S. officer authorities only, by the undersigned officer, whose telephone number is Munich Military 3341. (Signed) John R. McCarthy, Infantry, 0–1299833, U.S. Army."

It was even more extraordinary that McCarthy should have remained in continuous personal and "business" contact with "the Doctor" for the next five years, even though it had been long established that he was one of the most notorious racketeeers and dope traffickers in the Munich and Garmisch underworlds. "The Doctor," we have been told by American CID investigators, was "the clue to McCarthy"—though no matter how hard they tried they were never able to "get to him."

All that is past history. It is not difficult to imagine the kind of mutual advantages accruing from a working relationship between a crooked, high-ranking and strategically placed American officer in Property Control and an clever, ruthless, ex-Nazi criminal and gang leader in narcotics and big-time black marketeering. But the real question—the true heart of the mystery—is this: What actually transpired at the first meeting of McCarthy and "the Doctor" on the banks of the River Inn during the last days of the war in Europe that resulted in such a close and continuous relationship between them—a relationship all the more remarkable for the fact that McCarthy was the representative of the ruling power and "the Doctor" was an enemy subject and a wanted war criminal? Whatever it was it must have offered a unique and considerable advantage to both men. By the nature of things at that time, the source of this unique advantage—some hidden source of concentrated wealth, of money, diamonds, or even gold perhaps (we can only speculate)—would have been known to "the Doctor" rather than McCarthy and revealed to the American in return for the kind favors and protection only an American could provide in that part of occupied Germany and Austria in those days. Something momentous took place, but what it was was never discovered at the time and—short of a deathbed confession—will doubtless never be discovered in the future. McCarthy is dead and "the Doctor" has never uttered a word about those dubious days, and probably never will.

So McCarthy and "the Doctor" survived and prospered through all the choppy seas and sudden squalls of the Counter-Intelligence Corps (CIC), CID, and Inspector General's investigations—until McCarthy and his Property Control associates overstepped the mark one last time and finally capsized and foundered. The immediate cause of this ultimate debacle seems to have been the I.G. Farben case. When the time came for this former giant German chemical combine—one of the greatest in the world—

to be broken up and sold off to legitimate private bidders, the indomitable Property Control boys of OMGB, by now feeling invulnerable and over-whelmingly confident, decided to have a crack at this grandest of all Pro-perty Control prizes. The whole operation was underhand and illegal, as John McCarthy and his superior officer, Russell Lord, the Chief of the Finance Division, well knew. But they stood to make millions — or thought they did — if the deal came off and it was clearly a gamble these expert operators felt well worth the risk of taking.

It had been the rule under the Allied occupation that properties confis-cated by Property Control should be placed under the supervision of a qualified custodial supervisor who was in turn responsible to the Finance Division under Russell Lord. The ultimate goal was to return these pro-perties to their rightful owners or, in the case of new operations such as the big Perlon (nylon) plant near Augsburg, to sell them off to non-Nazi buy-ers and allocate the purchase money to war reparations. One provison of the regulations was that no member of Property Control, or any custodial supervisor, could buy into the property concerned. But this was not the sort of thing to deter the likes of McCarthy and Lord — nor their close as-sociate, a Property Control officer for Augsburg, who had supervision over the Perlon plant mentioned above.

When the break-up and sale of I.G. Farben were first discussed, it seems that McCarthy and Lord concocted a scheme to set up secret front corporations in Liechtenstein and Switzerland and have them buy the var-ious Farben plants, which apparently included the Perlon one. The general idea was that a stock-holding group composed of German financiers, cus-todial supervisors, and American members of Property Control would compose the syndicate. This was a very bold, indeed a breathtaking scheme. If it had gone according to plan, Lord and McCarthy would have become millionaires from their secret stock holdings in the denazified Ger-man companies — but only temporarily. Though they obviously had not foreseen it, they would eventually have been frozen out by stock manipula-tors and, as soon as Germany became autonomous (which in 1949 it did), they would, in the words of an American investigator on the case, "have lost their shirts."

But the scheme did not go according to plan, for it was shaken — as so often happens in such cases — by a surprise intervention from a completely unexpected direction. One of the CID agents involved in the ensuing in-vestigation, William C. Wilson, has described what happened:

The Augsburg Property Control Officer had a German mistress who virtually ran his office. For some reason or another he brought his wife over to live with him in Augsburg and he kept up his relationship with his mistress. It didn't take her long to catch on as to the state of affairs. One night they had a big row and he beat up his wife. She left him and returned to the States where she got in touch with her Congressman. She was a highly intelligent woman, who had found out a great deal of what was going on, and she told her Congressman everything she knew or suspected. A CID case was opened by the 15th Detachment at Augsburg (Agent Henry Coogan), but it soon became apparent that it was far too big and complex for him to handle alone. Also, it involved matters of finance and procedure that was beyond the scope of the CID.

In early December 1948 General Clay ordered an investigation to examine the entire performance of the property custodians and administrators in OMBG, the management by American personnel of properties under American control in Bavaria and procedures of control since May 1945. Clay also demanded an audit of the records of the more important properties. A Special Team of investigators from the Inspector General was set up. The team was headed by Lieutenant-Colonel William King. King was an experienced man. He had served many years with the fraud branch of the Department of Immigration, and later he was one of the early chiefs of the CID.

He was one of the most brilliant and astute investigators I have ever known [Wilson recalled]. He had as his team: Major Ross Black, who was an excellent interrogator and very tenacious; Major Robert Hensley, who was very thorough; a Captain Austin from military intelligence (who spoke fluent German); an auditor named Murray Feingold, and myself. King very wisely compartmentalized the case so that each investigator had his own area with King acting as coordinator and evaluator.

It soon became apparent that Lord and McCarthy were feathering their own nests, furthermore that "the Doctor," based in Garmisch, was McCarthy's chief contact man and advisor, and that another dubious figure—an Austrian named George Spitz, who had been sentenced to 20 years for embezzlement before the war, worked as a Nazi SD agent during the war, and purported to be a Munich cashier and U.S. citizen after the war—was Lord's fiscal advisor. Spitz had been one of the Nazis' leading "salesmen" of counterfeit British currency manufactured during the war as part of an SS project code-named "Operation Bernhardt." After the war he had become Lord's and McCarthy's front man in the I.G. Farben affair.

The investigation by the Special Projects Team into the wrongdoings of Lord, McCarthy, and their collegue from Augsburg took six months to complete. The resulting report ran into 26 volumes. The Inspector General was assisted not only by the men from the CID but by fiscal experts among whom were American and German auditors, and the case was the subject of almost daily conversations between General Clay and his Chief of Staff in Berlin, his Theater Inspector General in Heidelberg and his Director of Military Government in Bavaria. It was a *very* big case. All three of the officers investigated were found to be deeply implicated; their two German advisors, George Spitz and "the Doctor," skipped the country while the investigation was in process. According to CID Agent William Wilson, who wrote one of the 26 volumes, the investigators actually found the minutes of a meeting in which the American officers discussed how to buy themselves into the German companies then being made available through the break-up of the I.G. Farben cartel—by forming dummy companies in Liechtenstein with qualified German front men. "Having a piece of this kind of action would be better than stealing something that could be traced," wrote Wilson later, "but I doubt that any of them got away with anything much in the long run." While there was little doubt about McCarthy's guilt, that of his superior officer, Russell R. Lord—the American financial "godfather" in Bavaria—was more difficult to determine. It was generally felt that he was either naïve to the point of stupidity, or he was dishonest—though there was some disagreement as to whether he was an out-and-out crook or merely an accessory to McCarthy's criminal schemes.

As far as the Property Control case is concerned—the last great scandal involving some of the longest-surviving rascals who have appeared in this story—the spirit of cover-up seems to have prevailed in Washington to the present day. When the authors first applied to the U.S. Archives for copies of the 26 volumes of investigative records relating to the case, availability was denied on the grounds of invasion of privacy of the individuals principally involved. When the authors then submitted the death certificates of both McCarthy (died in 1978) and Lord (died in 1981) as submission that privacy could no longer be invaded, the U.S. authorities replied that they had now shredded the records of the Property Control case, and that these no longer existed. However, sufficient bits and pieces of documentation cross referenced in other files in different archives have survived to provide a picture of the scope and seriousness of the case, if not the fiscal minutiae of the evidence.

Thus in a letter to General Clay dated 22 March 1949 the Inspector General's office reported that "by concentrating on certain accounts... they expect to be able to trace various unethical and illegal transactions to those responsible at top level. It would appear at this time that Mr. Lord had knowledge, if not actual participation, in these manipulations."

A further letter from the Office of the Chief of Staff, European Command Headquarters, to the Headquarters of Military Government for Germany, dated 17 August 1949 and enclosing the report of the investigation for appropriate action, stated: "The investigation does show on the part of Mr. Lord and Mr. McCarthy flagrant indifference to the interests of the United States and a disregard for the obligations of an officer of the government, which is in effect a breach of trust."

On 31 August 1949 the Office of Military Government for Germany made their final pronouncement on the case. The Personnel Officer wrote:

1. I have reviewed the attached case involving Mr. Russell Lord *et al*. The file in my opinion clearly confirms Mr. Lord's weaknesses as an administrator, but does not show clearly that Mr. Lord gained personal benefits through the juggling of property and monies.

2. With respect to Mr. Lord, I repeat a recommendation that Mr. Lord not be given a position in the High Commissioner's Office.

3. With respect to Mr. John R. McCarthy, the extent of his involvement in the irregularities of property management is not very clear. His conduct before the investigating authorities, however, was such as to raise serious doubt as to the wisdom of retaining him in a position of responsibility. On the basis of the material on file, I would recommend that Mr. McCarthy not be given a position on the staff of the High Commissioner.

McCarthy and Lord, in other words, were out of a job—or, in clinical U.S. Army parlance, "terminated." But discretion was still the better part of justice under General Clay's troubled command. There was no public statement about the case, let alone a trial. McCarthy and Lord were not separated from the employ of Military Government dishonorably, but simply shipped quietly home—amazingly, Lord found subsequent employment in the State Department; McCarthy went back to Europe to sell insurance in Switzerland. They were not asked to apply for reemployment in the American High Commission (the organization representing the American presence in Germany which replaced Military Government after the formation of an autonomous West German state in September 1949—the date which spells the absolute conclusion of this tortuous tale). Such wrongdoers as had survived the total collapse of the German black market following currency reform did not survive the end of American rule in Germany. The wild old, bad old postwar days were over—and so were the careers of "the men who had enriched themselves."

There is perhaps no particular or subtle moral with which to end this story of the world's greatest robbery and its aftermath—only that war and the conquest and rule of one nation by another bring about their own exaggerated, frontier-style forms of corruption. But our main drift might be best summarized in the words of a man who was close to the action of this book during one of its most important periods — the Military Governor of Bavaria, Brigadier-General Walter J. Muller. General Muller made two statements when he finally relinquished his command and returned to the States — one public, the other private, the one after the other. The two statements are totally contradictory, and in their contradiction lies the paradox which is close to the crux of this book. In his formal valedictory to the Americans in Military Government under his command, General Muller proudly proclaimed:

It is difficult for me to find words to adequately express my appreciation for your able assistance to me during the past two years...The accomplishments of Military Government for Bavaria are a result of your efforts and cooperation. After all, you are a group of "All-Stars." Harmony gives strength and support to all undertakings and it has played a great part in the success of Military Government for Bavaria.

Then, in a private aside not intended for public consumption, the general confided to a crony: "I have just realized I was surrounded by knaves!"

Sources

CHAPTER 1

Page

4 "950 Flying Fortress bombers"
Roger A. Freeman: *Mighty Eighth War Diary*, pp. 432-3 (London, 1981)

5 "The city was ravaged"
For eyewitness accounts of the aftermath of the raid, see
Ursula von Kardorff: *Diary of a Nightmare* (London, 1962)
Ruth Andreas-Friedrich: *Berlin Underground* (London,1948)

6 "Photographs taken during the day"
Reproduced in Rolf Italiaander: *Berlin Stunde Null 1945* (Düsseldorf, 1979)
Gerhard Kiersch: *Berliner Alltag im Dritten Reich* (Düsseldorf, 1979)

6 "'Indescribable scenes occurred in Berlin'"
Quoted in Hans Dollinger: *The Decline and Fall of Nazi Germany and Imperial Japan* (London, 1968)

6 "the People's Court"
Fabian von Schlabrendorff: *The Secret War Against Hitler*, p. 325 (London, 1966)

6 "'I have just this minute taken refuge...'"
Martin Bormann: *The Bormann Letters* (London, 1954)

7 "'drop bombs into a pickle barrel'"
Freeman: op. cit.

7 "'It was only by a miracle...'"
Trial of the Major War Criminals at Nuremberg (HMSO, 23 vols, London, 1946-51)

8 "Puhl was a banker of the old school"
Major C.S.G. Bach: *In Search of the Reichsbank* Ministerial Collecting Center, Control Commission for Germany, 30 June 1945)
James Stewart Martin: *All Honorable Men*, p. 118 (Boston, 1950)

9 "*Aktion Reinhardt*"
Trial of the Major War Criminals at Nuremberg, vol. 21, p. 232

Page
10   "Bank for International Settlements"
     Martin: op. cit., p. 131
10   "a very extensive potassium mine at Merkers"
     For accounts of Merkers, see
     Lt. Col. Carl L. Morris: 65-page Report on Merkers Find
     (SHAEF, April 1945)
     R.A. Nixon: Report on Recovery of Reichsbank Precious Metals
     (HQ U.S. Group Control Council, Finance Division, 6 September
     1945)
     Earl F. Ziemke: *The U.S. Army in the Occupation of Germany, 1944-6*
     (Army Historical Series, Washington, 1975)
     Sunday Express, London, 8 April 1945
     Daily Telegraph, London, 8 April 1945
     Stars and Stripes, Paris, 11 April 1945, 4, 20 and 22 June 1945
     Robert Reed: War Report No. N143 (BBC German Service, 8
     April 1945)
11   "'One could tear one's hair'"
     Joseph Goebbels: *The Goebbels Diaries: The Last Days* (London,
     1979)
11   "the accidental discovery of the mine"
     There are several differing versions of the Merkers discovery. Not
     even the Supreme Commander's is entirely accurate. The
     definitive description is contained in Morris: op. cit.
13   "a Dr. Werner Veick"
     Stars and Stripes: op. cit.
13   "the value of the gold"
     R.A. Nixon: Report on Recovery of Reichsbank Precious Metals:
     op. cit.
14   "'The party was ushered into a primitive freight hoist'"
     Charles R. Codman: *Drive*, p. 281 (Boston, 1957)
14   "'Jesus Christ!'"
     Ziemke: op. cit.
14   "'The ones I saw'"
     George S. Patton: *War As I Knew it* (Boston, 1947)
14   "'I doubt,' interjected General Bradley"
     Gen. Omar N. Bradley: *A Soldier's Story*, p. 540 (London, 1951)

CHAPTER 2
16   "'Sad news from Mühlhausen'"

Page

Goebbels: op. cit., p. 321

16 "Friedrich Josef Rauch"
Biographical details and quoted letters and documents from Berlin
Document Center.
For Rauch's role as Hitler's security officer, see
Peter Hoffmann: *Hitler's Personal Security*, p. 173 (London, 1979)

17 "'Even as a boy'"
Berlin Document Center: op. cit. (Berlin, 26 November 1940)

17 "'The morale in the unit is fabulous'"
Berlin Document Center: op. cit. (Romania, 15 March 1941)

18 "'Rauch has proved himself first rate'"
Berlin Document Center: op. cit. (Berlin, 27 July 1941)

18 "'I nominate you, Friedrich Rauch'"
Berlin Document Center: op. cit. (Berlin, 20 April 1944)

19 "Rauch put his idea...Dr. Lammers"
Major Lionel C. Perera, Chief Mil. Govt. Finance Officer, HQ,
3rd U.S. Army, G-5 Section: Interrogation Report on Fritz Rauch
(Bad Tölz, 4 July 1945)

19 "an Alpine Fortress"
See Rodney G. Minott: *The Fortress That Never Was* (New York,
1965)

19 "Hotel Maison Rouge in Strasbourg"
Simon Wiesenthal: *The Murderers Among Us* (London, 1969)
Antony Terry: Operation Odessa (Internal memorandum to *Sunday Times* Insight Team, London, 20 February 1968)

19 "By the spring of 1945"
Wiesenthal: op. cit.

20 "one document purporting to list RSHA treasure"
Wiesenthal: op. cit.

20 "Rauch always insisted"
Perera: op. cit.

21 "The Führer figure that presented itself"
James O'Donnell: *The Berlin Bunker* (London, 1979)
Hugh Trevor-Roper: *The Last Days of Hitler* (London, 1981)

21 "Rauch might hand over all the reserves to Bavarian separatists"
Perera: op. cit.

21 "The closing balance of the Berlin Reichsbank's Precious Metal
Department"
Nixon: op. cit.

Page

22   "At two different stations in the southern suburbs"
     Kriminalabteilung beim Präsidium der Bayerischen Landpolizei:
     Final Report—Gold and Foreign Currency Assets of the Former
     German Reichsbank (Munich, January 1953) (hereafter referred
     to as Munich CID Report)

22   "'Two special trains'"
     Office of Strategic Services: Secret Report No. GB 4690. Source Z
     Liberation (Austria, 20 April 1945)

24   "OSS team code-named GREENUP"
     A. Cave-Brown: *The Secret War Diary of the OSS* (New York, 1977)

25   "the gold convoy"
     Munich CID Report
     Gottfried Arendt: Report Concerning the Transfer of Valuables
     from Berlin to Munich (April 1945)

26   "the treasure was believed to consist of"
     Munich CID Report

27   "The convoy rolled past"
     Henriette von Schirach: *The Price of Glory* (London, 1960)
     See also her article "Wo blieb das Gold der Reichsbank?" (*Wochen-
     end*, Nuremberg, 5 October 1950)

27   "the trains *Adler* and *Dohle*"
     Munich CID Report

27   "25 boxes containing 100 bars of gold bullion"
     Munich CID Report

28   "the erratic behavior of the Führer"
     See, among others
     James O'Donnell: *The Berlin Bunker*
     Hugh Trevor-Roper: *The Last Days of Hitler*

29   "Bormann intimated that the departure was scheduled for 22 April"
     Paul Manning: *Martin Bormann—Nazi in Exile* (Secaucus, 1981)
     Jochen von Lang: *Bormann* (London, 1970)

30   "the Chancellery staff took off in ten aircraft"
     O'Donnell: op. cit.

30   "One of these ten aircraft...was shot down"
     O'Donnell: op. cit.

31   "According to a SHAEF report"
     Rona L. Geib: Currency sent from the Reichsbank, Berlin to
     Southern Germany in April 1945 (FED, Frankfurt, 1947) Record
     Group 9404060 Box 168 2/11

Page

31   "Dr. Österreich"
Munich CID Report: op. cit.
It is possible that this is the same Dr. Österreich who was the
author of an official Nazi biography of Funk (according to Funk's
testimony at the Nuremberg War Crimes Trial). He may have
taken the Swiss francs at Funk's request—it is worth noting that
Funk was later to ask for a further quantity of Swiss francs from the
Reichsbank foreign currency reserves to be placed at his disposal.

31   "SS Brigadier-General Josef Spacil"
Robert A. Gutirrez (CIC Detachment, 970—45) and William J.
Connor (M11 Team 466—G): Memo to 307th CIC Detachment,
HQ 7th Army: Interrogation of Wilhelm [*sic*] Spacil, Head of Amt
II RSHA and Hitler—his Diaries, Relics and Buried RSHA
Assets (27 July 1945)
Also: Statement taken from Josef Spacil at Military Government
HQ Salzburg on 25 August 1945 in the presence of Capt. McNally,
Det. Sgt. Chadburn and Chief Inspector W. Rudkin
Special Investigation Squad, CIC Detachment 970: Memo on
ownership and disposal of effects recovered as result of
interrogation of William Spacil (4 February 1946)

32   "At Fischhorn Castle"
Glen B. Infield: *Secrets of the SS* (Chapter 17, Missing Nazi Treasure)
(New York, 1982)

32   "Disguised as an SS corporal named Gruber"
Spacil file: op. cit.
U.S. Army Intelligence Center: *History of the Counter-Intelligence
Corps*, vol. XXVI — *CIC in the Occupation of Germany* (Fort Holabird,
Baltimore, 1959)

33   "'a fanatical Nazi named Josef Spacil'"
History of the CIC: op. cit.

33   "On 9 June 1945 Lieutenant Nacke"
Spacil file: op. cit.

34   "'Then you must be the guy'"
Glenn B. Infield: *Otto Skorzeny — Hitler's Commando* (New York, 1981)

34   "He talked freely about professional business"
U.S. Army Intelligence Center: *History of the Counter-Intelligence
Corps*, vol. XXV — *The Occupation of Austria and Italy* (Fort Holabird,
Baltimore, 1959)

Page
34   "at Nuremberg and at Dachau"
Infield: op. cit.
See also: Charles Foley: *Commando Extraordinary* (London, 1954)
35   "Reichsbank officials holding keys"
Board for Valuation of German Bonds in the United States: Decision and Opinion in the Matter of the Registration by Mr. João Mendes Lyra [of Bonds] (Decision No. 58, Opinion No. 58, 26 February 1960)
Lorana Sullivan: The Weimar Bonds That Won't Go Away (*Observer*, London, 21 November 1982)
Antony Terry, Phillip Knightley, and Stephen Fay: Soviet Agents Try to Cache 27 Million German War Loot Bonds (*Sunday Times*, London, 31 January 1971)
Nixon: op. cit.
35   "Herman William Brann"
Board for Valuation: op. cit.
Sullivan: op. cit.
36   "In March 1979, three men were tried"
Reuters: 6 April 1977
The Brantford Expositor: 6 April 1977–1 June 1977
36   "Signal Life"
Board of Valuation: op. cit.
Sullivan: op. cit.
37   "Great Train Robbery"
Piers Paul Read: *The Train Robbers* (London, 1978)
37   "Captain John Taylor and Captain Olivier La Buze"
C.R. Boxer: 'The Count of Ericeira and the Pirates, 1721-2' (*History Today*, London, December 1974)
H. Deschamps: *Les Pirates à Madagascar aux XVII ' et XVII ' Siècles* (Paris, 1949)

CHAPTER 3
39   "At Walchensee the Post Hotel"
Jürgen Bungert and Armin Walter: Das Gold, die Nacht und der Nebel (in *Bild am Sonntag*, Hamburg, 2 June 1974)
40   "German mountain or Alpine troops"
James Lucas: *Alpine Elite* (London, 1980)
Bruce Quarrie: *German Mountain Troops* (Cambridge, 1982)
40   "Colonel Franz Wilhelm Pfeiffer"

Page

Interviews with Pfeiffer in Munich on 22 May 1974, 29 May 1978, 19 September 1982

41   "'Day after day, in countless battles'"
Helmuth Spaeter: *Die Brandenburger* (Munich, 1982)

41   "'Gentlemen,' Pfeiffer said gravely"
Jürgen Bungert and Armin Walter: Das Gold, die Nacht und der Nebel (*Bild am Sonntag*, Hamburg, 26 May 1974)
Albrecht Wieland: *Der Schatz am Walchensee* (*Wochenend*, 1952)

42   "Once a new Bavarian State had been formed"
Bungert and Walter: op. cit. 26 May 1974
Wieland: op. cit.

42   "A space for the treasure had been cleared"
For accounts of the handling of the Reichsbank treasure in Mittenwald see Bungert, Moss, Munich CID Report, Wieland, Schirach, Neuhauser interview, Pfeiffer interviews, Turicum Report

44   "'Push on and push hard'"
John Frayn Turner and Robert Jackson: *Destination Berchtesgaden* (London, 1975)

44   "'fantasy of violence and speed' "
7th Army: After Action Report, vol. iii, p. 831 (Heidelberg, 1946)

44   "On 24 April, Colonel Hörl"
For local military situation at end of war, see manuscript by Colonel Hörl on events of April 1946 in files of *Münchner Merkur*; diary of Lt. Hubert Gais (typescript, Garmisch, 15 May 1945); Col. Michael Pössinger — articles in the *Garmisch-Partenkirchner Tagblatt*, 29 April 1970 ("Das Schicksal des Wardenfelser Landes hing en einem Haar"), 24 April 1975 ("Mit gezogener Pistole standen Sie sich gegenüber"), 29 April 1975 ("200 Bomber stehen schon bereit")

45   "'The Party is finished'"
Gais: op. cit.

46   "'I can lead you up to the Vereinsalm'"
Wieland: op. cit.

47   "Captain Hans Neuhauser"
W. Stanley Moss: *Gold Is Where You Hide It* (London, 1956)

48   "11 mysterious oblong boxes"
Turicum: Report to Lt. DuBois concerning Reichsbank treasure (Mittenwald, 22 May 1945)
Also Lt. Herbert G. DuBois: In Quest of Gold, Silver and Foreign Exchange (Finance Branch, SHAEF, May 1945)

Page

Interrogation Report of Walter Funk, 26 June 1945

48   "25 boxes of gold bars"
Munich CID Report

48   "$50,000 worth of foreign currency"
Munich CID Report

49   "One of the rifelmen, Vitus Mayr"
Bungert and Walter: op. cit. 26 May 1974

49   "'I wouldn't mind swapping some of the gold'"
Ottmar Katz: Unpublished notes quoting Josef Pinzl (Munich, 1952)

49   "'We were proud to have our house selected'"
Moss: op. cit.

50   "20 airtight boxes"
Turicum Report.

50   "what the treasure actually comprised"
Munich CID Report
Turicum Report

51   "'I had not seen the gold'"
Bungert and Walter: op. cit. 9 June 1974

51   "The first hole"
First and second holes as seen on the Steinriegel by Douglas Botting in October 1982

52   "four *Zentner*"
Bungert and Walter: Unpublished notes on Reichsbank treasure affair (1974)

53   "Though it was a dark night"
According to Moss: op. cit.
Bungert and Walter claim that Forstreicher watched the mule trains by daylight on the last morning of the burial. It would be difficult to see the mules once they had entered the forest, whether by night or day. But it would be easy enough to see the beginning of the trail and to follow the hoof tracks to the caches afterwards.

53   "Walther Funk's house at Bergerhof"
Munich CID Report

54   "'It was really difficult,' Schwedler recalled"
Munich CID Report
Evidence by Schwedler

54   "the two missing bars of gold"
Munich CID Report

Page

55 "'Colonel Pfeiffer made a remarkable impression'"
Munich CID Report
Evidence by Schwedler

55 "three new currency caches"
Ottmar Katz: Unpublished notes quoting Capt. Hans Neuhauser
(1952)

56 "At night the captain slept in a cave"
Katz: op. cit. — Neuhauser's statement
Moss: op. cit.

56 "'The fate of the Alpine Fortress lies in your hands'"
Pfeiffer interview (Munich, 1982)

57 "'By order of Field-Marshal Kesselring'"
Gais: op. cit.

57 "Major Michael Pössinger"
Pössinger: op. cit.

58 "'Also bitte versuchen Sie es'"
Pössinger: op. cit.

CHAPTER 4

61 "'When and in what direction will you be running'"
V. Sevruk: *How Wars End*, p. 312 (Moscow, 1969)

62 "at about 7 P.M. on the evening of 30 April"
Lt.-Col. William E. Eckles: Correspondence

62 "Mittenwald was acutally under American artillery bombardment"
Michael Pössinger: "Artillerie-Saven auf Mittenwald und letztes
Gefecht bei Klais" (*Garmisch-Partenkirchen Tagblatt*, 30 April 1975)

62 "'He stated that he wanted to talk with an honorable American officer'"
Eckles: op. cit.

63 "a *Wehrmacht* sergeant and the local baker waving a white flag"
Pössinger: op. cit.

63 "a last special meeting...on the Klausenkopf"
Katz: op. cit. — Neuhauser's statement

63 "In an interview with a German journalist in 1952"
Katz: op. cit. — Neuhauser's statement

63 "Neuhauser believed that Colonels"
Katz: op. cit.

64 "On Pfeiffer's orders Captain Neuhauser"
Katz: op. cit.

Page
64 "Almost the last significant objective...Berchtesgaden"
    After the Battle, No. 9: *Obersalzberg* (London, 1975)
    Turner and Jackson: *Destination Berchtesgaden*
    Ziemke: *The U.S. Army in the Occupation of Germany 1944-6*
65 "They found vast stocks of arms"
    Percy Knauth: *Germany in Defeat* (New York, 1946)
65 "*Landrat* (or Prefect) Karl Theodor Jacob"
    Ziemke: op. cit.
65 "Funk had been drunk for months"
    John Kenneth Galbraith: *A Life in Our Times* (London, 1981)
65 "the facts of Jacob's case were submitted to the Public Prosecutor's
    Office'
    Munich CID Report
66 "2,000 important military and political prisoners"
    Rodney G. Minott: *The Fortress That Never Was*, p. 127
    Werner Maser: *Nuremberg—A Nation on Trial* (London, 1979)
    Percy Knauth: op. cit.
66 "'looked like a typical German tourist'"
    Public Records Office document WO 219 1700HM 09328
66 "personal physician, Dr. Morell"
    David Irving (ed.): *Adolf Hitler— The Medical Diaries*, p. 280 (London, 1983)
66 "a huge man standing nearly seven feet tall"
    Douglas M. Kelley, M.D. *Twenty-Two Cells in Nuremberg* (London, 1947)
67 "Positive idenfication of Kaltenbrunner"
    Minott: op. cit., p. 127
    History of the CIC, vol. XXV
67 "Kaltenbrunner had been caught"
    Charles de Jaeger: *The Linz File—Hitler's Plunder of Europe's Art*, p. 132 (London, 1981)
67 "Special Sections Sub-Division"
    Ziemke: op. cit., pp. 248, 314, 316
    Martin: *All Honorable Men*, pp. 27, 51
67 "T (Target) Forces composed in scientists in uniform"
    Martin: op. cit., p. 59
68 "Enemy Personnel Exploitation Section"
    Ziemke: op. cit.
68 "Alsos Mission"

Page

Prof. Samuel A. Goudsmit: *Alsos — The Search for the German Atom Bomb* (London, 1947)

68   "Goldcup teams"
     Ziemke: op. cit.

68   "Strategic Bombing Survey"
     Galbraith: op. cit., pp. 206, 226

68   "The Allied Monuments, Fine Arts and Archaeology Commission"
     de Jaeger: op. cit., pp. 90, 138

68   "The Decartelization Branch"
     Martin: op. cit., p. 109

68   "the Gold Rush teams"
     Martin: op. cit., pp. 73, 120, 121

68   "The closing balances"
     R.A. Nixon: Report on the Recovery of Reichsbank Precious Metals

69   "The Gold Rush"
     SHAEF: Report on Reconnaissance to Discover Further German Gold, Foreign Exchange and Loot (Frankfurt, *c*. May 1945)
     Martin: op. cit., p. 121

69   "all sorts of treasure hoards"
     Report on the Reconnaissance to Discover Further German Gold: op. cit.

69   "35 bags of gold coins"
     Public Records Office: Captured Currencies, WO 219 990

70   "a prodigious 32 million dollars worth of gold"
     Nixon: op. cit.

70   "'With something tangible like looted gold to take in hand'"
     Martin: op. cit., p. 73

70   "I.G. Farben in the industrial suburb of Hoechst"
     Martin: op. cit., pp. 56, 58, 74

70   "the super poison Tabun and the super-super poison Sarin"
     Martin: op. cit., p. 59

70   "The ruins of Frankfurt"
     Klaus-Jörg Ruhl: *Die Besatzer und die Deutschen-Amerikanische Zone 1945-8* (Düsseldorf, 1980)
     Knauth: op. cit., p. 9
     D.A. Spencer: Diary, vol. 3. Germany, 1945 (private manuscript)
     Martin: op. cit., p. 58

71   "Farben's suspected wartime connection"
     Martin: op. cit., p. 58

Page

Spencer: op. cit., p. 698

71 "Into its six wings and seven stories"
Frank C. Gabell: Essay on the FED and Letter (Bentonville, Arizona, 13 September 1982)

71 "'In case of fire'"
Major K.L. Walitschek: Reporting Fire in Reichsbank Premises (Currency Section for Germany, 30 May 1945)

72 "220 tons of Nazi gold"
Antony Terry: Operation Odessa, op. cit.

72 "the largest single collection of wealth in the world"
Paul S. McCarroll: Foreign Exchange Depository (HQ USFET Finance, typescript, 24 January 1946)

72 "The total value of all the assets"
Jack Bennett: Memo to OMGUS — Recommendation for Award to Frank C. Gabell (Berlin, 27 July 1948)

72 "Among the more spectacular sights in the FED"
McCarroll: op. cit.

72 "17,000 carats worth $10,000,000"
Pittsburgh Press: Pittsburgher Divides $500 Million in Nazi War Loot, Wins Citation. January 1949

73 "'not a simple problem'"
McCarroll: op. cit.

73 "the most elaborate security system possible"
McCarroll: op. cit.

74 "That still left over $14,000,000 of gold unaccounted for"
Nixon: op. cit.

74 "By now, Colonel Bernstein was deeply preoccupied"
Martin: op. cit., p.89

74 "he was working for Supreme Headquarters Allied Expeditionary Forces (SHAEF) Financial Intelligence Section"
SHAEF G-5 Division: Telephone Directory (classified) Issue No. 6, 10 April 1945

76 "400 million cubic feet of rubble"
Koch: *Fünf Jahre der Entscheidung — Deutschland nach dem Krieg, 1945-9.* See also Grosser, p. 35, Balfour and Muir, p. 7, Davidson, p. 66

76 "The autobahn down to Munich ran through a pastoral setting"
Spencer: op. cit.

76 "streets were still labeled 'Gruesome'"

Page

       Spencer: op. cit., p. 689

76   "'BRING   IN   YOUR   JEEP'...'WE   NEVER   SLEEP'...'BRIDGE
       OUT'"
       Knauth: op. cit., p. 124

76   "'SOLDIERS WISE DON'T FRATERNIZE'"
       Eugene Davidson: *The Death and Life of Germany*, p. 85 (New York,
       1959)

77   "this vast ragged army of people"
       W. Byford Jones: *Berlin Twilight*, p. 20 (London, *c.* 1946)

77   "The road was full of people"
       Knauth: op. cit., pp. 113, 123
       Spencer: op. cit.

77   "'YOU ARE NOW ENTERING 3RD ARMY TERRITORY'"
       Knauth: op. cit., p. 121

77   "'Paper is a passport to anywhere'"
       Spencer: op. cit., p. 8

78   "'The devastation of Munich was different from that of other
       cities'"
       Heribert Schwan and Rolf Steininger: *Besiegt, besetzt, geteilt* (Olden-
       burg, 1979)
       James Stern: *The Hidden Damage* (New York, 1947)

78   "Red Cross—or bivouac in the station yard"
       Spencer: op. cit., p. 688

78   "'Mielke...was very uncertain about the facts'"
       DuBois: op. cit.

79   "Half the streets in Germany"
       Knauth: op. cit., p. 11
       Spencer: op. cit.

79   "'Neuhauser professed to have little knowledge of the bags and
       boxes'"
       DuBois: op. cit., p. 4

79   "'Lt. DuBois hesitated to continue the reconnaissance to Jache-
       nau'"
       DuBois: op. cit.

80   "'The forest was infested with hungry soldiers'"
       Schirach: *The Price of Glory*
       Pfeiffer: Interview, 1982

80   "Fourteen German soldiers and two mules"
       Lt. K. Meyer, MII: Report on Civilians held in PWE

Page

(Mittenwald, *c.* 22 May 1945)

80 "a mother and her thirteen-year-old daughter"
Schirach: op. cit.

80 "DuBois made a breakthrough"
DuBois: op. cit.

80 "the Bergerhof"
Jack Fishman: *The Seven Men of Spandau*, p. 206 (London, 1954)

81 "on the morning of 14 May"
DuBois: op. cit.

81 "still chubby and round"
Victor H. Bernstein: *Final Judgement*, p. 24 (London, 1947)

81 "He had contracted a venereal disease when he was thirteen"
Fishman: op. cit., pp. 41, 49

82 "'It should be stated...that no pressure was exerted on Funk'"
DuBois: op. cit.

82 "'*Sagen sie die Wahrheit, sonst*'"
Ottmar Katz: Unpublished notes of interview with Veit, Munich, 1952

83 "He was quartered in a working-class block"
Maser: op. cit., p. 46

83 "even his diamond ring"
However, he kept three other rings, inset with opals and other precious stones, and ostentatiously wore a different one each day.
Douglas M. Kelley: *Twenty-Two Cells in Nuremberg*

83 "codeine addiction"
Galbraith: op. cit.
Douglas M. Kelley: op. cit.

83 "'I am convinced,' Funk told his interrogator"
Top Secret Report of Interrogation of Funk and Goering (7th Army Interrogation Center, 21 May 1945)

84 "Camp Ashcan"
Maser: op. cit., p. 56
Galbraith: op. cit., p. 192
Ziemke: op. cit., p. 278
Kelley: op. cit.

84 "'a pass from God and someone to verify the signature'"
Galbraith: op. cit., p. 192

84 "'Who'd have thought we were fighting the war against a bunch of jerks?'"

Page

Galbraith: op. cit.

85   "'Our investigation of foreign exchange can be explained'"
Interrogation of Funk and Goering (7th Army Interrogation Center, 26 June 1945)

85   "four bridges along the road had been blown"
DuBois: op. cit.

86   "But neither the intelligence officer with the 10th Armored detachment"
DuBois: op. cit.

CHAPTER 5

87   "*Gott behüte euch!*"
Jürgen Bungert and Armin Walter: Das Gold, die Nacht und der Nebel *(Bild am Sonntag,* 9 June 1974)
The account of Pfeiffer's movements is based on interviews with Pfeiffer in Munich in May 1974, May 1978, September 1982 and with Neuhauser in 1952 and von Blücher in 1982
Also:
Bungert and Walter: op. cit., 9 June 1974
Ottmar Katz: op. cit.
W. Stanley Moss: *Gold Is Where You Hide It*
Munich CID Report
Turicum Report
Schirach: *The Price of Glory* and article in *Wochenend* in 1950
Garmisch-Partenkirchen Tagblatt: Article entitled "Dunkle Rätsel aus dunklen Tagen"

87   "'I don't like to remember these bad times'"
Pfeiffer interview, September 1982

89   "Major-General Reinhard Gehlen"
Heinz Höhne and Hermann Zolling: *The General Was a Spy,* pp. 50-53 (New York, 1972)
Reinhard Gehlen: *The Gehlen Memoirs* (London, 1972)

89   "Like Germany, Austria had been divided into four zones"
Michael Balfour and John Muir: *Four-Power Control in Germany and Austria, 1945-6* (Royal Institute of International Affairs, London, 1956)

91   "The war between Finland and the Soviet Union"
Hubert von Blücher: Interview with Antony Terry in Düsseldorf, 27 April 1982

Page

Waldenman Erfurth: *The Last Finnish War* (Washington, 1979)

91 "seriously wounded at the fighting around Kuban bridgehead"
von Blücher: op. cit., 27 April 1982

91 "Hubert von Blücher"
Description of von Blücher from W. Stanley Moss, Ivar Buxell, and Berlin Document Center

92 "working for the *Abwehr*"
Moss: op. cit.

92 "According to his brother"
Ivar Buxell: Correspondence

92 "Your military records say"
Hubert von Blücher: Interview in Düsseldorf, 23 June 1982

93 "In fact, available records show"
Berlin Document Center

93 "'I turned up in Garmisch from Berlin'"
von Blücher: op. cit., 27 April 1982

94 "Colonel Pfeiffer was later to claim"
Pfeiffer: Interview

95 "38 Gsteigstrasse was bursting at the seams"
von Blücher: op. cit., 27 April 1982

95 "Mathias Stinnes"
Berlin Document Center

95 "according to Hubert von Blücher"
von Blücher: op. cit.

95 "Hugo Stinnes, Sr."
Robert Wistrich: *Who's Who in Nazi Germany* (London, 1982)
Who's Who in Germany and Austria (Foreign Office, London, 1945)

96 "Stinnes had sent an extraordinary letter"
Berlin Document Center

97 "the Reich Security Police...were asked to check out Mathias Stinnes' credentials"
Berlin Document Center

97 "'From this journey,' reported the Berlin SD"
Berlin Document Center

98 "'it is not expected that it will produce a profit'"
Berlin Document Center

98 "a grandiose scheme for irrigating the Sahara...The Berlin SD summed Stinnes up thus"
Berlin Document Center

Page
98 "'He was a very fine man'"
von Blücher: op. cit., 27 April 1982
99 "'When I arrived back at Gsteigstrasse'"
Moss: op. cit.
99 "'Up to this day,' Mathias Stinnes wrote"
Moss: op. cit.
99 "'The first scenario was Rauch's'"
von Blücher: op. cit., 27 April 1982
99 "'Colonel Pfeiffer took me into his confidence'"
Moss: op. cit.
99 "Another idea put forward by Pfeiffer"
von Blücher: op. cit., 27 April 1982

CHAPTER 6
101 "In case the two ex-Colonels, Rauch and Pfeiffer, met anyone on the way"
Wieland: op. cit.
101 "'The former head of the Gebirgsjäger School in Mittenwald'"
Munich CID Report
102 "'Every night,' he related afterwards"
Moss: op. cit. — Stinnes quoted
102 "'We would start counting'"
Ivar Buxell: Correspondence
102 "After the notes had been stacked"
Moss: op. cit.
Bungert and Walter: op. cit.
Garmisch-Partenkirchen Tagblatt: op. cit.
102 "'No mine detector would ever have found them'"
Moss: op. cit. — Stinnes quoted
103 "'The von Blücher brothers,' Bremme related"
Moss: op. cit. — Bremme quoted
103 "Bremme posted an OFF LIMITS sign"
Garmisch-Partenkirchen Tagblatt: 'Dunkle Rätsel aus dunklen Tagen' (Pt. 3)
(Garmisch, 28 January 1956)
103 "According to a statement made by Bremme in 1978"
Ivar Buxell: Correspondence
104 "Hubert von Blücher...does not concur with this account"
von Blücher: op. cit., 27 April 1982

Page
105   "Turicum had been formed towards the end of the war"
       "Die Sauhund hau'n wir wieder 'naus," Die Geheimakten der
       U.S.—Militärregierung in Bayern, 1945 bis 1949 (Pt. 3, *Der
       Spiegel*, 1 December 1980)
106   "In a memo to Captain Walter R. Dee"
       Lt. DuBois: Memo on Reichsbank Treasure (Private papers of
       Captain Walter R. Dee)
106   "Turicum had prepared a complete report"
       Organization Turicum to Lt. DuBois: Subject Reichsbank Gold
       (Mittenwald, April 1945)
107   "'I had no wish to conceal anything from them'"
       Moss: op. cit.
107   "'24 May 1945—Sent patrol'"
       61st Armored Infantry Battalion: After Action Report 11-31 June
       [*sic*] 1945 (Mittenwald, 12 June 1945)
107   "A few days later"
       idem
108   "'After some while I had the impression'"
       Munich CID Report. Testimony of Will
108   "In an extensive search and arrest operation"
       Garmisch-Partenkirchner Tagblatt: "Dunkle Rätsel aus dunklen Tagen"
       (Pt. 3) (Garmisch, 28 January 1956)
109   "He began to collect unused headed notepaper"
       Ivar Buxell: Correspondence
       Garmisch-Partenkirchner Tagblatt: op. cit.
109   "Hubert von Blücher...was still the proprietor of a deposit of wine"
       Garmisch-Partenkirchner Tagblatt: op. cit.
       Moss: op. cit.
109   "At 8:30 on the evening of 21 May"
       G-2 Journal: 10th Armored Division, Garmisch-Partenkirchen, 22
       May 1945
110   "'Never in my life have I been so tight'"
       Moss: op. cit.
110   "they allegedly made tens of thousands of marks and dollars"
       Garmisch-Partenkirchner Tagblatt: op. cit.
110   "dressed in the uniform of an officer of the Chasseurs Alpins"
       Ottmar Katz: Unpublished notes, quoting Frau Stöttelmeier of the
       Hotel Einsiedl (Munich, 1952)

CHAPTER 7

Page

111 "his trousers were amazingly baggy"
Moss: op. cit.
Katz: Unpublished notes—Neuhauser's statement

111 "Captain Neuhauser's mother"
Moss: op. cit.

111 "'a highly cultivated man'"
von Blücher: op. cit., 27 April 1982

112 "War Office representative...one of the liaison officers at SHAEF"
Public Records Office files FO 371 50804, HM 09328

112 "'I had been down in the Garmisch and Mittenwald'"
Brigadier Michael Waring: Transcript of telephone interview (Zimbabwe, September 1978)

112 "Word that Brigadier Waring was looking for him"
Pfeiffer interviews: op. cit.

113 "the two officials were subjected to an intensive interrogation"
Munich CID Report. Testimony of Will

114 "'The search once again looked like proving a great waste of time'"
Munich CID Report. Testimony of Will

114 "'When I stood in amazement'"
Will: op. cit.

114 "Will succeeded in making his getaway"
Will: op. cit.

115 "Arrested in Mittenwald on 22 May"
Lt.-Col. W.E. Eckles: Secret Intelligence Bulletin (10th Armored Division, Garmisch, 23 May 1945)

115 "'Er weiss auch nichts'"
Katz: Unpublished notes

115 "'Of course...it is generally assumed...The only thing I got out of it'"
Moss: op. cit.

116 "Mittenwald on 6 June"
Katz: Unpublished notes—statement by Josef Veit

116 "Pinzl was not in the best of shape"
Statement by Pinzl to *Bild am Sonntag* (Mittenwald, 1974)

116 "they met a platoon of C Company, 55th Armored Engineering Battalion"
For the recovery of the gold see:
Moss: op. cit.

Page

　　　　Bungert and Walter: op. cit.

　　　　Ottmar Katz: op. cit.

　　　　Tiger's Tales

　　　　Munich CID Report

　　　　Statements by Dee, Geiler, Graziano, Veit, Pinzl, *et al.*

116　"One of the Americans told Veit"

　　　　Bungert and Walter: op. cit.

117　"Captain Rüger gave the order for the mine detectors to be switched on"

　　　　Katz: op. cit. — statement by Josef Veit

117　"Major Geiler in his subsequent report"

　　　　Major William R. Geiler: Report on Gold Recovery (HQ 7th Army, Augsburg, 9 June 1945)

118　"'I'd sure like to have just a little of it'"

　　　　Tiger's Tales, vol. 4, no. 5 (10th Armored Division, 23 June 1945)

119　"'The operation took one complete day'"

　　　　Louis J. Graziano: Correspondence

120　"*Tiger's Tales*"

　　　　Tiger's Tales, vol. 4, no. 5 (10th Armored Division, Garmisch, 23 June 1945)

121　"'Regarding the 'Ten Tons of Gold''"

　　　　Albert Singleton: Correspondence

121　"But in the course of two lengthy interviews"

　　　　Albert Singleton: Telephone interviews, Cleveland, Ohio, 7 October 1977 and 28 April 1978

122　"Major Adolf ('Adi') Weiss"

　　　　Obituary, *Garmisch-Partenkirchner Tagblatt*: 1979

125　"'When the Americans marched into Mittenwald'"

　　　　Col. L. Stautner: Letter to Melanie Bryan (Grainau, 19 March 1981)

125　"all were different"

　　　　So was the weather. Singleton's recovery took place on a "damned hot day" when the sun was shining brilliantly. But the weather forecast for 7 June (according to the 3rd Army Weekly Intelligence Report of 6 June) was "partly to mostly cloudy" — and there is no sunshine in the photos.

125　"'I'll be honest with you'"

　　　　Singleton: Telephone interviews, op. cit.

130　"Among the accused who were tried and sentenced"

Page

Hans Dollinger: *Deutschland unter den Besatzungsmächten 1945-9*, p. 100 (Munich, 1967)

130 "A secret gold hoard in the German Foreign Ministry"
Robert M. W. Kempner: *Das Dritte Reich in Kreuzverhör*

132 "a statement about the German Foreign Office Gold...three recoveries of Foreign Office gold"
Frank J. Roberts: Data re German Foreign Office Gold reflected by Records of Foreign Exchange Depository (FED, Frankfurt, 3 May 1949

132 "the *Goldzug*"
Wiesenthal: Telephone interview with Antony Terry, Vienna, 4 July 1983

133 "in 1950 he decided to lobby the U.S. Congress"
Wiesenthal: op. cit.
Kempner: op. cit.

133 "Congressman Lindley Beckworth"
Lindley Beckworth: Letters to Congressional Interstate and Foreign Commerce Committee (House of Represenatives, Washington, DC, 6 and 21 June 1950)

133 "As Sir Ronald Wingate"
Sir Ronald Wingate: *Not In the Limelight* (London, 1959)

CHAPTER 8

134 "'The crucial problem in the first month'"
Pfeiffer: Interview, Munich, September 1982

135 "'I was amazed how many people knew about it'"
Pfeiffer: op. cit., September 1982

135 "'I received a call from Colonel Oscar Koch'"
Col. William E. Eckles: Correspondence

136 "'In the morning, after the recovery of the money'"
Eckles: op. cit.

137 "Kenneth Asa McIntyre"
U.S. Army Records—file on Major Kenneth A. McIntyre

137 "'He was a likeable guy'"
Eckles: op. cit.

138 "'no more than a million dollars'"
Sieglinde Odorfer: Correspondence (Munich, 14 August 1976)

138 "'The accused is charged with the 95th Article of War'"
Lt.-Col. Alexander A. Lafleur: Case of Kenneth A. McIntyre (Of-

Page

169 "'A very funny thing happened'"
     Hubert von Blücher: op. cit. 27 April 1982
171 "Frederick Siegfried Neumann"
     U.S. Army 201 file — F. S. Neumann
172 "'Subject made an excellent impression'"
     U.S. Army 201 file — F. S. Neumann
172 "'Officer is well suited for interrogation'"
     U.S. Army 201 file — F. S. Neumann
172 "'He went about everywhere with a dog whip'"
     von Blücher: op. cit., 27 April 1982
173 "'The grotesqueness of the situation only struck me'"
     von Blücher: op. cit., 27 April 1982
174 "'The general stayed for about two hours'"
     Moss: op. cit.
175 "'It was just as if you were digging up an Easter egg'"
     von Blücher; op. cit., 27 April 1982
175 "'on Friday 3 August 1945'"
     Major Melvin W. Nitz: Military Government Annual Report
     (Garmisch, June 1946
176 "'The most fantastic search...then started'"
     Moss: op. cit., quoting statement by Klaus Bremme, 28 March
     1956, pp. 150-54
177 "TO WHOM IT MAY CONCERN"
     Moss: op. cit.
     Lüder von Blücher: Correspondence
     Ivar Buxell: CIC dossier
178 "he has consistently denied"
     Pfeiffer: op. cit., September 1982
178 "'My signature was refused by Captain Neumann'"
     Moss: op. cit., quoting Klaus Bremme, p. 153

CHAPTER 11
179 "'Of course, saying we were confined to the house'"
     von Blücher: op. cit., 27 April 1982
180 "'Everything was black market'"
     von Blücher: op. cit., 27 April 1982
181 "'they flashed slowly and intermittently like the revolving lamp'"
     Moss: op. cit. (Preface)
183 "Were you ever told later"

Page

von Blücher: op. cit., 27 April 1982

183   "You were with the American newsreel company"
      von Blücher: Interview with Antony Terry, op. cit.

185   "'These parties were the most harmless things'"
      von Blücher: op. cit., 27 April 1982

CHAPTER 12

187   "'I want those civilian bastards handed over"
      Farago: op. cit.

188   "the nature of the American Occupation"
      For broad accounts of the Allied occupation of Germany in general
      and American Military Government in particular, see, *inter alia*,
      Michael Balfour and John Muir: *Four-Power Control in Germany and
      Austria, 1945-6* (London, 1956)
      F.S.V. Donnison: *Civil Affairs and Military Government in North-West
      Europe, 1944-6* (London, 1961)
      Klaus-Jörg Ruhl: *Die Besatzer und die Deutschen-Amerikanische Zone,
      1945-8* (Düsseldorf, 1980)
      Ziemke: *The U.S. Army in the Occupation of Germany, 1944-6*
      Harold Zink: *The United States in Germany, 1944-55* (New York,
      1959)
      General Lucius D. Clay: *Decision in Germany* (London, 1950)
      Edward N. Peterson: *The American Occupation of Germany* (Detroit,
      1977)
      Eugene Davidson: *The Death and Life of Germany* (New York, 1959)
      Oliver Frederickson: *American Military Occupation of Germany,
      1945-53* (Darmstadt, 1953)
      Franklin Davis: *Come as a Conqueror* (New York, 1967)

189   "'The apparently unanimous judgment of contemporary critics'"
      Peterson: op.cit, pp. 84-5

189   "'a variety of feudal kingdoms'"
      Harold Zink: *American Military Government in Germany* (New York,
      1967)

190   "'Germany was deluged with intelligence teams'"
      Quoted in Peterson: p. 110

190   "the intelligence agencies were not functioning well"
      Peterson: p. 89

190   "'they lacked really first-class men'"
      Alfred Gosser: *Germany in Our Time* (New York, 1971)

Page

190 "a top salary of $10,000 per annum"
Peterson: op. cit., p. 90

191 "'the wine, women, and song boys'"
Zink: *The United States in Germany*, p. 76.

191 "'The background checks of some of the people'"
William C. Wilson: Correspondence

191 "a series of pen portraits"
William C. Wilson: op. cit.

192 "'Brigadier-General George H. "Pappy" Weems'"
William C. Wilson: Correspondence, 17 August 1979
Lt.-Col. Lester J. Zucker, former Executive Officer of CID HQ at
EUCOM, formed a rather more charitable view of General
Weems: "I liked General Weems," he wrote to the authors on 29
May 1979. "He was always nice to me. He had no real knowledge
of Military Police or CID, but he managed."
Born in 1891, Weems was promoted to Brigadier-General in 1942
and served on Special Missions to the Philippines as well as
Hungary. He was Provost Marshal, European Command, 1947-9.

193 "It was a fucked-up mess!'"
Wilson: op. cit.

193 "'I tried to stay away from the CIC'"
Buck Wardle: 6 May 1978

193 "'I have nothing to add to this statement'"
Robert B. Shaw, Agent 13th CID: Report to Office of the Provost
Marshal, Criminal Investigation Division, EUCOM, 27 June
1947

194 "'Too many fingers in the pie'"
Wilson: op. cit.

195 "'They had considerable testimony'"
Wilson: op. cit.

195 "At a subsequent inquiry"
Lt.-Col. Leonard H. Smith: Testimony before the Inspector General into Allegations by Guenther Reinhardt. Exhibit 'B-3' (Berlin,
20 January 1948)

196 "two gold shipments down to Mittenwald"
Wilson: op. cit.

196 "near Füssen"
Wilson: op. cit.

196 "Goering's palace at Valhalla"

Page

Wilson: op. cit.

196   "As for the rumors"
Wilson: op. cit.

196   "'I had all this stuff in the safe'"
Charles I. Bradley: Telephone interview (Redondo Beach, California, 19 January 1980)

197   "'Ketcham and I were there'"
Ward Atherton: Telephone Interviews (Lafayetteville, North Carolina, 4 and 27 March, 26 April and 2 May 1978)

197   "'It was an awful lot'"
John L. Ketcham: Telephone interviews (Concrete, Washington State, 28 March and 29 April 1978)

197   "'These things had taken place in June or July of '45'"
Atherton: op. cit.

198   "'I was asked whether I would mind going to a place in Garmisch'"
Leo de Gar Kulka: Correspondence, taped statements, and telephone interviews (San Francisco, 1978)

199   "'Utter piffle, Pure nonsense'"
von Blücher: op. cit., 27 April 1982

200   "'I wish to Christ I *had* gotten some — if there had been some'"
Melvin Nitz: Interview with Colin Simpson, *Sunday Times* (Fresno, California, January 1982)

CHAPTER 13

201   "The first recovery, totalling $251,374"
Major Melvin W. Nitz: Military Government Annual Report, Detachment E-236. 1 May 1945-30 June 1946. Section 1): Finance and Property Control, p. 92.

201   "The second recovery...worth 'about $50,000'"
Ibid.

201   "'I believe that it was one of Oscar Koch's officers'"
Charles W. Snedeker: Correspondence, 4 October 1977

201   "Captain Snedeker received an official receipt'"
Receipt signed Lt.-Col. William A. Brown, Fiscal Section Officer. Military Government Detachment E-205, Munich, 27 August 1945 (in the private papers of Charles W. Snedeker)

201   "The third and final recovery...the $104,956"
Nitz: op. cit.

202   "Third Army Weekly Intelligence Report"

Page

Col. Oscar W. Koch: G-2 Secret Weekly Intelligence Report No. 14 for week ending 29 August 1945, p. 4 (Third U.S. Army, Bad Tölz)

202 "Deposit No. 18"
Consolidation of Reports of Deposit of Foreign Exchange (OMGB, Munich, 2 May 1947)

202 "The correct procedure for the handling and shipment of recovered funds"
Lt.-Col. F.S. McFadzean: Seized Enemy Funds (SHAEF Financial Branch, 10 March 1945)

203 "a wooden box containing $141,225"
Nitz: op. cit.

203 "$4,000 found by Lt. Roger Ernst"
Captain Benjamin S. Schilling: Reference Shipment No. 60 – Receipt for $4,000 (HQ USFET G-5 Financial Branch, Currency Section, Frankfurt, 11 August 1945)

203 "The detailed gold and currency inventories of the FED"
Register of Valuables in the Custody of the Foreign Exchange Depository, Frankfurt am Main, Germany, 15 April 1945 to 29 November 1950

203 "and the Federal Reserve Bank"
Office of Alien Property, U.S. Department of Justice: Vesting Orders for U.S. currency recovered in Germany (Washington, DC, letters dated 7 December 1978 and 18 April 1979)
Federal Reserve Bank in New York: Letters dated 11 April 1977 and 15 December 1978

204 "Deposit No. 10"
Reports of Deposits: op. cit.

205 "in a handwritten reply"
Albert Thoms: Memo – Gold Stocks, Reichsbank Berlin (no date)

205 "the FED seems to have lain almost completely dormant"
McCarroll: op. cit.

206 "The purpose of the visit, according to Rona Geib"
Rona L. Geib: Liaison Visit to G-2 – List of Germans Connected with Seized Valuables in FED (Frankfurt, 13 August 1946)

206 "the final inventory of Shipment 52A"
FED Currency Section: Inventory of Shipment 52A (Frankfurt, 22 July 1946)

206 "On 12 September the Deputy Director"

Page

213 "Two months later"
Edwin P. Keller: Secret Memo—U.S. Dollars Discussions on 3 January (Office of Finance Adviser, OMGUS, FED Group, Frankfurt, 3 January 1949)

213 "'The United States'"
Murray D. Van Waggoner: Letter to Major-General George P. Hays re Military Government Law No. 53. (Munich, 3 February 1949)

213 "'U.S. policy has reached the stage'"
Eugene K. Bird: *Prisoner No. 7—Rudolf Hess* (New York, 1972)

215 "90 bars of gold and 4,580,878 gold coins taken from the Reichs-bank in Berlin"
Nixon: op. cit.
Terry: op. cit.

215 "Gold Currency Bonds...taken from the Berlin Reichsbank"
Board for Valuation of German Bonds: op. cit.
Sullivan: op. cit.
Terry: op. cit.

215 "Jewels, diamonds, securities, and foreign currency worth $9,131,000 taken at gunpoint"
Spacil file: op. cit.—interrogation reports and statements
Infield: *Secrets of the SS*, op. cit.

215 "1 bag of SS foreign currency taken from the Munich Reichsbank"
Munich CID Report
Geib: Currency Sent from Berlin, op. cit.

215 "12 sacks of SS foreign currency"
Geib: op. cit.

215 "85,000 Swiss francs"
Munich CID Report

215 "$5,000 taken by Reichsbank official Mielke"
Munich CID Report
Geib: op. cit.

215 "$67,120 U.S. dollars"
Munich CID Report
FED Register of Valuables: op. cit.

215 "2 gold bars worth $30,000"
Reports of deposits: op. cit.
FED Register of Valuables: op. cit.

215 "One truck-load of foreign currency"

Page

      Eckles: op. cit.

      Ordorfer: op. cit.

      FED Register of Valuables: op. cit.

216   "11 boxes weighing 330 pounds each"

      Turicum Report

      DuBois: op. cit.

      Goering and Funk interrogation report

216   "25 boxes containing 100 gold bars"

      Munich CID Report

      FED Register of Valuables: op. cit.

216   "6.5 tons of Ribbentrop gold"

      Wiesenthal: op. cit.

      Kempner: op. cit.

216   "17 bags of foreign currency from the Berlin Reichsbank"

      Geib: op. cit.

216   "the Brinks robbery"

      David Wallechinsky, Irving Wallace, and Amy Wallace: *The Book of Lists* (Sensational Thefts, p. 16) (London, 1977)

217   "Great Train Robbery"

      Piers Paul Read: *The Train Robbers* (London, 1978)

218   "On 27 November he was arrested"

      Siegfried F. Feld, Special Agent, CIC: C.I. Arrest Report (Tegernsee, 28 November 1945)

218   "Subsequent investigations...He was, however, sufficiently in funds"

      Confidential Source

219   "a sum of between 100,000 and 150,000 dollars"

      Buenos Aires Police records

219   "according to the Innsbruck police"

      Munich CID Report

219   "According to Pfeiffer"

      Bungert and Walter: *Bild am Sonntag* op. cit., 9.6.74

219   "in his application for a visa to the Innsbruck Police"

      Munich CID Report

219   "according to the Registry of Births in Munich"

      Idem

219   "sailed with his wife from Cannes"

      Bungert and Walter: op. cit., 9.6.74

219   "to the tune of some 100,000 U.S. dollars"

Page

Buenos Aires Police records

220   "'That is a lot of lies...'"
Telephone interview with Colonel Pfeiffer, 1 September 1983, Munich

221   "'I am completely unqualified to say anything...'"
Telephone interview with Colonel Rauch, 1982, Graz

221   "In 1951 it seems he made his way to the United States"
Buenos Aires Police Department.
von Blücher: op. cit., 27 April 1982

221   "Walt Disney film set in the Amazon"
Who's Who in Germany

221   "he wrote several...novels and"
Who's Who in Germany
Ivar Buxell: Correspondence

222   "he bought a large farm near Pretoria"
von Blücher: Telephone interview with Antony Terry (Düsseldorf, 4 February 1983)

222   "Helmut Groeger"
Charles S. Dimarino, CIC Special Agent: Secret Report re Helmut Groeger — Illegal Possessions of Large Quantities of American Money" (CIC Region IV, 17 June 1948)

222   "'hidden by the Nazis shortly after World War Two'"
Dimarino: op. cit.

222   "'Helmut Groeger lives exceedingly well'"
Lt.-Col. Ellington D. Golden: Secret Report re Helmut Groeger (HQ CIC Region IV, 970th CIC Detachment, 17 February 1948)

222   "part of a packet of $5,000"
Max L. Marshall, Special Agent: Secret Memo re Helmut Groeger (CIC Tegernsee, 25 May 1948)

223   "'This investigation was inaugurated'"
Max L. Marshall, Special Agent: Report on Helmut Groeger and Illegal Possession of Large Quantities of American money (HQ CIC Region IV, 17 June 1948)

223   "'You will never, never find out'"
Confidential source in Garmisch

CHAPTER 14
227   "It had not been envisaged that the Germans would fight to the last"
Zink: op. cit., p. 88

384   NAZI GOLD

Page

227 "'The world had never known before'"
     Balfour and Muir: op. cit., p. 116

227 "The problems confronting Military Government"
     Zink: op. cit., p. 82

227 "these were often looked down"
     Peterson: op. cit.
     Zink: pp. 10-11, 23-6

227 "average age of officers"
     Zink: op. cit. pp. 8, 31-2

228 "an immensely powerful prewar Porsche"
     Wilson: op. cit.

228 "19,000 U.S. Army deserters"
     Stars and Stripes (Paris, 1945)

229 "indulging in gang warfare"
     Stars and Stripes (Paris, June 1945)

229 "armed gangs of deserters"
     Byford-Jones: op. cit., p. 151

229 "American train bandits"
     Public Records Office File WO 171

229 "seen to loot rare antiquarian books"
     Charles L. Mee: *Meeting at Potsdam* (London, 1975)

229 "'a couple of thousand bucks'"
     Mee: op. cit.

229 "Reichspost stamp collection"
     Wilson: Correspondence

230 "their own private trains"
     Guenther Reinhardt: 55-page memorandum on American Occupation of Germany (Washington, December 1947, p. 49)

230 "'We became an "India Service"'"
     Arthur Kahn: *Betrayal—Our Occupation of Germany* (Warsaw, 1950), p. 123-4

231 "a sense of sheer horror"
     George Kennan: *Memoirs 1925-50*, p. 452 (Boston, 1967)

231 "'I decided to get out'"
     Quoted in Peterson: op. cit.

231 "universal concubinage"
     Peterson: op. cit.

231 "regular bed checks"
     Davidson: op. cit.

232   "'Beware of *V*eronika *D*ankeschön'"
Communication from Antony Terry, *Sunday Times* (London, April 1983)

232   "'our first 19-year-old Rhineland blonde'"
Byford-Jones: op. cit., pp. 25-6

232   "'Moral standards have crashed to a new low'"
Byford-Jones: op. cit., p. 44

232   "One Camel or Lucky Strike"
Byford-Jones: op. cit., p. 35

232   "$12,000 a year on the cigarette economy"
Koch: *Fünf Jahre der Entscheidung — Deutschland nach dem Kreig, 1945-9* (*c*.1969)

232   "$5.5 million more than they had been paid"
Byford-Jones: op. cit., p. 37
Davidson: op. cit., pp. 84-5

232   "'Those conditions...created an atmosphere so unreal'"
B.U. Ratchford and W.D. Ross: *Berlin Reparations Assignment*, p. 3 (Chapel Hill, North Carolina University Press, 1947)

232   "'it was common gossip that Mrs. Clay'"
Wilson: Correspondence

233   "Brigadier-General...Walter Muller"
Peterson: op. cit., p. 226

234   "'What a collection of carpetbaggers'"
Wilson: Correspondence

234   "3,500 had been illegally disposed of"
Agent George O. Muse: Alleged Illegal Traffic in German Automobiles (14th CI Detachment CID, 14 May 1947)

234   "inefficient or dishonest"
Col. Thomas H. Young: Final Report of Investigation of Transportation Branch, OMGB (EUCOM, 31 March 1948)

235   "'was the most poorly administered detachment I have seen'"
Captain Elwood J. Pennetto: Inspection Report of Inspecting Colonel, OMGB (Munich, 4 May 1946)

235   "'They changed like a revolving door'"
Paul O. Bruehl: Telephone interview (Long Island, 10 December 1977)

235   "24 American personnel ordered out of Bavaria"
Col. Fred A. Mayer: Report on Personnel Ordered out of the Occupation Zones for Prejudicial Acts (P and A Division, OMGB,

Page

Munich, 30 October 1974)

CHAPTER 15

238 "many Germans of real wealth"
     Wilson: Correspondence
239 "the daily fat ration"
     Frank Grube and Gerhard Richter: *Die Schwarzmarktzeit*, pp. 25-6
     (Hamburg, 1979)
239 "a rigid monetarist policy"
     Balfour and Muir: op. cit., pp. 110-11
239 "A Bokhara rug could be bought"
     Grube: op. cit., p. 75
239 "Germany became a cigarette civilization"
     Byford-Jones: op. cit., p. 35
239 "Each train had its black-market nickname"
     Koch: op. cit.
240 "the *Scheiber*"
     Grube: op. cit., pp. 77-8
240 "penicillin, or 'white gold'"
     Wilson: op. cit.
240 "The Duisburg Railway Station Gang"
     Grube: op. cit., pp. 77-8
240 "Another gang stole complete trains"
     Grube: op. cit., p. 76
240 "One of the most successful black-marketeers"
     Wilson: op. cit.
240 "In Garmisch-Partenkirchen there was no 'Mr. Big'"
     Wilson: op. cit
241 "Zenta Hausner"
     Garmisch Police files
     CIC Reports
     Personal recollections
     Articles in *Wochenend, Garmisch-Partenkirchener Tagblatt*
244 "Why don't we keep quiet about the past?'"
     Confidential U.S. sources
245 "'the worst concentration of international gangsters'"
     James A. Rutter: Interview with Lt. Col. E. Van Buskirk (66th
     CIC Group, 1 August 1957)
245 "in addition to the Reichsbank reserves"

Page

Garmisch-Partenkirchner Tagblatt: "Dunkle Rätsel" Pt. 4 (Garmisch, 2 February 1956)

246 "Ten cases of platinum"
Moss: op. cit.

246 "Much of the uranium disappeared"
Moss: op. cit.
Garmisch-Partenkirchener Tagblatt
CIC files
CID and CIC agents

247 "'We put a big hush-hush on it'"
Buck Wardle: Telephone interview (6 May 1978)

248 "the postwar narcotics trade"
Victor H. Peccarelli, Chief Agent: Secret Preliminary Report on Narcotics Trafficking in Upper Bavaria (Project Garpeck, EUCOM, 2 December 1947)
Ivar Buxell: Correspondence

248 "a huge deposit of cocaine"
Ivar Buxell: Correspondence

248 "other sources had to be found"
Peccarelli: op. cit.

249 "'While no concrete evidence exists'"
Philip P. Benzell, Chief Agent: Concluding Report on Narcotics Trafficking in Upper Bavaria (Project Garpeck, EUCOM, 10 January 1948)

CHAPTER 16

255 "Ivar Buxell"
For the episode involving Ivar Buxell the authors are indebted to Dr. Buxell (who now lives in Caracas, Venezuela) for information concerning his remarkable life contained in his correspondence (Caracas, 1976-83), in his taped interviews (London, 1976) and manuscript autobiography (Caracas, 1983)
Reference has also been made to Buxell's CIC file from the U.S. Army Intelligence Agency, Fort Meade, Maryland.

256 "I did not care for Hitler'"
Ivar Buxell: Taped interview

256 "I was a member of the *Abwehr*'"
Ivar Buxell: Correspondence

256 "'General Shandruk supplied me with all necessary documents'"

Page

Ivar Buxell: Correspondence

257   "'Are you a spy or something?'"
Ivar Buxell: Taped interview
257   "'The CIC lieutenant was very confused'"
Ivar Buxell: Unpublished autobiography (Caracas, 1983)
257   "'You can only survive in times after war or revolution'"
Ivar Buxell: Correspondence

CHAPTER 17
267   "'It is recommended that the proper authorities in France'"
Bruehl: cop. cit.
268   "'The same man turned up in both places'"
Lt.-Col. Leonard H. Smith: Transcript of telephone interview
(Clearwater, Florida, 1 December 1979)
268   "'an aggregation of homesick Americans'"
Raymond Daniell: *New York Times*, 16 December 1945, quoted in
Peterson: p. 92
268   "'The ragged German'"
Peterson: op. cit., p. 90
268   "'The most competent man in the executive departments'"
Peterson: op. cit., pp. 56-7
269   "'During this period of unavoidable confusion'"
General Lucius D. Clay: *Decision in Germany*, p. 63 (London, 1950)
269   "'I was just trying to find out what was going on'"
Leonard H. Smith; Transcript, op. cit.
270   "'imbued with a spirit of creating a *magnum opus*'"
Lt.-Col. Leonard H. Smith: Report of Investigation: Conditions
in Garmisch. Interim Report 3 (Inspector General's Division,
EUCOM, 14 July 1947)
270   "'It didn't cost the U.S. Government a penny'"
Frank J. Gammache: Transcripts of telephone interview (Sante Fe,
New Mexico, 13 December 1977)
270   "'Where did the money come from?'"
Leonard H. Smith: Report, op. cit.
270   "'I was told that the nightclub'"
Lt.-Col. Lester J. Zucker: Correspondence, 27 May 1979
270   "'The Army to this day'"
Bob Shaw: Transcript of telephone interview (Pebble Beach,
California, 28 February 1978)
270   "British urinals"

Page

Leo de Gar Kulka: Taped reminiscences (Tape No. 1, San Francisco, 21 June 1978)

271   "Agoston's story continues"
Tom Agoston: Transcript of telephone interview (Hamburg, 3 December 1977)

272   "HUGE DOPE RING PROBED IN BAVARIA"
Tom Agoston: *Stars and Stripes* (Frankfurt, 13 January 1948)

272   "Ed Hartrich had filed a similar story"
Ed Hartrich: Army Reveals Huge Bavarian Drug Traffic, *New York Herald Tribune*, 13 January 1948

272   "'all possible influence'"
Message concerning Gammache case from HQ EUCOM, Frankfurt, signed Huebner, 7 January 1948 CSO 19 3339

272   "'the original tip'"
Ibid.

273   "After a bugging assignment in Garmisch"
Kulka: op. cit., Tape No. 1

273   "'I could not help but sense'"
Lt.-Col. Leonard H. Smith: Testimony before Inspector General's Investigation into Allegations by Guenther Reinhardt. Exhibit "B-3", p. 15 (Berlin, January 1948)

273   "In his report to General Clay"
Leonard H. Smith: Report of Investigation, op. cit.

274   "'The first time we left our hotel room'"
Lt.-Col. Leonard H. Smith: "She Came By Night" (unpublished manuscript, Clearwater, Florida, October 1980)

274   "'Once physically installed'"
Leonard H. Smith: "She Came By Night"

275   "'Accustomed to the German habit'"
Leonard H. Smith: "She Came By Night"

275   "'My conclusion...was that this was not an ordinary housebreaker'"
Leonard H. Smith: Testimony, op. cit., p. 13. Record Group No. 159 333.9 Guenther Reinhardt. Box 527

275   "Zenta Hausner"
Leonard H. Smith: Testimony, op. cit.

276   "What he remembered most about that time"
Leonard H. Smith: Telephone transcript, op. cit

276   "'Several attempts were made on my life'"
Kulka: op. cit., Tape No. 1

Page

276 "'I decided that the way to sanity'"
Kulka: op. cit., Tape No. 1

277 "imprisonment without trial"
OMGB Intelligence, Historical and Reports Branch: Time Necessary for Trial of Minor Cases after Arrest (Munich, 6 January 1947) Nat. Archives Record Group No. 260

277 "'I knew through Counter-Intelligence Corps (CIC) channels'"
Lt.-Col. Leonard H. Smith: Testimony, op. cit., p. 16

277 "Smith then took a most unusual step"
Smith: Testimony, op. cit.

277 "'that gold and dope deal'"
Telex, HQ CIC Region IV, Munich, 4 June 1947

278 "'All of a sudden'"
Kulka: op. cit., Tape No. 2 (San Francisco, January 1979)

278 "One night...Ivar was picked up from the *Rathaus* cells"
Ivar Buxell: Correspondence, 28 September 1976 and June 1983
Garmisch-Partenkirchner Tagblatt: "Dunkle Rätsel" Pt. 7 (Garmisch, 11 February 1955

278 "'I arranged for him to be released into my custody'"
Kulka: op. cit., Tape No. 2

279 "In Buxell's memory"
Garmisch-Partenkirchner Tagblatt: op. cit.

279 "'I brought up the subject of a certain Garmisch resident'"
Kulka: op. cit., Tape No. 2

280 "'The gold bullion...which was in mahogany boxes'"
Kulka op. cit., Tape No. 2

281 "'I disappeared for 18 days'"
Ivar Buxell: Correspondence, 18 June 1976

281 "'The noncommissioned officers of the Military Police detachment in Garmisch'"
Kulka: op. cit., Tape No. 2

282 "'The Military Police claimed'"
Kulka: op. cit., Tape No. 2

283 "the 'almost incredible power'"
Guenther Reichardt: 55-page memorandum (Washington, December 1947), p. 20

283 "'I didn't feel that I had cooperation in the Post'"
Smith: Telephone transcript, op. cit.

283 "Colonel Smith testified in 1948"

Page

Smith: Testimony, op. cit.

284 "'I felt like a mushroom'"
Kulka: op. cit., Tape No. 2

284 "One morning Kulka telephoned Smith in Garmisch"
Smith: Testimony, op. cit.

284 "'The amount of information we received was overwhelming'"
Kulka: op. cit., Tape No. 2

285 "'My investigation led to the pointing of suspicion'"
Smith: Testimony, op. cit.

286 "'The preliminary evidence alone'"
Guenther Reinhardt: 55-page memorandum, p. 20

286 "On 18 July General Clay expressed an order"
Smith: Testimony, op. cit., p. 14

286 "'I had reasonable concern for my own life'"
Smith: Telephone transcript. op. cit.

287 "'The entire story got awfully hot'"
Kulka: Transcript of telephone interview (San Francisco, 20 March 1978)

287 "must have gotten too close to home"
Kulka: Correspondence, 24 April 1978

287 "'When Colonel Smith and I were ordered back'"
Kulka: Telephone transcript, op. cit.

287 "'I found him sitting there putting them all in the fireplace'"
OMGB Officer Elmer Pralle commented on the phone from Stuttgart on 23 March 1978, 'A lot of the files just disappeared, you know'

287 "For 26-year-old Lt. Kulka, worse was to follow"
Kulka: Telephone transcript and taped reminiscences (San Francisco, 1978)

288 "'Even while I was separated from the Service'"
Kulka: Telephone transcript, 20 March 1978 and Tape No. 1

288 "'my first gut reaction was to let sleeping dogs lie'"
Kulka: Correspondence, 3 March 1978

289 "'I wonder if at my age'"
Kulka: Correspondence, 14 April 1978

CHAPTER 18

290 "Frank Gammache's court martial"
Record of Trial: Frank J. Gammache (General Court Martial, Bad

Page

Tölz, 9-11 September 1947

291 "The charges against Frank Gammache were so trivial"
Record of Trial: op. cit.

291 "U.S. Army Judiciary's Pre-Trial Report"
Record of Trial: op. cit.

291 "I think it was General Eisenhower'"
Col. Clifton H. Young: Transcript of telephone interview (New Harbor, Maine, 18 November 1978)

292 "Peccarelli was a 'typical BTO'"
William C. Wilson: Correspondence, 12 July 1979

292 "'very, very bombastic type'"
Bob Shaw: Transcript of telephone interview (Pebble Beach, California, 28 February 1978)

292 "WANTED! $2.50 REWARD"
In the possession of William C. Wilson, Douglasville, Georgia

293 "It was gold from the German National Treasury'"
Alice Peccarelli: Transcript of telephone interview (Stockton, New Jersey, 20 December 1981)

293 "'We were not investigating narcotics'"
Frank Purcell: Transcript of telephone interview (Granada Hills, California, 24 January 1982)

293 "Philip Benzell confirmed"
Philip Benzell: Testimony before Inspector General's inquiry into allegations by Guenther Reinhardt (Munich, January 1948) (Exhibit "B-7," pp. 30-32, National Archives Record Group 159. 333.9)

294 "It was in Switzerland that we lost control of that'"
Elmer Pralle: Transcript of telephone interview (Stuttgart, 23 March 1982)

294 "Even Colonel Franz Pfeiffer"
William C. Wilson: Correspondence

295 "subject: Frederick Siegfried Neumann"
FBI; Memorandum to Director, FBI (San Francisco, 19 September 1947) (FBI Archives, Washington, DC)

296 "'absolute rock-bottom factual information on McCarthy...This reluctance...was attributed to fear'"
Benzell: Testimony before Inspector General, op. cit. (Exhibit "B-7," p. 31

296 "'McCarthy suddenly moved out'"

Page

Benzell: idem (B-7)

296 "'MG PRESSING WIDE SEARCH FOR HIDDEN NAZI TREASURE'"
Stars and Stripes, Frankfurt, 28 December 1947

297 "Victor Peccarelli reported"
Victor H. Peccarelli, Jr.: Preliminary Report of Narcotics
Trafficking in Upper Bavaria (Garmisch, 2 December 1947)
Exhibit "O" in IGD investigation of Reinhardt allegations.

297 "Five hundred grams of cocaine"
Philip P. Benzell: Concluding Report on Narcotics Trafficking in
Upper Bavaria (Office of the Provost Marshal, EUCOM, 10 January 1948)

297 "Guenther Reinhardt"
Guenther Reinhardt: Dossier XI 446319 (Investigative Records
Repository, CIC, U.S. Army)

298 "Loyalty and Character Report"
War Department, Office of the Provost Marshal General, 29 November 1943

299 "six Hungarian SS guards"
Guenther Reinhardt: "I Spy...You Spy...He Spies...(*Pageant*, November 1948)

299 "A confidential report on Reinhardt"
Col. F.J. Pearson: Reports of Investigation of Allegations Made by
Mr. Guenther P. Reinhardt (Office of the Inspector General,
EUCOM, 22 April 1948)

300 "'General Gailey told me'"
Reinhardt: *Crime Without Punishment*, p. 229 (New York, 1952)

301 "'full of crap'"
William C. Wilson: Correspondence

301 "'He was unbalanced up to a point'"
Tom Agoston: Transcript of telephone interview (Hamburg, 6
February 1948)

301 "'There was a crazy German girl'"
Agoston: op. cit.

301 "He would react strangely"
Pearson: Reports of Investigation, op. cit.

301 "'Chief of the American Intelligence in Germany'"
Paul H. Marvin: Letter to Commanding General, CIC Center,
Camp Holabird, Baltimore, Maryland (8 December 1948)

302 "'Being on the operations level'"

Page

Guenther Reinhardt: Correspondence with Tom Agoston (New York, 12 February 1949)

304   "'another Pearl Harbor in Germany'"
Quoted in Orville J. Taylor: "Reinhardt Report" 9th Part, 29 March 1948

304   "'I met Mr. Reinhardt at the billets of the 13th CID'"
Phillip Benzell: Testimony before Inspector General. Exhibit "B-2" (Munich, January 1948)
For another version of this meeting, Dave Gallant: Testimony in Exhibit "B-6" of the Reinhardt papers (National Archives Record Group No. 159 333.9 Guenther Reinhardt. Box 527)

305   "According to Reinhardt, "there were terrific personnel shake-ups'"
Reinhardt: Letter to Agoston: op. cit.

305   "a floating appendage of the U.S. Occupation Zone"
Reinhardt: 55-page memorandum, p. 4

305   "'When I got back to the States'"
Reinhardt: Letter to Agoston, op. cit.

306   "Gray was later Secretary of the Army"
Stephen E. Ambrose: *Ike's Spies* (New York, 1981

306   "Reinhardt's second and principal memorandum"
Guenther Reinhardt: 55-page memorandum (National Archives Record Group No. 159. Decimal File 333.9)

306   "'greedy American wives'"
Reinhardt: Memorandum, op. cit., p. 11

307   "'the lavish private railroad trains'"
Reinhardt: Memorandum, op. cit., p. 49

307   "'an exceptionally beautiful and clever German woman'"
Reinhardt: Memorandum, op. cit., p. 26

307   "'there were available on 1 October 1947'"
Reinhardt: Memorandum, op. cit., p. 28

307   "'Organized large-scale black-market activities'"
Reinhardt: Memorandum, op. cit., p. 19

308   "'The CID investigation by a special team'"
Reinhardt: Memorandum, op. cit., p. 23
In subsequent testimony during the Inspector General's inquiry into the Reinhardt allegations, the charges against Peccarelli and other CID agents were denied (see Exhibits "B-2" and "B-6")

309   "'It was established that one of the headquarters'"
Reinhardt: Memorandum, op. cit., p. 21

Page

309   "'Also implicated were three colonels'"
      Reinhardt: Memorandum, op. cit., p. 22

309   "'I dictated everything'"
      Reinhardt: Letter to Agoston, op. cit.

CHAPTER 19

311   "When it was reported that she was taking dope"
      Carl Sussmann: Memorandum for the Commanding Officer, Gar-
      misch Sub-Region, CIC, 19 October 1946

311   "When she was on the point of being arrested"
      Carl Sussmann: op. cit.

311   "clandestine meetings of the local Communist Party"
      Carl Sussmann: op. cit.

312   "*Was gescheht mit unserer Liebe?*"
      William C. Wilson: Correspondence

312   "'She was just about to pull off a big schnapps deal'"
      Moss: op. cit., p. 115

312   "it was established that five other people"
      Orman: op. cit. *Wochenend*, 12 November and 19 November 1952
      According to the Bavarian State Prosecutor, the Munich CID file
      on the case — "Diary—München Staatsanwaltschaft beim Landge-
      richt II Gn 2Js 1142/48"—has been destroyed.

313   "Karl Roesen"
      CIC File X-2771-IV-G

315   "A reward notice"
      Original in Sayer archives in German, English, French, Polish,
      and Greek

316   "struck him across the face with her riding crop"
      Garmisch-Partenkirchner Tagblatt: "Dunkle Rätsel," Pt. 11 (Garmisch,
      17-18 March 1956)

316   "made a crime plan of the White Horse flat"
      Original plan in Sayer archives

317   "the little black notebook"
      Wochenend: "Dunkel bleibt um Zenta Hausner" (Nuremberg, 26
      November 1952)

317   "Zenta Hausner's diary"
      Philip Benzell: Concluding Report on Narcotics Trafficking in Up-
      per Bavaria (Office of Provost Marshal, EUCOM, 10 January
      1948)

Page

317 "Michael Hugo Knoebel"
CIC File on Knoebel, XE 216143-I-9A-059

317 "A CIC report on Knoebel"
CIC: op. cit.

318 "'not in control of his mental faculties'"
CIC: op. cit.

318 "'as a threat to German society'"
CIC: op. cit.

318 "Ernst Virnich"
Charles B. Dyer: Narcotics Situation in Garmisch-Partenkirchen
(Public Health Branch, OMGB, Munich, 3 April 1948)

319 "In 1950 it seemed a breakthrough had been made"
Wochenend: op. cit.

319 "Then in the summer of 1952 came a fresh development"
Wochenend: op. cit.

319 "'I was hearing Christmas Eve Mass in a little church'"
Edward E. Bird: Transcript of telephone interview, Maryland, 26
November 1977

319 "Michael Knoebel was rearrested"
Wochenend: op. cit.

320 "The Germans believe she was murdered at the instigation of an
American"
Ivar Buxell: Correspondence

320 "'Five hundred people cleared out of Garmisch'"
Moss: op. cit., p. 115

322 "A Soviet-run East German newspaper"
The document in the National Archives is a translation and carries
no title or clue as to the provenance of the article. It was, however,
located with papers relating to a raid on the offices of the SED
(Socialist Unity Party) in the Soviet sector of Berlin

323 "The American Embassy in Prague immediately protested"
Note of Protest from the Office of Political Affairs in the American
Embassy in Prague, forwarded to Public Safety Branch, OMGUS,
4 February 1948

CHAPTER 20

324 "New Year's Day"
Col. F. J. Pearson: Reports of Investigation of Allegations made by
Mr. Guenther P. Reinhardt (Office of the Inspector General,

Page

EUCOM, 22 April 1948) AG Box 16

324 "through Army channels to Berlin"
Ibid.

325 "the sensational Kronberg jewel robbery"
Trial by General Court Martial, Frankfurt, 11 December 1946–
30 April 1947 CM 234235. United States *v.* Jack W. Durant
Also:
David F. Watson, Charge Sheet, Frankfurt, 31 August 1946
David Rowan: *Famous European Crimes* (London, 1955)

325 "Captain Victor J. Haig"
Record of Trial: General Court Martial of Captain Victor J. Haig,
Garmisch, 11-18 March 1947

327 "Secret message to the European Command"
Lt.-Col. Clarke: Secret Message War Department from CSGID
Security Group to HQ EUCOM, Frankfurt, 12 January 1948

327 "134 separate incidents grouped into nine main categories"
Pearson: op. cit.

328 "'exerting all possible influence'"
Message concerning Gammache case from HQ EUCOM, Frankfurt. Signed Huebner, 7 January 1948. CSO19 333.9

328 "'There is no factual basis for the allegations'"
Major General Louis A. Craig: Report of Investigation of Allega-
tions of Guenther Reinhardt Covering Suppression of Information
(Office of the Inspector General, EUCOM, 3 February 1948)

328 "Major Hensley's investigation"
Major Robert B. Hensley: Alleged Blackmarket Activities of
American Personnel (Office of the Deputy Inspector General,
EUCOM, February 1948)

328 "'It is evident...that the writer'"
Hensley: op. cit., p. 15

329 "'Germany...still is in the backwash of World War II'"
Hensley: op. cit., p. 15

329 "'By such generally unfounded and fanatical allegations'"
Hensley: op. cit., p. 16

329 "'General Conclusion'"
Ibid.

329 "'That the matters contained in the allegations'"
Ibid.

331 "Recommendations"

Page

Ibid.

331   "The vast majority of Mr. Reinhardt's allegations'"
      Pearson: op. cit., p. 2

332   "While serving in Munich'"
      Pearson: op. cit., p. 3

334   "I always felt that Peccarelli'"
      Zucker: Correspondence, 3 and 29 May 1979

334   "Rives came back on 18 January'"
      Reinhardt: Letter, op. cit., p. 4

335   "FOR RELEASE IN A.M. PAPERS'"
      Taylor Report: Department of the Army, Public Information Division, Press Section, 6 May 1948

335   "The first Taylor Report"
      Orville J. Taylor: Reinhardt Report 1 (9th part) Wholesale Irregularities in the Counter-Intelligence Corps in the European Theater (29 March 1948)

336   "It is regrettable'"
      Taylor Report: op. cit., p. 24

336   "Ninety percent of the newspapers refused to print it'"
      Reinhardt: Letter, op. cit., p. 6

338   "if $3 million in gold'"
      General Lucius D. Clay: Letter to H. L. Hammond-Seaman (New York, 2 January 1978)

338   "I don't have any recollection'"
      Gordon Gray: Transcript of telephone interview (2 December 1977)

338   "That's all news to me'"
      Murray van Waggoner: Transcript of telephone interview (26 November 1977)

338   "Based upon repeated research of the official records'"
      Lt.-Col. Hugh G. Waite, Chief, News Branch, Public Information Division, Department of the Army: Letter to Norris McWhirter, Editor, *Guinness Book of Records* (Washington, DC, 10 January 1975)

339   "That no further action be taken"
      Hensley: op. cit.

CHAPTER 21

340   "In December 1948'"
      Reinhardt: Letter, op. cit., p. 6

SOURCES

Page
341   "For ten years he worked as a private eye"
      Reinhardt obituary in *New York Times*, 3 December 1968

342   "One of the five was…now roaming Europe"
      Young: op. cit., p. 75

342   "'The defense is willing to call several high-ranking officers'"
      Young: op. cit., p. 76, quoting Lt.-Col. Marion Beatty of OMGB
      Legal Field Team, Augsburg Area, at the Court Martial of
      Sergeant Helen C. Cobb in Munich

342   "'the confusion and dismay'"
      Young: op. cit., p. 78

343   "'There has been a failure'"
      Young: op. cit., p. 80

343   "We have already seen"
      Philip Benzell: Testimony before the Inspector General's inquiry
      into allegations by Guenther Reinhardt (Exhibit "B-7," pp. 30-32)

344   "so when the CCD tapped his private phone"
      Benzell: op. cit.

344   "McCarthy was forewarned and destroyed them"
      Benzell: op. cit.

344   "'not much doubt as to his dishonesty'"
      William C. Wilson: Correspondence

344   "McCarthy had provided false testimony"
      Benzell: op. cit.

344   "The circumstances leading to the denazification of 'the Doctor'"
      Exhibit "K," Reinhardt papers. Includes denazification
      "Certificate" from Major John R. McCarthy and related charge
      sheet of denazification court in Garmisch

344   "It is highly desirable'"
      This certificate appears as Exhibit "K" in the papers relating to the
      IGD investigation into the allegations made by Guenther Rein-
      hardt.

345   "'The Doctor'…'the clue to McCarthy'"
      William C. Wilson: Correspondence, 12 July 1979

345   "the I. G. Farben case"
      The official papers relating to this case have been destroyed. Infor-
      mation comes from surviving correspondence between Clay,
      EUCOM, OMGB, and the IGD, and from William C. Wilson,
      one of the investigators on the case.

346   "Lord and McCarthy would have become millionaires"

William C. Wilson: Correspondence, 26 November 1979

346   "'The Augsburg Property Control officer had a German mistress'"
William C. Wilson: Monograph — Property Control (Douglasville, Georgia, October 1979)

347   "In early December 1948 General Clay"
Col. Harold R. Booth: Letter to General Clay re: Investigation of Property Control Officer (Office of Inspector General, Berlin, 22 March 1949) AG 49 Box 64 6

347   "'He was one of the most brilliant and astute investigators'"
Wilson: op. cit., fourth monograph

348   "'Having a piece of this kind of action'"
Wilson: Correspondence, 26 November 1976

348   "'by concentrating on certain accounts'"
Booth: op. cit.

349   "'The investigation does show on the part of Mr. Lord and Mr. McCarthy'"
Brigadier General W. B. Palmer: Investigation Report re: Lt.-Col. Russell R. Lord et. al. (Office of Chief of Staff, EUCOM, 17 August 1949)

349   "I have reviewed the attached case involving Mr. Russell Lord *et al.*'"
Robert M. Barnett: Memo re: Mr. Russell Lord (Office of the Personnel Officer, OMGUS, 31 August 1949) 102-3/19 259 9

350   "'It is difficult for me to find words'"
Brigadier General Walter J. Muller: Parting Address to Members of OMGB (OMGB Munich, n.d.) 143-2/1 263 14

350   "I have just realized I was surrounded by knaves!'"
Wilson: Correspondence, 17 February 1983

Bibliography

PUBLISHED SOURCES

After the Battle, No. 9: *Obersalzberg* (London, 1975)

Robert S. Allen: *Lucky Forward — The History of Patton's Third U.S. Army* (New York, 1947)

Stephen E. Ambrose: *Ike's Spies* (New Yorik, 1981)

Ruth Andreas-Friedrich: *Berlin Underground* (London, 1948)

Michael Balfour and John Muir: *Four-Power Control in Germany and Austria, 1945-6* (Royal Institute of International Affairs, London, 1956)

Victor H. Bernstein: *Final Judgement — The Story of Nuremberg* (London, 1947)

General Antoine Béthouart: *La Bataille pour l'Austriche* (Paris, 1966)

Eugene K. Bird: *Prisoner No. 7 — Rudolf Hess* (New York, 1972)

Douglas Botting: *The Aftermath: Europe* (Time-Life, Virginia, 1982)

Tom Bower: *Blind Eye to Murder* (London, 1981)

C.R. Boxer: "The Count of Ericeira and the Pirates, 1721-2" (*History Today*, London, December 1974)

Omar N. Bradley: *A Soldier's Story* (London, 1951)

W. Byford-Jones: *Berlin Twilight* (London, *c*.1946)

A. Cave-Brown: *The Secret War Diary of the OSS* (New York, 1977)

Gen. Lucius D. Clay: *Decision in Germany* (London, 1950)

Charles R. Codman: *Drive* (Boston, 1957)

Eugene Davidson: *The Death and Life of Germany* (New York, 1959)

Franklin Davis: *Come as a Conqueror* (New York, 1967)

H. Deschamps: *Les Pirates à Madagascar aux XVIIIᵉ et XVIIIᵉ Siècles* (Paris, 1949)

Documentation Center of the State Archives Administration of the German Democratic Republic: *Brown Book — War and Nazi Criminals in West Germany* (Dresden, n.d.)

Hans Dollinger: *Deutschland unter den Besatzungsmächten, 1945-9* (Munich, 1967)

Hans Dollinger: *The Decline and Fall of Nazi Germany and Imperial Japan*

(London, 1968)

F.S.V. Donnison: *Civil Affairs and Military Government, North-West Europe, 1944-6* (HMSO, London, 1961)

Dwight D. Eisenhower: *Crusade in Europe* (London, 1948)

Dwight D. Eisenhower: *The Papers of Dwight D. Eisenhower*, vol. VIII, *The Chief of Staff* (Baltimore-London, 1978)

Waldeman Erfurth: *The Last Finnish War* (Foreign Military Studies Branch of the Historical Division, HQ European Command, Washington DC, 1979)

Jeffrey Ethell and Alfred Price: *Target Berlin* (London, 1981)

Ladislas Farago: *The Last Days of Patton* (New York, 1981)

Joachim Fest: *Hitler* (London, 1974)

Jack Fishman: *The Seven Men of Spandau* (London, 1954)

Charles Foley: *Commando Extraordinary* (London, 1954)

Oliver Fredericksen: *American Military Occupation of Germany, 1945-53* (Darmstadt, 1953)

Roger A. Freedman: *The Mighty Eighth* (London, 1978)

Roger A. Freedman: *The Mighty Eighth War Diary* (London, 1981)

John Kenneth Galbraith: *A Life in Our Times — Memoirs* (London, 1981)

Reinhard Gehlen: *The Gehlen Memoirs* (London, 1972)

Dr. Joseph Goebbels: *The Goebbels Diaries — The Last Days* (London, 1979)

Samuel A. Goudsmit: *Alsos — The Search for the German Atom Bomb* (London, 1947)

Alfred Gosser: *Germany in Our Time* (New York, 1971)

Frank Grube and Gerhard Richtens: *Die Schwarzmarktzeit* (Hamburg, 1979)

Guinness Book of Records (1957 et seq)

History of the Counter-Intelligence Corps: Vol. XXV, *Occupation of Austria and Italy* (Fort Holabird, Baltimore, 1959)

Peter Hoffmann: *Hitler's Personal Security* (London, 1979)

Heinz Höhne: *The Order of the Death's Head* (New York, 1972)

Edward J. Huntington: *The 388th at War* (USA, 1979)

Glen B. Infield: *Otto Skorzeny — Hitler's Commando* (New York, 1981)

Glen B. Infield: *Secrets of the SS* (New York, 1982)

David Irving (ed.): *Dr. Morrell, The Medical Diaries* (London, 1983)

Rolf Italiaander: *Berlins Stunde Null 1945* (Düsseldorf, 1979)

Charles de Jaeger: *The Linz File — Hitler's Plunder of Europe's Art* (London, 1981)

Arthur Kahn: *Betrayal — Our Occupation of Germany* (Warsaw, 1950)

Ursula von Kardorff: *Diary of a Nightmare — Berlin, 1942-5* (London, 1962)

Douglas Kelley: *Twenty-Two Cells in Nuremberg* (London, 1947)

Robert M. W. Kempner: *Das Dritte Reich in Kreuzvehör*

George Kennan: *Memoirs, 1925-50* (Boston, 1967)

Gerhard Kiersch, Rainer Klaus, Wolfgang Kramer, Elisabeth Reichardt-Kiersch: *Berliner Alltag im Dritten Reich* (Düsseldorf, 1979)

Percy Knauth: *Germany in Defeat* (New York, 1946)

Hildegard Knef: *The Gift Horse* (London, 1971)

Thilo Koch: *Fünf Jahre der Entscheidung—Deutschland nach dem Kreig, 1945-49*

Jochen von Lang: *Bormann* (London, 1979)

James Lucas: *Alpine Elite—German Mountain Troops of World War II* (London, 1980)

Paul Manning: *Martin Bormann—Nazi in Exile* (Secaucus, NJ, 1981)

James Stewart Martin: *All Honorable Men* (Boston, 1950)

Werner Maser: *Nuremberg—A Nation on Trial* (London, 1979)

Charles L. Mee: *Meeting at Potsdam* (London, 1975)

Paul Meskil: *Hitler's Heirs* (New York, 1961)

Rodney G. Minott: *The Fortress That Never Was* (New York, 1965)

Lester M. Nichols: *Impact—The Battle Story of the Tenth Armored Division* (New York, 1967)

James O'Donnell: *The Berlin Bunker* (London, 1979)

George S. Patton: *War As I Knew It* (Boston, 1947)

Edward N. Peterson: *The American Occupation of Germany* (Detroit, 1977)

Bruce Quarrie: *German Mountain Troops* (Cambridge, 1982)

B.V. Ratchford and W.D. Ross: *Berlin Reparations Assignment* (N. Carolina University Press, 1947)

Guenther Reinhardt: *Crime Without Punishment* (New York, 1952)

Piers Paul Read: *The Train Robbers* (London, 1978)

Report of Operations: *The Seventh United States Army in France and Germany*, Vol. III (Heidelberg, 1946)

David Rowan: *Famous European Crimes* (London, 1955)

Klaus-Jörg Ruhl: *Die Besatzer und die Deutschen-Amerikanische Zone, 1945-8* (Düsseldorf, 1980)

Cornelius Ryan: *The Last Battle* (London, 1966)

Antony Sampson: *The Sovereign State—The Secret History of ITT* (London, 1974)

Henriette von Schirach: *The Price of Glory* (London, 1960)

Fabian von Schlabrendorff: *The Secret War Against Hitler* (London, 1966)

Heribert Schwan and Rolf Steininger: *Als der Krieg zu Ende ging* (Frankfurt, 1981)

Heribert Schwan and Rolf Steininger: *Besiegt, besetzt, geteilt* (Oldenburg, 1979)

V. Sevruk (ed.): *How Wars End* (Moscow, 1969)

SHAEF: *Counter-Intelligence Handbook — Germany* (April, 1945)

Harry E. Slater: *The Big Square — 94th Bomber Group, 1942-45* (USA, 1980)

Louis B. Snyder: *Encyclopedia of the Third Reich* (London, 1976)

Helmuth Spaeter: *Die Brandenburger — eine deutsche Kommandotruppe zbV800* (Munich, 1982)

Albert Speer: *Inside the Third Reich* (London, 1970)

W. Stanley-Moss: *Gold Is Where You Hide It* (London, 1968)

James Stern: *The Hidden Damage* (New York, 1947)

John Toland: *The Last Hundred Days* (London, 1968)

Trial of the Major War Criminals at Nuremberg (HMSO, 23 vols., London, 1946-51)

Hugh Trevor-Roper (ed.): *The Bormann Letters* (London, 1954

Hugh Trevor-Roper: *The Last Days of Hitler* (London, 1981)

John Frayn Turner and Robert Jackson: *Destination Berchtesgaden* (London, 1975)

David Wallechinsky, Irving Wallace, and Amy Wallace: *The Book of Lists* (London, 1977)

Simon Wiesenthal: *the Murderers Among Us* (London, 1969)

Robert Wistrich: *Who's Who in Nazi Germany* (London, 1982)

Earl F. Ziemke: *Stalingrad to Berlin — The German Defeat in the East* (Army Historical Series, Washington, 1971)

Earl F. Ziemke: *The U.S. Army in the Occupation of Germany* (Army Historical Series, Washington, 1975)

Harold Zink: *The United States in Germany, 1944-1955* (New York, 1956)

Harold Zink: *American Military Government in Germany* (New York, 1967)

UNPUBLISHED ARCHIVE SOURCES

U.S. Army: Military records of Frederick Siegfried Neumann and Kenneth Asa McIntyre.

Major E.S.G. Bach: In Search of the Reichsbank (Control Commission for Germany, 30 June 1945)

Berlin Document Center and U.S. Archives: Documents relating to Fritz Rauch, Helmut Schreiber, Helmut Groeger, Mathias Stinnes, Klaus Bremme, and Gottlob Berger

SHAEF, Finance Branch: Report on Reconnaissance to Discover Further German Gold, Foreign Exchange, and Loot (Unsigned undated secret typescript, c May 1945, Frankfurt)

Bibliography

"Reichsbank Building, Frankfurt am Main" Currency Section for Germany, U.S. Army Branch, 13 May 1945

SHAEF: Captured Currencies (typescript, May 1945, PRO)

Berlin Document Center: Documents relating to Hubert von Blücher

Kriminalabteilung beim Präsidium der Bayerischen Landpolizei: "Final Report — Gold and Foreign Currency Assets of the Former German Reichsbank" (Munich, January 1953)

SHAEF: Hiscovery of Hidden German Gold Reserves. Appendix "B" to Weekly Field Report (Secret) April 1945

Organization Turicum: Report Lt. DuBois, G-5 Financial SHAEF (Mittenwald, 22 May 1945

Third Army G-2: Secret Weekly Intelligence Report, No. 4, 29.8.45

Register of Valuables in Custody of the FED, Frankfurt-am-Main, Germany, 15.4.45-29.11.80

Office of Alien Property, U.S. Department of Justice: Vesting Orders for U.S. currency recovered in Germany 7.12.78 and 18.4.79

CIC file on M. H. Knoebel — Dossier XE216143-1

FED Currency Section. Inventory of Shipment 52A, 22.7.46

FED: Inventory of Shipments 1-115 (Frankfurt 1947-48)

Civil Censorship Division: Transcripts of telephone intercepts Memo to 307th CID Detachment HQ 7th Army. Interrogation of Wilhelm Spacil, Head of Amt II, 27.7.45

970th CIC Detachment: Memo on ownership and disposal of effects recovered as a result of interrogation of Wilhelm Spacil, 4.2.45

61st Armored Infantry Battalion: After Action Report, 12.6.45

OMGB Finance Division: Briefing Notes of Meeting with General Dwight D. Eisenhower, 14/15.10.46

OMGB Intelligence, Historical and Reports Branch: Time Necessary for Trial of Minor Cases after Arrest, 6.1.47.

CIC Dossier on Guenther Reinhardt (Dossier XI 446319)

National Archives: Papers relating to raid on the Socialist Unity Party in Soviet Sector of Berlin

American Embassy, Prague — Note of protest from Office of Political Affairs to Public Safety Branch, OMGUS, 4.2.48

Record of Trial — General Court Martial of Jack W. Durant CM 234234, 11.12.46-30.4.47

Record of Trial — General Court Martial of Captain Victor J. Haig, 11.3.47–18.3.47

FED: Memo from Deputy Chief of Currency Section to Assistant Director, Financial Division, U.S. Group Control Council 10.7.45

U.S. Group Control Council: 31-page secret report — Report on Recovery of Reichsbank Precious Metals

Major R. M. Allgeier: Report of incident to Provost Marshall, 3rd U.S. Army (HQ 512 MP Battalion, Bad Tölz, 29.6.45

Rona L. Geib: Currency sent from Reichsbank, Berlin, to Southern Germany in April 1945 (FED, Frankfurt, 1947)

Rona L. Geib: Liaison Visit to G-2 (FED, Frankfurt, 1947)

Lt. Hubert Gais: 537 Gebirgsjäger Regiment. Diary entries prior to American Occupation of Garmisch-Partenkirchen, 15 May 1945)

Gottfried Arendt: Report concerning the transfer of valuables from Berlin to Munich, April 1945

R. A. Nixon, Chief Financial Intelligence and Liaison Branch, OMGUS: Report on Recovery of Reichbank Precious Metals (HQ U.S. Group Control Council, Finance Division, 6 September 1945)

Lt. Herbert G. DuBois: In Quest of Gold, Silver, and Foreign Exchange (Finance Branch, SHAEF, May 1945)

Paul S. McCaroll: Foreign Exchange Depository (HQ USFET Finance, typescript, 24.1.46

Lt.-Col. F. S. McFadzean, SHAEF Finance Branch: Seized Enemy Funds, 10.3.45

Capt. Benjamin S. Schilling, HQ USFET G-5 Financial Branch: Shipment No. 60, 11.8.45

Frank J. Roberts: Data re: German Foreign Office Gold Reflected by Records of Foreign Exchange Depository, 3.5.49

Lindley Beckworth: Letters to Congressional Interstate and Foreign Commerce Committee, 6.6.50 and 2.6.50

Col. Roy L. Dalferes, 3rd Army, G-5; Delivery of Treasure, 6.7.45

Major Melvin W. Nitz: Military Government Annual Report, June 1946

Robert B. Shaw, 13th CID: Report to Office of the Provost Marshal, CID, EUCOM, 27.6.47

Lt.-Col. Leonard H. Smith: Testimony before Inspector General into allegations by Guenther Reinhardt, 20.1.48

Major Lionel C. Perera, HQ 3rd Army G-5 Section: Interrogation Report on Fritz Rauch, 4.7.45

Russell R. Lord: Letter to Director of Finance Division, OMGUS re: Direct Contact betweeen OMGUS and German Officials, 8.3.47

Edwin P. Keller: Report on Visit to OMGB Munich, 31.7.47

Edwin P. Keller: Memo re: U.S. Dollars Discussions on 3 January, 3.1.49

Joseph A. Angotti: Internal memo — Item 37, Shipment 109, 2.11.48

Murray D. Van Waggoner: Letter to Major-General George P. Hays re:

BIBLIOGRAPHY

Military Government Law No. 53, 3.2.49

Siegfried F. Field, CIC Special Agent: C.I. Arrest Report, 28.11.45

Charles S. Dimarino, CIC Special Agent: Secret Report re: Helmut Groeger—Illegal Possession of Large Quantities of American Money, 17.6.48

Ellington D. Golden, 970th CIC: Secret Report re: H. Groeger 17.2.48

Max L. Marshall, CIC Agent: Secret memo re: Helmut Groeger, 25.5.48

Guenther Reinhardt: 55-page memorandum on American Occupation of Germany, December 1947

George O. Muse: CID Agent: Alleged Illegal Traffic in German Automobiles, 14.5.47

Col. Thomas H. Young: Final Report of Investigation and Transportation Branch, 31.3.48

Captain Elwood J. Pennetto: Inspection Report, 4.5.46

Col. Fred A. Mayer: Report on Personnel Ordered Out of the Occupation Zones for Prejudicial Acts, 30.10.47

James A. Rutter, 66th CIC Group: Interview with Lt.-Col. E. Van Buskirk, 13.8.57

Col. William G. Brey, Chief, FED: Letter to Mr. Jack Bennett, Finance Advisor, OMGB, 23.4.48

Victor H. Peccarelli, Chief Agent: Secret Preliminary Report on Narcotics Trafficking in Upper Bavaria (Project Garpeck), 2.12.47

Charles B. Dyer, Narcotics Officer, OMGB: Narcotics Situation in Garmisch-Partenkirchen, 3.4.48

Philip P. Benzell, Chief Agent: Concluding Report on Narcotics Trafficking in Upper Bavaria (Project Garpeck), 10.1.48

Major Earl S. Browning, 970th CIC: Report on Boleslaw 'Kasimierski', 27.2.47

Lt.-Col. Leonard H. Smith: Report of Investigation of Conditions in Garmisch, 14.7.47

HQ EUCOM, Frankfurt: Message (signed Huebner) concerning Gammache case, 7.1.48

Record of Trial: Frank J. Gammache, 9.9.47-11.9.47

Col. F.J. Pearson, Inspector General's Office: Reports of Investigation of Allegations made by Mr. Guenther Reinhardt, 22.4.48

Orville J. Taylor: Reinhardt Report. Wholesale Irregularities in the Counter-Intelligence Corps in the European Theater, 29.3.48

Carl Sussmann: Memo for CO Garmisch Sub-Region CIC, 19.10.4

Lt.-Col. Clarke: Secret Message from CSGID Security Group to HQ EUCOM, Frankfurt, 12.1.48

Major-General Louis A. Craig, Inspector General's Office: Report of Investigation of Allegations of Guenther Reinhardt covering Suppression of Information, 3.2.48

Major Robert B. Hensley, Deputy, Inspector General's Office: Alleged Black Market Activities of American personnel, 3.2.48

Col. Harold R. Booth, Inspector General's Office: Correspondence with General Clay re: Investigation of Property Control Officer, 22.3. 49

Brigadier-General W. B. Palmer: Investigation Report re: Lt.-Col. Russell R. Lord, 17.8.49

Robert M. Barnett, Personnel Officer, OMGUS: Memo re: Russell R. Lord. 31.8.48

Receipt from Lt.-Col. Robert P. Rowe, G-5, HQ 7th Army to Major William R. Geiler and Captain Walter R. Dee, 9.6.45

Dr. Robert M. W. Kempner: Letter to Mr. Perry Lankhuff, Political Division, OMGUS, 28.12.48

CIC Munich: Telegram to other CIC stations re: Kasimierski, 12.3.47

Chief of FED: Letter to Fiscal Officer, OMGB, Munich, April 1945

Frank J. Roberts, Acting Chief, FED: Secret Report U.S. Dollars Found in Germany, 28.3.49

NEWS SOURCES

Antony Terry, Philip Knightley, and Stephen Fay: Soviet Agents Try to Cache 27 Million German War Loot Bonds (*Sunday Times*, 31.1.71)

Lorana Sullivan: The Weimar Bonds That Won't Go Away (*Observer*, 21 November 1982)

Ottmar Katz: Interviews with Colonel Franz Pfeiffer, Captain Hans Neuhauser, Josef Veit, and Josef Pinzl

Garmisch-Partenkirchner Tagblatt: "Dinkle Rätsel aus Dunklen Tagen" (Garmisch-Partenkirchen, January/February 1956)

Jürgen Bungert and Armin Walter: Das Gold, die Nacht und der Nebel (*Bild am Sonntag*, May-June 1974)

"Die Sauhund" hau'n wir wieder "naus" Die Geheimakten der U.S.-Militärregierung in Bayern 1945 bis 1949 (Part III, *Der Spiegel*, 1 December 1980

Frank Orman: "Was geschah in diesem Haus" (*Wochenend*, Nuremberg, 1952)

Robert Reed: War Report No. N143 (BBC German Service, 8 April 1945)

Guenther Reinhardt: "I Spy, You Spy, He Spies" (*Pageant*, 1948)

Henriette von Schirach: "Wo blieb das Gold der Reichsbank" (*Wochenend*,

5 October 1950)
Hochlande Bote (Bavaria, 8.5.48)
Chicago Herald Tribune
New York Herald Tribune
Rude Pravo
New York Times
Brantford Expositor
Tiger's Tales
Stars and Stripes
Daily Telegraph
Sunday Express
Antony Terry: Operation Odessa (memo to *Sunday Times* Insight Team, 20.2.68)

CORRESPONDENCE, INTERVIEWS, AND DIARIES
Correspondence with the Deutsche Bundesbank, Frankfurt, and Landeszentralbank in Bayern (Munich, 1979-82)
Correspondence with Federal Reserve Bank, New York, 11.4.77 and 15.12.78
Correspondence from Guenther Reinhardt to Tom Agoston, 1949
D.A. Spencer: 1945 Diary, vol. 3, Germany: Post-Armistice (T-Force Manuscript — Air Photographs Research Committee)
Correspondence, interviews, telephone interviews with the following individuals:
Paul Bruehl; telephone
General Lucius D. Clay; correspondence
Murray van Waggoner; telephone/correspondence
Lt. Hugh G. Waite; correspondence
Edward E. Bird; telephone/correspondence
Elmer G. Pralle; telephone/correspondence
Gordon Gray; telephone
Col. Clifton H. Young; telephone/correspondence
Alice Peccarelli; telephone/correspondence
Lt.-Col. Leonard H. Smith; telephone/correspondence
Frank C. Gammache; telephone/correspondence
Lt.-Col. Lester J. Zucker; correspondence
Bob Shaw; telephone
Tom Agoston; telephone/correspondence
Frank C. Gabell; correspondence
Col. L. Stautner: correspondence

Sieglinde Odorfer; correspondence
William C. Wilson; telephone/correspondence
Buck Wardle; telephone/correspondence
Charles I. Bradley; telephone/correspondence
Ward Atherton; telephone
John L. Ketcham; telephone/correspondence
Leo de Gar Kulka; tapes/telephone/correspondence
Melvin W. Nitz; interview
Charles W. Snedeker; telephone/correspondence
Ivar Buxell; tapes/telephone/correspondence
Captain Walter R. Dee; telephone/correspondence
Brigadier M. H. F. Waring; telephone
Colonel William Eckles; telephone/correspondence
Sergeant Albert Singleton; telephone/correspondence
Captain G. Garwood; telephone/correspondence
Major William Geiler; correspondence
Alfred Geiffert III; correspondence
Louis Graziano; correspondence
Colonel Franz Pfeiffer; interview
Hubert von Blücher; interview
Major R. M. Allgeier; correspondence
Simon Wiesenthal; telephone
Ian K. T. Sayer: Documents and other material relating to the Great
    Reichsbank Robbery and its sequel.

Index

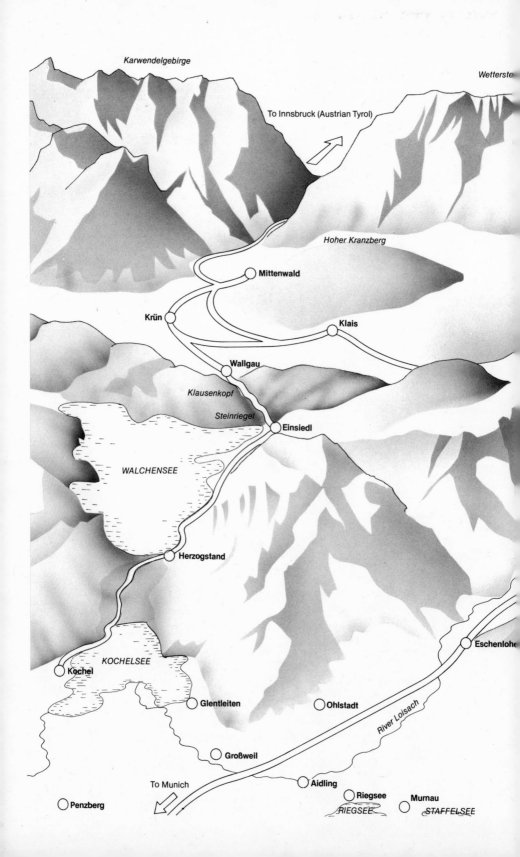